The de Havilland
Mosquito

Part 2: Fighter, Fighter-Bomber & Night-Fighter (including Sea Mosquito)

by Richard A. Franks

Airframe & Miniature No.10
The de Havilland Mosquito
Part 2: Fighter, Fighter-Bomber & Night-Fighter (inc. Sea Mosquito)
by Richard A. Franks

First published in 2017 by Valiant Wings Publishing Ltd
8 West Grove, Bedford, MK40 4BT
+44 (0)1234 273434
valiant-wings@btconnect.com
www.valiant-wings.co.uk
Facebook: valiantwingspublishing

ISBN: 978-0-9935345-8-4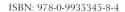

Acknowledgments

One of the main sources of inspiration and images for this title is sadly no longer with us: Stuart Howe will always be remembered for his love of the Mosquito and I remain indebted to him for the numerous images he supplied to me back in 1998 when I did my first title on the type, many of which have been used once again here.

I would also like to give a special word of thanks to J.J. Petit, Nigel Perry and George Papadimitriou for their invaluable help with photographs. Special thanks must go to Steve A. Evans, Libor Jekl and Dani Zamarbide for their excellent model builds, and Jerry Boucher, Richard J. Caruana and Wojciech Sankowski for their superb artwork.

Note

There are many different ways of writing aircraft designation, however for consistency throughout this title we have used one style for the pre-1948 period (e.g. FB Mk VI, NF Mk XIII etc.) and another for the post-1948 period when the RAF adopted the Arabic system of numbering (e.g. TR Mk 33) that is still in use today.

Author's Note

There are many contradictions in documentation about the Mosquito series, both in genuine documents as well as all written accounts since the end of WWII. As a result of this throughout the title you will find details of contradicting information that was discovered by myself during the compilation of this book. I have done this to give you as much data as possible, so that you can make your own decision as to the most likely scenario.

Cover

The cover artwork depicts an FB Mk XVII 'Tse Tse', NT225, 'O' of No.248 Squadron attacking shipping. This artwork was specially commissioned for this title. ©Jerry Boucher 2017

An FB Mk VI during final assembly (©BICC)

Contents

Airframe Chapters

1	Evolution – The Fighters (including Night-Fighters)	40
2	Evolution – Fighter-Bombers and Photo-Reconnaissance	51
3	Evolution – Trainers, Target-Tugs and the Sea Mosquito	59
4	Camouflage and Markings	66
	Stencils	99

Miniature Chapters

5	Mosquito Fighter, Fighter-Bomber, Night-Fighter and Sea Mosquito Kits	101
6	Building a Selection	108
7	Building a Collection	131
8	In Detail:	155

	Cockpit & Canopy	155
	Radio & Radar	166
	Cameras	171
	Miscellaneous	172
	Access Panels	173
	Wings	175
	Mid & Aft Fuselage	179
	Tail	182
	Engines, Propellers & Cowlings	184
	Undercarriage	188
	Armament , Ordnance & Drop Tanks	191

Appendices

I	Mosquito Kit List	199
II	Mosquito Accessory List	201
III	Mosquito Decal & Mask List	204
IV	Bibliography	207

1/48th Scale Plans Fold-out

Glossary

A&AEE . . . . . . .Aeroplane & Armament Experimental Establishment
ACM . . . . .Air-Chief Marshall (RAF)
A.I. . . . . .Airborne Interception (radar)
AID . . . . .Airworthiness Inspection Directorate
AM . . . . .Air Marshall (RAF)
AVM . . . . .Air Vice Marshall (RAF)
B . . . . .Bomber
BOAC . . . . .British Overseas Airways Corporation
BS . . . . .British Standard
BSDU . . . . .Bomber Support Development Unit
CAACU. . . . . . .Civilian Anti-Aircraft Co-operation Unit
CAM ship . . . . .Catapult, Aircraft Merchant ship
CBE. . . . . .Commander of the Most Excellent Order of the British Empire
CO. . . . . .Commanding Officer
CSE. . . . . .Central Signal Establishment
DFC. . . . . .Distinguished Flying Cross
DFM . . . . .Distinguished Flying Medal
D.H. . . . . .de Havilland Ltd
D.H.C.. . . . . . . .de Havilland (Canada)
DTD . . . . .Department of Technical Directorate
FB . . . . .Fighter-Bomber
F/O . . . . .Flying Officer (RAF)
Flt . . . . .Flight
Flt Sgt . . . . .Flight Sergeant
FRAeS . . . . .Fellowship of the Royal Aeronautical Society
FS . . . . .Federal Standard
ft . . . . .Foot
Gp Capt . . . . . .Group Capitan (RAF)
He . . . . .Heinkel
HQ . . . . .Headquarters
HUD . . . . .Head-Up Display
IFF. . . . . .Identification Friend or Foe
Imp. Gal.. . . . . .Imperial Gallon
in . . . . .Inch
lb . . . . .Pound
Ju . . . . .Junkers

MAC . . . . .Mediterranean Air Command
MAP . . . . .Ministry of Aircraft Production
Me . . . . .Messerschmitt
Mk. . . . . .Mark
Mod. . . . . .Modification
MoS. . . . . .Ministry of Supply
mph . . . . .Miles Per Hour
MU . . . . .Maintenance Unit (RAF)
NF . . . . .Night-fighter
No.. . . . . .Number
Oblt . . . .*Oberleutnant* (Luftwaffe)
OTU . . . . .Operational Training Unit
P/O . . . . .Pilot Officer (RAF)
PR . . . . .Photo Reconnaissance
PRU. . . . . .Photo Reconnaissance Unit
RAAF. . . . . .Royal Australian Air Force
RAE . . . . .Royal Aircraft Establishment
RAF . . . . .Royal Air Force
RCAF. . . . . .Royal Canadian Air Force
RNAS . . . . .Royal Naval Air Station
RNZAF . . . . . . .Royal New Zealand Air Force
R.P. . . . . .Rocket Projectile
Sgt . . . . .Sergeant
SOC. . . . . .Struck Off Charge
Sqn . . . . .Squadron
Sqn Ldr . . . . . . .Squadron Leader (RAF)
TF . . . . .Torpedo/Fighter
TR . . . . .Torpedo/Reconnaissance
TT . . . . .Target Towing
UK. . . . . .United Kingdom
USAAF . . . . . . .United States Army Air Force
VC. . . . . .Victoria Cross
Wg Cdr . . . . . . .Wing Commander (RAF)
WWII . . . . .World War II (1939-1945)
/G. . . . . .Suffix letter added to aircraft serial number denoting that it carried special equipment and was to be guarded at all times

F Mk II production at Hatfield (©DH)

Preface

NF Mk II W4052 flies over the bomber prototype W4057 at Hatfield *(©DH)*

The events that would lead up to the first two prototype Mosquitos have already been recounted in Part 1, as the Mosquito initially was seen as a photo-reconnaissance and bomber platform, so we will restrict ourselves here to just the development and production of the fighter series and all the variants that would be developed from it.

The third prototype Mosquito to fly was W4052 and it was completed as a night-fighter. The Air Ministry was still debating the actual role of the Mosquito even at this late stage, but W4052 was completed to Specification F.21/40 and it differed from the previous two prototypes by having Rolls-Royce Merlin 21 engines producing 1,460hp each, a bullet-proof (flat) windscreen and crew entry and exit via a door in the starboard side of the fuselage, instead of via an access door in the floor of the cockpit, as had been the case with W4050 and W4051, and the type was also envisaged to be fitted with the highly secret Airborne Interception (A.I.) Mk IV radar. The type had a compressor fitted to the port engine, which charged the pneumatic system for the wheel brakes and to cock and fire the machine-guns and cannon. The yoke style control column of the bomber and PR version gave way to a simple stick-type unit. To save the month or so it would have taken to move the components of W4052 to Hatfield from Salisbury Hall it was flown out of an adjacent field by Geoffrey de Havilland Jr on the 15th May 1941, even though the field was only 450yds (1,350ft) long. Numerous problems were encountered with the new fighter: the blast from the nose-mounted machine-guns would blind the crew at night, so these were soon fitted with blast eliminators

and the 'saxophone' exhaust system proved to overheat after prolonged use, and even burn through on some occasions. The first bomber prototype, W4050, joined W4052 in trying to overcome some of the problems encountered, and although shrouded exhausts were eventually fitted, these slowed the Mosquito slightly and it was not until much later when various ejector-style exhausts were fitted to later variants that these actually augmented the top speed. The Air Ministry made a final decision on the variants to be built for the contracts already awarded to de Havilland on the 21st June 1941. Apart from the one bomber (W4050), one photo-reconnaissance (W4051) and three fighter prototypes, nineteen

John de Havilland in the cockpit of a Fighter-Bomber Mosquito, sadly he was killed in a collision between HX849 and HX850 near Hatfield on the 23rd August 1943 *(©DH)*

Early NF Mk IIs W4090, W4092 and W4088 awaiting delivery at Hatfield 12th February 1942 with delivery crews including Jim Mollinson 2nd from right *(©DH)*

F Mk II DZ230 YP•A flown by Wg Cdr P.G. Wykeham-Barnes, No.23 Squadron, Luqa, Malta *(©Middle East Command)*

would be built as pure photo-reconnaissance machines and 176 as fighters. There were another fifty machines on order, but the Air Ministry did not specify what variant these were to be built as at this point and it was not until July that they confirmed they were to be completed as bombers. They also went on to say that the last ten (W4064-W4072) ordered as photo-reconnaissance variants against Contract 69990 (1st March 1940) could be converted to bombers.

At this stage in the war serious consideration was given, against Specification F.21/40, for the use of the Mosquito as a long-range fighter to combat the Focke-Wulf Fw 200 Condor that was hunting Allied shipping in the Atlantic. In this guise the Mosquito would have weighed 20,124lb at take-off, have a 600 Imp. Gal. fuel capacity, 200rpg for the four 20mm cannon and 700rpg for the four 0.303in machine-guns, and would have operated from the Southern Irish ports of Queenstown and Beerhaven, had the British Government not abandoned the right to use these ports in April 1938. In the end the Mosquito was not used at this time in the long-range fighter role, instead the task was initially taken by the Hurricats on the merchant CAM ships, then by the fighters on the escort carriers.

The powers that be also persisted in wanting the Mosquito to have rearward-facing armament in the form of a turret and although de Havilland protested against it, stating it would have a serious detrimental effect on performance, the requirement remained. As a result several studies were undertaken into fitting a turret on the dorsal spine of the type, the first being a faired mock-up fitted to the very first prototype W4050 (in which form it flew on the 24th July 1941). Later a four-gun Bristol Mk X turret was installed just behind the cockpit on the first NF Mk II W4053 and when test flown it proved to be unsuitable, as it caused drag and the poor gunner had to turn the turret fully forwards before he could bale out, as there was no escape hatch in the lower rear fuselage! Many accounts state that a second NF Mk II W4073 was converted in a similar way, but no photographic evidence has come to light of this, and both W4053 and W4073 went on to be converted as trainers, acting as the prototypes for the T Mk III series, so it is not known if W4073 ever undertook flying trials with the turret installed? Other heavy armament installation were considered, including six fixed upward-firing machine-guns in the dorsal spine (later tested in a Douglas Havoc) and two or four cannon in the turret, but in the end these were all deemed unnecessary.

Once W4052 had completed its trials with the A&AEE at Boscombe Down, it was fitted for the first time with A.I. radar and started to undergo a series of trials to overcome the exhaust problems and to look at other factors that had caused concern. One of these was the whole question of how the fast Mosquito would quickly decelerate when making an interception at night. To slow the airframe W4052 tested two different types of air brake towards the end of 1941, the first being the Youngman 'frill' brake, which comprised a frill of metal around the rear fuselage, just aft of the wing trailing edge, which could be brought out into the airstream by means of linkage arms behind it. This system was tried in various forms, with 10in, 13in and 16in chords and with and without the drag-inducing serrations, although each had a section missing on the dorsal spine to try and reduce buffeting of the vertical fin and rudder when deployed. When deployed the braking time in flight from 250mph to 150mph was reduced by a third and these trials were followed by the fitment of bellows type air brakes around the rear fuselage of W4052. These were inflated by a venturi under the fuselage that acted as a pressure head to activate them in 3 seconds at 250mph indicated air speed. As with the frill version they were not adopted, due to fears about structural integrity as a result of the forces being exerted on the aircraft with the frill brakes, and the severe vibrations that the bellow type brakes caused where it was felt there was a real risk of their causing a total structural failure. In the end, once the Mosquito was being used in the night fighter role, the crews soon found that lowering the undercarriage had the desired effect, without any of the risks inherent in either air brake system. W4052 went on to test a variety of other proposed improvements and modifications from 1942 which included carrying a 40mm cannon in place of the four 20mm ones, under-wing bomb racks and drop tanks, cable cutters on the wing leading edges, strengthened engine cowls for the new exhaust flame dampers, front-glow exhaust shrouds, fuel coolers, negative-G carburettors, Hamilton-Standard propellers, governors for the propellers, braking propellers, the new 'sandwich' windscreen construction and a set of three flashing downward identification lamps. The control systems also came in for modification including the ailerons drooping slightly in conjunction with the flaps for a steeper approach, convex trailing-edge ailerons and a larger rudder trim tab to help with one-engine-out configuration below 140mph.

Converted for Photo-Reconnaissance

As an odd little aside to operational use as a night-fighter, four early production NF Mk IIs were obtained by No.1 PRU at RAF Benson, where they were modified to carry cameras and were used as armed photo-reconnaissance aircraft. In May 1943 B Flight of No.333 (Norwegian) Squadron would operate F Mk IIs that carried cameras in the long-range day-reconnaissance and anti-shipping role along the Norwegian coast until they re-equipped with the FB Mk VI in September 1943.

In January 1943 No.60 (South African) Squadron converted a pair of F Mk IIs with the addition of a camera beneath each crew seat and operated them in North Africa. These machines were diverted to North Africa after General Montgomery contacted Prime Minister Winston Churchill, having failed to obtain the Mosquitos he desperately needed, and told him the planned attack on the Mareth Line would not go ahead without them. The first sortie was flown on the 15th February 1943 with DD744 and the two modified F Mk IIs were later joined by a PR Mk IV and an FB Mk VI, before the unit finally received PR Mk IXs in August 1943.

Into Action

The first unit to become operational with the night-fighter Mosquito NF Mk II was No.157 Squadron at Debden, when it reformed there under Wg Cdr Gordon Slade on the 13th December 1941. It did not actually receive a Mosquito (T Mk III prototype W4073) until the 17th January 1942 (some sources state it was the 26th January), by which time it had moved to Castle Camps. Deliveries were slow however

and by the end of March the squadron only had fourteen aircraft. These were joined by six more in April, but three of these had no A.I radar installed and only seven crews were fully trained to fly the Mosquito. The squadron made a few modifications to controls and lights in the cockpit to ease night operations, plus they developed flash eliminators for the nose-mounted machine-guns. Other modifications were made thanks to the development work being undertaken by de Havillands, and these included modified cowlings and exhausts to overcome the overheating and burning of the exhausts, and a twin-contact Marstrand tailwheel tyre was used in place of the standard balloon unit to overcome tail-wheel shimmy. The second unit to be allocated the type, No.151 Squadron at RAF Wittering

F Mk IIs of No.456 Squadron at Middle Wallop 5th June 1943 *(©Crown Copyright)*

under the command of Wg Cdr Irving S. Smith DFC, was also awaiting Mosquitos to replace its Boulton-Paul Defiant NF Mk Is and it was not until the 6th April that the first (DD608) arrived and was allocated to A Flight. The need for effective night interceptors was paramount at this stage because the Luftwaffe's Baedeker raids were in full swing, as a reprisal for Bomber Command's raid on Lubeck on the night of the 28th/29th March. No.157 Squadron undertook its first patrol with the NF Mk II on the night of the 27th/28th April, with three machines operating alongside Beaufighters and Spitfires against Lufwaffe bombers attacking Norwich. Although radar contact was made on several occasions, none of the attacking aircraft were intercepted

F Mk II, DZ238, YP•H delivered to No.23 Squadron on the 9th December 1942 made the last F Mk II sortie with the unit on the 17th August 1943 *(©DH)*

NF Mk II DD609 of
No.151 Squadron
(©British Official)

and the problems with gun muzzle flash, and exhaust overheating/burning made themselves felt once again. The next night, the Luftwaffe attacked York, killing eighty-three people, but again, no interceptions were achieved. The raids continued and No.151 Squadron undertook their first night operations with the Mosquito NF Mk II on the night of the 29th/30th April against various Luftwaffe raids across the UK. Exeter was bombed on the night of the 3rd/4th May and the next night, Cowes on the Isle of Wight was attacked in two waves, resulting in the death of sixty-six people and the injuring of another seventy. Norwich was hit again on the night of the 8th/9th May, followed by Hull, Poole and, on the 29th/30th May Grimsby was the target. Having had no success thus far the NF Mk II started to enjoy success at night, when Flt Lt Pennington of No.151 Squadron, intercepted and damaged a Heinkel He 111, even though he lost the port engine and had to fly some 140 miles back home on one engine. P/O John Wain and Flt Sgt Thomas S.G. Grieve, also from No.151 Squadron, attacked a Dornier Do 217 of KG2 and saw it fall away into the sea on fire (it was claimed as a 'probable'), while Sqn Ldr G. Ashfield of No.157 Squadron got another probable on a Do 217 south of Dover. During

the failed raid against Nuneaton on the night of the 24th/25th June No.151 Squadron scored their first kills with the NF Mk II, when Wg Cdr Smith and Flt Lt Kernon-Sheppard intercepted three bombers during a 30-minute period, claiming two Do 217s as destroyed and one He 111 as a probable. The squadron gained yet more victories the next night, when P/O John Wain and Flt Sgt Tom Grieve shot down a He 111, and then on the night of the 26th/27th, Flt Lt Moody and P/O Marsh shot down a Do 217.

The next squadron to receive the NF Mk II was No.85 at Hunsdon in August 1942, but it was not until October that they achieved their first kill with the type. By this stage the Luftwaffe had revised tactics and started to send single aircraft on daylight low level (or by cloud cover) 'pirate' raids against selected targets. No.157 Squadron had its first success against such raiders on the night of the 22nd/23rd August and in September No.151 Squadron destroyed two more Do 217s. The first victory in daytime was achieved by No.157 Squadron on the 30th September and by October they added another three victories to their increasing tally. No.151 Squadron got its first kill of the New Year on the night of the 15th/16th January 1943 and No.85 Squadron had success on the night of

NF Mk XII HK129 was
built as an F Mk II and
converted by Marshall of
Cambridge *(©MofS)*

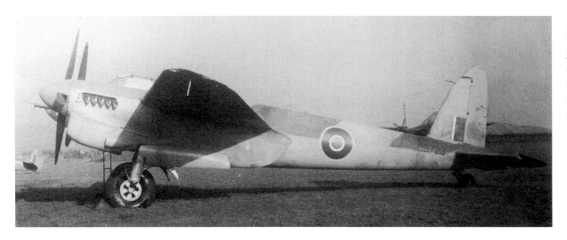

NF Mk II DD723 with Rolls-Royce Merlin XX units with their underslung radiators being tested by Rolls-Royce at Hucknall

(©Rolls-Royce)

the 17th/18th January.

The next unit to receive the NF Mk II was No.307 (Polish) Squadron in December 1942 and it went operational with the type on the 14th January 1943. This was followed by No.410 (Canadian) Squadron, who converted from the Beaufighter in January 1943 and it soon claimed a victory with the type the same month. No.25 Squadron had started to re-equip with the Mosquito on the 21st October 1942 and finally relinquished its last Beaufighters in February 1943. The next unit to get the NF Mk II was No.605 Squadron at Ford in February 1943.

Turbinlite

Mosquito NF Mk II W4087 was fitted with a 2,600 million candlepower Helmore/GEC airborne searchlight during October/November 1941. The unit was powered by twenty-four batteries stowed in the bay aft of the cannon and was intended to supplement the existing A.I. radar, as these early sets were not precise enough to obtain a good visual contact with an enemy except on the clearest of nights. The Helmore unit was huge, using some 1,400 amps when the largest searchlights then in use by the Army and Navy used a mere 150 amps, and it was developed by GEC under the sponsorship of Air Commodore W. Helmore CBE, FRAeS, the Ministry of Aircraft Production's Scientific Advisor. The reflector produced a sausage-shaped beam some 950yds (2,850ft) wide at one mile. The original intention was to fit the Helmore-equipped aircraft with A.I. radar to guide it to a target that it would then illuminate, so the following single-seat fighters could engage and shoot it down. The light was also installed in a number of Douglas Havocs and when single-engine types were withdrawn from the night-fighter role, other Havocs were intended to act as the 'killer' element of this hunter/killer combination. In the end, though, the development of better centimetric radars such as the A.I. Mk VIII fitted to the Mosquito NF Mk XII from January 1943 meant that the Helmore concept was outdated and it was never adopted nor used operationally with the Mosquito. W4087 was used for operational trials with Nos.25, 85 and 151 Squadrons until early 1943, when it returned to No.1422 Flight at Heston, having never

achieved a night interception. It later went on to undertake radio and radar flights for the National Physical Laboratory.

One-off Modifications

NF Mk II DD723 was fitted by Rolls-Royce at Hucknall with Merlin engines that had the chin-type radiators similar to those seen on the Beaufighter Mk II and Lancaster. This installation removed the need for the standard radiators mounted in the leading-edge of the inboard wing. Although the adoption of these 'power eggs' would have simplified supply, the units did nothing as far as the Mosquito's performance was concerned, as they created more drag, so in the end the use of this type of engine unit was never adopted by the Mosquito and DD723 remained a single prototype.

DZ714 was apparently fitted with a special H2S radar scanner, however as we can find no photographs of this installation, it is impossible to tell where the scanner was situated (was it under the bomb bay or the rear fuselage?).

On the Offensive

Even though by this stage just about every night-fighter that could be mustered was needed to defend the UK from the nightly raids of the Luftwaffe, there was a call to use the type offensively across occupied Europe in both the pure night-fighter and intruder roles. With mounting losses in Bomber Command, it was felt that intruder aircraft over the Luftwaffe bases in France and the Low Countries would help to reduce the losses. The first such operation was undertaken during the 1,000 bomber raid on Cologne on the night of the 30th/31st May, but this involved Hawker Hurricanes and Douglas Bostons and Havocs because the use of A.I. radar was still strictly forbidden over enemy territory. The NF Mk II was ideal for such tactics, though, so some machines had the A.I. radar removed and in this form took on the guise of pure intruder F Mk IIs. The first unit to operate the type was No.264 Squadron based at RAF Colerne in Wiltshire. Previously the squadron had used the Boulton-Paul Defiant as a night-fighter, but on the 3rd May 1942 it received its first Mosquito (a T Mk III) and undertook its first operations with the F Mk II on the 13th June. The unit

NF Mk XIII, HK382, RO•T of No.29 Squadron seen at their base at Hunsdon (*©Crown Copyright*)

made its first claim on the night of the 27th/28th June, a Do 217 was forced down on the night of the 28th/29th June, but it was not until the night of the 30th/31st July that a Ju 88 was shot down by the squadron.

On the 7th June 1942, No.23 Squadron at Ford received a T Mk III and this was later followed by twenty-three F Mk IIs. The unit would later move to Malta, but for now it used a single machine for its first intruder sortie on the night of the 6th/7th July and the next night its pilot Wg Cdr Bertie R. 'Sammy' O'Bryen shot down a Do 217 over Montdidier, east of Chartres. The same aircraft, this time flown by Sqn Ldr K.H. Salisbury-Hughes, shot down another Do 217 and an He 111 near Evreux two nights later. The

NF Mk XIII of No.604 Squadron, complete with invasion stripes, lands at Hurn

squadron moved to Malta in December 1942 and did not return to the UK until June 1944. On the 6th December, though, the squadron was withdrawn from action and their aircraft had 150 Imp. Gal. fuel tanks fitted in the bay aft of the cannon. The aircraft also received tropical equipment and filters and the standard tailwheel tyre was replaced with a twin-contact Marstrand version to reduce shimmy. The squadron's eighteen Mosquitos flew out to Malta via Gibraltar on the 20th December. There the squadron would be used against Italian and Luftwaffe bases in Sicily in support of the 8th Army offensive against Tripoli. The squadron began operations over Sicily and undertook night attacks of the retreating Afrika Korps vehicles as they moved towards Tunisia. By May 1943 the unit had accounted for

fifteen enemy aircraft and 200 trains. The unit found the reflector gunsight then fitted to the Mosquito no use at night against ground targets, so they removed the glass reflector of the GM2 sight and used it to project the ring and red dot onto the inside of the windscreen, a bit like a primitive HUD. The unit gained FB Mk VIs in May 1943 and returned to the UK in May 1944.

After the fitment of the big tanks inside the fuselage of No.23 Squadron's machines, it was decided to do this to the aircraft of another five night-fighter squadrons in the UK to allow them to be used for daylight cloud-cover patrols. These machines received *Gee* navigation aids and the space left by the removal of the A.I. radar resulted in more room for cannon shells. It is said that these machines were called NF Mk II (Special), but it is unlikely that was ever adopted as an official designation, the type being identified as NF Mk II or F Mk II with their role as intruder defining their true nature. Six aircraft each in Nos.25, 85, 151, 157 and 264 Squadrons were modified in this manner. By December 1942 the type of sorties undertaken by the type was divided into different sorts. The *Instep* patrols were flown over the Bay of Biscay against Luftwaffe fighters in wait for Coastal Command aircraft doing anti-submarine patrols, while *Ranger* sorties were for a specific target area and the crews were given free reign to attack any target of opportunity that would thus force the Luftwaffe to maintain a large fighter force in the West to counter them. Both *Day Ranger* and *Night Ranger* sorties were undertaken, each taking off at predetermined times. The first *Instep* sortie was undertaken by No.264 Squadron on the 15th December 1942 and this squadron also undertook the first *Ranger* sortie on the 4th February 1943. No.151 Squadron started to undertake *Night Ranger* sorties over the continent on the 16th February 1943, their NF Mk IIs now equipped with rearward looking *Monica* radar. The unit also undertook high-level patrols protecting the bomber streams. During the same month No.410 Squadron moved from Acklington to its new base at Coleby Grange, where it too undertook its first *Night Ranger* sortie on the 26th. A detachment was sent to Predannack to work with Coastal Command in June, along with another intruder detachment at Hunsdon, although this latter unit was only temporary.

Protecting the Bombers

In 1942 Sir Arthur Harris CinC of Bomber Command suggested that Mosquitos be mixed in with the bomber streams to attack any Luftwaffe night-fighters. The application of radar and other electronic countermeasures were becoming more effective by 1943, so on the 8th November that year No.100 (Bomber Support) Group was formed to control electronic countermeasures and night-fighters within the bombers. Bristol Beaufighters were first used for the role, armed with A.I. Mk IV radar and *Serrate* that could home in on Luftwaffe *Lichtenstein* SN-2 airborne radar from up to 100 miles away. The combination of A.I. and *Serrate* was necessary because the latter gave the enemy aircraft's bearing, but no range, so the A.I. completed the search. With the success of the Beaufighters of No.141 Squadron it was decided that a faster aircraft was needed, so the F Mk II intruders of No.605 (County of Warwick) Squadron undertook the role initially. They were joined by *Serrate*-equipped F Mk II intruders of No.141 Squadron on the 3rd November, and these machines were also fitted with the fuel tank in the ventral bay aft of the cannon. Two Mosquitos from No.239 squadron joined operations and these machines are quoted as having early A.I. with special aerials mounted on the wing leading-edges; if this is the case, then this is the first example of the 'toasting fork' style of antenna array used by Luftwaffe night-fighters; sadly no photos survive so we are unable to illustrate this type elsewhere in this title. The third unit with *Serrate*-equipped Mosquitos, No.168 squadron, joined No.100 Group shortly afterwards and the first success by these machines was achieved by No.141 Squadron, who shot down a Bf 109 on the 28th January 1944. The Group now undertook three types of sortie, the first being flights over the target areas during or after an attack (the latter usually proving to be the more successful), the second being sorties against the Luftwaffe night-fighter assembly points to force them into combat (these were codename *Mahmoud*), and thirdly as fighter escorts to the bomber streams from a point some forty miles from the target. Intruder patrols (codename *Flower*) were also undertaken by the NF Mk IIs and FB Mk VI squadrons

outside of No.100 Group. Back in late 1942 specially modified B Mk IVs (DZ375, 376 and 410) were delivered to No.1474 Flight and these machines were equipped to detect the enemy radio and radar transmissions before they were jammed. The unit was renamed No.192 Squadron in January 1943 and at the end of February 1944 it was joined by No.515 Squadron flying NF Mk IIs in the jamming role; the unit received FB Mk VIs at the end of February as most NF Mk IIs were getting very old by this stage and many elsewhere were re-engined with Merlin 22s. The three *Serrate*-equipped squadrons soon relinquished their NF Mk IIs for FB Mk VIs and those operated by No.169 Squadron also had *Perfectos II* fitted. The 100th No.100 Group kill was achieved by No.169 Squadron, when NT113 shot down a Bf 110 near Coutrai on the night of the 20th/21st July 1944.

New Radar, New Variants

NF Mk II DD715 was taken off the production line on the 22nd July 1942 and fitted with the new centrimetric A.I. Mk VIII radar. This radar was housed in a revised 'thimble' radome, which took the place of the machine-guns usually installed in the nose region. The installation made DD715 the first of the new NF Mk XII series and in the end ninety-seven NF Mk IIs were converted by Marshall's Flying Services Ltd between January and June 1943, beginning with HJ945. The type became operational with No.85 Squadron on the 28th February 1943. The type achieved its first kills on the night of the 14th/15th April, when two Do 217s were shot down whilst attacking Chelmsford. The Luftwaffe were by then using single-seat Focke-Wulf Fw 190s in hit-and-run raids and it was against such a raider that the NF Mk XII had its first success on the night of the 16th/17th April. No.85 Squadron used the type to succeed in shooting down one of the new Messerschmitt Me 410s being used in hit-and-run raids on the night of the 13th/14th July, and it was also the first to shoot down over the UK a Junkers Ju 188 on the night of the 15th/16th October. The type was first used abroad by No.256 Squadron when they moved to Malta in July 1943, and their aircraft all carried long-range tanks in the bay aft of the cannon bay.

The use of the A.I. Mk VIII or American SCR.720 known as the A.I. Mk X was first test

NF Mk XVII, DZ659 marked as ZQ•H with the Fighter Interception Unit at Ford in October 1944

(©Air Ministry)

fitted into the nose of an NF Mk II, DZ659/G, although the radome adopted on this machine was not exactly the same as the later Universal ('bullnose') unit you will find on the NF Mk XIII and NF Mk XIX. It undertook trials with the FIU at Ford from the 1st April 1943 and was later fitted with the slightly different SCR.729 radar system. After trials DZ659 was converted to NF Mk XVII standard and used by the FIU at Ford where it received the codes ZQ•H. The NF Mk XIII was based on the fighter-bomber FB Mk VI with its strengthened wing capable of carrying drop tanks, plus it had the bomb-carrying capacity of the FB Mk VI in the fuselage and had an endurance of 5 3/4 hours, so was ideal for the intruder and bomber escort roles. The type could use the Merlin 21 or 23, as well as the more powerful Merlin 25. The early production machines had the A.I. radar housed in the same 'thimble' radome as seen on the NF Mk XII, but later machines adopted the new universal 'Bull-nose' radome, which could accommodate either the Mk VIII or Mk X radars without modifica-

tion. The first unit to use the NF Mk XIII was No.488 (New Zealand) Squadron and they undertook the first patrol with the type on the 8th October 1943 and scored the first kill (a Me 410) on the 8th November. Operations with the NF Mk XII and XIII had shown the need for some improvements, not least of which was better performance above 20,000ft. To this end nitrous-oxide injection was tested on the Merlin 23s of two Mosquitos with the RAE (one was operationally tested by the FIU, whilst the other HK374 'L' was flown by No.85 Squadron) and this system was retrofitted to fifty NF Mk XIIIs by Heston Aircraft Ltd. These machines were mainly operated by Nos.96 and 410 Squadrons and the system boosted speed by as much as 47mph at 28,000ft. The system had enough nitrous-oxide for six minutes' use and it was also later fitted to an unknown number of the later NF Mk XXX. It is also known that NF Mk XIII HK508 with No.256 Squadron was modified to carry 500lb bombs under each outer wing panel during the unit's operations in Italy, so it is likely

that other such field modifications took place on other machines in the squadron, and maybe with other units. It was No.256 Squadron that again operated this variant abroad first, when their NF Mk XIIs were supplemented by Mk XIIIs in late 1943.

The NF Mk XIV was never built, as it was a proposed high-altitude development of the NF Mk XIII fitted with Merlin 67 engines and, in the end, it was superseded by the NF Mk XIX and XXX series.

With the availability of the American SCR 720 and 729 radar, both called A.I. Mk X in RAF service, it was fitted into existing NF Mk II airframes. The installation, albeit with a slightly different profile radome to later machines, was first tested in NF Mk II DZ659/G, but the true prototype of the NF Mk XVII was HK195/G and one hundred NF Mk IIs were converted in this manner by Marshall's Flying Services Ltd. The type undertook its first patrol on the 4th January 1944 with No.25 Squadron and on the 20th February the unit achieved its first kill with the type, shooting down a Ju 188 on its way to attack London. The type was also used to counter the new V1 pilotless bombs which were being launched against the UK, and from the 14th June the night-fighter Mosquitos started to achieve success against them. Gauging the distance to fire on these weapons, especially at night, was not easy as the bright flame coming from the pulse-jet was blinding, so a number of devises were tried, including photo-cell indicators, and the type even tried to flip the V1 over purely by rushing past with the slipstream causing such air disturbance as to the topple the bomb. Many of these V1s were air-launched in the Channel from Heinkel He 111s and so these became the target of night-fighter Mosquitos before they could release the weapon. One NF Mk XVII, HK324/G, was fitted with

rearward-looking radar and a Perspex tail cone, although sadly no images seem to have survived of this installation, so it is not one we can illustrate elsewhere in this title. The NF Mk XIX was first used outside the UK by No.600 Squadron in Italy at the end of 1944 and this was followed by No.255 Squadron, who moved from Foggia Main to Rosignamo in February 1945 to re-equip with the NF Mk XIX and remained the only night-fighter squadron to cover the Italian airspace until the end of the war.

The next night-fighter version to be produced was the NF Mk XV, so we will cover that separately later on. The next variant to reach series production was the NF Mk XIX, which was basically similar to the NF Mk XIII (late), but could use either the A.I. Mk VII or SCR720/720 (A.I. Mk X) radar fitted in a universal 'Bullnose' radome. The series prototype was HK364 and in all 280 were built, Later machines, mainly operated by Nos.85 and 157 Squadrons, had the rearward-looking *Monica I* (and later *Monica VI*) radar fitted for use over Europe in the bomber-support role. No. 85 Squadron also had *Perfectos Mk II* fitted to their NF Mk XIXs, which homed in on the IFF signals of Luftwaffe aircraft and became available in November 1944. At the beginning of 1945 *Serrate* IV was fitted to the NF Mk XIXs operated by No.157 Squadron and this homed in on the Luftwaffe's SN-2 airborne radar system. The Mosquito squadrons of No.100 Group received the NF Mk XIX in January 1945, with No.169 squadron being the first recipient. Even with all the countermeasures being undertaken by No.100 Group, bomber losses were high enough that in May 1944 Nos. 85 and 157 Squadrons were transferred to the group as pure night-fighter squadrons operating the NF Mk XIX. These machines all had *Monica IV* rear-looking radar installed, which gave a warning note to the crew of an aircraft approach-

NF Mk XV prototype MP469 after modification in November 1942 with A.I. Mk VIII radar in the nose and a gun pack under the fuselage *(©BAE)*

NF Mk XV DZ385 in flight
(©Ministry of Supply)

ing them from the rear (no indication of range, speed or bearing, though). Neither unit remained for long, as they were diverted to deal with V1s at the end of June. It was during one of these low-level chases of a V1 that the radome of an NF Mk XIX collapsed, so all other NF Mk XIX had their radomes subjected to a series of strengthening modifications. Further modifications to their machines came in July, when they were withdrawn for the engines to be adjusted to allow 24lb boost and the use of 150 octane fuel, along with the removal of the exhaust shrouds, which all resulted in these machines having a top speed of 360mph at sea level. Whilst these modifications were taking place the anti-diver (as the V1 was codenamed) duties were taken on by pioneering intruder unit No.23 Squadron. It was No.141 Squadron with its NF Mk XIXs that on the 14th April 1945 used the first of a new weapon that was to gain infamy in the Korea and Vietnam wars, when they dropped 100 Imp. Gal. drop tanks filled with Napalmgel on Neububurg airfield outside Munich. This was the first of a series of *Firebash* raids that were to take place against Luftwaffe landing grounds in the latter stages of the war.

The last wartime Mosquito night-fighter variant was the NF Mk XXX and it was also the first high-altitude night-fighter to enter production (NF Mk XVs were all conversions, none were built from new). It was similar to the NF Mk XIX and had the same A.I. Mk X (SCR 720/729) radar in a 'Bullnose' radome but was fitted with two-stage Merlin 72 engines initially, with Merlin 76s or 113s in later machines. The prototype MM686 first flew in April 1944 and the type entered service with No.219 Squadron on the 13th June. In all 580 NF Mk XXXs were built and the first kill was achieved by a No.410 Squadron machine on the night of the 19th/20th August, when it shot down two Ju 88s. Problems with the exhaust flame dampers led to the type being grounded not long after entering squadron service, and they only returned to flying when an interim modification was made to the outer

shrouds. This did not work, however, and problems soon arose with the inner shrouds and it was not until a lot of tests had been undertaken that louvred shrouds were all fitted retrospectively to the entire NF Mk XXX fleet. The type could carry a 250lb bomb or 50 or 100 Imp. Gal. drop tanks under each outer wing panel, although you will rarely see the former carried. Some aircraft had the *Perfectos II* homing device installed, whilst others had rearward-looking *Monica VI* radar for bomber support sorties. The NF Mk XXX was allocated to No.100 Group before the war's end, being allocated to Nos.169 and 239 Squadrons. The type was also operated by pure night-fighter squadrons Nos.85, 141 and 157 before the war's end, and ex-Fighter Command squadrons Nos.151, 307 and 406 were handed over to Bomber Command for offensive missions in the light of no more Luftwaffe bombing attacks against the UK. Both Nos.151 and 406 Squadrons' machine had *Monica* rearward-facing radar installed. In late 1944 the radar jamming No.192 Squadron had W4071, a B Mk IV Series I, join it to undertake jamming missions with the new *Piperack* device installed. This device caused 'clutter' on the enemies' A.I screens and was first used over Hannover on the 5th January 1945.

Unique High-Flyer

Development of the two-stage, high-altitude Merlin 61 meant that there was potential to develop high-altitude versions of the bomber and photo-reconnaissance Mosquito, however at that stage of the war the engine was needed for the Spitfire, so no great urgency was attached to the task. In March 1943 however an unidentified bomber airframe with Merlin 61s and a pressurised cockpit joined prototype W4050 with its Merlin 61s. This machine was not unlike the new B Mk XVI series, but it was not identified as any particular variant, being a pure test-bed for the engines and pressurisation system. This machine was MP469 and it first flew in bomber configuration on the 8th August 1942. That same month the Luftwaffe started high-altitude bombing and reconnaissance operations over the UK with the 84ft span Junkers Ju 86P and 105ft span Ju 86R. Such was the altitude that these machines operated at, that when they first appeared it was felt they were beyond reach of any existing aircraft type used by Fighter Command. The Ju 86s operated above 36,000ft and on its return from a raid on Luton one passed over Hatfield at 40,000ft. Many D.H. personnel watched the aircraft fly over, including R.M. Clarkson the head of aerodynamics, who soon got into conversation with his colleagues about potentially modifying a Mosquito to operate at that height. Forty-eight hours later D.H. asked the Director of Technical Development if they could produce one high-altitude Mosquito fighter. Work started almost at once to convert the high-altitude MP469 into a fighter; the nose was removed and replaced with the fighter nose of NF Mk II DD715, which had been removed from it when it was fitted with centimetric radar as the NF Mk XII prototype. A fighter-style control column was installed and the armour bulkhead aft of the nose gun bay was replaced with a duralumin one with just plywood replacing the pilot's back armour. Initially the Merlin 61s had three-blade propellers, but on the 13th September these were replaced with non-feathering, four-blade units that had been tested on W4050. The wing tips were extended to give a total span of 62ft 2in and the main wheels were replaced with ones of smaller diameter and tyres that lacked any tread pattern. The outer wing and fuselage fuel tanks were removed to lighten the airframe, leaving the aircraft with just 287 Imp. Gal. of fuel in the inner wing tanks, with the bullet-proofing also being removed from these tanks to further save weight. Radio equipment was reduced to a minimum and the bomb bay doors were replaced with lighter ones with simplified operating jacks. One week after the Director of Technical Development Mr N.E. Rowe had visited Hatfield and given the go-ahead on the project, MP469 rolled out, weighing in at just 16,200lb with 2,000 rounds of ammo, 287 Imp. Gal. of fuel and pilot (it carried only one crew at this point), when the standard MP469 in bomber configuration had weighed 22,485lb. Two test flights were made

on the evening of the 14th September and the next morning a height of 43,000ft was achieved. In anticipation of the arrival of suitable types, Fighter Command had set up the High Altitude Flight at RAF Northolt and MP469 was flown there on the 16th by F/O Sparrow from No.151 Squadron. There MP469 waited, but the Ju 86s did not return and summer turned to autumn. Test flights saw MP469 achieve 42,000ft in 35 mins and it had a two-hour endurance at a true air speed of 360mph. On one occasion a height of 45,000ft was achieved, but the Ju 86s never returned over the UK and in fact high-altitude flights over the UK were not to occur again until the Arado Ar 234 Blitz (see Airframe Album No.9, ISBN: 978-0-9935345-0-8) undertook a few such sorties in late 1944 and early 1945.

With no sign of the Ju 86s, MP469 was returned to Hatfield during the winter and was modified with the fitment of A.I. Mk VIII radar in the nose, which relocated the machine-guns there into a gun pack underneath the fuselage. A second crew member was also added and the two 24 Imp. Gal. outer wing tanks were reinstalled. In late November the decision had been made to create four more NF Mk XVs and these were all converted from B Mk IVs (DZ366, DZ385, DZ409 and DZ417). All four had A.I. radar and the ventral gun pack; while DZ366 had Merlin 61s, the other three had Merlin 77s. All four then joined the FIU at Ford with MP469 and from March to August 1943 they formed the special C Flight of No.85 Squadron at Hunsdon for operational trials. It was during such trials that MP469 achieved an altitude of 44,600ft. With no Ju 86s to intercept once the trials were over some of the NF Mk XVs went to RAE Farnborough for research into cabin pressurisation, but the ultimate fate of all the NF Mk XVs is unknown.

A Trainer

The fitment of dual controls was considered from a very early stage in production, with these controls being fitted to a limited number of NF Mk IIs. To that end the two turret-armed prototype W4053 and W4073 were modified to become dual-control trainers, the first flying on the 30th January 1942. These were followed by four more converted NF Mk IIs W4075,

T Mk III, HJ880, built at Leavesden in March 1943, note the fighter scheme complete with yellow wing leading edges and the Sky band round the rear fuselage

(©Crown Copyright)

All-yellow T Mk III, VT589,OT•Z of No.58 Squadron in flight

FB Mk VI prototype HJ662/G at A&AEE during the summer of 1942 for handling and diving trials
(©Crown Copyright)

FB Mk VI, HR135, from No.248 Squadron carrying 250lB Mk XI* depth charges for trials with A&AEE
(©A&AEE/Crown Copyright)

W4077, W4079 and W4081 and series production of the type started with the serial number batch HJ851 to HJ899 at Hatfield. Later batches were constructed at Leavesden with 358 being built before production ceased in 1948; all the post-war machines were built once more at Hatfield. Of these twenty were delivered to the Royal Navy to help train pilots of the Sea Mosquito, twenty-four went to Canada from April 1943 and fourteen went to Australia, although four of these were later shipped on to New Zealand.

After the war a number of T Mk IIIs were supplied to foreign air forces that already operated other variants of the Mosquito. Seven went to the Belgian Air Force and three to the Royal Norwegian Air Force, with an unknown number supplied to the Israeli, Yugoslavian and Turkish Air Forces. The Turkish examples had the option to carry 500lb bombs under the wings, and this was also an option available in the late-production examples used by the RAF. The Belgian Air Force went on to convert some of their T Mk IIIs to target tugs, where they were designated the TT Mk III.

Fighter-Bomber

The FB Mk VI was a natural progression in development from the intruder F Mk IIs with the extra fuel tankage, navigational aids such as *Gee* and the removal of the A.I. radar. The type featured the strengthening of the wing at Rib 8, so that a 50 Imp. Gal. drop tank or bomb could be carried under each outer wing panel. The first 200 FB Mk VIs were Series I, in that they could only carry two 205lb bombs with the shortened tails in the bay aft of the cannon and two more under the wings. The remainder were Series II machines that could carry two 500lb bombs in the bomb bay and two more under the wings. Options included the carriage of two extra 151 Imp. Gal. fuel tanks in the bay aft of the cannon, or the carriage of two 250lb bombs with a 50 Imp. Gal. fuel tank. The type was also tested with and could use operational SCI (Smoke laying) containers in place of the bombs under the wings.

The first FB Mk VI was converted from B Mk IV DZ434 and it first flew on the 1st June 1942 (later it was allocated the new serial number HJ662/G). On the 13th June it went to A&AEE Boscombe Down for trials, including the fitment of mustard gas distribution canisters under the wings. At this time there were actually plans to produce two versions of the Mk VI, the first was the NF Mk VI (which was previously entitled the Mk IVA), which had 403 Imp. Gal. fuel capacity and no bomb load, and the LRF Mk VI long-range fighter and

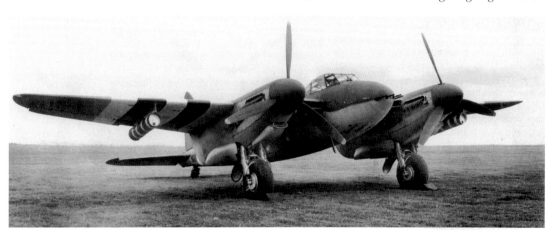

intruder (previously the Mk IVB), which had 520 Imp. Gal. fuel capacity. In the end though, neither version was built as all these roles could be undertaken by the FB Mk VI and other night-fighter versions. The FB Mk VI could be powered by the Merlin 21, 22, 23 or 25 engines, the latter with improved +18lb boost for better low- and medium-altitude performance. The first FB Mk VI airframe to be fitted with Merlin 25s was HJ679, which undertook radar trials at Boscombe Down and the Air-Sea Warfare Development Unit. Overall fuel tankage in the type was also increased, with overload tanks available for the fuselage and 100 Imp. Gal. drop tanks. This meant that in total the FB Mk VI could carry 66 1/2 Imp. Gal. overload tanks in the fuselage, a 50 Imp. Gal. tank in the fuselage between the spars, 131 Imp. Gals in two tanks, two more of 156 Imp. Gals. inboard of the nacelles in each wing and two 24 and 34 Imp. Gal. tanks outboard of the nacelles in each wing, giving a maximum internal tankage of 519 1/2 Imp. Gal. The type could carry a variety of ordnance and is probably best known for the carriage of 3in rocket projectiles; this became available in late 1944. These rockets usually carried one of two head types, either the 25lb semi-armour piercing (SAP) or the 60lb high explosive (HE), with the type fitted dependant on the intended target; the 60lb HE heads often went right through things like the hull of a ship before exploding. The first FB Mk VI to carry 3in rockets was HJ719 and it first flew with four of them under each wing in October 1943, and the ideal angle for launch was 20°. Later a two-tier rail was developed to allow the carriage of eight rockets with drop tanks, thus extending the range of these machines as they undertook strikes along the coast of Norway etc. The FB Mk VI could also carry a Mk XI depth charge or Mk VIII mine under each wing in the coastal-strike role, and dropping trials were undertake by a No.248 Squadron machine at Boscombe Down in 1944, although in the end

the Mosquito was never used for mine-laying by Coastal Command. Delays due to ever changing demands and orders for the various versions of the Mosquito meant that the first production FB Mk VIs did not fly until seven months after the prototype, in February 1943.

A number of FB Mk VIs were used for trials with A.I. Mk IV and V radar, NS997/G is known to have undertaken trials with the latter. In June 1944, the first American A.I. Mk XV, known as ASH (Air to Surface Home) radar arrived with the Bomber Support Development Unit at Foulsham. There a nose installation within the FB Mk VI was devised and these were subsequently installed in the machines of Nos.23, 143 and 515 Squadrons. The first kill achieved with the installation came on the 1st January 1945, when a Ju 88 was claimed near Ahlhorn. A further fourteen kills were achieved before the war ended in Europe, although the ASH radar needed a great deal of skill to be effective. Some of the FB Mk VIs used in the bomber support role were fitted with *Gee* or *Gee-H* navigational aids, whilst others used *Serrate*, *Perfectos* and *Monica* electronic countermeasures. The BDSU developed the installation of the *Monica III* radar in the nose of FB Mk VI NT181, which it was

An FB Mk VI of No.29 Squadron fires all its guns at night in the stop butts at Hunsdon for the official photographer (©Air Ministry)

FB Mk VI. PZ338 of No.515 Squadron at Little Snoring with Wg Cdr F.F. Lambert DSO DFC on the left (©Air Ministry)

This still taken during the Amiens prison raid shows the second wave of Mosquitos bombing the walls *(©Crown Copyright)*

hoped would allow accurate ranging radar for targeting V1s.

A Merlin 61 powered version of the FB Mk VI was planned as the FB Mk XI, but it was never built.

Fighter-Bomber into Action

The very first unit to get the FB Mk VI was No.418 (City of Edmonton) Squadron, based at Ford, when it received its first one on the 11th May 1943 to replace the night-fighter Mk IIs it had previously operated. The second unit to get the FB Mk VI was not based in the UK, it was No.23 Squadron on Malta, who got the type in the later stages of May 1943 and first used it on the 17th July. The second UK-based ex-intruder unit to get the FB Mk VI was No.605 (County of Warwick) Squadron based at Castle Camps, when it received them in July 1943. The FB Mk VIs on Malta were supplemented when No.108 Squadron also flew the type alongside its existing Beaufighters during February-July 1944.

Nos.464 (RAAF) and 487 (RNZAF) Squadrons started to re-equip with the FB Mk VI when they each received a pair of them on the 21st August 1943, and they were joined soon afterwards when No.21 Squadron swapped its Venturas for the type. All three of these units were part of the newly-formed 2nd Tactical Air Force, which was set up to co-ordinate attacks on tactical targets in Europe, especially in the build-up for D-Day. All three units operated from Sculthorpe to form No.140 Wing and it undertook its first operation with the type on the 2nd October when Nos.464 and 487 attacked the power stations at Guerleden and Pont-Château. Nos.21 and 464 Squadrons later went on to undertake *Day Ranger* and *Flower* sorties with the FB Mk VI. The Wing undertook the first of many attacks against the V1 sites in France on the 22nd December 1943. A fourth FB Mk VI squadron, No.613 based at Lasham, made its first sortie on the 19th December and was soon joined by Nos.107 and 307(Polish) Squadrons to form No.138 Wing. No.140 Wing moved south to Hunsdon during the New Year period, to make them nearer the continent.

One of the most famous raids in which the FB Mk VI was key, was Operation Jericho, a precision attack on Amiens jail in an attempt to help numerous French Resistance workers held there to escape before they were executed. At 11am on the 18th February 1944 (the raid having been postponed from the 17th due to dense cloud and snow) eighteen FB Mk VIs of No.140 Wing took off accompanied by a B Mk IV (DZ414) of the Wing's Film Unit. The raid was led by Gp Capt P.C. Pickard, DS and two bars, DFC, who was already well known to the British public having been in the film *Target for Tonight*, with his navigator Flt Lt J. A. Broadley DSO, DFC, DFM. The first wave of No.487 Squadron aircraft were to breech the 20ft high, 3ft thick

FB Mk VIs of No.47 Squadron on the Arakan Front, Burma with skull and crossbones on the crew door, where they operated against Indonesian Nationalists in Java *(©British Official)*

FB Mk VIs of No.618 Squadron in the DH-Australia Mascot facility being re-assembled after shipment from the UK. These were intended operationally to safeguard the squadron's Highball-carrying B Mk IVs, they were also used for training purposes; HR578 is in the foreground
(©DH-Australia)

prison walls on the north and east sides, while the second wave of No.464 Squadron aircraft were to attack the quarters of the guards at either end of the prison and a very strict time-table had to be followed to avoid collisions. The Mosquitos were escorted by Hawker Typhoons and as planned the walls were breached by the first wave, then the second attacked the guards, whilst the B Mk IV circled and filmed the whole thing. The third wing of No.21 Squadron ma-chines was there as a back-up, but they were not needed and were ordered not to attack. Pickard circled the prison to ensure that the objectives were achieved and he engaged Focke-Wulf Fw 190s that came on the scene, as the Typhoon escorts had turned for home. Sadly in the ensu-ing dogfight Pickard's aircraft was shot down and both he and Broadley were killed; he was buried adjacent to the prison and for years the graves were maintained by locals in thanks for the many who escaped. One more FB Mk VI was shot down by Flak and two Typhoons were also lost, and 258 of the 700 prisoners, including half of those due to be executed. 102 prisoners were either killed by the bombs or machine-gun fire from the guards and some of those that escaped were later recaptured.

The FB Mk VI also undertook another well-known low-level precision attack, when they helped destroy the Gestapo records for the Dutch Resistance. The raid, which took place on the 11th April 1944, was made against the Dutch central Population Registry in the Schven-ingsche Wegg in the Hague by six FB Mk VIs of No.613 Squadron, led by Wg Cdr R.N. Bateson. The five-storey house in the midst of others was completely destroyed with 500lb bombs and incendiaries with the loss of a single Mosquito. After a series of precision raids on known and suspect Gestapo and SS barracks, a raid was mounted on the Gestapo HQ housed within two buildings of the Aarhus University at Jutland on the 31st October 1944. Twenty-four Mosquitos of Nos.21, 464 and 487 Squadrons were led by Gp Capt P.G. Wykeham Barnes, DSO and Bar, DFC and they dropped their time-delayed bombs

on target having attacked in four waves of six aircraft. Surprise was complete and only one air-craft had to divert to land in Sweden, while the rest made it home safely. These squadrons made a second raid on the 21st March 1945 against the Gestapo HQ in the Shellhaus building in Copenhagen. The attack was led by Gp Capt Bateson and although the attack was precise and the building set ablaze, one Mosquito crashed into an adjacent school killing both children and teachers. In all four Mosquitos and two of the escorting Mustangs were lost in the attack.

Having undertaken precision bombing raids, it was no surprise that the FB Mk VI was chosen for the task of dropping markers for No.617 Squadron. The first such operation was under-taken by Gp Capt Leonard Cheshire, DSM and two bars, DFC on the marshalling yards at Juvisy near Paris, but his markers hung up. Cheshire flew lead to a group marking railway yards near Munich on the 24th April 1944 and once over the target he dived from 10,000ft to 3,000ft to drop his markers on the yard, then circled at top speed at only 1,000ft to tell the bombers of the fall of their bombs, whilst the flak burst all around him. As none of the Mosquitos had overload tanks available for this flight, they were unsure of their fuel reserves, but all reached base safely with just 10 minutes of fuel remaining. For this attack and for his long history of leadership

FB Mk VI, RF942, KU•H of No.47 Squadron being loaded with RPs during operations in Java
(©British Official)

Built as an FB Mk VI HJ732/G was modified as the prototype FB Mk XVIII and is seen here with the A&AEE in August 1943 for firing trials on Salisbury Plain that started on the 2nd July 1943 *(©A&AEE)*

and courage, Cheshire was awarded the Victoria Cross. An interesting aside to this is the Mosquito flown by Cheshire on that raid, NS993, force-landed at Dubendorf on the 30th September 1944, whilst serving with No.515 Squadron and was interned by the Swiss, before being passed to the Swiss Air Force, where it was flown marked as 'B-5'.

The Far East

Four Mosquito NF Mk IIs were in India by May 1943 for weathering trials, two of them featuring the new formaldehyde glue instead of the usual casein glue. By August an FB Mk VI was in India and two F Mk IIs with cameras installed were being used by No.681 Squadron at Dum Dum airfield, Calcutta and it was one of these that made the first Mosquito sortie against the Japanese, when it did a photo-reconnaissance flight over the Mandalay region on the 23rd August. An FB Mk VI with a camera in the nose (HJ730) soon joined the unit, whilst a second unit, No.684 Squadron, was formed at Dum Dum in October with two F Mk IIs and three FB Mk VIs on strength. The trials, along with the limited use of the type in the region had proved that the structure and formaldehyde glue were resistant to the high temperatures (103°+) and humidity (88%+), so a big expansion of the type in the region was planned for the beginning of 1944 but this involved a complex service and repair infrastructure. Little or no wood could be held in Bengal and only minor repairs could be done at unit level, so two RAF depots near Calcutta did the major repairs while a subsidiary of de Havillands was set up at Karachi to make components like flaps and tailplanes.

The first units to receive the FB Mk VI in the region were ex-Vengeance squadrons Nos.45 and 82, with their crews being converted to the type by No.1672 Conversion Unit, which had a couple of T Mk IIIs. No.45 was the first to go into operations, with a tactical reconnaissance flight on the 28th September, followed by No.82 Squadron the next month. On the 20th October though, a No.82 Squadron FB Mk VI was making a shallow practice bombing run when the outer half of the starboard wing failed and collapsed, causing the aircraft to crash with the loss of both crew. An investigation revealed that the climate was starting to effect the structure of the Mosquito, with the glue and fabric cracking and skins lifting from the spars. All Mosquitos in India were grounded along with any that had been in the Far East for more than three months. All were flown to maintenance units for inspections, where it was discovered that the formaldehyde glued machines were structurally sound, so no modification programme was needed; it is assumed it was those with casein glue that were unsound, and thus probably scrapped or rebuilt by de Havillands? The ban on flying came at a

Well-known in-flight shot of FB Mk XVIII, NT225, 'O' of No.248 Squadron taken in June 1944

(©Crown Copyright)

bad time, as the Mosquitos were needed to keep up the pressure on the Japanese in support of the 14th Army's advance, and it was not until February 1945 that Nos.45 and 82 Squadrons resumed operations, joined by a third squadron, No.47. At some point towards the end of 1944 the FB Mk VIs operated by No.45 Squadron had a F.24 camera installed in the nose, presumably in a vertical position, to allow them to undertake tactical reconnaissance missions to supplement the long-range PR versions now being operated in the region. Two more units, Nos.84 and 110, began to re-equip with the FB Mk VI in March 1945, and all of them were operational by the fall of Rangoon in May. A sixth unit, No.211, began to convert to the type in June, but it did not see any operations with the type before the cessation of hostilities. The last operational sortie undertaken by the type in the region was flown by eight FB Mk VIs of No.110 Squadron on the 20th August 1945 against a pocket of resistance at Tikedo.

Operations with the type soon resumed in the East Indies though, as Dr Sukarno had proclaimed the Republic of Indonesia to resist Dutch colonial rule with Japan's defeat. The anti-Dutch insurgents took advantage of the lack of Allied formal control in the region and started to use discarded Japanese weapons, ordnance and even aircraft to attack the Allied forces. When Brigadier A.W.S. Mallaby was killed in his car at Jembatan Merah (Red Bridge) in Surabaya on the 30th October 1945 some Mosquitos of Nos.84 and 110 Squadrons began to do reconnaissance flights over likely insurgent hideouts from the 9th November, where they were joined by rocket-firing FB Mk VIs from Nos.47 and 82 Squadrons. These machines made attacks on radio stations used by the insurgents and against them in the field, as well as flying in support of British troops on the ground. All such operations ceased in the region by March 1946, but it was not until December 1949 that the Dutch Government formally recognised Indonesian independence and all political and military action ceased.

Highball

The Royal Navy was allocated nineteen FB Mk VIs for crew training in preparation for the projected use of the *Highball* weapon by B Mk IVs of No.618 Squadron in the Pacific. In the end though, the weapon was never deployed in the Pacific, with all of them being blown up in situ and the unit was officially disbanded at RAAF Narromine on the 14th July 1945, with all the Mosquitos being sold as scrap.

At least one aircraft, PZ281, was used to test the proposed *Highball 2* system for the Sea Mosquito TR Mk 33 and D.H. Hornet (see Airframe Album No.8 ISBN: 978-0-9930908-0-6), via a quickly detachable crate in the bomb bay. Although neither type ever used the weapon this aircraft was used for nearly three years by Vickers-Armstrong Ltd for *Highball* development work from April 1945.

FB Mk VIs of No.143 Squadron attack shipping in Sandefjord 2nd April 1944 *(©Crown Copyright)*

Tsetse & Banff

With the Mosquito having been proven to be effective against shipping, on the 19th March 1943 Mr R.E. Bishop the chief designer at de Havillands received a letter from the Ministry of Aircraft Production asking if it was feasible to install the 1,800lb 6-pounder (57mm) QF (quick-firing) gun into the Mosquito. His reply was that there would be little problem dealing with the forces exerted by the weapon in the airframe, and so less than three months after receiving the letter an FB Mk VI (HJ732/G) was fitted with the gun to become the prototype FB Mk XVIII. The big gun, modified for in-flight use by Molins, was a modified anti-tank gun and it could fire twenty-five rounds in 20 seconds. Initial tests on the effect of the blast of the gun were carried out by de Havillands in the nose cut from a crashed Mosquito, with test-firing into the butts at Hatfield on the 29th April. The prototype fired its gun in the butts on the 6th June, where blast, recoil and ammunition feeds were all found to be satisfactory, so it flew for the first time on the 8th, before moving for trials at Boscombe Down on the 12th.

A decision was made to take thirty FB Mk VIs off the production line and complete them as FB Mk XVIIIs, but in the end only eighteen, in addition to the prototype, were built and only three of these (HX902-904) were converted from FB Mk VIs. An additional 900lb of armour plate was added to protect the crew and engines, and to save weight most of the later machines only retained two of the four machine-guns in the nose. In addition to the cannon, the type retained the capacity of the FB Mk VI, so could carry 500lb bombs, or eight 3in rocket projec-

Banff with Strike Wings FB VIs taxying past No.143 Squadron machines and the station hack Proctor in the foreground (©British Official)

FB Mk VI, G-AGGC at Leuchars on the 6th August 1944 for part of filming 'de Havilland presents the Mosquito' with FB Mk VI, G-AGKP (ex-LR296) in background (©BAE)

tiles or 50 or 100 Imp. Gal. drop tanks under the wings. The type could also be fitted with a 65 Imp. Gal. fuel tank in the bay aft of the cannon and with 100 Imp. Gal. drop tanks this gave a total fuel capacity of 668 Imp. Gal. Trials with the gun at Boscombe Down were generally good, but the rifling in the barrel wore out after between 300 and 500 rounds had been fired and there were problems with the ammunition feed. The first machines (HX902/G, HX903/G and HX904/G) were issued to No.248 Squadron at Predannack on the 22nd October 1943 and the first sortie was made by HX902 and HX903 on the 24th October in search of U-Boats in the Bay of Biscay. The first loss was experienced on the 4th November, when Sqn Ldr C.F. Rose DFC, DFM, the CO of No.618 Squadron on secondment to No.248 for experience in operating the Mosquito at low-level over the sea (the unit was intended to drop *Highball* bombs in the Pacific – see elsewhere), was killed when his aircraft disintegrated on ditching. After a number of attacks on U-boats on the surface as they returned to base, escort armed trawlers and flak ships had to be provided. The extent of this protection was clearly seen during an attack on a U-boat on the 11th April 1944, when it was accompanied by a flak ship, two armed trawlers and two Ju 88s, but it was to little avail, as all the ships were

damaged and the two Ju 88s were shot down. By this stage No.248 Squadron also operated the FB Mk VI in support of the FB Mk XVIIIs that now formed a special detachment in the squadron. On the 16th June 1944 a second strike unit operating the FB Mk VI, No.235 Squadron, was re-equipped and alongside No.248 Squadron moved up to Banff in Scotland in September. There the FB Mk VIs and FB Mk XVIIIs operated alongside one another and with the FB Mk VIs of No.333 (Norwegian) Squadron on strikes against shipping in Norwegian coastal waters. A third FB Mk VI unit, No.143, joined the rest at Banff in November 1944 and one of the Beaufighter squadrons at Banff, No.404, re-equipped with the FB Mk VI in April 1945. The FB Mk XVIIIs of No.248 Squadron were withdrawn from service in January 1945, mainly because rocket projectiles had proved to be more effective against shipping, but five FB Mk XVIIIs served with No.254 Squadron at North Coates in the last two months of the war, attacking U-boats in Belgian and Dutch waters.

There are two other FB Mk XVIIIs that warrant mention, the first being PZ467, which was fitted with an arrestor hook and tested by the US Navy at Patuxent River (as BuNo.91106) having been flown there from RAF Pershore on the 30th April. This was later on the civil register as NX66422 and was damaged in a ground-loop incident on landing at Lake Wales Municipal Airport, Florida on a ferry flight from WAA storage field, Augusta, Georgia in 1946 (registered to Allison Perry). It was then registered to Marvin Dunlavy, Birmingham, Alabama in 1946/47, before moving to the ownership of Al K, Rozawick/World Air Shows in 1947. Jean P. Doar of Around the World Inc., Charlotte, North Carolina owned it from 20-09-47 to 1948. The aircraft was modified for a world record flight named 'The Silver Streak', but swung on landing at Charlotte Municipal Airport on the 27th January 1948. It was never repaired and was eventually burnt by the airport fire service there at some time in 1948. The other machine

F Mk IIs of No.333 Squadron, B Flight, at Banff with DZ754, 'F' in the background
(©British Official)

is NT220, which was fitted with a torpedo rack under the fuselage for trials. It also had rocket projectiles under the wings and was fitted with a clear nose cone, behind which was probably a camera to record the torpedo drops. This machine is listed as arriving at A&AEE Boscombe Down in July 1945 and was used for 'armament demonstrations'.

It should be noted that originally it was intended to rename this version of the Mosquito the 'Tsetsefly', but it was felt that this would just cause confusion, as it was obviously a Mosquito variant. Many sources quote 'Tsetse' as the name given to this version, but it was never officially so, and was either therefore adopted by the crews or has been applied to the type by post-war historians.

Other Big Guns & Weapons

Other large calibre weapons considered for the Mosquito include the 3.7in anti-tank gun developed from the anti-aircraft gun of the same calibre. The gun would fire its 32lb projectile at 2,880ft/sec, but the 4,000lb weapon was still not fully developed by the time the war ended. The main problem with a gun of this size was recoil, so it was fitted with a Galliot muzzle brake. This was shaped like a thimble with a number of spiral slots around it, and the muzzle blast spun it around to exert a forward pull on the barrel and thus reduce recoil. Although the system worked well on the prototype, producing the muzzle brake proved difficult in mass production, but with the war's end fast approaching that was academic anyway. One was actually fitted to a Mosquito at the end of the war and some successful air firing was undertaken.

The FB Mk VI was also used for trials with the American Tiny Tim rocket projectile, which weighed 1,050lb and was called Uncle Tom by

FB Mk VI (ex-HK691), G-AGGD with BOAC in April 1943 on final approach to Leuchars
(©British Official/DH)

the British. The projectile was tested here under a Grumman Avenger and it was fired by it on a number of occasions. Pictures do exist of a Mosquito with two Tiny Tim rockets under the fuselage and it is believed these were taken at A&AEE Boscombe Down, but there seems to be no record there of these actually being fired, so the photos may just be of the intended installation. The main problem with the Tiny Tim was its size and the resulting blast from the rocket motor. This had caused damage to launch aircraft in the USA and it may go some way to explain the extended period of time to which the weapon was subjected in the UK (it was being shown at the School of Air Support, Old Sarum in May 1947) as well as the fact that it was never adopted operationally in the UK or the USA.

Airliner

BOAC operated four Lockheed Hudsons and two Lockheed Lodestars on their Leuchars to Stockholm route to collect much needed ball-bearings, fine springs and machine-tool steel needed by the British. These were supported by DC-3s of AB Aerotransport, which operated from Stockholm to Scotland. The difficulties the crews experienced were huge, as no radio contact was

FB Mk VI G-AGGF (ex-HJ720) of BOAC about to depart Leuchars (©BOAC)

Navalised FB Mk VI, LR359, acted as a test airframe for the projected Sea Mosquito and although it had the four-blade propellers, arrestor hook etc., it did not have wing-fold (©DH)

allowed, nor were navigational aids much use, plus the slow aircraft had to avoid clear nights and even the Northern Lights. When the long summer nights began BOAC had to devise more northerly routes to avoid the ever present risk of icing. On top of this the Nazis knew every landing at Bromma (Stockholm), as Deutsche Luft Hansa operated Ju 52s from there. Strict routes to and from Bromma were in force and any aircraft that strayed was shot at, this extended to Swedish aircraft and was brought home when two of ABA's DC-3s were shot down in August and October 1943. The need for faster aircraft on the route was obvious, so BOAC started to demand the Mosquito. The first flight to Bromma was undertaken by a No.105 Squadron FB Mk VI (DK292) on the 6th August 1942; carrying a diplomatic bag the crew were in civilian clothes and all the RAF markings were temporarily removed from the aircraft. After further pressure from BOAC and them turning down slower types such as the Whitley and Albemarle, a Mosquito PR Mk IV (DZ411) was supplied and it became G-AGFV on the 15th December 1942. Captain C.B. Houlder and Radio Officer F. Frape made the first flight to Bromma on the 4th February 1943. With the need for fast delivery of the ball-bearings etc. BOAC was allocated six new FB Mk VIs (HJ680, 681, 718, 720, 721 and 723) and these were registered as G-AGGC to G-AGGH respectively. G-AGFV was attacked by Fw 190s on the night of the 23rd/24th April over Skagerrak and had to force-land at Barkaby near Stockholm. The aircraft was repaired in situ by D.H. engineers, but it did not return to service for eight months.

After the USAAF 8th AF's attack on the ball-bearing factories at Schweinfurt on the 17th

August 1943 the Nazis sought to make up the shortfall in these by buying them from Sweden. The need to negotiate a deal in favour of Britain was urgently sought and two BOAC Mosquito FB Mk VIs were hastily modified in a matter of hours to carry a passenger. Once modified the machines carried negotiators to Sweden hours ahead of the Nazis and a deal was struck to sell all of Sweden's ball-bearing production to the UK. The modifications were pretty basic: the passenger lay on a reclining mattress above the bomb bay doors, which were lined with plywood, he faced forward and wore a flying suit, life preserver, flying boots and a parachute harness. He was provided with electric light and temperature control plus an intercom link with the pilot, who could advise him when to adjust his oxygen settings or to warn him of impending evasive manoeuvres. The 3-hour flight must have been a nerve-racking experience and there are accounts of the bomb bay doors not closing properly, or another of an hour long pursuit at wave top height! Sadly two passengers were lost, one of them a BOAC pilot returning as a passenger. Many VIPs were flown in this manner, including Sir Kenneth Clark, the conductor Sir Malcolm Sargent and the Danish nuclear physicist Professor Niels Bohr and his son Aage (Bohr was a leading nuclear scientist who had a Jewish mother, so he needed to get away from the Nazis should they force him to work on their nuclear programme instead of going to the concentration camps). He later went to the USA and worked on the Manhattan Project under the codename Nicholas Baker.

Operating the Mosquito was not without loss for BOAC, as G-AGGF crashed on high ground near Invermairk on the 17th August 1943, killing Captain L.A. Wilkins and Radio Officer Beaumont. G-AGGG crashed a mile from Leuchars on the 25th October, with the loss of the crew, Captain Hamre and Radio Officer Haug, as well as their passenger Mr Carl Rogers. Three more FB Mk VIs were supplied to replace the losses in April 1944; G-AGKO (ex-HJ667), G-AGKP (ex-LR296) and G-AGKR (ex-HJ792). G-AGKP ditched about nine miles off Leuchars on the night of the 18th/19th April 1944 with the loss of Captain Rae, Radio Officer Roberts and Captain B.W.B. Orton, who was a passenger, and the reason for the crash still remains a mystery. On the night of the 28th/29th April G-AGKR was lost without trace after leaving Gothenburg, with the loss of Captain White and Radio Officer Gaffeny. Operations by BOAC ended on the 17th May 1945 and G-AGGE, G-AGGH and G-AGKO were handed back to the RAF on the 22nd June, with G-AGGC on the 9th January 1946. G-AGGD was never returned to the RAF, as it was reduced to spares after a landing accident on the 3rd January 1944.

The Sea Mosquito

The Royal Navy already had Mosquitos for training, so it was a logical step for them to con-

sider the type in regard to frontline operations. Although various alternatives were considered, in the end the Royal Navy went for a simple 'navalised' version of the FB Mk VI with an A-frame arrestor hook and folding wings. An existing FB Mk VI LR359 was modified to become the first navalised Mosquito, and although many state it was the Sea Mosquito TR Mk 33 prototype, it was really only a proof of concept with regard to the suitability of the Mosquito for carrier operations. Built to Specification N.15/44, it did not feature folding wings, but it did have an arrestor hook (which was later modified and reinforced) and additional strengthening at its attachment point in the fuselage, plus further strengthening via additional longerons in the lower half of the rear fuselage. Powered by Merlin 25 engines, this drove four-blade propellers, which in this prototype, were non-feathering and had a blade diameter of 12ft 6in to improve thrust by between five and ten percent. Deck-landing trials were undertaken on HMS Indefatigable on the 25th and 26th March 1944 and were undertaken by Lt Cmdr (later Capt) Eric 'Winkle' Brown OBE, DSC with Lt Cmdr Everett acting as batsman. The twin-engine configuration made it difficult for the pilot to see the batsman, so in this case Everett had to stand right in the middle of the deck, in the path of the aircraft, and made a very quick exit to one side to avoid being hit by the propellers. Seven take-offs and landings were made during the two days, however on the eight the arrestor hook fractured, but the pilot was able to take-off and then land on shore. Later, once the arrestor hook was repaired and reinforced, during one landing the hook missed all the wires, but the aircraft was stopped safely within the deck limits purely on the brakes alone, proving the type was ideally suited to carrier operations.

The first navalised FB Mk VI was followed by LR387, another converted FB Mk VI, but it had manually folding outer wing panels and as such was the first true Sea Mosquito prototype. A powered wing fold was ruled out early on, as it would have required a complete redesign of the hydraulic system, plus the folded width achieved was only 27ft 3in, which was much wider than the 20ft lifts fitted to carriers at that time, but this could not be overcome. It should be noted that the first thirteen production machines did not have this wing fold system installed. The fold dispensed with any need for rivets, as the wood/metal plates were secured via Redux-bonding, thus transferring all loads to the top and bottom wing surfaces. The TR Mk 33 could carry an 18in Mk XV or XVII torpedo, a mine or a 2,000lb bomb under the fuselage. The type retained the four 20mm cannon, but the ASH radar pod in the nose meant the machine-guns in this location were dispensed with. Two 500lb bombs could be carried in the bay aft of the cannon, and the wings were such that four 3in rocket projectiles and a 50 Imp. Gal. drop tank could also be carried. The need for extra power

on take-off from a carrier meant that the rear fuselage had attachment points for and was reinforced for the stresses of Rocket-Assisted Take-Off (RATO). The original rubber-in-compression block undercarriage system gave far too great a rebound rate, so was replaced with oleo-pneumatic legs made by Lockheed. From the fourteenth production machine, the main wheels were also of a slightly smaller diameter than previously fitted. Two more pre-production TR Mk 33s were built at Leavesden, TS444 and TS449, to undertake handling trials. In all fifty production machines were built, TW227-257 and TW277-295, but another forty-seven were cancelled. The Sea Mosquito was also envisaged to carry the revised Mk 2 version of *Highball* and

FB Mk VI LR359 approaches HMS Indefatigable on the 25th March 1943 to make the first landing on a carrier at sea by a two-engined aircraft *(©FAA/FAAM)*

TR Mk 33 TW230/G was used for trials with the original version, whilst TW228 was used for trials with *Card*, a development of the *Highball*. In the end neither weapon ever saw service with the Royal Navy.

The first unit to operate the type was No.811 Squadron at their base at Ford in August 1946, having operated the Mosquito FB Mk VI initially there from September 1945. In January 1947 it moved to RNAS Brawdy, but disbanded in July that year. A great many more served with the Fleet Requirements Units, non-operational squadrons that provided aircraft for such roles as target-towing, training and communications. These comprised No.762 at Ford from 1946 to 1949, No.711 at RNAS Lee-on-Solent from 1947 to 1950, No.772 at RNAS Arbroath during 1946-7 and Nos.778 and 790. No.728 at Hal Far, Malta also operated the Mosquito during

The TR Mk 37 prototype TW240 was converted from a TR Mk 33

(©Crown Copyright)

The first true Sea Mosquito prototype was FB Mk VI LR38, which had wing-fold, ASH radar and the capacity to carry a torpedo
(©Ministry of Aircraft Production)

A TR Mk 33 approaches for a deck landing
(©FAA/FAAM)

1948, but only the TT Mk 39, which is a conversion based on a bomber airframe.

During 1954-55 fourteen surplus TR Mk 33s were taken out of storage at Colerne (some state fourteen, whilst IAF sources quote only three TR Mk 33s being used as trainers?) and refurbished by Eagle Aviation Ltd at Blackbushe. The refurbishment also included the removal of the arrestor hooks and other naval equipment, then the aircraft were flown to Israel for operation by the Israeli Air Force until finally retired after the Suez Crisis in early 1957.

The second Sea Mosquito fighter variant was the TF/TR Mk 37, which differed in having the British ASV Mk XIII radar in an elongated nose radome. The prototype, TW240, was modified from a TR Mk 33 and another fourteen production machines (VT724-737) were built at Chester. The type only saw very limited service with the Royal Navy, most being operated by No.702 Squadron for a short period.

Post-War

No.21 Squadron operated a courier service between Blackbushe and Furth in Germany during the Nuremburg war crimes trials under the British Air Forces of Occupation (BAFO). It, along with No.71 Squadron (later renumbered No.11 Squadron), operated the FB Mk VI in occupied Germany during the post-war era for varying periods as part of BAFO, along with No.613 (later renumbered as No.69 Squadron).

The installation of the Merlin 113s into a Mosquito night-fighter was first done in NF Mk XXX MT466, and some late production NF Mk 30s used this engine, but the more common use was in the post-war NF Mk 36 variant. The new engines were some 9in longer than the previous ones, so to overcome the resulting slight nose-heaviness larger balance weights were added to the elevators. The prototype RK955 first

The last night-fighter variant to see RAF service was the NF Mk 36, with RL261 of No.29 Squadron seen here
(©Crown Copyright)

FB Mk VIs of No.4 Squadron (ex-605 Squadron) at Wünstorf in 1949 with PZ165 UP•E, NT181 UP•H, TA639 and RS667 in background; Sqn Ldr C.P.N. Newman DFC, the squadron CO is in the white flying suit

flew in May 1945 and another 163 were built, all at Leavesden. The type entered service with Nos.23, 23, 29, 85, 141 and 264 Squadrons in the UK. In Egypt the Suez Canal Zone was protected by No.39 Squadron from their base at Fayid and Kabrit. The type stayed in RAF service until 1951, when the Meteor NF Mk 11 replaced them first with No.29 Squadron at the beginning of 1951 and the Vampire NF Mk 10 with No.25 Squadron in September 1951. A small number were converted for target-towing duties as TT Mk 36s, being similar to the TT Mk 35, and some were converted for weather-reconnaissance as MET Mk 36s.

The last night-fighter variant was the NF Mk 38, which differed from the NF Mk 36 by having British A.I. Mk IX radar and a cockpit canopy that was 5in longer and 4in higher; this being caused by the need for greater headroom behind the pilot to install additional radio and radar equipment. The prototype RL248 was converted from an NF Mk 36 and first flew on the 18th November 1947. It underwent service trials with the Central Fighter Establishment at West Raynham, but the type never entered RAF service due to the instability caused by the longer engines and the extended canopy. However, another 101 were built after the prototype, most going straight into store, but sixty were later sold to the Yugoslavia Air Force from 1952.

Most post-war production returned to Hatfield and Leavesden, but the new factory at Chester was used for the NF Mk 38 and the Sea Mosquito TF/TR Mk 37. The last FB Mk VI was produced by Standard Motors in December 1945 and the very last (of 7,781) Mosquito to be built was an NF Mk 38, VX916, completed at Chester on the 15th November 1950.

Canadian Production

The Canadian Minster of Munitions and Supply, Hon. C.D. Howe, was in the UK in December 1940 to discuss Canadian war production and on the 29th of that month, he saw the Mosquito being flown. It took until the 7th July 1941 before the final decision was made to produce the Mosquito in Canada by the de Havilland Aircraft of Canada Ltd factory at Downsview, outside Toronto. Power was to come from engines built in Detroit by the Packard Motor Co., Ltd, who in September 1940 had agreed to build these engines under licence from Rolls-Royce for both the American and British Governments. When production at Downsview was agreed, the factory was building Tiger Moths and Avro Ansons and it was estimated that forty Mosquitos a month could be produced, so a target of two aircraft completed by September 1942 and fifty

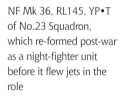

NF Mk 36, RL145, YP•T of No.23 Squadron, which re-formed post-war as a night-fighter unit before it flew jets in the role

The first of only three FB Mk 21s KA100 seen at the at Downsview plant
(©DH Canada)

The FB Mk 24 variant never went into production, with KA102 seen here being the only prototype (©DH Canada)

per month by 1943 was agreed. Two engineers from Hatfield went out to Canada in September, Harry Povey, the chief production manager and W.D. Hunter a senior engineer. The latter took on the task of converting the Mosquito to local materials and Canadian equipment, but quite a lot of the airframe remained compatible with the British-built examples. The first batch of production drawings went to Canada, while fuselage and wing jigs were made ready for shipment, however delays and losses were inevitable in war and so by the time the fuselage jigs had arrived at Downsview, local ones had already been made. Certain specific production tools were lacking and other equipment could not initially be easily found locally, so it was quite a while before the first production bombers started to roll of the assembly lines.

FB Mk 40, A52-1, was the first Australian-produced example and is seen here at Bankstown in mid-1943. Only the tail was painted Foliage Green and Earth Brown, the rest of airframe was aluminium due to the emergency nature of the flight test programme (©DH Australia/BAE)

To help train those who would fly the Mosquito, as well as those that would ferry them to the UK, the Ministry of Aircraft Production released twenty-four British-built T Mk IIIs from April 1943, while the first Canadian-built T Mk 22s (KA873-876 and KA896-897) did not arrive until September 1944. Initial fighter production was the FB Mk 21, which was similar to the British-built FB Mk VI, but used Canadian and American-built equipment and Merlin 31 engines. In the end only three (KA100 to KA102) were built. Another variant that came to nothing was the proposed high-altitude FB Mk 24, a version of the FB Mk 21 with Merlin 301. The next fighter type to reach production was the FB Mk 26 with its Packard Merlin 225 engines, and this engine also powered the two-seat version, the T Mk 27. In all three-hundred FB Mk 26s were built, of which thirty-seven

were converted into T Mk 29s due to a shortage of cannon and radio equipment. Forty-nine T Mk 27s (KA877-895 and KA898-927) were built and the FB Mk 28 was allocated to Canadian production, but was never actually built. By May 1945 only fifty-nine FB Mk 26s had been delivered to the UK and most of these saw service with No.249 Squadron at Habbaniya, Iraq in the post-war era. Many FB Mk 26s were refurbished and sold to China, see the Foreign Service section elsewhere for more details.

Australian Production

Production in Australia was considered from an early stage in the history of the Mosquito, although all machines produced in this country were based on the fighter/fighter-bomber airframe. The very first machine was British-build NF Mk II DD664, which was shipped to Australia in June 1942 to serve as a pattern aircraft for Australian production. It was re-assembled and first flew at Bankstown on the 17th December 1942 and was allocated the RAAF serial number A52-1001. Later it was re-engined with Packard-built Merlin 31s, as all subsequent FB Mk 40 and PR Mk 40 aircraft would be. It first flew with these engines on the 23rd March 1943 before moving to Mascot for evaluation, and production in Australia moved a step closer when a new assembly hangar and flight shed at Bankstown near Sydney was available by April 1943.

The first Australian-produced machine was an FB Mk 40, A52-1, which first flew on the 23rd July 1943 with Wg Cdr Gibson Lee at the controls. The FB Mk 40 was based on the British-built FB Mk VI and the first one-hundred were built with the Packard Merlin 31, whilst the reminder had Merlin 33s fitted with paddle-blade propellers. In all 212 FB Mk 40s were built, 108 of them before VJ-Day on the 15th August 1945. It was in fact the only version actually built in Australia, because all subsequent machines were converted from FB Mk 40s. The second FB Mk 40 A52-2 was actually completed with cameras and entered service as a PR Mk 41, where it was later followed by A52-2, 4, 6, 7, 9 and 26.

With twenty-one Mosquitos completed a fault arose with a blind joint in the wing and this stopped all production until non-destructive testing could take place. Whilst modifications and corrections were made to the built airframes and stock-piled wings, thirty-eight British-built FB Mk VIs were supplied to supplement the FB Mk 40s, where they received serial numbers in the A52-500 to 537 range and were all used by No.1 Squadron from the beginning of 1945.

A single FB Mk 42 was built with two-stage engines, this being converted from FB Mk 40 A52-90 and it later was further modified to become the prototype of the PR Mk 41.

Twenty-two British-built PR Mk XVIs were supplied to Australia as well, to bridge the gap before the PR Mk 41 could go into service and these machines received serial numbers in the A52-600 to 622 range, where they mainly served with No.87 Squadron. The PR Mk 41 was the first Australian-built variant with two-stage Merlin 69s and twenty-eight were converted from FB Mk 40s during the 1947-8 period; these were re-numbered A52-300 to A52-327. All joined No.87 Squadron, where they undertook the aerial surveying of 2/3rd of Australia in the 1946-1953 period. The squadron was disbanded in June 1953, when the remainder of the task was taken on by civil aerial-survey firms, who then took another ten years to complete the last 1/3rd!

The Australian-built trainer, the T Mk 43 was delayed, so eight British-built T Mk IIIs were shipped out minus their engines at the end of 1943, then fitted with Merlin 31 or 33 engines. Later two more lots of three airframes were supplied, bringing it to a total of fourteen, and these were allocated serial numbers in the A52-1002 to A52-1015 range. Four of these were later passed to New Zealand, where they became NZ2301 to 2304. These machines had the cannon removed, but many retained the machine-guns if their intended use was for gunnery training. A total of twenty-two were converted from FB Mk 40s, where they were allocated new serial numbers in the A52-1050 to A52-1071 range. As with the British-supplied T Mk IIIs, four T Mk 29s were later supplied to New Zealand, where they received new serial numbers NZ2305 to NZ2308.

Foreign Service

Australian Civil
Two PR Mk 41s were entered for the speed section of the 1953 air race from London to Christchurch, NZ. One was VH-KLG (ex-A52-62/A52-324) and was flown by Sqn Ldr A.J.R. 'Titus' Oates DFC (who owned the aircraft) and Flt Lt D.H. Swain DFC, and the other was VH-WAD (ex-A52-210/A52-319), which was christened 'The Quokka' and flown by Capt J. Woods; although he later had to withdraw due to lack of money. Both machines had armament and cameras removed and whilst VH-WAD retained its original Packard Merlin 69s, VH-KLG

FB Mk 40s of No.1 Squadron, with A52-513 on the left and A52-510 ('H') on the right, taken 5th August 1945 the day after the Squadron arrived at Amberley
(©RAAF)

PR Mk 40 A52-2 after one of its first missions
(©J. Love)

FB Mk 40, A52-50, with No.5 OTU at Williamtown, NSW in overall Foliage Green before disposal in 1949
(©Hawker-DH Australia)

was modified by the fitment of Rolls-Royce Merlin 77s as well as long-range tanks in the bomb bay and 100 Imp. Gal. drop tanks under the wings. Neither took part in the end though, as Woods withdrew and VH-KLG crashed 25 miles south of Mergui in southern Burma en route to the UK to start the race on the 3rd October 1953. The aircraft was brought down on a mud flat and both crew were unhurt, but the airframe was submerged by the high tide and inaccessible, so it was written off. VH-WAD remained at Perth until as late as 1968. It was purchased by James A. Harwood in January 1969, but badly damaged during dismantling, so it remained stored in a warehouse at Perth from 1969 to 1972, changing ownership during this period to Ed A. Jurist. The remains were bought by David M, Kubista from Tucson Arizona in June 1971 and shipped to the USA on the *SS Manora*, but off-loaded en-route at Melbourne due to fees owed. It remained stored at Port Melbourne from 1972 to 1979, where it was auctioned to recover shipping and storage fees on the 22nd January 1979. Acquired by the Australian War Memorial, its static restoration began in 1979 and was completed in 1996. It was rolled out for display as A52-319 in the AWM Mitchell Annex on the 22nd January 1997, where it remains to this day.

Other Australian-registered machines included PR Mk 41 VH-WWS (ex-A52-197/A52-306), which was purchased by World Wide Surveys (a join operation by Aero Service Corp of Philadelphia and Fairchild Aerial Surveys of Los Angeles) on the 17th May 1954. It was registered as N1596V (note: two ex-crew state it was N1597V – see elsewhere) by them and departed Sydney for Labuan. Borneo in June 1954 to undertake US Army Map Service work. It returned to Sydney via Darwin on the 21st September 1954 and was parked at Camden during the 1954-56 period. The aircraft passed to the sole ownership of Fairchild Aerial Surveys on the 27th April 1956 and was struck off the US civil register on the 17th July 1956. It was registered to Sepal Pty Ltd from Sydney as VH-WWS on the 2nd November 1956, having been test flown by them at Camden on the 16th October. The crew access door flew off at 25,000ft over Tumut, NSW on the 11th January 1957 and the aircraft was unused ar Camden by August

1957, where it was struck off the civil register on the 20th August. The aircraft was stripped of parts and burnt at Camden in 1960. The other machine was PR Mk 41 N1597V (ex-A52-204/ A52-313). This too was registered to World Wide Surveys on the 17th May 1954 and it also undertook survey work for the US Map Service from Labuan. Borneo. It later went on to survey at Broome, WA and returned to Camden on the 3rd September 1955 before departing in August 1956 to do survey work in Tamworth, NSW. It returned to Camden on the 30th October 1956 and never flew again, being stripped of parts and burnt there at some stage in 1960.

Belgium

Seven T Mk 3s, as well as an instructional airframe, were used by the Belgian Air Force. At first they were used at the Advanced Flying Training School at Brustem, but were soon replaced with the Airspeed Oxford, so they moved on to the JVS/EC (Fighter Training School) at Koksijde where they took the place of Miles Martinets used in the target-towing role. They were allocated serial numbers as follows: MA-1 (ex-VR333 – B2•A), MA-2 (ex-VR335 – B2•B), MA-3 (ex-VR338 – B2•C), MA-4 (ex-VR339 – B2•B/B2•D), MA-5 (ex-VR341 – B2•E), MA-6 (ex-VR342 – B2•F) and MA-7 (ex-VR343, ND•A). The latter aircraft was used by No.10 Squadron, who operated the NF Mk 30, as a trainer and communications aircraft

They also operated three FB Mk VIs converted to TT Mk 6s by Fairey Aviation Ltd, which were allocated serial numbers MC-1 (ex-TE614), MC-2 (ex-TE663) and MC-3 (ex-TE771). All three were supplied in March 1954 with MC-1 lost in a landing accident at Koksijde on the 4th June 1954, but the other two remained in service until August 1954. Another FB Mk VI, NS857 (instructional airframe 5265M) had been transferred to Belgium in June 1945 and was used as an instructional airframe at Wevelgem.

Under the terms of the Western Defence Pact the Belgian Air Force received twenty-six NF Mk 30s in 1948, all of which were refurbished by Fairey Aviation Ltd at Ringway. Two of these, NT450 and NT563, were used as instructional airframes at the Technical Training School at Tongres (scrapped there in 1953), while the

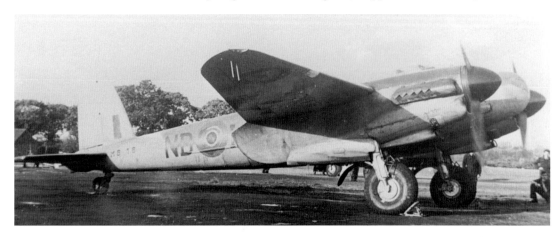

NF Mk 30, MB18, (ex-MM757), ND•I of the Belgian Air Force

(via Rudy Binnemans)

NF Mk 30s, MB1 (KY•V) and MB19 (ND•A) in the maintenance hangar at Beuuvechain in 1952 *(©Rudy Binnemans)*

remainder were allocated Belgian Air Force serial numbers as followed: MB-1 (ex-NT446 – ND•B/KT•V), MB-2 (ex-NM768) – ND•H/ KT•Q), MB-3 (ex-NT322 – ND•K), MB-4 (ex-NT300 – ND•C), MB-5 (ex-NT368 – ND•P/ ND•D), MB-6 (ex-MT465), MB-7 (ex-MV559 – ND•E), MB-8 (ex-MT491 – ND•H), MB-9 (ex-NT314), MB-10 (ex-MT499), MB-11 (ex-NT377 – KT•O), MB-12 (ex-NT384 – ND•C), MB-13 (ex-NT317 – KT•S), MB-14 (ex-NT362 – ND•A), MB-15 (ex-NT375 – ND•J), MB-16 (ex-NT387 – ND•K), MB-17 (ex-NT501 – KT•R), MB-18 (ex-MM757 – ND•I), MB-19 (ex-NT275 – ND•A), MB-20 (ex-NT-330 – ND•E), MB-21 (ex-MM687 – ND•J) and MB-22 (ex-NT332 – KT•M).

Two additional machines were delivered in 1953; MB-23 (ex-RK935, written off on delivery so supplied as a spare parts source in December 1953) and MB-24 (ex-RK952, ND•N, today displayed at the Royal Belgian Army Museum). They were all operated by Nos.10 and 11 (night-fighter) Squadrons of the 1st Wing at Beauve-chain from 1948 through to 1956-7, when all NF Mk XXs were struck off charge and scrapped and their role taken on by the Gloster Meteor NF Mk 11.

It should be noted that the Belgian Air Force also had an NF Mk XVII and XIX on strength for a while. These were NF Mk XVII, HK327 (Instruction Airframe 6343M) and NF Mk XIX, MM631 (Instructional Airframe 6157M), both of which were used to train ground personnel at the Technical School at Tongere from July 1947 to 1952, after which they were scrapped.

Burma

Regardless of what every other book on the Mosquito has ever said, no Mosquitos of any variant were ever supplied to, or served with the UBAF (Union of Burma Air Force).

Canadian Civil

Two Canadian-built T Mk 29s were registered to Kenting Aviation Ltd as CF-GKK (ex-KA202) and CF-GKL (ex-KA244), fitted with cameras and used for aerial survey work by Kenting, and later in 1955-59 by Spartan Air Services Ltd. GKK was retired and struck off charge on the 26th February 1959, whilst GKL was stripped for spares and struck off the register on the 20th December 1955.

Today a Canadian-built FB Mk 26 is one of the few airworthy Mosquitos in the world. This is KA114, which was taken on charge by the RCAF on the 22nd February 1945 and struck off on the 13th April 1948. It was sold to a local farmer, who towed it to his farm and it remained there until 1978. The shattered hulk was acquired by the Canadian Museum of Flight and Transportation in August 1978, before passing to Anglo-American Cedar Productions in Mission,

BC for restoration in July 1979. For a time it was registered C-GMGM, but this registration was cancelled in December 1979 and the airframe remained unrestored until 2012, when it was purchased by Gerald Yagen for his Fighter Factory at Virginia Beach, CA, USA. The remains were shipped to New Zealand, where they were incorporated into a new-build fuselage by Avspecs Ltd in Auckland. The aircraft was registered as ZK-MOS and restored to airworthiness, first flying from Ardmore on the 27th September 2012 marked as KA114, EG•Y. Dismantled in February 2013 and shipped aboard the Bahia Negra to the USA, it arrived at Virginia Beach on the 15th March 2013 and was re-assembled and test flown there on the 7th April 2013 where it remains airworthy to this day.

Czechoslovakia

With the end of WWII a new Czechoslovakian air force (*Ceskoslovenske Letectvo*) was formed using personnel and aircraft from Czech RAF squad-

A TT Mk 3 of the Belgian Air Force with a target-towing winch under the fuselage *(©Rudy Binnemans)*

FB Mk VIs of the Czechoslovakian Air Force with IY-10 of the Atlantic Squadron at Pilzen in the foreground (©Stan Spurny via Stuart Howe†)

rons. The FB Mk VI was used by the new air force, where it was designated the B-36, or LB-36 when fitted with cannon and machine-guns of German origin. Both types served with 24th Bomber Regiment and the 47th Air Regiment and remained so until the Communist takeover of the country in 1948. The type remained in service though, under Communist control, until finally withdrawn from use around 1950 and replaced by types of Russian origin.

China

With the defeat of Japanese forces in the Far East, the civil war that had started in the early 1930s between the Nationalist forces (Kuomintang) led by General Chiang Kai-shek and the Sino-Communists of Mao Tse-tung came to a climax. Once American attempts to reconcile the Kuomintang and Communists failed in 1947, Chiang began to loose control of the mainland, so a total of 250 (other sources state "around 200") surplus FB Mk 26s and T Mk 27/29s were bought by American for the Chinese Nationalist Air Force at a cost of $10,000 each (other sources state a total of $12 million). These were taken out of storage in Canada, refurbished and then shipped to Shanghai via the Panama Canal, where they joined about 1,000 ex-USAAF aircraft in the region that the Chinese Government had purchased at the end of WWII. Nine FB Mk 26s and T Mk 27/29s remained in Toronto during this period, operated by CNAC (China Nationalist Aviation Corps), to train Chinese pilots, although later pilot training transferred to Hankow in China. The aircraft were re-erected in a factory set up at Tazang airfield near Shanghai, with Eddy Jacks of de Havilland Canada as shop superintendent. By 12th November 1948 179 aircraft had been assembled and test flown, with the last, KA440, taking to the air on the 18th November 1948 (all were test flown by DHC test pilot Fred Offord). By this stage the factory had to be closed down because of approaching

FB Mk VI, TE794, 'Yellow 33' of GC 2/6 (©J.J. Petit)

Communist forces. All aircraft were flown to Hankow, where pilot and groundcrew training continued and where the type would become operational with No.1 Bombardment Group. The Chinese pilots, used to aircraft with a nose-wheel undercarriage, found the type very difficult to control on the ground and many airframes were written off in training in Canada. The type did not fair much better in China, especially when the Chinese insisted on taking over control of training in May 1948, with at least sixty being written off in various training accidents (mainly during taxying, take-off and landing). All of the Nationalist machines received serial numbers in the 001 to 180 range, with the type codes of 'FB' for the fighter-bombers and 'T' for the trainers being applied on the fuselage (e.g. T•19 or FB•40). The type also carried the serial on either side of the vertical fin, in the format of 'B-MO' [MO stands for Mosquito] and then the full serial number, e.g 019.

Dominican Republic

In 1947 a group of exiled Dominicans living in Cuba threatened to invade and overthrow the country's president, General Rafael Trujillo Molina, and they had a substantial air force (*Fuerza Aerea del Ejertico de la Revolution Americana* – FAERA) made up of Catalinas, Mitchells and Lightnings. With no fighter force in Dominica, the president sought to purchase aircraft elsewhere, but America was unwilling to assist in case any attack on FAERA forces caused a war with Cuba, so the president's agents managed to purchase aircraft elsewhere, including Mosquitos from the UK. Six FB Mk VIs were delivered for use by the Dominican Air Force (*El Cuerpo de Aviacion Militar*) after being refurbished and tested by Fairey Aviation Co. Ltd at Ringway between July and September 1948. They were flown to the Dominican Republic by Airwork Ltd pilots via Iceland, Canada and the USA and they all featured four-blade propellers. The serial numbers given to these machines in Dominican service were as follows: 301 (ex-TE612), 302 (ex-T909), 303 (ex-TE822), 304 (ex-TE873), 305 (ex-RF939) and 306 (original serial number unknown). The type first saw action against an FAERA Catalina and landing craft in Luperon Bay on the 14th June 1949. These were supplemented by three ex-RCAF T Mk 29s (KA172, KA206 and KA423) in February 1952 and the Mosquito was withdrawn from service in 1954.

France

The *Armée de l'Air* (French Army Air Force) operated the T Mk III, FB Mk VI, PR Mk XVI and NF Mk XXX from 1947 through to 1953. A total of seventeen T Mk IIIs and fifty-seven (some sources state 139) FB Mk VIs were supplied to France and fifteen of the latter were sent out to Indo-China in January 1947 for use against the Viet-Minh by 10/Group de Chasse 1/3 'Corse', having been ferried to Saigon from

FB Mk 26 'FB1' of the
Chinese Nationalist Air
Force retained in Canada
to train pilots before
being sent out; it carries
the emblem of the 1st
Bombardment Group

FB Mk 26s being
prepared for shipment to
China with B-M008 in the
foreground (©DH Canada)

T Mk 29 'T-85' (ex-
KA155) being refuelled
at Hankow. T=Trainer
and 85 was the shortened
CAF serial B-M085

(©G. Stewart via Stuart Howe†)

T Mk 29 'T-38' (ex-
KA203) at Hankow with
Canadian instructor
George Stewart standing
by it

(©G. Stewart via Stuart Howe†)

A T Mk 29 at Hankow
in 1949 after the
undercarriage was wiped
off whilst being flown by
Canadian instructor John
Turnbull

(©G. Stewart via Stuart Howe†)

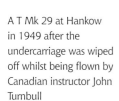

FB Mk VIs of GC 2/6, note the Normandie-Niemen badge on the nose of the nearest (©J.J. Petit)

An NF Mk 30 of GCN 1/31 'Lorraine' at Rabat-Sale, Morocco (©J.J. Petit)

Mosquitos of the French Air Force in the graveyard at Rabat in 1950; some were bought by the Israeli Air Force and refurbished before flying to the Middle East in 1951 (©J.J. Petit)

Rabat in Morocco. They undertook their first offensive operation on the 23rd January 1947 and by the end of May that year had flown 345 sorties and dropped 169,000lb of ordnance. In May 1947 the unit moved to Rabat where it became Groupe de Chasse 1/6 'Corse' and continued to use the type until withdrawn in July 1949. The type was also operated by GC 2/6 'Normandie-Niemen'.

The T Mk IIIs were operated by GC 1/3 'Corse', GC/GCN 1/20 'Lorraine' and GC 2/6 'Normandie-Niemen' and remained in ser-

vice the longest. Many were retained by the PR Mk XVI unit Groupe de Chasse 1/20 'Lorraine' in North Africa (Agadir and Rabat) before returning to Tours in April 1952 and being withdrawn from service in 1953/4.

Twenty-three surplus NF Mk XXXs were also supplied to France after the war and these operated from Rabat with GR 1/31 Groupe Lorraine from 1947 until withdrawn and replaced by the Meteor in 1953.

Israel

The Israeli Air Force took delivery of an unknown number of Mosquitos of various marks (a total of eighty-seven is probably the most accurate), many of them coming from France. The very first Mosquito in Israel was a PR Mk XVI salvaged from wrecks left at Ekron airfield in early 1948 and despite repeated attempts to get it airworthy, it never flew and was used to train mechanics before it was scrapped in June 1949. Two ex-RAF PR Mk XVIs were purchased in England from Gp Capt G.L. Cheshire VC in mid 1948 by Israeli agent Emanuel Zur; these machines were NS811 and 812, which were registered as G-AIRU and AIRT. In the end only one reached Israel, because the other was destroyed after a ground-loop at Ajaccio airfield in Corsica (the cause was thought to be sabotage). The remaining aircraft served with No.103 Squadron at Ramat David but crashed on the 21st September 1948, was repaired and returned to service in November, continuing in use until January 1957 when it broke up on landing.

A deal was made with the French Government on the 17th February 1951 to sell sixty-seven ex-Armée de l'Air Mosquitos to the IAF, which would be refurbished by Société Nationale de Construction (SNCAN) and Hispano for a cost of $387,000. These aircraft (thirty-nine FB Mk 6s, twenty NF Mk 30s and four PR Mk 16s), which were ex-RAF and had operated in French Indo-China, were in very poor condition, hence their very low selling price. Later an additional two ex-Armée de l'Air T Mk 3s were acquired and four of the original FB Mk 6s (2161 to 2164) were converted to dual-control in France before being ferried to Israel (thus becoming T Mk 6s). The refurbishment was undertaken at Chateaudun and Rennes and it took until the 11th June 1951 before the first aircraft began to arrive in Israel. They initially operated from Ekron (Tel-Nof) airfield, but quickly moved to Hazor to form No.109 Squadron, 4th Wing with three sections for operations, training and reconnaissance. A fourth night-fighter section was created with the arrival of the NF Mk 30s in 1952. The squadron undertook its first flights in February 1952 and its first operational (reconnaissance) sortie in May. The first Mosquito training course was started in August, where crews flew ground-attack missions and air-combat with other IAF types such as the Spitfire and Mustang. This training section became a squadron in its own right on the 23rd August 1953, when it became No.110 Squadron and had a number of each Mosquito variant assigned to it.

The FB Mk. VI was the mainstay of the IAF's ground-attack force whilst it remained in service. Quite a few were lost in accidents through, with the poor condition and maintenance of the aircraft plus the havoc the Mediterranean conditions wrought on it being the main causes. In all some fourteen IAF Mosquito crews were killed. The fifty-eight NF Mk 30 night-fighters were all acquired without any radar fitted, these having been removed by the French before the aircraft were sold, so they were fitted with American APS-4 radar instead. Only fifty-seven NF Mk 30s ever reached Israel though, as the last (2156) crashed at Chateaudun on the 18th July 1952, killing the IAF test ilot Captain John Harvey. The remaining machines formed the first IAF night-fighter squadron in 1953 but the radar performed badly, and poor maintenance coupled with the effect of local weather hampered their operational use. In truth the type never became an effective night-fighter force, this role only eventually being fulfilled with the arrival of the

FB Mk VI '2135' at the head of a row of machines at Wing 4 Day on the 9th July 1953 (©IDF/IAF)

Gloster Meteor NF Mk 13 in Israel in 1955. Another fourteen ex-Royal Naval Sea Mosquito TR Mk 33s were purchased in Britain in 1954 from scrap-dealer R.A. Short (many were low-hours airframes). Once refurbished by Eagle Aviation Ltd and devoid of arrestor hooks and all Royal Navy equipment, they were allocated fictitious ferry markings in the 4x3171 to 4x3190 range and flown to Israel from the 4th November 1954 through to August 1955.

When the jets started to arrive in the IAF, the Mosquito was demoted from frontline service and with Hazor now home to jet aircraft, in September 1955 the Mosquitos moved to Sirkin and Ekron airfields. In October Nos.109 and

TR Mk 33 marked as 'IDFAF 4x 3186' being ground run in the UK prior to delivery

110 Squadrons were combined as one (No.109), and with the imminent arrival of the Dassault Mystère IVA in May 1956 the squadron was disbanded and its aircraft put into storage. The PR version remained in service with No.115 Squadron, but with escalating tension in the area once the Suez Crisis broke out in 1956, all the Mosquitos were taken out of storage and re-formed as No.110 Squadron at Ramat David, to take part in Operation Kadesh, Israel's part in the crisis. They were tasked with attacking the farthest Egyptian airfields, such as Cairo-West,

FB Mk VI '26' of the Israeli Air Force (©IAF)

FB Mk VI NZ2328 of
No.75 Squadron, RNZAF
(©RNZAF)

An unidentified FB Mk VI
of No.75 Squadron with
one RP still hung up,
comes in to land
(via Internet)

FB Mk VIs of No.75
Squadron are re-armed in
the field *(via Internet)*

Faid and Abu-Sweir, however in the event the
only operations undertaken by the Mosquito
at this stage, were by the PR versions as all
propeller-driven aircraft were excluded from the
battles over the Sinai Desert. It was not until the
31st October that Mosquitos began to undertake ground-attack missions in the Sinai Desert
region, where they often attacked Egyptian
armour and army encampments. They were also
extensively involved in the fighting around the
Egyptian stronghold at Sharm-A-Sheik, which
they attacked for four consecutive days from

the 1st November. In all seventy-four Mosquito
sorties were flown during Operation Kadesh, for
the loss of two aircraft (most accounts state none
were lost to enemy action, so these were probably losses from other causes).

The end of Operation Kadesh also brought
about a final end of Mosquito service with the
IAF and in January 1957 No.110 Squadron
disbanded and all its remaining Mosquitos were
placed in storage and later scrapped.

New Zealand

A number of T Mk IIs and T Mk 43s, along with
FB Mk 40s were sold to New Zealand by Australia, however the bulk of the RZNAF's Mosquito force was made up of seventy-six ex-RAF
FB Mk VIs. The first batch of ten flew to New
Zealand from RAF Pershore on the 10th December 1946 and the 11,800 mile trip took 10-12
days. All aircraft were intended for use by No.75
Squadron at Ohakea, but very few actually flew
with the squadron due to a shortage of maintenance staff. In fact many aircraft never flew again
in New Zealand, remaining in store until broken
up for scrap in 1955-56. These machines were
allocated serial numbers NZ2321 to NZ2396.

Six survived the scrap-man and were added
to the civil register in July 1953, having been
inspected by Arthur Kaplan and Bob Bean,
American representatives of Aircraft Sales Inc.
of California on the 16th October 1952. They
were purchased from the Government Stores
Board by Aircraft Supplies (NZ) of Palmerston
North in July 1953 and destined for export.
In September 1953 they were all placed on
the civil register and allocated the registrations
ZK-BCT to ZK-BCY, then overhauled in preparation for ferry flights to the USA. ZK-BCV
(ex-PZ474/NZ2384) departed for America in
February 1955, but the New Zealand Government then stopped the export of the remaining Mosquitos, fearing they were destined for
overseas military use. ZK-BCV was allocated
the US civil registration N9909F and owned by
the Insurance Finance Corporation of Studio
City, California. Its subsequent use is unknown, but there are rumours that it was used
for intelligence gathering by the CIA in South
America. It ending up at Whiteman Air Park,
San Fernando, California, and was cancelled
from the civil register in December 1970. The
aircraft was left and started to deteriorate with
the fuselage cut behind the main wing at some
stage. In 1970 Jim Merizan heard about the aircraft and acquired it, moving it to his home in
Placentia, California, then to Yorba Linda. He
apparently traded ownership of the aircraft with
the Swedish Air Force Museum in 1984, but
for some reason the remains never left the USA
and today the wings (in a very poor condition)
and both engines and nacelles are stored outside
at Chino Airport, California. ZK-BCT (ex-
PZ413/NZ2381) was registered in the USA as
N4935V to Aviation Export Company Ltd. Inc.
in Los Angeles on the 18th September 1953,
but because of the ban imposed by the government, it never left New Zealand. The registration was cancelled on the 28th September 1954
and it and the remaining four were scrapped at
Palmerston North in May 1957, having found
no buyers within New Zealand because of the
export ban.

Norway

During WWII only one Norwegian unit operated the Mosquito, that being B Flight of No.333

(Norwegian) Squadron at RAF Leuchars, where they operated the FB Mk VI on anti-shipping reconnaissance flights over Norway. The unit moved to Banff in September 1944, where they flew in advance of the main Strike Wing on anti-shipping strikes along the Norwegian coast. With the end of the war B Flight was redesignated No.334 Squadron on the 26th May 1945 and returned home the following month, where they were based at Gardermoen. The unit was passed to Royal Norwegian Air Force (*Luftforsvaret*) control on the 21st November 1945 and an additional eighteen FB Mk VIs were acquired by the *Luftforsvaret*. Most of the newer machines had the landing light in the starboard wing leading edge, while the older ones that came over from the UK at the end of the war, were a mix of those with and those without. In 1950 three of them were fitted with A.I. radar in a thimble radome in place of the machine-gun armament. The type was grounded on the 21st February 1951 after a fatal crash caused by the failure of the wing on TE908 and all remaining airframes were maintained on an emergency use basis only (due to the Cold War and Korean War). The type was retired by the *Luftforsvaret* on the 12th January 1952 and the majority of them were scrapped at Sola.

Sweden

After the war sixty surplus NF Mk XIXs were supplied to the *Flygvapnet* (Swedish Air Force), where they were designated J 30 'Hunter'. These machines were all refurbished by Fairey Aviation Co. Ltd at Ringway, with the first test flown there in July 1948 and the last in October 1949. They were all ferried from Ringway to Hatfield, where they would be ferried to Sweden by Swedish crews. All the Swedish machines adopted the four-blade propellers first used operationally on the Sea Mosquito and had a landing light built into the leading edge of the starboard outer wing. These aircraft were allocated serial numbers in the 30001 to 30060 range whilst in *Flygvapnet* service, the first being ex-TA286, which arrived at Vasteras on the 16th July 1948. The type entered service with Nos.1, 2 & 3 Squadrons of F1 Wing and a number were lost in service due

J30, S/No.30031 as 'Red N' at Vasteras

(©P Kempfe via Stuart Howe†)

J 30 ex-TA286 as 3001, this was the first Mosquito delivered to the *Flygvapnet* at Vasteras in July 1948

(©P. Kempfe via Stuart Howe†)

A nice posed shot of NF Mk 19s refurbished by Fairey Aviation at Ringway with *Flygvapnet* delivery crews on the 25th February 1946
(©DH/BAE)

T Mk III '541' for the Turkish Air Force at Hatfield prior to delivery. It, like all the others, had been refurbished by Fairey Aviation Ltd
(©DH/BAE)

T Mk IIIs had the option to carry 500lb bombs under the wings, an option that had already been available in the late-production examples used by the RAF. All ten of the T Mk IIIs supplied to Turkey were newly built, not refurbished airframes and they were all completed at Hatfield. They were allocated production serial numbers 6601 to 6610 and received the codes 533 to 542 in Turkish service. Over £47,000 worth of spares was also bought from de Havillands in February 1952. The Mosquito only had a very limited service in Turkey, based at Izmir and Diyarbakir, and later serving at Malatya, primarily tasked with anti-shipping and light bombing. They were replaced by the Republic F-84 Thunderjets (supplied under the Marshall Air Plan) in 1954.

United States
The USAAF did operate a number of PR Mk XVIs during WWII, some of them fitted with H2X radar in a revised nose, but all of these were based on the bomber airframe, so were covered in Volume 1.

A few NF Mk XXXs were given to the US Army Air Force under reverse lend-lease and they were operated by one unit in North Africa, the 416th NFS (Night Fighter Squadron). The unit converted to the type at Pisa during December 1944 and operated the type until it was replaced by the Northrop P-61 Black Widow in June 1945. All of these machines were tropicalized and carried a variety of desert survival equipment, plus some can be found in photos fitted with non-louvred exhaust shrouds.

Yugoslavia
Seventy-six FB Mk VIs were allocated to the Yugoslavia Air Force under the Mutual Defence Air Programme, with the first machines arriving in that country in 1951. From 1952 these served with the 32nd Bomber Division at Zagreb, until they re-equipped with other types in 1956 and passed their aircraft to the 184th Aviation Reconnaissance Regiment, who continued to use the type until 1960 alongside its

to the structural failure of the elevator static balance weight. The type remained in service until 1954 when they were replaced by the de Havilland Venom.

Turkey
Turkey originally ordered 108 FB Mk VIs and ten T Mk IIIs, but later added another twenty-four FB Mk VIs to equip two more squadrons. In all 135 FB Mk VIs were supplied to Turkey, including three to replace those lost in accidents. They were all refurbished by Fairey Aviation Co., Ltd at Ringway, with the first flight tested on the 13th November 1946 and the last in June 1948. They were ferried to Turkey by British Aviation Services Ltd crews and both FB Mk VIs and

NF Mk 38s. The type also saw service with the 97th Aviation Regiment and with a sea reconnaissance squadron for the anti-aircraft school at Zagreb, mainly in the target-towing role before retiring in 1963. One machines was converted to carry a TR-45/A torpedo, which was full of water ballast (which could be drained in flight in an emergency), whilst in 1957 another three machines (8084, 8106 and 8122) were converted to carry a LETOR-2 torpedo, which was a Yugoslavia-built version of the TR-45/A.

Although most English-language publications do not list them, the JRV also operated the trainer variant. Three of these (8101, 8102 and 8103) were ex-RAF T Mk IIIs, whilst the others were FB Mk VIs converted to trainers (S/No.8168, 8169 and an unknown example).

A total of sixty NF Mk 38s were also supplied, all out of storage in the UK, and these were allocated serial numbers in the 8001 to 8060 range. The type served with the 103rd Reconnaissance Regiment at Pancevo near Belgrade, as well as with the 97th and 184th Aviation

Reconnaissance Regiments. Yugoslavia was the only nation to use the NF Mk 38 operationally and it retired the type in 1960 when the 184th Aviation Reconnaissance Regiment relinquished their examples.

FB Mk VI '8074' with the 32nd Bomber Division at Zagreb

(©M Micevski via Stuart Howe†)

JRV NF Mk 30 '8030' of the 103rd Recon Regiment approaches to land; note the enlarged elevator horn balances

(©M Micevski via Stuart Howe†)

Yugoslavian FB Mk VI (ex-RF610) as '8114' was converted to a T Mk III by the JRV. NF Mk 38 '8052' (ex-VX897) can be seen in the background

(©M Micevski via Stuart Howe†)

Chapter 1: Evolution – The Fighters (including Night-Fighters)

F Mk II W4052 in flight from A&AEE Boscombe Down, note the early exhaust outlets on cowls and the lack of any radio hatch in the lower rear fuselage, aft of the wing trailing edge

(©Crown Copyright)

Although the Mosquito was always envisaged as a fast bomber *(See Airframe & Miniature 8 ISBN: 978-0-9935345-1-5 from Valiant Wings Publishing Ltd)*, development in the fighter role was always considered. Both day and night-fighter were therefore considered side-by-side, with the first such prototype a day fighter, even though it was painted overall black.

Note: See Chapter 4 for details of the in-service schemes applied to the Mosquito.

F Mk II prototype (W4052)

Initial Form

Built to Specification F.21/40 this aircraft first flew on the 15th May 1941. It was powered by two Rolls-Royce Merlin 21 engines in the new 'long' nacelles and was the first Mosquito to be built with these.

Camouflage & Markings

This machine remained in Special Night overall with Type B roundels on the upper wings and Type A1 on the fuselage with a Type A fin flash. The serial number was applied in Dull Red characters 8in high forward of the leading edge of the tailplane, using its centreline as the base-line for the characters. The aerial mast looks to be unpainted.

F Mk II prototype (W4052)

Revised Form

The only changes here were that W4052 received the revisions to the engine cowlings to allow the shrouded exhausts that would be used in all subsequent production machines.

Camouflage & Markings

The overall scheme remains uncharged, the only things that were different related to the new shrouded exhausts, which were left in a light primer colour. It is also interesting to note that when it did a wheels-up landing on the 19th April 1942, the inboard port engine had the entire cowling around the shrouded exhaust in primer, whilst the outer starboard side only had the shroud itself in primer; we thus assume both inboard starboard and outboard port sides were restricted to primer on the new shrouded exhausts only.

F Mk II (W4053)

with dorsal turret

At the time the Mosquito was fighting for acceptance by the powers that be at the Air Ministry, the call was constantly for the fitment of a powered turret, because the older high ranking officers could not see a twin-engine aircraft being manoeuvrable enough to bring fixed guns to bear on nimble single-seat fighters. As a result a mock-up on W4053 saw a Bristol B Mk XI turret containing four Browning 0.303in machine-guns being fitted to it, in the dorsal spine just aft of the cockpit. Flights with the turret soon proved it to be unsuitable, as it caused drag and the poor gunner had to turn the turret fully forwards before he could bale out, as there was no escape hatch in the lower rear fuselage! It is also stated that the second production F Mk II, W4073, was fitted with such a turret and although we have found no photographic evidence to support this, that machine can be considered to be the same as W4053.

F Mk II prototype (W4052) – Initial Form

F Mk II prototype (W4052) – Revised Form

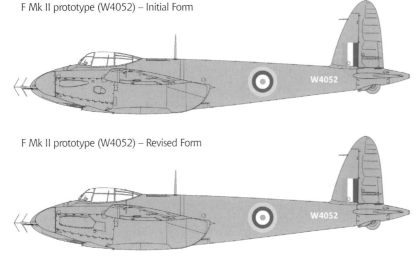

Camouflage & Markings

By this stage the aircraft was still in the very sooty Special Night overall, so the finish was more akin to a dusty black than pure black. The markings remained unchanged and the area where the radio hatch would be added on the lower, starboard rear fuselage, was a very dirty looking area that we assume to be a combination of primer and a very rough coat of Special Night, as that colour had to be flooded onto the surface to get a smooth finish, so spraying a patch like this would have resulted in a very poor finish and colour density. It is not known if the prototype 'P' marking was applied, but it is very likely considering that the aircraft undertook flight tests in this configuration.

F Mk II (W4052)

with 'frill' speed brake

In an attempt to allow the Mosquito to decelerate as it came up behind an enemy aircraft at night, a number of air brakes were tested. This was the first, produced by Youngman and comprising metal petals that were attached around the rear fuselage, aft of the wing trailing edge. They were operated by rods and by this time W4052 had also gained the radio access hatch on the lower starboard side of the rear fuselage. These brakes were not adopted due to a combination of fears about the structural integrity of the airframe due to the stresses and the fact that it was soon found dropping the undercarriage was a much safer way of quickly decelerating.

Camouflage & Markings

The overall scheme remained uncharged, the only addition was a prototype 'P' marking applied aft of the fuselage roundel on both sides. This had the P facing the rear of the aircraft on the port side and the front on the starboard and the outer ring was larger in diameter than the 36in fuselage roundel, so we assume it to be 40in. The aerial mast looks to remain unpainted.

F Mk II (W4052)

with bellows-style speed brake

These inflatable air brakes were again situated around the rear fuselage, aft of the wing trailing edge, and a venturi under the fuselage acted as a pressure head to activate them in 3 seconds at 250mph indicated air speed. As with the frill version they were not adopted, although this time it was due to the fact that during testing they were found to cause such severe vibrations that it was felt there was a real risk of their causing a total structural failure.

Camouflage & Markings

We have to assume that the overall markings were the same as when this machine had the 'frill' air brakes installed because only close-up

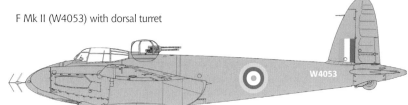

F Mk II (W4053) with dorsal turret

F Mk II W4052 (note the glazed oval port in access door) with Geoffrey de Havilland Jr. about to board for a test flight *(©DH)*

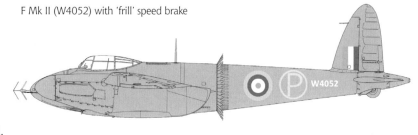

F Mk II (W4052) with 'frill' speed brake

F Mk II (W4052) with bellows-style speed brake

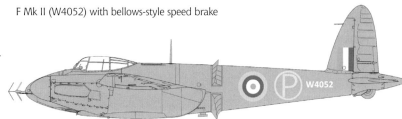

F Mk II W4052 after it was forced landed by Geoffrey de Havilland Jr. on the 19th April 1942. Note the unpainted shrouded exhausts now fitted *(©DH)*

(partial) images exist. There is no way to determine if the prototype 'P' marking remained, but it is a pretty safe bet to assume it was, considering the nature of the work being undertaken. It is interesting to note that there is a darker band running around the fuselage in the region on the aerial mast, as a wide band, and that the aerial itself is now painted black.

F Mk II prototype W4052) – Final Form

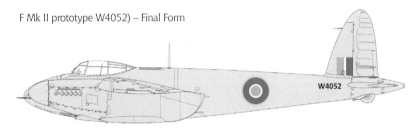

F Mk II prototype (W4052)

Final Form

By this stage the Mosquito was accepted as a day fighter, so W4052 adopted a day fighter colour scheme and had the shrouds removed from the exhausts. It had the A.I. radar 'bow and arrow' antenna in the nose, but oddly no dipoles at the wing tips, nor the swept-back pair at mid-span on the starboard wing.

Camouflage & Markings

By this stage W4052 adopted the day fighter scheme of Medium Sea Grey overall with a disruptive camouflage pattern of Dark Green on the upper surfaces. The vertical fin and rudder remained in Medium Sea Grey, with no Dark Green. The demarcation between upper and lower colours was determined by a hypothetical

NF Mk II with A.I. Mk IV radar

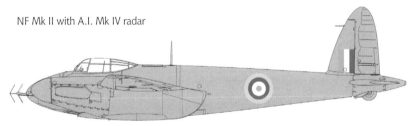

line running along the nose and fuselage through the centreline of the wing and tailplane. Demarcation on the engine cowlings was done by following the lower edge of the top cowling. The camouflage pattern has a tight edge to it, it is not feathered, but the demarcation along the nose, fuselage and tail are all slightly wavy. Type B roundels (54in dia.) were applied above the wings, with a 36in diameter Type C1 roundel on the fuselage sides and 27in x 24in Type C fin flash. The serial was applied in black 8in high characters on either side of the rear fuselage, forward of the tailplanes and using their centreline as the baseline for the characters.

NF Mk II with A.I. Mk IV radar

All the lessons learnt with the prototype led to this the first production series. The airframe was basically similar to W4052 in its revised form, with shrouded exhausts and the dipoles for the A.I. radar above and below each wing tip, plus the staggered antenna on the upper starboard wing at the mid-span point, and the 'bow and arrow' antenna in the nose. Armament consisted four Browning 0.303in machine-guns in the nose and four Hispano 20mm cannon in the ventral bay. The type retained the aft bomb bay of the bomber version.

Serial numbers W4072, W4076, W4078-W4088 and W4090-W4099, DD600-644, DD659-691, DD712-759, Dd777-800, DZ228-272, DZ286-310, DZ653-661, DZ680-727, DZ739-761, HJ642-661, HJ699-715 & HJ911-944 for all F Mk II/NF Mk II production.

NF Mk II (W4096)

with tropical filters

This prototype tested the revised lower engine cowls with the elongated intakes that accommodated the filters necessary for operations in a tropical climate.

Camouflage & Markings

The only photos that survive that are confirmed as being of W4096 are close-ups and thus do

Early production NF Mk IIs W4090, W4092 and W4088 awaiting delivery at Hatfield on the 12th February 1942, the extremely matt nature of the Special Night scheme evident by the way the Type B roundels look positively bright in comparison (©DH)

The 'Turbinlite' NF Mk II W4087 was evaluated by No.151 Squadron in December 1942

not show her overall scheme. It does look as if the Night scheme overall was retained, although it was the 'smooth' Night Type S not the very matt RD2A Special Night. All other markings are presumed to be the same as the production machines and we doubt this aircraft had the prototype 'P' marking, as it was being used for in-service trials and was based outside the UK.

NF Mk II

with Helmore/GEC Turbinlite

The installation of a 2,700 million candle power light was envisaged to 'illuminate' targets at night, but co-ordinating Turbinlite and fighter proved to be complex and in the end A.I. radar did the job much more effectively. In the end, only one such installation was undertaken in the Mosquito, that being in NF Mk II W4087.

Camouflage & Markings

Few images survive of this installation; one is well known as it was an official image of the period, but nowadays a few others snaps have appeared. These all confirm that the airframe was Medium Sea Grey overall with the disruptive pattern of Dark Green on the upper surfaces and fuselage sides. The Dark Green did not extend up the vertical fin and rudder, instead it ended ahead of it on the dorsal spine, with the demarcation as a sweeping line from the lower edge of the rear fuselage up to it. The entire front end seems to be only in Medium Sea Grey, with no sign of Dark Green on the upper edges at all. Markings are confirmed in photos as Type C1 fuselage roundel and fin flash, but there are no clear images to confirm the upper wing roundels, although we suspect these were Type B. Even when evaluated by No.151 Squadron in December 1942, this machine was devoid of any squadron codes.

NF Mk II (W4096) with tropical filters

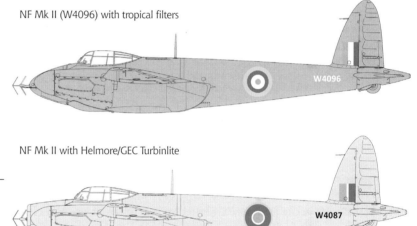

NF Mk II with Helmore/GEC Turbinlite

F Mk II (Intruder)

Singling out the F and NF Mk IIs is not a simple task, as production of both went hand-in-hand and many NF Mk IIs were used in the intruder role. Basically the F Mk II was an NF Mk II with the A.I. radar and all associated antenna removed. The type was then used in a pure fighter role, operating late in the evening or early morning in hit-and-run operations in regions like the Bay of Biscay etc. Note that there are various ways of describing the intruder version of the Mk II, so the terms F Mk II, F Mk II In-

F Mk II (Intruder)

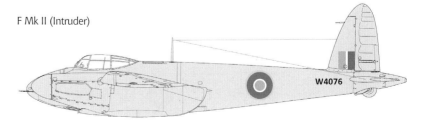

An F Mk II with No.68 Squadron with the crew boarding prior to an intruder sortie

(©British Official)

remained throughout testing. In the end the engine units were not found to offer any benefit over the existing ones, and offered more drag etc., so the whole project was dropped and no other airframes were thus converted.

Camouflage & Markings

This machine was in Medium Sea Grey overall with a disruptive camouflage of Dark Green on the upper surfaces, fuselage sides, but not the vertical fin and rudder, as these were left in Medium Sea Grey. The demarcation along the nose and fuselage was typical for a fighter and thus followed a hypothetical line from nose to tail through the centreline of the wing and tailplanes and the demarcation on the engine cowls simply followed the join line between upper and side cowls. The spinners were Medium Sea Grey and each propeller blade was black with the tips painted yellow. Photos confirm that a Type C1 roundel was applied to each side of the rear fuselage with a matching fin flash on each side of the vertical fin. The serial number was applied in the usual 8in high black characters on either side of the rear fuselage, all of it being within the regions of the upper camouflage on either side. The demarcation along the fuselage is soft, whilst those on the engines are hard-edged, because they follow a panel line. Oddly, the aircraft did not carry a prototype 'P' marking, nor was the serial concluded with the addition of the '/G' element.

truder, NF Mk II (Intruder) and even NF Mk II (special) have been associated with it over the years and this is because the type was only distinguished in service by its use and the fitment of things like the larger (150 Imp. Gal.) tank behind the cannon bay and the removal of the A.I. radar, but some NF Mk IIs were also fitted with the tanks for intruder sorties, so being pedantic about the term 'Intruder' and the airframes that it relates to, is purely academic.

Serial numbers W4072, W4076, W4078-W4088 and W4090-W4099, DD600-644, DD659-691, DD712-759, DD777-800, DZ228-272, DZ286-310, DZ653-661, DZ680-727, DZ739-761, HJ642-661, HJ699-715 & HJ911-944 for all F Mk II/NF Mk II production.

F Mk II (DD723)

with Merlin XX engines

F Mk II DZ659/G was used for the first trials installation of the American SCR 720 radar, the revised bulbous nose being evident in this port side shot *(©BAe)*

This machine was experimentally fitted with Rolls-Royce Merlin XX power-eggs complete with chin-mounted radiators, as seen fitted to the Beaufighter Mk II and Lancaster. This resulted in the deletion of the radiators in the inboard wing leading edges and the use of revised shape spinners and propellers. The airframe retained the bow and arrow antenna of the A.I. on the nose and the dipoles at each wing tip, but did not seem to have the swept-back antenna at mid-span on the starboard wing. All armament was retained, This conversion was undertaken by Rolls-Royce at Hucknall, where the aircraft

F Mk II (DZ659/G)

with SCR 720 radar

This machine was test-fitted with the American SCR 720 radar scanned in a revised nose radome that is unique to this machine, although not unlike the later universal 'Bullnose' unit in some respects. This machine was later converted to NF Mk XVII standard and went on to serve with the FIU at Ford, where it received the codes ZQ•H.

Camouflage & Markings

This machine was Medium Sea Grey overall with a disruptive camouflage of Dark Green on the

F Mk II (DD723) with Merlin XX engines

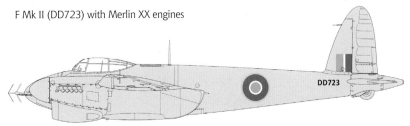

upper surfaces, fuselage sides, but not the vertical fin and rudder, as these were left in Medium Sea Grey as was usual for the Mosquito fighter. The demarcation along the nose and fuselage was typical for a fighter and thus followed a hypothetical line from nose to tail through the centre-line of the wing and tailplanes, and the demarcation on the engine cowls simply followed the join line between upper and side cowls. The spinners were Medium Sea Grey and each propeller blade was black with the tips painted yellow. Photos confirm that a Type C1 roundel was applied to each side of the rear fuselage with a matching fin flash on each side of the vertical fin (its base line on the upper line of the fillet at the base of the fin, and its back edge forward of the rudder hinge line). The serial number was applied in the usual 8in high black characters on either side of the rear fuselage, just forward of the tailplanes and using the centreline of the tailplanes as its baseline, so that it was partially in the camouflage, and partially below it. The secret nature of this machine meant that a '/G' was applied after the serial, to denote that it should be guarded at all times when on the ground.

NF Mk XII

Developed from the NF Mk II, this version used Merlin 21 or 23 engines and adopted the A.I. Mk VII centimetric radar that was installed in a 'thimble' radome in the nose. The type also only had the standard wing, so could only carry 50 Imp. Gal. drop tanks.

Serial numbers HJ945-946, HK107-141, HK159-204, HK222-236.

NF Mk XIII (Early)

This was a night-fighter variant developed from the fighter-bomber Mk VI and it had the A.I. Mk VIII radar in a 'thimble' nose radome.

Serial numbers HK362-382, HK396-437, HK453-481, HK499-536, MM436-479, MM491-534, MM547-590 and MM615-623 for all NF Mk XIII production.

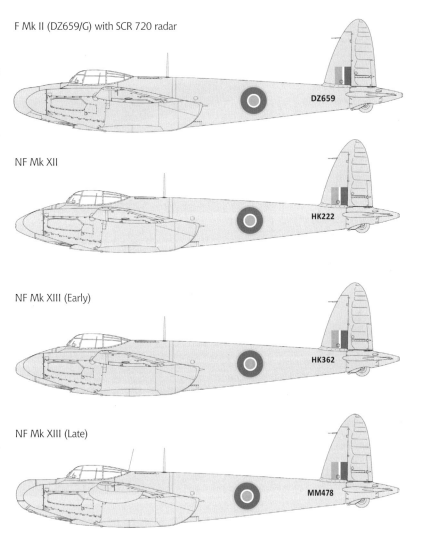

F Mk II (DZ659/G) with SCR 720 radar

DZ659

NF Mk XII

HK222

NF Mk XIII (Early)

HK362

NF Mk XIII (Late)

MM478

NF Mk XIII (Late)

In its later form the NF Mk XIII used the A.I. Mk VIII radar, but this time in the new 'universal' Bullnose radome. As the serial numbers for these machines do not seem to follow any logical set of 'batches', we are pretty sure that this state was one to which the earlier machines could be modified, so you will find early machines fitted with the new radome, as well as ones built from new with them.

See NF Mk XIII (Early) for serial numbers.

The narrow 'thimble' radome of the NF Mk XII is well illustrated in this photo of HK117

(©Air Ministry)

The early production batches of the NF Mk XIII also had the 'thimble' radome, as seen here in this shot of HK382 that served with No.29 Squadron

(©British Official/Crown Copyright)

The later production NF Mk XIIIs adopted the universal 'Bullnose' radome, seen here on MM466 with No.409 Squadron at a forward airfield in France in January 1945

(©British Official)

NF Mk XIV

This variant number was intended for a high-altitude development of the NF Mk XIII with Merlin 67 engines, but it was never built.

NF Mk XV prototype (MP469)

Initial Form

This high-altitude development was actually based on the PR Mk VIII and was achieved in just seven days. The basic airframe retained all the 'bomber' elements of its PR Mk VIII nature, but a fighter nose unit taken off F Mk II

NF Mk XV prototype (MP469) – Initial Form

NF Mk XV prototype (MP469) – Revised Form

DD715 was grafted on in place of the glazed version. To allow better control at higher altitude the wing span was increased to 62ft 2in by adding extended tips and it was one of the first Mosquito variants to be fitted with four-blade propellers, which were then being considered for the new naval version of the FB Mk VI (later to become the TR Mk 33). The outer fuel tanks in the wings were removed, as was the fuselage tank, leaving just 287 Imp. Gal. of fuel. Much equipment was removed to lighten the airframe and the type only had a pilot, no second crew member at this stage. The main wheels were replaced with ones of a smaller diameter, with tyres that lacked any tread pattern, and the bomb bay doors were lightened and their retraction system simplified.

Camouflage & Markings

The overall scheme of this machine in its initial form is one that is very contentious, as no period documents survive to confirm the exact colours used. Many colours are listed for it, including Ocean Grey and Dark Green, Ocean Grey and Dark Grey or Sky Grey and Dark Slate Grey, all of which were applied over Deep Sky. Considering the bomber heritage of MP469 and the obvious loose nature of the camouflage demarcation clearly seen in period images, it is most likely this machine was quickly repainted in the then night-fighter scheme of Medium Sea Grey and Dark Green on the upper surfaces, but with the application of Deep Sky underneath to cope with the type's intended high-altitude role. Both patterns and demarcation are at odds with the regulations at the time, although it does carry the regulation markings of Type B upper wing roundels, Type C1 fuselage roundel and fin flash and a serial number in 8in high black characters on the rear fuselage.

NF Mk XV prototype (MP469)

Revised Form

In its revised state MP469 gained A.I. Mk VIII radar in a nose radome replacing the existing machine-gun armament. Being based on a bomber, it never had ventral 20mm cannon, so the loss of the machine-guns was compensated for by adding them in a ventral gun pack mounted

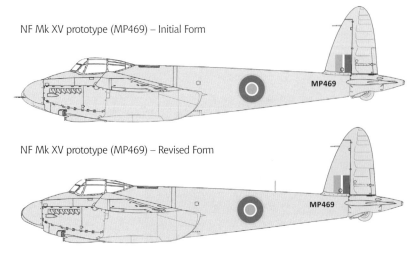

The prototype NF Mk XV MP469 in its original form with the gun nose of DD715 grafted onto its bomber fuselage, make this the only Mosquito fighter variant with the 'V' windscreen and lower crew access door of the bomber series *(©DH)*

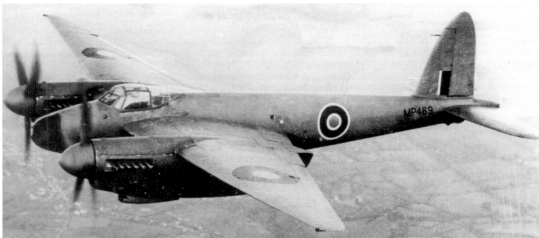

The prototype NF Mk XV MP469 after modification in November 1942 with A.I. Mk VIII radar in the nose and a gun pack the under fuselage *(©DH/BAe)*

below the forward bomb bay. The outer 24 Imp. Gal. fuel tanks were returned and a second crew-member was now carried.

Camouflage & Markings

By the time the A.I. radar and gun pack were added MP469 adopted the scheme that the other four conversions would also use, namely one of Deep Sky overall with the top of the radome in Special Night and its extreme tip in bare metal. A 54in diameter Type B roundel was applied above each wing, with a 36in diameter Type C1 roundel on either side of the rear fuse-lage and a 27in x 24in Type C fin flash on either side at the base of the vertical fin.

NF Mk XV – Conversions

The four airframes (DZ366, DZ385, DZ409 & DZ417) converted only differed from MP469 in its revised state by DZ366 using the Merlin 61, whilst the other three used the Merlin 77. Many sources state these machines reverted to the standard wing span, but period images prove this to be incorrect, as they all had the extended wing tips. Sources also claim both three- and four-blade propellers were used, but all surviving images show four-blade propellers installed.

NF Mk XV

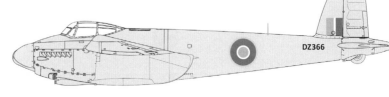
DZ366

Camouflage & Markings

These machines are all in the same overall scheme as MP469, although it is claimed that when these machines underwent operational trials with No.85 Squadron, each had an indi-vidual aircraft number allocated to it that was applied 'under the radome'. With no surviv-ing images to support this, the exact location, along with the character style, size and location remain unknown.

This port side view of NF Mk XV DZ366 shows the overall Deep Sky scheme of it and all other NF Mk XVs, along with the radome in the 'sooty' Special Night and the unpainted extreme tip *(©DH)*

DZ659 started life as a NF Mk XII, but was converted to a Mk XVII and served with the FIU at Ford, as seen here
(©British Official)

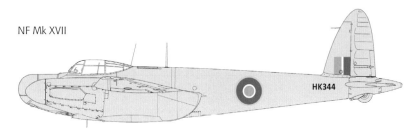

NF Mk XVII

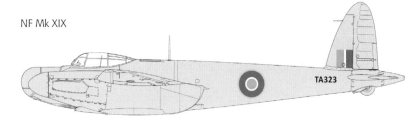

NF Mk XIX

J 30 'Hunter' (NF Mk XIX)

An NF Mk XIX of No.68 Squadron readies itself for a night intruder mission
(©British Official/Crown Copyright)

NF Mk XVII

This variant was similar to the NF Mk XII but it used A.I. Mk X radar, which was the American-built SCR.720, and this was fitted in the 'universal' (Bullnose) radome.

Serial numbers HK237-265, HK278-327 & HK344-362.

NF Mk XIX

This variant was similar to the NF Mk XVII and the first one to allow the fitment of either A.I. Mk VII or A.I. Mk X radar, and both of these used the 'universal' (Bullnose) radome.

Serial numbers MM624-656, MM669-685, TA123-156, TA169-198, TA215-249, TA263-308, TA323-357, TA389-413 & TA425-449 for all NF Mk XIX production.

J 30 'Hunter' (NF Mk XIX)

These were refurbished RAF NF Mk XIXs sold to Sweden, so they had all the features of the RAF examples and only differed in the fitment of a landing light in the leading edge of the starboard wing. The first three machines had the shrouded exhausts, but the remainder had exposed five-stack exhausts. The radio altimeter 'T' antenna can be seen under the wings and a universal shackle for a bomb rack or drop tank was also fitted under each outer wing panel, although in service you will rarely see these machines with anything under the wings.

See NF Mk XIX for all serial numbers.

NF Mk XXX

This variant adopted the two-stage Merlin 72 or 76 and initially the type used a simple shroud on each exhaust, but after much modification and trials, these were replaced with the 'slotted' covers instead. The type used the A.I. Mk X radar in the universal (Bullnose) radome and later machines had the landing light in the leading edge of the starboard wing. The type was in service past the change from Roman to Arabic numbering systems in 1948, so machines in use after this date were designated the NF Mk 30.

Serial numbers MM686-710, MM726-769, MM783-822, MT456-500, MV521-570, NT241-283, NT295-336, NT349-393, NT415-458, NT471-513, NT526-568, NT582-621 & RK929-954.

NF Mk XXXI

This variant number was intended for a Packard-Merlin powered night-fighter, but it was never produced.

NF Mk 36

Adopted for service after the 1948 change-over, this variant was thus always the NF Mk 36 and it used the fuel-injected, two-stage Merlin 113 and 114. It had the A.I. Mk X in the universal (Bullnose) radome and the landing light in the starboard wing leading edge. The type usually carried 100 Imp. Gal. drop tanks in service and most you will see with rearward-looking 'Monica' radar underneath the tailcone. You will also find a number of images showing the NF Mk 36 with the upper clear plastic element of the radome left unpainted.

Serial numbers RK955-960, RK972-999, RL113-158, RL173-215 & RL229-268 for all NF Mk 36 production.

NF Mk XIX '18' (ex-TA242) awaiting delivery to Sweden at Hatfield. The four-blade propellers fitted to these machines are evident *(©DH)*

NF Mk XXX

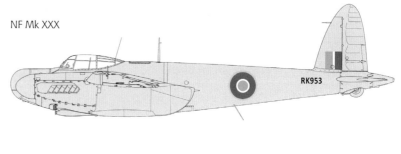

NF Mk 36

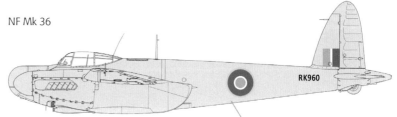

This shot of NF Mk XXX MM687 clearly shows the simple tube exhaust shrouds initially fitted to this series; these would prove to be very problematic, and were replaced after much effort was expended on trials and modifications

(©Ministry of Aircraft Production)

The official photo of NF Mk XXX RK953 clearly shows the 'slotted' exhaust stacks that were fitted to solve the problems experienced with the early tube shrouds

(©Air Ministry/Crown Copyright)

A nice shot of NF Mk 36, RK980, ZK•E with No.25 Squadron, where you can see the unpainted upper half of the radome, the gaps in the serial number under the wings where the drop tanks go and, in this instance, the repeating of the individual aircraft letter on the radome

(©British Official/Crown Copyright)

NF Mk 36 (Hookah)

These machines adopted the new 'Hookah' wide-band homing device and thus had its two 'T' antennae on each wing leading edge.

Serial numbers RK955-960, RK972-999, RL113-158, RL173-215 & RL229-268 for all NF Mk 36 production.

NF Mk 38

The final production night-fighter used the Merlin 113/114 or 113A/114A combination and some of them removed the slotted exhaust dampers in service, as they tended to burn out. Changes to

equipment meant that the type risked being nose-heavy, so to overcome this the cockpit was moved 5 inches aft and the canopy itself was raised by 4 inches. Apart from various whip antennae and dipoles, the type was otherwise just an upgrading of the NF Mk 36, although the type saw only limited RAF use, with a lot being sold directly out of storage to nations such as Yugoslavia. The type can often be seen with the clear upper section of the radome left unpainted.

Serial numbers VT651-63, VT691-707, VX860-879 & VX886-916 for all NF Mk 38 production.

NF (Met) Mk 38

With the night-fighter role being undertaken by interim jet designs before the RAF got its purpose-made all-weather fighter, those NF Mk 38s that remained in RAF service were operated by Meteorological Flights and were thus designated NF (Met) Mk 38. Little changed with them other than they carried various meteorological equipment in the cockpit to undertake their new role.

Serial numbers VT651-63, VT691-707, VX860-879 & VX886-916 for all NF Mk 38 production.

Note: The MET Mk IX variant was based on the B Mk IX so is not included here as it was covered in Volume 1.

NF Mk 36 (Hookah)

RK995

NF Mk 38

NF (Met) Mk 38

NF (Met) Mk 38 with Flt Lts Corrie and LcFarlin about to board for the last MET flight by a regular RAF crew, on the 30th April 1951 *(©British Official)*

The relocated and raised canopy is very evident from this angle of NF Mk 38 VY653 seen in March 1948 at Hatfield

(©DH)

Chapter 2: Evolution – Fighter-Bombers and Photo-Reconnaissance

The very first FB Mk VI, HJ662/G was converted from B Mk IV DZ434 and is seen here with 250lb bombs and Merlin 21 engines at A&AEE Boscombe Down during initial trials; it crashed and was destroyed there on the 30th July 1942
(©A&AEE)

Note: See Chapter 4 for details of the in-service schemes applied to the Mosquito.

Fighter-Bombers

FB Mk VI (Series I)

Powered by single-stage Merlin 22, 23 or 25 engines, the FB Mk VI retained the four 0.303in machine-gun and four 20mm Hispano cannon armament of the night-fighters, the main revision being that they had a wing that allowed a universal carrier to be fitted under each outer panel and a bomb of up to 250lb to be carried on each.

Serial numbers HJ662 (Prototype), HJ663-682, HJ716-743, HJ755-792, HJ8080-833, HP848-888, HP904-942, HP967-989, HR113-162, HR175-220, HR236-262, HR279-312, HR331-375, HR387-415, HR432-465, HR485-527, HR539-580, HR603-648, HX802-835, HX851-869, HX896-901, HX905-922, HX937-984, LR248-276, LR289-313, LR327-340, LR343-389, LR402-404, MM3989-423, MM426-431, NS819-859, NS873-914, NS926-865, NS977-999, NT112-156, NT169-199, NT201-207, NT219-223, NT226-238, PZ161-203, PZ217-250, PZ253-259, PZ273-299, PZ302-316, PZ330-358, PZ371-419, PZ435-466, PZ471-476, RF580-625, RF639-681, RF696-736, RF749-793, RF818-859, RF873-915, RF928-966, RS501-535, RS548-580, RS593-633, RS637-680, RS693-698, SZ958-999, TA113-122, TA369-388, TA469-508, TA523-560, TA575-603, TE587-628, TE640-669, TE683-725, TE738-780, TE793-830, TE848-889, TE905-932 & VL726-732 for all FB Mk VI production.

FB Mk VI (Series II)

These machines differed in that they had the modified wing that allowed either 500lb bombs or a 50 or 100 Imp. Gal. drop tank to be carried under each outer wing panel.

See FB Mk VI (Series I) for all serial numbers.

FB Mk VI (RP)

During 1944 the wing was further modified with strengthening and wiring etc. to allow four 3in 60lb SAP (or 25lb AP) rocket projectiles on staggered rails to be fitted under each outer wing panel (available in 1944).

See FB Mk VI (Series I) for all serial numbers.

FB Mk VI (Series I)

FB Mk VI (Series II)

FB Mk VI (RP)

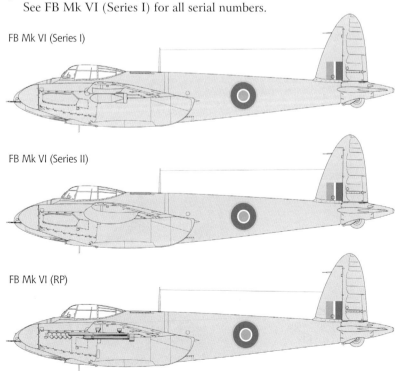

FB Mk VI LR355 of No.487 Squadron at RAF Swanton Morley in April 1944 with 500lb bombs on trolleys in the foreground *(©British Official)*

FB Mk VI (Series I – Banff)

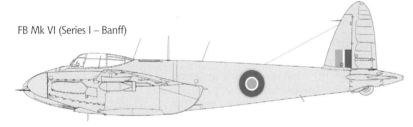

FB Mk VI (100 Group)

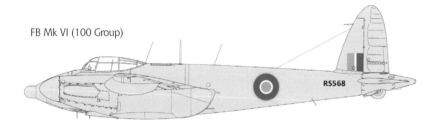

FB Mk VI (Series I – Banff)

These machines, operated by the Banff Strike Wing, were identical to the standard Series I machines, the only difference being the fitment of various whip and dipole antennae for the radio equipment that these machines used in their long-distance strike role.

See FB Mk VI (Series I) for all serial numbers.

FB Mk VI (100 Group)

These machines were used by Nos.23, 141 and 5151 Squadrons as part of 100 Group in early 1945 and they had the nose armament replaced with an ASH radar pod mounted in a thimble radome. They also had 'Monica' warning radar under the tail cone and usually operated with 100 Imp. Gal. drop tanks under each outer wing panel.

See FB Mk VI (Series I) for all serial numbers.

FB Mk VI PZ446 of No.143 Squadron being rearmed with 60lb RPs mounted on the early rails at Banff *(©British Official)*

FB Mk VI RS566 with ASH radar installed in the nose and operated by No.515 Squadron at RAF Little Snoring as part of 100 Group

An FB Mk VI used in the anti-shipping role with the prominent camera in the centre of the nose cone and the two-tier Mk IIIA rails for the RPs that also allowed the carriage of 100 Imp. Gal. drop tanks (©DH)

FB Mk VI (Series II – Banff)

Initial Form

As with the Banff Strike Wing's Series I machines, these Series II machines were identical to the standard ones except they had the strengthened outer wing panels with the wiring to carry four 3in rocket projectiles with either 25lb AP or 60lb HE warheads. They also had the larger camera fitted centrally in the nose cone.

See FB Mk VI (Series I) for all serial numbers.

FB Mk VI (Series II – Banff) – Initial Form

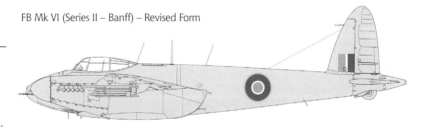

FB Mk VI (Series II – Banff)

Revised Form

These machines were modified to allow the carriage of four 3in RPs on 'tier-carriage' Mk IIIA rails outboard under the wings in combination with a 100 Imp. Gal. drop tank inboard of them.

See FB Mk VI (Series I) for all serial numbers.

FB Mk VI (Series II – Banff) – Revised Form

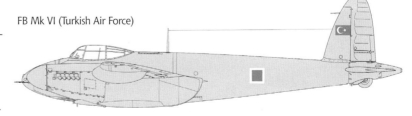

FB Mk VI (Turkish Air Force)

These refurbished machines used four-blade propellers and had a landing light fitted in the leading edge of the starboard wing (not all machines did, so check your references). They could carry 50 or 100 Imp. Gal. drop tanks under each outer wing panel, or four 3in RPs on Mk IIIA rails.

See FB Mk VI (Series I) for all serial numbers.

FB Mk VI (Turkish Air Force)

A FB Mk VI marked as '55' with the Turkish Air Force. Note the four-blade propellers and the fact that this machine does not have a landing light in the starboard wing leading edge

below: A well-known image from C.E. Brown, this time showing FB Mk VI, RS650, AK-F of No.334 Squadron, Royal Norwegian Air Force in flight over some typical scenery (©C.E. Brown)

FB Mk VI (Royal Norwegian AF)

These machines had three-blade propellers with the wide 'paddle' propeller and a landing light fitted in the leading edge of the starboard wing. They could carry a 250lb bomb on a universal carrier under each outer wing panel, and you will see most in later life with the shrouds removed from the exhausts and separate stake exhausts fitted.

See FB Mk VI (Series I) for all serial numbers.

FB Mk VI (Dominican Air Force)

These refurbished machines were like those for Turkey in that they had four-blade propellers and had a landing light fitted in the leading edge of the starboard wing. They could carry drop tanks or bombs (up to 250lb) under each outer wing panel.

See FB Mk VI (Series I) for all serial numbers.

FB Mk VI (RAAF)

The RAAF initially had a batch of British-built FB Mk Vis prior to delivery of Australian-built FB Mk 40s and these had the extended intakes under each engine nacelle, with tropical filters inside. Most of them are seen with 100 Imp. Gal. drop tanks of local manufacture fitted, as they are pressed metal and have a pronounced raised flange around the middle, which also means the filler cap is off-set to port.

See FB Mk VI (Series I) for all serial numbers.

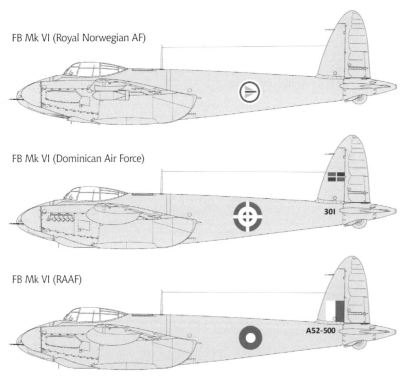

FB Mk VI (Royal Norwegian AF)

FB Mk VI (Dominican Air Force)

FB Mk VI (RAAF)

FB Mk X

This variant number was for a projected Packard Merlin 67 powered version of the FB Mk VI, but it was never built.

FB Mk VI '301' of the Dominican AF during the delivery flight in July 1948, seen en route at USAF Barsarssuak, Greenland (©A.G. Harwin via Stuart Howe†)

FB Mk XVIII NT225 was the subject of a series of photos for official purposes, this one nicely shows off the underside, with the bulge for the 57mm gun in the gun doors, the ejector ports behind it, the fitment of only two machine-guns in the nose and what look to be reinforcing ribs added to the inboard flaps *(©Air Ministry)*

FB Mk XVIII (Early)

The first of the 'Tse Tse' used the Merlin 25 and had the ventral cannon replaced with a single 6-pdr (57mm) Molins cannon. This gun had a rate of fire of 25 shells in 20 seconds, although prolonged use usually resulted in the ventral bay being rebuilt as the recoil pushed the gun further and further aft! The type usually carried 50 Imp. Gal. drop tanks and the fitment of the gun led to various bulged, reinforcing plates and ejector ports in the underside, as the four (cannon/bomb bay) doors were replaced with single ones on each side.

Serial numbers HJ732 (prototype) and HX902-904, MM424-425, NT200, NT224-225, NT592-593, PZ251-252, PZ300-301, PZ346 & PZ467-470.

FB Mk XVIII (Late)

In later service you will find FB Mk XVIIIs with two of the four nose-mounted machine-guns removed, to save weight, but to still allow the remaining guns to be used to sight the Molins. From surviving photos there also looks to be ribs added to the underside of the inboard flaps, maybe to strengthen them as a result of blast damage with earlier examples?

Serial numbers HJ732 (prototype) and HX902-904, MM424-425, NT200, NT224-225, NT592-593, PZ251-252, PZ300-301, PZ346 & PZ467-470.

FB Mk 21 (Canada)

These machines were Canadian-built examples of the FB Mk VI, which used the single-stage Packard Merlin 33 in the first example, and the Packard Merlin 31 in the second and third examples. Only three FB Mk 21s were ever built (Serial numbers KA100 to 102, the latter later being converted to the FB Mk 24 prototype).

FB Mk XVIII MM424 is an early machine, which retains all four machine-guns and is seen here with 50 Imp. Gal. drop tanks fitted

(©Crown Copyright)

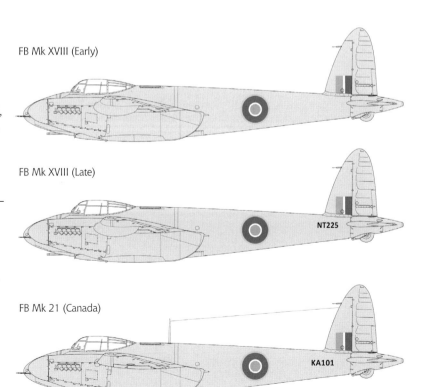

FB Mk XVIII (Early)

FB Mk XVIII (Late)

NT225

FB Mk 21 (Canada)

KA101

FB Mk 21 KA100 was one of two pre-production machines fitted with Packard Merlin 33 engines. although the type never entered series production *(©BAc)*

The single FB Mk 24 development aircraft (KA102) with its two-speed, two-stage supercharged Packard Merlin engines; this type was never to see production in Canada *(©DH Canada)*

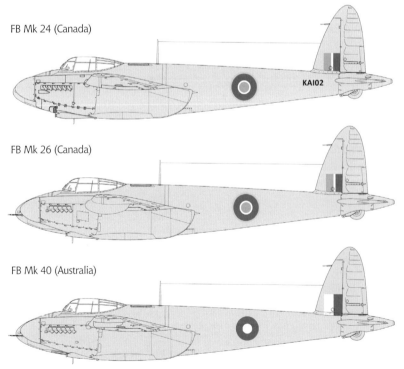

FB Mk 24 (Canada)

FB Mk 26 (Canada)

FB Mk 40 (Australia)

FB Mk 24 (Canada)

Only a single example of this Canadian-built development of the FB Mk 21 was ever built (KA102). It had the two-stage Packard Merlin 301 engines with their six-stack exhausts and three-blade Hamilton-Standard 'paddle' propellers. This machine remained unarmed throughout its career, mainly due to acute shortages of 0.303in machine-guns and, especially, 20mm Hispano cannon.

FB Mk 26 (Canada)

including Chinese examples

These machines used the two-stage Packard Merlin 225 engine with five-stack exhausts and were fully armed with four 0.303in Browning machine-guns in the nose and four 20mm Hispano cannon in the ventral bay. Once again the trailing aerial fairlead was fitted under the nose and you will often see these machines with 100 Imp. Gal. drop tanks fitted. The type used a combination of American and Canadian-produced equipment (e.g. radio) in lieu of British examples.

Serial numbers KA103-450, although many were cancelled and a great number were completed as T Mk 29s.

FB Mk 28 (Canada)

This number was allocated to a Canadian-built variant that never went into production.

FB Mk 40 (Australia)

The first 100 machines used the Packard Merlin 31, whilst the remainder had the Merlin 33. Both used the long single-stage nacelles and had six-stack exposed exhausts. Three-blade (narrow) Hamilton Standard of Australian-built de Havilland Hydromatic propellers were used and the wing allowed either bombs (up to 500lb) or drop tanks (50 or 100 Imp. Gal.) to be carried. As with the Canadian-built machines, all the Aus-

Surplus FB Mk 26s being prepared for shipment to China at the Downsview plant in Canada
(©DH Canada)

A52-1 the first Australian-built FB Mk 40 in flight
(©DH Australia)

tralian ones also had the trailing aerial fairlead tube situated under the nose, just aft of the crew access door, offset to starboard.

Serial numbers A52-1 to A52-212 were allocated to the FB Mk 40, although not all of these were completed as the type.

FB Mk 42 (Australia)

This variant started out as a fighter-bomber, but the type was soon dropped and developed as the PR Mk 41 (see elsewhere in this section).

Photo-Reconnaissance

PR Mk 40 – A52-2 (Australia)

This machine was converted from an FB Mk 40 and had Packard Merlin 31 engines in long single-stage nacelles with six-stack exposed exhausts. All the armament was removed and the ports plated over, while an additional strengthening strake was added to the port fuselage side (from Bulkheads 4 to 5) as a mirror image of the one that already existed on the star-

board side. The camera fit in this machine was two split F.24 8in camera in the nose and one oblique F.52 20in camera in the rear fuselage, slightly off the centreline to port, with a square shutter and rail assembly visible on the outside of the fuselage.

PR Mk 40 – remainder (Australia)

As with A52-2 these were all converted from FB Mk 40s and all seem to have used the Packard Merlin 31 in long single-stage nacelles with six-stack exposed exhausts. The armament was

One of the remaining PR Mk 40s, A52-4, seen here at Noemfoor in late August/ early September 1944 (©RAAF/T. Jay)

The first PR Mk 40, A52-2, seen here during one of its first missions *(©RAAF/J. Love)*

PR Mk 40 – A52-2 (Australia)

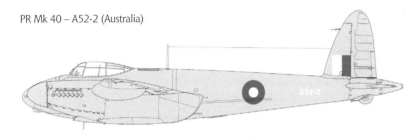

PR Mk 40 – remainder (Australia)

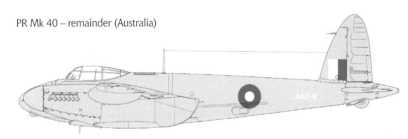

PR Mk 41 (Australia)

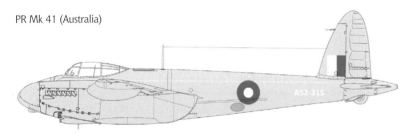

removed and the additional strake was added to the port rear fuselage side. The camera layout was for one in the nose in the vertical position, two vertical cameras in the rear fuselage staggered slightly to port and starboard and two oblique cameras either side of the rear fuselage. The last five machines (A52-4, A52-6, A52-7, A52-9 and A52-26) had provision for the following combinations of cameras: 1. Reconnaissance – vertical F.52 (36in. lens) in rear fuselage plus vertical K.18 (24in. lens) in the nose and oblique F.24 (8in. lens) in the port rear fuselage; 2. Aerial Photographic Survey – vertical K.17 (6in. lens) in the nose, two K.17 (6in. lens) mounted obliquely, to port and starboard, in the rear fuselage and a vertical F.52 (20in. lens) in the rear fuselage.

Serial numbers A52-4, A52-6, A52-7, A52-9 and A52-26.

PR Mk 41 (Australia)

This variant was originally intended to be a fighter-bomber (FB Mk 41), but was dropped and developed as a photo-reconnaissance version instead. It used the Packard Merlin 69 engine in long nacelles with six-stack exhausts and had three-blade (paddle) D.H. Hydromatic Type 500 propellers. All armament was removed and the ports covered over. It too had the additional strengthening strake on the port side, plus a third one below this. A single K.18 camera was carried in the nose, with a shutter and rail assembly visible externally. Two oblique F.52 cameras were installed in the rear fuselage with another two oblique ones to port and starboard with only the starboard one having an external shutter and rail plate visible.

Serial numbers A52-300 to A52-327, all of which were reallocations from the FB Mk 40 production batch.

PR Mk 41 A52-302 with No.87 (Survey) Squadron at Broken Hill airfield in 1948 *(©RAAF)*

Chapter 3:   Trainers, Target-Tugs and the Sea Mosquito

T Mk III TV959 marked as 'Y', this machine is now airworthy with FHC in the USA after rebuild in New Zealand

The two-seat nature of the Mosquito meant that it lent itself to use in a number of other roles, including that or trainer and target-tug. Its stout construction also meant that sea trials soon proved it suitable for operations from Royal Naval carriers, the first twin-engine aircraft to do so, and the type therefore saw limited production and service with the FAA.

Note: See Chapter 4 for details of the camouflage and markings applied to all in-service Mosquitos.

Trainers

T Mk III (Early)

This machine was basically an unarmed, dual-control Mk II, with Merlin 21, 23 or 25 single-stage engines with narrow-blade propellers and shrouded exhausts. The machine-guns in the nose were usually removed unless the particular aircraft was used primarily in the gunnery role. The ventral cannon were always removed and their ports covered over. Dual controls were fitted in the cockpit with the tutor situated on a sliding seat where the navigator used to be. The type retained the universal carrier under each outer wing panel, so could carry bombs or drop tanks.

Serial numbers W4053 (prototype) and W4073, W4075, W4077 plus HJ851-899, HJ958-999, LR516-541, LR553-585, RR270-319, TV954-984, TW101-119, VA871-894, VA923-928, VR330-349, VT581-595 & VT604-631 (production).

T Mk III (Late)

These machines differed in that they had exposed five-stack exhausts and 'paddle' blade

propellers. A landing light was installed in the leading edge of the starboard wing and the engine cowls had the deeper/longer intakes with the shutters inside but no side vents, nor filter units inside.

See T Mk III (early) for serial numbers.

T Mk III and TT Mk III (Belgian AF)

These machines were identical to the late versions of RAF T Mk IIIs, but in the target-towing

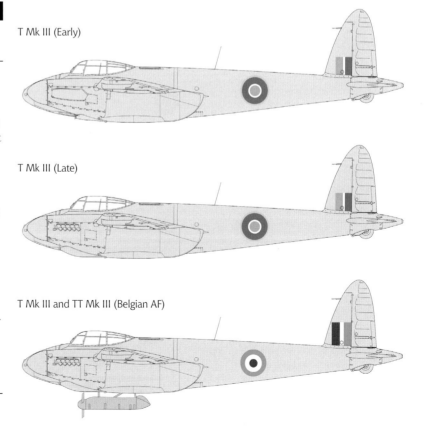

T Mk III (Early)

T Mk III (Late)

T Mk III and TT Mk III (Belgian AF)

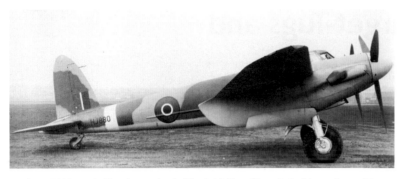

T Mk III HJ880 was built at Leavesden in March 1943 and is typical of the early machines, with their shrouded exhausts and narrow blade propellers *(©Crown Copyright)*

role they had a wind-driven winch mounted in a pod below the forward section of the ventral bay; these usually lacked the aerodynamic fairing around the base. Behind this was a buffer unit for the towed cable and the sleeves (banners) were held in place on either side of the rear of the bomb-bay with horizontal bars that could be removed in flight to let the sleeves fall free.

See T Mk III (early) for serial numbers.

TT Mk 6 (Belgian Air Force)

These were FB Mk VI (Series II) machines modified for the target-towing role. Being export machines they had the landing light added to the leading edge of the starboard wing, and like the TT Mk III they had the wind-driven winch and cable buffer under under the fuselage. Not all machines used these latter items, though, so some probably streamed the sleeve by towing them from the ground and simply cutting the cable over the airfield to release it.

See FB Mk VI (Series I) for all serial numbers relating to the FB Mk VI series.

TT Mk 6 (Belgian Air Force)

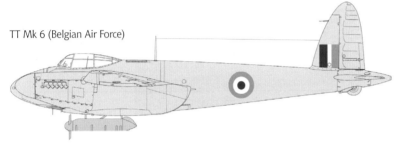

TT Mk 6 of the Belgian Air Forcing whilst visiting Evere-Brussels in 1947 *(©Rudy Binnemans)*

T Mk 22 (Canada)

This was a dual-control version of the FB Mk 21 and it used the Packard Merlin 33 engine with the longer/deeper ventral intakes with the two-position shutter system inside (there were no vents on the outside, so doubt they had tropical filters fitted). All armament was deleted and the ports covered over and the tutor was situated in a sliding seat where the navigator used to be. The type retained the universal carrier under each outer wing panel, so could carry bombs or drop tanks and was usually seen with 100 Imp. Gal. drop tanks attached. Only six T Mk 22s were built.

Serial numbers KA873-876 & KA896-897.

T Mk 22 (Canada)

KA874

T Mk 27 (Canada)

This version was similar to the T Mk 22 but used the single-stage Packard Merlin 225 with short intakes, exposed five-stack exhausts and three-blade 'paddle' propellers.

Serial numbers KA877-895 & KA898-927.

T Mk 27 (Canada)

KA898

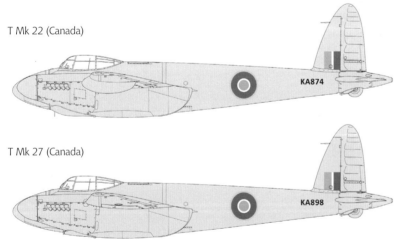

One of only six T Mk 22s comes in to land, note the blanked-off nose gun ports and the 100 Imp. Gal. drop tanks

(©DH Canada)

Nice shot, probably taken at the Downsview plant, of T Mk 27 KA888

(©DH Canada)

T Mk 29 (Canada) – Early

This was a dual-control version of the Canadian-built FB Mk VI and many of them were in fact FB Mk 26s built without armament due to a shortage of Hispano cannon. The type used the Packard Merlin 225 with short intakes, shrouded exhausts and three-blade 'paddle' propellers. Once again the tutor was situated in a sliding seat where the navigator used to be and the type retained the capacity to carry bombs or drop tanks, although most images will show the type rarely carried either.

Although the exact serial numbers for the T Mk 29 are unknown, these machines were all converted from the KA117 to KA314 production batches.

T Mk 29 (Canada) – Late

These later machines can be seen fitted with exposed six-stack exhausts and most will be seen with 100 Imp. Gal. drop tanks under each wing.

See T Mk 29 (Canada) – Early for serial numbers.

T Mk 43 (Australia)

This was a dual-control version of the FB Mk 40 and used the Packard Merlin 33 with long/deep intakes, exposed six-stack exhausts and three-

T Mk 29 (Canada) – Early

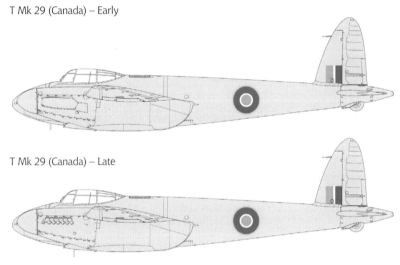

T Mk 29 (Canada) – Late

above: This late production T Mk 29 complete with exposed exhausts and wide-blade propellers is seen being towed in after a test flight at the Downsview factory

(©National Museum of Science and Technology)

This early T Mk 29 KA117 later went on to serve with No.85 Squadron

(©Ministry of Aircraft Production)

T Mk 43 (Australia)

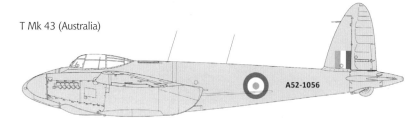

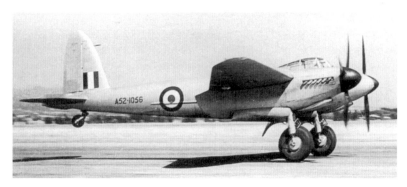

T Mk 43, A52-1056, with No.87 (PR) Squadron at Fairbairn in 1952, this machine was originally built as FB Mk 40 A52-8 (©N. Sparrow)

blade 'narrow' propellers. Once again the tutor was situated in a sliding seat where the navigator used to be and all armament was removed. The type had twin trim tabs fitted to the elevators and retained the capacity to carry bombs or drop tanks, although most images will show the type rarely carried either.

Serial numbers A52-1050 to 1071, all re-allocated from the FB Mk 40 production.

[Naval] FB Mk VI (LR359)

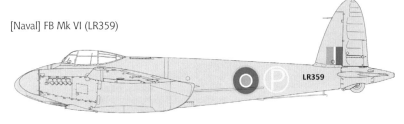

Naval FB Mk VI LR359 acted as the first prototype of the Sea Mosquito TR Mk 33 series and differed in many ways, most noticeable having no wing fold nor ASH radar (©BAe)

Sea Mosquito

[Naval] FB Mk VI (LR359)

TR Mk 33 prototype

Used to test the concept of a Naval version of the Mosquito, this FB Mk VI had the Merlin 25 engine with five-stack exhausts and was fitted with non feathering experimental four blade propellers. The guns in the nose and ventral bay were removed and their ports covered over and reinforcing strips were added to each side of the fuselage, aft of the wing trailing edge. An arrestor hook was installed underneath the rear fuselage with the interior of the rear fuselage also strengthened to withstand the forces of deck landings. This first prototype never had folding wings.

Camouflage & Markings

Being a true prototype, this aircraft was painted yellow underneath, whilst the upper surfaces were in the Temperate Sea Scheme of Extra Dark Sea Grey and Dark Slate Grey in a disruptive camouflage pattern. Type B roundels were applied above the wings, with Type C (36in dia.) underneath. The Type C1 roundel was also repeated on either side of the fuselage. The prototype 'P' marking was applied aft of the fuselage roundel and because of the yellow underside, the lower half of the outer ring was applied in Dark Slate Grey to contrast on the yellow. A Type C fin flash (27in x 24in) was applied to either side of the base of the vertical fin and the upper surface camouflage colours covered both vertical fin and rudder, unlike the RAF Mosquitos with these areas left in the underside colour. The serial number was applied in 8in black characters either side of the rear fuselage, forward of the tailplane and using a hypothetical line from the centreline line of the trailing edge of the wing to the leading edge of the tailplane as the baseline for the characters. The legend 'Royal Navy' was applied in 6in high black capital letters directly below the serial number. Both spinners and propellers were Night, with yellow tips to each propeller blade.

[Naval] FB Mk VI (LR387)

TR Mk 33 second prototype

This machine was basically similar to LR359, and also acted as a proof of concept airframe. The machine-gun armament in the nose was replaced with an AN/APS-4 (ASH) (ASV Mk XI-IIb) radar pod, whilst the ventral 20mm Hispano cannon were retained. It was also the first to have manually-operated folding outer wing panels, and crutches under the fuselage allowed the carriage of a single 2,000lb 18in Mk XV or XVII torpedo. Even with a torpedo a 50 Imp. Gal. drop tank could be still carried under each outer wing panel. Initially retaining the rubber-in-torsion undercarriage legs, this machine later went on to test the Lockheed long-stroke oleo-pneumatic legs that would be used on the production machines.

Camouflage & Markings

This airframe had the full Temperate Sea Scheme of Extra Dark Sea Grey and Dark Slate Grey, but the undersides do not have the contrast of yellow, so it looks as if they were Sky (some claim them to be Medium Sea Grey, but that seems unlikely). The demarcation along the fuselage sides is odd, in that although it follows a hypothetical line from the leading edge of the tailplane, this is actually slightly below it, and it is in a straight line projecting forward. This results in the front edge being well above the centreline of the wing trailing edge, so about 6in ahead of the forward edge of the roundel, the line goes diagonally downwards to meet the wing trailing edge. All Sea Mosquitos had the vertical fin and rudder painted in the upper surface camouflage pattern, with LR3878 being no exception. The wings had Type B roundels on top and Type C underneath, whilst the fuselage has a Type C1 roundel that has a thin darker outer ring, that we presume to be Dark Slate Grey or Extra Dark Sea Grey. The prototype 'P' marking aft of the fuselage roundel is slightly larger in diameter, but it too has a darker ring, although in this instance it is for both the inner and outer edge of the outer yellow ring. The serial number is applied in 8in black characters on either side of the aft fuselage, but this is positioned centrally in relation to the

centreline of the leading edge of the tailplane. This time the 'Royal Navy' legend is applied well above the serial. A Type C fin flash is applied to the base of both sides of the vertical fin and the tip of the ASH pod is painted black.

[Naval] FB Mk VI (LR387)

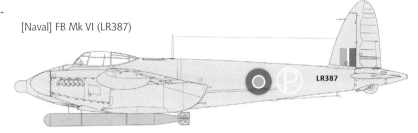

TF/TR Mk 33

(inc. pre-production TS444 and TS449)

These production machines were basically similar to LR387, but had single-stage Merlin long nacelles with long intakes and exposed five-stack exhausts. TS444 and production machines had the ASH radar pod mounted in the nose, whilst TS449 only had an (empty?) ASH pod that was more extensively faired in. The fighter canopy had a bulged panel on the starboard side only and the type used the long-stroke Lockheed oleo-pneumatic undercarriage legs, as they dealt better with the sink rates on an aircraft carrier, along with reduced size main wheels. RATO bottle attachment points were installed on either side of the rear fuselage, just below the mid-point of the reinforcing strips, and enlarged mass balances were added to the tips of the elevators to give better low-speed response. From the fourteenth production machine, the main wheels were of a slightly smaller diameter than previously fitted.

Serial numbers TS444, TS449, TW227-257 and TW277-295.

Camouflage & Markings

The second pre-production machine (TS449) was almost certainly in the same scheme as applied to LR359, complete with yellow underside. It may be that this is Sky, but the contrast is very high, so we suspect yellow is more likely (especially when you consider the outer ring of

The first true TR Mk 33 was LR387, which was the second prototype for the series and included production elements such as the wing fold, ASH radar and capacity to carry a torpedo under the fuselage

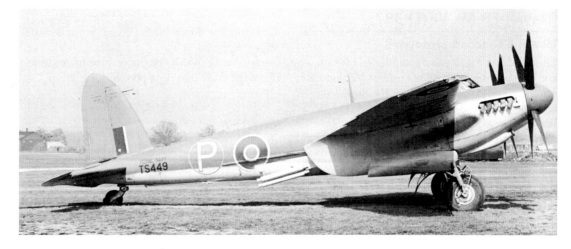

the prototype 'P' marking is once again given an additional dark edge to it). Roundels are Type B above and Type C below the wings, and the serial number is applied in 30in high black characters under each outer wing panel, read from the trailing edge of the port and leading edge of the starboard wing. There is the usual gap in these numbers for the fitment of a drop tank, so they are split 'TS', then a gap, then '449'. The fuselage roundel is Type C1 with that

it. The 'Royal Navy' legend is in smaller (4in?) characters above the serial number and a Type C fin flash is at the base of the vertical fin, on each side. The area in which the RATO bottle reinforcing plate is attached to the rear fuselage has been roughly sprayed with the under surface yellow, so this goes onto the lower quarter of the fuselage roundel on both sides. The spinners look to be Extra Dark Sea Grey, whilst the blades are black with a yellow tip. TS444 had a slightly different scheme, but period images have too much contrast in them to be sure. It looks to be the same as LR387, although the roundels under the wings are right out under the tip and no serial numbers are applied under the wings. The fuselage demarcation is low down as is the case with TS444 and this machine had the ASH pod in place, which looks to be painted white.

TF/TR Mk 33

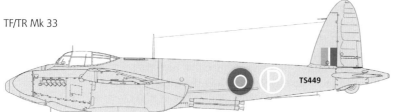

darker outer element to the outer yellow ring on those areas that overlap the underside (yellow) colour. The prototype 'P' marking is aft of the roundel and oddly does not have its centre in the same place as the roundel ahead of it, it is slightly above. The lower yellow ring is once again edged in a thin dark shade, probably Dark Slate Grey. The demarcation along the fuselage is lower than usual, and soft edged, so it is actu-

TF/TR Mk 33 – Late

These later machines can all be seen with the antennae for the Hookah wide-band homing device on the leading edge of each wing, halfway between where the drop tank carriers would be (not usually fitted) and the wing tips. These comprised aerials mounted in a vertical 'T' con-figuration from bulges that projected from the wing leading edge.

Serial numbers TS444, TS449, TW227-257 and TW277-295.

TF/TR Mk 37

(including prototype TW240)

The final Sea Mosquito variant used Rolls-Royce Merlin 25 (single-stage) engines in long nacelles with long intakes and exposed five-stack ex-hausts. Four-blade propellers were also installed and the machine-gun armament in the nose was replaced with an APS-4 (ASH) (ASV Mk XIIIb) radar in an elongated and bulbous radome. The outboard two 20mm Hispano cannon were delet-ed from the ventral bay, although some machines had all four cannon removed. A pitot tube was installed in the starboard wing tip and the fighter canopy had a bulged panel on the starboard

TF/TR Mk 33 – Late

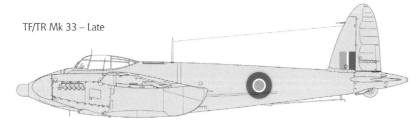

ally below the centreline of the trailing edge of the wing or leading edge of the tailplane, and thus the upper surface colours go underneath the tailplanes and continue out to the tail cone. The serial number is applied in the usual manner ahead of the tailplane, but again the characters are not applied on a hypothetical line from the centreline of the tailplane trailing edge, they just about have their upper edge in line with this, but even then, the characters are slightly below side. As with the others, this type had manually-operated folding outer wing panels and the radio access hatch on the starboard side of the mid-fuselage was relocated to the underside. The long-stroke Lockheed oleo-pneumatic undercarriage legs were used along with reduced diameter main wheels. A small intake can be seen on the leading edge of the port wing, just outboard of the engine and this is probably to do with cooling air for the radar. Three dipoles were fitted above and below the wing tips, along the centreline and a reinforcing strip was added to each side of the rear fuselage side, just aft of the wing trailing edge. Attachment points for RATO bottles were added on either side of the rear fuselage, just below the mid-point of the reinforcing strips and the arrestor hook under the rear fuselage was deleted, although the prototype (TW240) retained it throughout its life. As with the TR Mk 33, this version had the enlarged mass balances on the tips of the elevators and it was intended to carry a 1,000lb 'Uncle Tom' rocket projectile on a special rack under each outer wing panel although only TW240 was photographed with either racks or rockets installed. Uncle Tom was the British designation for the American 'Tiny Tim' rocket and was probably never adopted for use due to the damage the big rocket motor's exhaust blast was found to cause to the launch aircraft.

Serial numbers TW240 (prototype) and VT724-737.

Camouflage & Markings

The prototype TW240 went through two series of markings in its life, although the overall scheme remained the same as Extra Dark Sea Grey and Dark Slate Grey over Sky, with a soft-edged demarcation that was low down on the rear fuselage, thus going underneath the tail-planes. Markings consisted of Type B roundels above the wings and Type C underneath, initially without serial numbers under the wings. A Type C1 roundel was applied to the rear fuselage with a Type C fin flash on either side of the vertical fin. The serial number (8in) and 'Royal Navy'

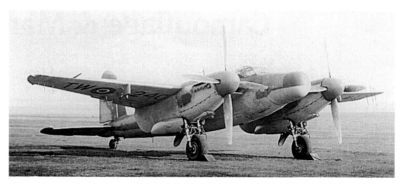

legend (4in) was applied on either side of the rear fuselage, all contained within the upper camouflage portion due to the low demarcation. The demarcation around the forward fuselage and nose continues along the same line, but it is interesting to note that there is a distinct step in this line around the crew access door, with the line on the door being quite a bit higher than the surrounding area. The spinners were Dark Slate Grey, whilst the propeller blades were black with yellow tips. The revision made to the scheme once this machine was involved in Uncle Tom rocket trials was the addition of the serial

TF/TR Mk 37

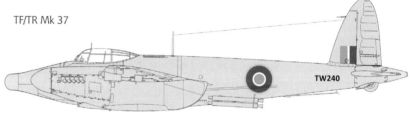

number under each wing, read from the trailing edge of the starboard and leading edge of the port wing. The fitment of the big pylon for the rocket meant that the Type C roundel was just outboard of it and this meant that the code was split either side of the pylon/roundel, thus being 'TW' (roundel/pylon) '240' under each wing.

TR Mk 37 prototype TW240 seen at A&AEE Boscombe Down in December 1947 with underwing pylons for Uncle Tom rockets and the application of serial numbers under each wing (©Crwon Copyright)

Production TF/TR Mk 37 VT724 was built at Chester and served with No.703 NAS

Chapter 4:   **Camouflage & Markings**

All profiles and top-views
©Richard J Caruana 2017

Let us first start by saying that nothing is certain when trying to deduce colours from old black and white photographs. The best you can make is an educated and, with luck, intelligent guess using both photographic and documentary evidence. The regulations with regard to the camouflage and markings of RAF aircraft during the war period are well known and all survive, the problem is that at the front line when the regulations changed it was highly unlikely that the ground crew rushed out to paint every aircraft in their charge, it was simply not practical. So be warned, nothing is an absolute when it comes to camouflage and markings, and therefore what follows is what should have been according to the regulations.

For the *schemes applied to the various Mosquito prototypes and one-off test airframes, please see Chapters 1, 2 and 3 respectively.*

Note: We have decided to approach the whole subject of camouflage and markings differently this time, so instead of pages of words (OK, there are still lots of words!) we thought it would be better, and thus more usable, to offer colour profiles and other visual guides combined with a detailed narrative.

Night-Fighters & Fighters

Shades of Black

The initial scheme used by the fighter variant was that of night-fighter and this called for the application of Special Night overall. This colour was developed by the RAE during the 1935 to 1939 period and it was officially cleared for use by Bomber Command in September 1939. Only a relatively small number of machines were finished in this colour, though, mainly those in the W-serial range which were delivered between January and March 1942. The Hatfield photo dated February 1942 with W4088, W4090 and W4092, clearly shows them in this scheme. The

upper wing roundels were Type B (54in diameter), none were carried underneath and the roundels on either side of the fuselage were oddly the very visible Type A1 (42in diameter) with its wide outer yellow ring. It is believed that many of the machines delivered to the units with this style of roundel were modified by painting out a proportion of the outer yellow ring, thus making it more akin the new Type A2 roundel with its 1:3:5:6 ratio. The tail fin flash was Type A (24in x 27in), with equal bands of red, white blue and the serial number was applied in 8in characters on either side of the rear fuselage in Dull Red. Few if any photographs survive of these Special Night-painted machines with squadron codes, although these too theoretically would have also been done in Dull Red.

NF Mk II

Tests undertaken by de Havillands with W4082 in February 1942 proved that the Special Night colour was reducing the top speed of the Mosquito. The colour was applied over a base layer of standard Night, so de Havillands flew W4082 in just the Night base coat and then with the Special Night on top, and proved that with the latter paint applied the Mosquito was 26mph slower! This caused alarm bells with the Controller of Research and Development, who requested the DTD investigate and advise the Air Staff accordingly. Without waiting for the de Havilland tests to be confirmed the Directorate of Operational Requirements advised Fighter Command, so on the 5th February 1942 CinC Fighter Command agreed that the night-fighter scheme should immediately be changed from Special Night to 'smooth black'. The adoption of the new Night Type S (as 'smooth black' was known) is believed to have occurred with the delivery of the DD-serial batch of NF Mk IIs around the 12th March 1942 and the new rules for the colour were circulated by the Air Ministry on the 6th March 1942. Although the aircraft retained the Type B roundel on the upper wing,

NF Mk II, DD673, YP•E, No.23 Squadron, summer 1942. Night Type S (smooth) overall with Dull Red codes and serials; Blue/Red (Type B) roundels above wings

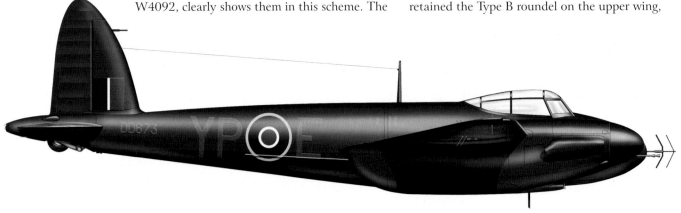

Mosquito FB Mk VI, G-AGGC, British Overseas Airways Corporation. Extra Dark Sea Grey/Dark Slate Grey upper surfaces with Night undersides; registration letters in Medium Sea Grey, outlined in light grey, in all positions. Tricolour beneath fuselage registration and below wings; red/blue only beneath registration above wings

Mosquito FB Mk VI, G-AGGD (ex-HJ681), British Overseas Airways Corporation. Extra Dark Sea Grey/Dark Slate Grey upper surfaces with Sky undersides; registration letters on fuselage sides and above wings in Medium Sea Grey with light grey outline; registration repeated below wings in Night only. Tricolour bands on fuselage sides and below wings; Red/Blue only beneath registration above wings

the fuselage roundel changed to the new Type C1 (36in diameter), with its 3:4:8:9 ratio in comparison with the 1:3:5:7 ratio of the Type A1. Adoption of this roundel style was confirmed in the amendment to the marking regulations on the 30th April 1942, although it was applied to aircraft prior to this date. The fin flash also changed to Type C1 (24in x 24in), with the narrow central white segment.

BOAC

The Mosquitos operated by BOAC on the 'ball-bearing run' and for VIP transport carried a variety of schemes, as they used both bomber and fighter-bomber variants. All adopted the Temperate Sea Scheme of Extra Dark Sea Grey and Dark Slate Grey over Sky initially, although later the Sky was overpainted with Night and the registration number under the wings was applied in Light Slate Grey instead of Night. The camouflage patterns applied to these machines differs greatly from the standard factory patterns, but match almost exactly the diagram for large twin-engine aircraft in the AMO, and that is probably down to the fact that just such aircraft types were operating from Bramcote where the BOAC Mosquitos were maintained. For a long time it was stated that the registration letters were outlined in silver, but it now seems there were actually outlined in a light grey. The stripes under the registration were applied in red (top), white and blue, whilst those on top of the wings were red and blue only. No serial number was applied to the rear fuselage, instead the legend 'British Overseas Airways Corporation' was applied in 4in high black characters, on two rows, with the bottom baseline a hypothetical line from the tailplane centreline. The BOAC 'Speedbird' emblem was sometimes applied on either side of the nose, overlapping the crew access hatch on the starboard side, but it was not always applied, so check references; again for many years this was said to be outlined in silver, but now is thought to be more likely light grey.

Move to Grey

Trials with the new Ocean Grey and Dark Green colours in July 1942 made it quite clear that these colours were preferable on the upper surfaces of night-fighters in place of Night Type S. The Air Ministry was informed of the trials on the 28th July 1942 and on the 31st July the DOR advised HQ Fighter Command that night-fighters were to adopt the Day Fighter Scheme of Pattern A (comprising Ocean Grey and Dark Green upper surfaces) over standard Night undersides. All manufacturers were informed on the 6th August 1942, with the scheme applied to Patterns AD 1159 and AD 1160 to uneven and odd serial numbers respectively. The propeller

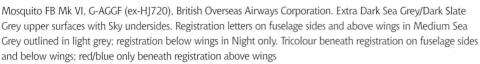

Mosquito FB Mk VI, G-AGGF (ex-HJ720), British Overseas Airways Corporation. Extra Dark Sea Grey/Dark Slate Grey upper surfaces with Sky undersides. Registration letters on fuselage sides and above wings in Medium Sea Grey outlined in light grey; registration below wings in Night only. Tricolour beneath registration on fuselage sides and below wings; red/blue only beneath registration above wings

Prototype fighter W4052 seen here at Hatfield on the 29th April 1943 clearly shows the final overall Medium Sea Grey scheme, with a disruptive camouflage pattern of Dark Green on the upper surfaces. The entire vertical fin and rudder remained in Medium Sea Grey, whilst demarcation on the engines was simply a case of following the panel line of the top cowl (©DH/BAe)

spinners were to be painted in Ocean Grey and the roundels and serial numbers were to remain the same as those applied to the Night Type S scheme. Concerns were voiced by many commanders as to the use of Night on the undersides, and after much consultation and trials, a revision was made to the night-fighter scheme by the AOC in C of Fighter Command on the 23rd August 1942.

The new regulation, circulated on the 25th August 1942, required the application of Dark Green and Medium Sea Grey on the upper surfaces; the under surfaces, fin, rudder and spinners to be in Medium Sea Grey; all national markings were to be in accordance with AMI A.664/42, with no further tactical fighter markings to be carried. To clarify the term 'under surfaces', it was defined as "all surfaces below a line from the centre of the nose to the centre

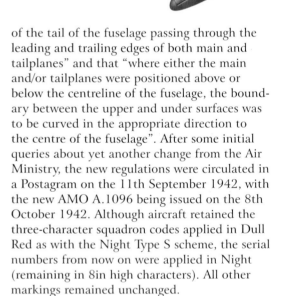

of the tail of the fuselage passing through the leading and trailing edges of both main and tailplanes" and that "where either the main and/or tailplanes were positioned above or below the centreline of the fuselage, the boundary between the upper and under surfaces was to be curved in the appropriate direction to the centre of the fuselage". After some initial queries about yet another change from the Air Ministry, the new regulations were circulated in a Postagram on the 11th September 1942, with the new AMO A.1096 being issued on the 8th October 1942. Although aircraft retained the three-character squadron codes applied in Dull Red as with the Night Type S scheme, the serial numbers from now on were applied in Night (remaining in 8in high characters). All other markings remained unchanged.

NF Mk XII, HK419, ZJ•B, No.96 Squadron, West Malling, 1943. Medium Sea Grey overall with Dark Green camouflage on upper surfaces; Dull Red codes and Night serial. Blue/Red roundels above wings. On this machine the serial number was applied after the camouflage and thus straddles the demarcation

Mosquito NF Mk II, DZ269, RX•U, No.456 Squadron (RAAF), June 1943. Medium Sea Grey overall with Dark Green camouflage on upper surfaces; Dull Red codes, Night serials. Type B roundels above wings; 'kill' markings showing locomotives, rolling stock and a truck carried on the port side of the nose

NF XII, HK197, ME•F, No.488 Squadron, Bradwell Bay, September 1943. Medium Sea Grey overall with Dark Green camouflage on upper surfaces; Dull Red codes, Night serials. Blue/Red roundels above wings

NF Mk XIII, HK479, PS•F, No.264 Squadron, Twenthe (Holland), 1945. Medium Sea Grey overall with Dark Green camouflage on upper surfaces; Dull Red codes; Night serial. Blue/Red roundels above wings
    The squadron codes on this machine follow a more level baseline than most and the serial number was obviously applied using the demarcation of the upper and lower colours as its baseline

NF Mk XIII, MM466, ME•R, No.488 Squadron, Gilze-Rijen, April 1945. Medium Sea Grey overall with Dark Green camouflage on upper surfaces; Dull Red codes and Night serials. Yellow/Blue/White/Red (similar to those on fuselage sides) roundels above wings; Red/White/Blue roundels on front of spinners
    The application of the Type C roundel (3:4:8 ratio) was adopted by 2nd TAF aircraft from the 7th January 1945 in place of the Type B roundel on the wings

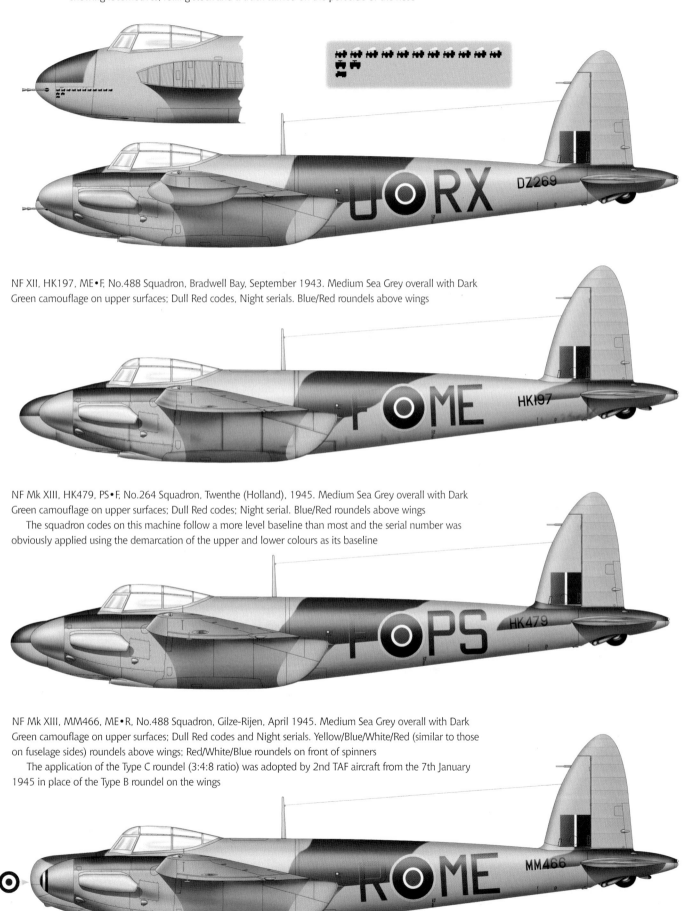

NF Mk XIX, TA429/G, JT•E, No 256 Squadron, Deversoir, Egypt, 1946. Medium Sea Grey/Dark Green finish with Red codes and Night serial; Blue/Red roundels above wings

Note the application of the '/G' after the serial number, denoting this machine had to be guarded at all times when on the ground. The style and thickness of the characters used for the codes are much thinner than usual, and probably a local variation

The Intruder Scheme

In late August 1942 the Air Commodore Night Operations paid a visit to RAF Manston, where No.23 Squadron was using the Mk II in the intruder role. Camouflage came in for discussion during the visit, so trials were agreed to see what scheme best suited the type in this role. On the night of the 17th September 1942 three machines operated over the Bay of Biscay, each in a different scheme; one was Night overall, another Medium Sea Grey and Dark Green over Night

and the third was Dark Green and Dark Earth over Night. The trials proved that the new nightfighter scheme of Medium Sea Grey overall with Dark Green disruptive camouflage on the upper surfaces was very visible in searchlights from both the ground and in the air, whilst the overall Night scheme was easily seen in searchlights from the ground. The Dark Green/Dark Earth over Night scheme was adjudged the best for this type of operation, but this was not well received by Fighter Command, who felt that the intruders should adopt the same scheme as the night-fighters, to

NF Mk II, DZ230, YP•A, flown by Wg Cdr Wykenham-Barnes, No.23 Squadron RAF, Luqa (Malta), December 1942. Medium Sea Grey/Dark Green/Night finish with Dull Red codes; serial in black. Blue/Red roundels above wings; personal emblem and 'A' in red on nose

Note the way the demarcation of the upper surface colours is visible underneath the serial on the rear fuselage, with the Night undersides applied around it

NF Mk II, DZ726, TW•Z, No.141 Squadron, late 1943. Medium Sea Grey/Dark Green upper surfaces with Night undersides; Dull Red codes. Night serials; Blue/Red roundels above wings

Note the straight-edged demarcation of the upper colours along the fuselage sides, with the Night undersides applied around the codes to give a very low demarcation. Unusually the spinners are in Night on this machine instead of the usual Medium Sea Grey, so this must have been applied at squadron level

FB Mk VI, NT115, TH•J, No.418 Squadron (RCAF), Ford, March 1944. Medium Sea Grey overall with Dark Green camouflage on upper surfaces; undersides overpainted in Night. Dull Red codes, Night serial; Blue/Red roundels above wings. Nose art includes 25 red swastikas; 'City of Edmonton Squadron' is carried in black within the blue circle of the marking on the crew access door

With the FB Mk VI used in the intruder role you can see how the underside black was applied after the markings and codes, although the wavy demarcation in this instance is limited to the area immediately around the codes

Mosquito FB Mk VI, HX914, SB•O, No.464 (RAAF) Squadron, Hudson, December 1943. Medium Sea Grey overall with Dark Green camouflage on upper surfaces; undersides overpainted in Night. Dull Red codes, Night serials; Blue/Red roundels above wings

With this machine, you can see how the original demarcation of the green and grey on the rear fuselage still exists, resulting in the serial on the port side looking rather odd sitting in a patch of green that has its own demarcation

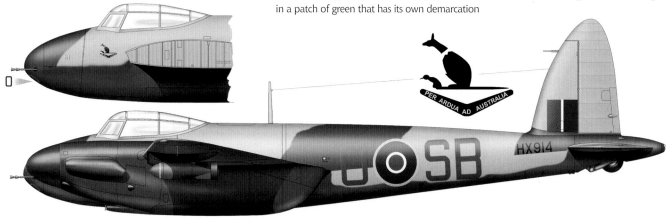

NF Mk XIX, MM850, RS•J of No 157 Squadron, RAF Swannington, late 1944. Ocean Grey/Dark Green finish with undersides overpainted in Night; black/white stripes around wings and fuselage. Ident Red codes, Night serial; Blue/Red upper wing roundels

The invasion stripes are applied to the wings and rear fuselage and considering their precise application under existing markings these are the permanent ones used by the advancing forces in Europe after the invasion. The wavy demarcation of the Night undersides around the existing codes and serial number is common, the way the rear section of the invasion stripes is applied around the serial number is less so

Posed, but nonetheless interesting as this photos shows invasion stripes being applied to an intruder Mosquito and you can see the chalk lines applied first (still visible on the extreme of the port wing) and the very basic equipment used to apply the black and white distemper; straight lines were optional! *(©British Official)*

reduce confusion with the manufacturers. As no compelling reason could be given for the adoption of yet another scheme for the Mosquito, on the 10th October 1942, HQ Fighter Command wrote to the DOR at the Air Ministry to set out the new requirements for intruder aircraft as Medium Sea

Grey with Dark Green disruptive camouflage on the upper surfaces and Night underneath. Because all Mosquitos by this stage were being delivered in overall Medium Sea Grey with Dark Green disruptive camouflage, the Night undersides were applied in service and this resulted in a great variation in the demarcation along the rear fuselage. Markings remained unchanged.

Fighter-Bombers

FB Mk VI – Initial Scheme

In January 1942 in a meeting held at the Air Ministry it was proposed to split the schemes applied to Mosquito production into two distinct types: the unarmed bomber/PR aircraft and the night-fighter/fighter-bomber. The latter was initially envisaged to be Dark Earth and Dark Green over Azure Blue in accordance with the Temperate Land Scheme, with those machines used by Coastal Command units to be painted in the Temperate Sea Scheme of Extra Dark Sea Grey and Slate Grey replacing the upper colours at the Aircraft Servicing Units prior to issuing to each unit. Fighter Command however felt that the Day Fighter Scheme of Dark Green and Ocean Grey over Medium Sea Grey gave

Exceptions

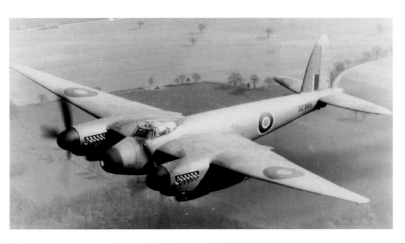

The NF Mk XV was an odd exception to the rule as far as night fighter C&M is concerned. This shot of MP469 the prototype, seen at Hatfield, clearly shows the odd manner of camouflage. Many colours are listed for it, including Ocean Grey and Dark Green, Ocean Grey and Dark Grey or Sky Grey and Dark Slate Grey, all of which were applied over Deep Sky. There is no authoritative source to clarify things, as no documents survive to confirm the colours used on this machine, other than that of the RAE-supplied Deep Sky for the undersides. I feel that considering the bomber heritage of MP469 and the obvious loose nature of the camouflage demarcation clearly seen in period images, that this machine was quickly repainted in the then night-fighter scheme of Medium Sea Grey and Dark Green on the upper surfaces. Both patterns and demarcation are at odds with the regulations at the time, although it does carry the regulation markings of Type B upper wing roundels, Type C1 fuselage roundel and fin flash and a serial number in 8in high black characters on the rear fuselage *(©DH/BAe)*

When MP469 was modified with the new radar nose and ventral gun pack, the scheme was changed to Deep Sky overall and the remaining four NF Mk XV conversions were also painted in this scheme. Roundels and markings remained the same, the radome was painted in Special Night (with the extreme tip in bare metal), whilst the spinners were standard Night. It is believed that whilst operated by No.85 Squadron, these machines had an individual aircraft code letter that was applied in black under the radome, although the exact style and location of this is unknown, as no photographs survive *(©Ministry of Supply)*

FB Mk VI, LR275, SY•B, No.613 Squadron, Hartford Bridge, January 1944. Ocean Grey/Dark Green/Medium Sea Grey finish with Sky codes, rear fuselage band and spinners; Night serials. Blue/Red roundels above wings

Note the very low demarcation with the swooping line from the wing trailing and tailplane leading edges to allow the upper surface colours to extend below the codes. The serial numbers remains in the same location as would be the case with the demarcation high up, and the Sky band is applied underneath. The Sky squadron codes are applied in 30in high characters, although there was no standard for this, so you will find variations in the size used. Wing roundels are Type B (54in), whilst the fuselage one is Type C1 (36in) with a Type C fin flash (24in x 24in)

FB Mk VI, HX917, EG•E, No.487 Squadron, Gravesend, April 1944. Ocean Grey/Dark Green/Medium Sea Grey finish with Sky codes; Ocean Grey spinners. Blue/Red roundels above wings

In comparison with LR275 you can see that the demarcation at the root of the vertical fin has been done by following the top edge of the fillet. The demarcation runs along the middle of the fuselage, as per the regulations, with the serial just below it because it uses an imaginary line from the centre of the leading edge of the tailplane as its baseline. The codes and spinners are in Sky, but this machine lacks the 18in wide Sky fuselage band

the most effective compromise for day operations and both Bomber Command and Coastal Command ultimately agreed. It was also felt that the fighter-bomber and night-fighters should carry the same squadron markings as those seen by pure fighter squadrons, to fool the enemy, and again both Bomber and Coastal Commands eventually agreed to this. The regulations were circulated in a Postagram on the 6th March 1942, which stated that all Fighter, Bomber and Coastal Command Mosquitos used in the day role were to be painted in the Day Fighter Scheme. The serial number was applied in 8in high black characters on either side of the rear fuselage, with an 18in wide Sky band applied vertically around the rear fuselage forward of the serial number. Sky spinners and yellow bands on the leading edges of each wing were also specified. This latter marking was to be applied at unit level and was to be within 3ft of the outboard side of the engine nacelle and 7in wide when measured around the curve of the leading edge, tapering to 3in at the wing tip.

There is something rather odd about this scheme, though, as it was replaced and all Mosquitos were supposed to be supplied in overall Medium Sea Grey with Dark Green camouflage on the upper surfaces? To this day no documents have come to light that cast any light on why Mosquitos can be seen clearly with the

Dark Green/Ocean Grey over Medium Sea Grey scheme, complete with Sky band on the rear fuselage? It is thought that some organisation/s undertook the painting by adding the Ocean Grey elements, although whether this was a civilian contractor, or an RAF Maintenance Unit, remains unknown. The confusion probably lies in the fact that the only day-flying Mosquitos in service at the time the orders were initially released, were B Mk IVs, it was not until early 1943 that the FB Mk VI started to come off the production line and it may have been the case that some MUs viewed these new machines as being covered by the older regulations, so applied the Day Fighter scheme complete with Sky fuselage band and yellow wing leading edges?

The 'Brown and Green' scheme

Little is known of this scheme, and although images of LR275 claim to show such a scheme applied, we are not convinced. Headquarters, Allied Expeditionary Air Force (HQ AEAF) complained about the two schemes applied to the Mosquitos they were receiving at No.2 Group. These comprised the Day Fighter and Night Fighter schemes, both of which were considered unsuitable for the low-level operations now undertaken by the FB Mk VI. In cooperation with RAE, No.2 Group undertook trials with a scheme they called 'light brown and green' over 'light grey' with a 'very light grey or white' vertical fin and rudder. Two weeks after the proposed new scheme was given to the Air Ministry they replied stating that it was not practical to introduce a special scheme for the fighter-bomber Mosquito and that application of different colours at MU or unit level was also impossible due to a lack of man-power and the adverse effect the extra paint would have had on the performance of the type. Whilst it is true that the image of LR275 seems to show levels of contrast between the fuselage and vertical fin that denote colours other than Ocean Grey or Medium Sea Grey, the difference in these colours in black and white images is so marginal as to make the whole subject academic until such times as documentary evidence comes to light, if indeed it ever does. No.2 Group certainly carried out C&M

trials with their Mosquitos, but the real nature of colours such as 'light brown and green' are open to such huge debate as to make it impossible to make anything but a complete guess as to their nature/tonal quality, and that is not something we are willing to do until (or if) sufficient period evidence appears.

Overall Medium Sea Grey

Further discussions in early March 1942 led to the agreement that an overall scheme should be applied to all Mosquitos on the production lines, to ease allocation to any command thereafter. It was therefore agreed on the 15th March 1942 that an overall scheme of Medium Sea Grey, with a disruptive pattern of Dark Green on the upper surfaces, should be adopted.

Mosquito FB Mk VI (fitted with American ASH radar), PZ459, 3P•D, No.515 Squadron, Little Snoring, December 1944. Medium Sea Grey overall with Dark Green camouflage on upper surfaces; Dull Red codes, Night serials. Night/white bands below rear fuselage, those under the wings overpainted (but partially showing through); Blue/Red roundels above wings

Here you can see the basic scheme applied in the official manner, with the slight up-turn in the demarcation as it approaches the tailplane. The entire fin and rudder remain in Medium Sea Grey, with the demarcation in this case following the fillet at the base of the fin and the hinge line at the base of the rudder. The ASH radar pod was either painted Medium Sea Grey or left in the base colour, which was a very pale grey with a slight creamy tint to it. Fuselage roundel is Type C1 with 30in codes and a Type C fin flash. The upper wing roundels remained Type B and the invasion stripes were obviously applied and then the markings re-applied, as the latter items are on top of the stripes. Although the orders about invasion stripes had existed in April 1944, the actual order to apply them was only given on the 3rd June, so initial applications varied in 'finesse'. The order to remove the wing stripes came on the 25th August 1944, to be completed by the 10th September 1944 and it was not until the 6th December (effective by the 31st December) that the order was issued to remove all stripes. This is why this profile shows the old stripes overpainted on the wings, but retains partial ones on the fuselage as many interpreted the August order to remove the stripes from all 'upper surfaces'.

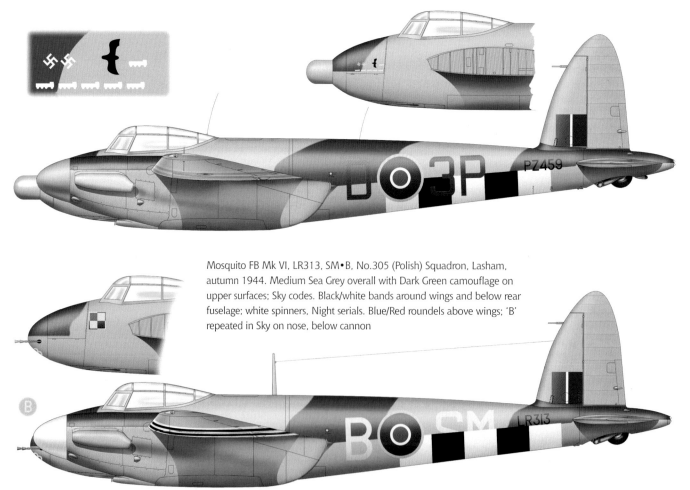

Mosquito FB Mk VI, LR313, SM•B, No.305 (Polish) Squadron, Lasham, autumn 1944. Medium Sea Grey overall with Dark Green camouflage on upper surfaces; Sky codes. Black/white bands around wings and below rear fuselage; white spinners, Night serials. Blue/Red roundels above wings; 'B' repeated in Sky on nose, below cannon

Mosquito FB Mk VI, RF838, EO•A, No.404 Squadron, Thorney Island, April 1945. Medium Sea Grey overall with Dark Green camouflage on upper surfaces; Night codes, outlined in yellow. Night serials, Sky spinners; Blue/White/Red roundels above wings

This Mosquito carried codes outlined in yellow, which was common on Mosquitos used in the maritime strike role. The move by such units within Coastal Command to a two-letter squadron code system was reinstated by an order issued on the 19th October 1943 and No.404 Squadron became 'EO' having previously been 'EE'. The use of the standard Medium Sea Grey/Dark Green scheme by this strike squadron is unusual and why they repainted some, if not all, their aircraft in it by 1945 remains unknown, but you can see the remains of an original colour under the serial number

FB XVIII

Mosquito FB Mk XVIII, NT225, 'O', No.248 Squadron (Special Detachment), Portreath, 6th June 1944. Ocean Grey overall with Dark Green camouflage pattern on upper surfaces only; Night/white bands around wings and fuselage. Code in Dull Red, outlined in white; serial in Night. Sky spinners

This machine carried the standard Medium Sea Grey/Dark Green scheme plus full invasion stripes, with these painted around the serial number. The drop tanks are often listed as being white, which is unlikely, and are depicted here in Medium Sea Grey, but the numerous photos of this machine seen to show a sheen on the tanks that may well mean they were aluminium

Mosquito FB Mk XVIII, PZ468, QM•D, No.254 Squadron, North Coates, June 1945. Medium Sea Grey overall with Dark Green camouflage on upper surfaces; Dull Red codes. Night serials; Blue/White/Red roundels above wings. Aluminium slipper tank; Night nose cone. White band around spinners; note overpainted D-Day stripes below rear fuselage

The official type photos for the Tse-tse were of this machine, so there are various angles of it and they all show that the invasion stripes were painted out in a dark colour, probably Ocean Grey and the nose cone was also dark, but even darker than the painted-out stripes, so this could be Ocean Grey (darkened by shadow) or Extra Dark Sea Grey? Much debate runs about the spinner colours, as No.254 Squadron were supposed to be Sky with a white band, but the period black and white images show the same tonal contrast as Medium Sea Grey, so that is what we have plumped for here

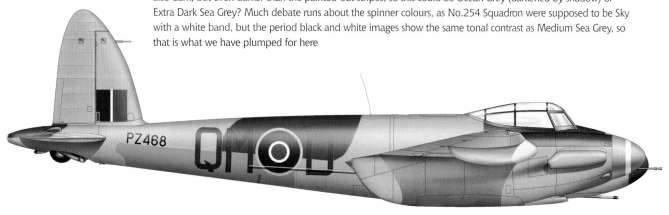

Banff

Mosquito FB Mk VI, HP862, KK•K, No.333 (Norwegian) Squadron, Banff, summer 1943. Medium Sea Grey overall with Dark Green camouflage on upper surfaces; Sky codes, Night serials. Blue/Red roundels above wings; Norwegian flag on port side of nose

Standard grey/green scheme as applied to all Mosquitos by this time, with the only real difference from any RAF unit being the application of the Norwegian flag on the side of the nose. Later the unit would go on to apply the national colours as bands around the spinners

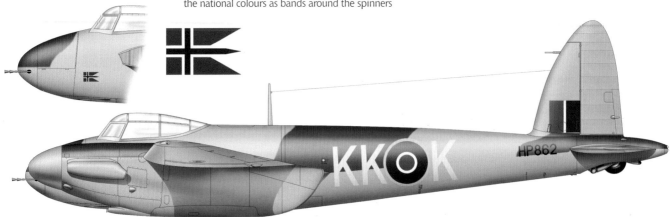

Mosquito FB Mk VI, RF610, DM•H, No.248 Squadron, Banff, March 1945. Extra Dark Sea Grey/Sky finish with Night serial and codes; spinner Night with white tip. Blue/White/Red roundels above wings; note original Dark Green base under serial (Ocean Grey under that on starboard) and a faint 'R' beneath the 'H' in the code

This aircraft was delivered in the standard grey/green scheme, but was repainted at an MU in the Special Coastal Duties Scheme A in accordance with the technical order issued on the 30th March 1944. The serial number remains within a region of the original upper surface colours and the demarcation along the fuselage is low, sweeping back up to the wing and tailplane, whilst that around the nose and tail follows a hypothetical straight line running through the centre of the wing

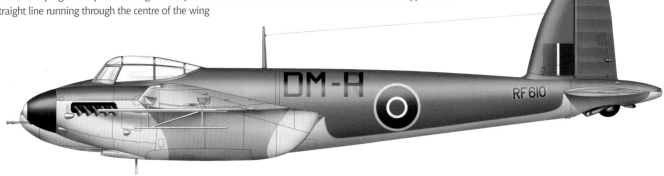

Mosquito FB Mk VI, HR130, LA•E, No.235 Squadron, Banff, late 1944. Extra Dark Sea Grey upper surfaces and Sky undersides; Night/white bands around wings and below rear fuselage. White codes, outlined in yellow; Night serials. Red spinners; Blue/Red roundels above wings

This machine is also in the Special Coastal Duties Scheme A, but is also retains the 24in invasion stripes under the rear fuselage and around the wings. It is odd to note how the last portions of the stripes on the fuselage have been deliberately 'stepped down' to clear the serial number, whilst the codes were moved up above them (in smaller, 24in characters). Separating the squadron codes from the aircraft letter with a dash was common on maritime strike Mosquitos in this scheme, but the use of white outlined in yellow was not common in No.235 Squadron and there are other colour combinations, as well as solid colour codes on other aircraft.

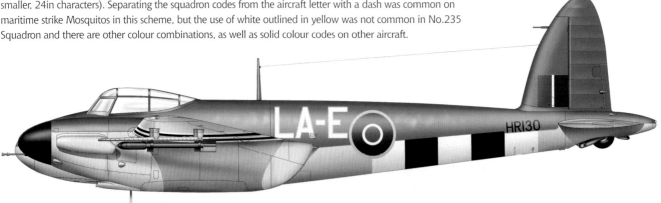

Far East

Plans were to equip over twenty squadrons in the ACSEA (Air Command, South East Asia) with the Mosquito. The first aircraft to be shipped into the Far Eastern theatre transited through India and images showing one of the first, F Mk II DZ695 being ferried by No.1 Overseas Aircraft Despatch Unit, confirm that it was in the overall Medium Sea Grey scheme with Dark Green camouflage on the upper surfaces. Although the aircraft had the machine-guns in the nose, there were no cannon fitted and all the ports were covered over. This region, as well as back across the bomb bay doors on the underside, is painted a uniform darker shade than the surrounding Medium Sea Grey, so it is likely to be a red oxide primer, although some may opt for Ocean Grey, and it is roughly applied (probably with a brush). All other markings remained as the UK-based machines but no codes were applied whilst being ferried.

Some of the FB Mk VIs allocated to the Far East were in the Day Fighter Scheme of Ocean Grey and Dark Green over Medium Sea Grey and some retained the Sky spinners and band around the rear fuselage. The whole question of the red dot in the roundel, and this leading to mis-identification with Japanese types, led to India Command passing the whole problem over to the Air Ministry on the 29th April 1943. They replied on the 15th May stating that a roundel similar to that already adopted by the RAAF to stop confusion with the red Hinomaru of the Japanese, would be suitable. Trials soon highlighted the fact that a blue roundel with a white centre was too obvious, as the white compromised the camouflage. As a result a light blue mixed from four parts white and one part blue was used to substitute the white and the new SEAC roundel was born. The fin flash was also revised, with the red and white element of the older fin flash now replaced with the new shade of blue, and these marking were adopted for all SEAC aircraft from the end of June 1943. Initially the sizes of the markings were in accordance with the existing AMOs for Europe, but after consultation with the RAAF new dimensions were adopted in line with those used by the RAAF and this came into effect from about September 1943. Being classed as a 'medium' aircraft the Mosquito received roundels of 32in diameter with a 12in diameter centre and a fin flash 24in high and 22in wide, divided equally into 11in side bands. The 54in Type B roundels were modified with the red centre replaced with the new mix of blue, but you will see many aircraft with this roundel replaced completely with a new SEAC one of 32in diameter and this especially applies when the Mosquito was later to adopt the aluminium scheme.

When the FB Mk VI was allocated to the ex-Vultee Vengeance units Nos.45, 47, 82. 84 and 110 Squadrons in 1944, these were seen as bomber aircraft, so they adopted the Temperate Land Scheme of Dark Green and Dark Earth disruptive

F Mk II DZ695 in India after delivery by No 1 Overseas Aircraft Despatch Unit, this aircraft was one of first in the Far Eastern theatre and it retains the overall Medium Sea Grey with Dark Green camouflage
(©Crown Copyright)

camouflage over Azure Blue undersides (the instructions stated 'Sky or azure', so was most likely Sky Blue or Azure Blue because Sky had been considered unsuitable for the Middle East back in 1940). The aircraft all came out the factory in the grey/green scheme, but when they were repainted the Dark Earth was applied to meet the Temperate Land Scheme to either the A or C pattern, with the demarcation running down the centreline of the fuselage, whilst others had the colours applied to Pattern 1 with the demarcation further down the fuselage sides. Squadron codes tended to be a mix of just individual aircraft letters, or a full set of squadron codes and the aircraft letter and you will find these applied in Sky, black and the new blue usually in 24in high characters (HP914 'H' of No.45 Squadron, had the letter applied in black, 33in high). White identification bands 24in wide were applied around the wings, but not crossing over the ailerons, and 18in bands were applied around the vertical fin and tail, again not crossing onto the control surfaces (often the band on the vertical fin was wider than the specified 12in, though).

Close-up of the nose of F Mk II DZ695 in India after delivery by No 1 OADU and you can see the blanked off cannon ports and the dark painted area under the nose and extending back along the fuselage
(©Crown Copyright)

After the loss of an FB Mk VI operated by No.82 Squadron on the 20th October 1944, due to wing failure in a dive, it became apparent that the dull nature of the camouflage schemes applied to Mosquitos in the Far East led to the deterioration of the structure due to differential shrinkage of the parts because of high temperatures. The solution was to remove all camouflage paint and adopt an overall aluminium scheme, which was confirmed by ACSEA on the 20th January 1945. With the development of better aluminium dope in the UK underway it was not felt worth changing the production lines to aluminium at the time. The Air Ministry offered ACSEA a pre-war glossy specification instead and ACSEA confirmed it preferred a glossy aluminium scheme on the 1st February 1945. Initially only day fighters were to be in the scheme, with

NF Mk XIX, TA230, 'N', No.176 Squadron, Baigachi, April 1945. Aluminium overall with Night codes and serials (note serial repeated on fin flash port side, and above fin flash on starboard); 18in. bands around fin/ rudder, tailplane (not overlapping onto control surfaces) and wings. Standard SEAC markings in all positions; light blue/dark blue spinners. Note this unit never became operational on the Mosquito, being disbanded on 1st June 1946

the night-fighters scheduled soon to go out to the theatre not being effected, however by the end of February 1945 the decision had been made to finish the night-fighters in the overall aluminium scheme as well.

The pre-war aluminium to DTD 63A was used overall on the Mosquitos in the Far East, with the existing aluminium to DTD 83A being used on the control surfaces. The paint was applied over the factory-applied grey/green scheme and was done by No.41 Group Maintenance Command in the theatre. Special identification markings took the form of 28in wide bands around the wings and 18in wide bands around the tailplanes and vertical fin/rudder and these were done in dark blue on aluminium aircraft (and white on camouflaged ones), but there are instances of black being used instead. As our profile shows, their application could be inconsistent because many were applied before the official notification was made to not extend them over flying controls, so here they go over the rudder and ailerons, but not the elevators and you will find others with or without them extending over the flying controls. This identification marking was no longer to be carried by the Mosquito from 9th March 1945, but those that already had them applied, seemed to retain them. Squadron identification colours were also to be applied to the spinners, but they are not consistent, therefore you will see No.82 Squadron machines with aluminium or light blue spinners, No.45 with red spinners, No.211 with

aluminium and, as shown here, No.176 with light and dark blue spinners. The squadron code was applied in Night or dark blue and the serial was applied in the usual 8in black characters on either side of the rear fuselage (usually sitting on a hypothetical line running from the centre-line of the tailplane or above it). This serial was often repeated on the vertical fin in a variety of manners, the most common being 3in black characters between the fin flash and dark blue band, but others (as seen here) had it applied in 2in black characters over the front portions of the fin flash. The reason for repeating the serial number on the tail remains unknown.

Highball

The FB Mk VIs operated by No.618 Squadron in Australia for the potential use of Highball in the Pacific theatre were painted in the standard Medium Sea Grey overall scheme with a disruptive camouflage pattern of Dark Green on the upper surfaces but these machines had the Dark Green camouflage extended up over the vertical fin and rudder as well (whether this was applied in the UK or on arrival in Australia is unknown). The existing roundels were all modified to the RAAF dark blue/white version on both fuselage (36in diameter with 16in white centre) and upper wings (54in diameter with 21.5in white centre) and the fin flash was also modified to these colours in a 24inx24in format equally split into 12in bands of dark blue and white (white

Mosquito FB Mk VI, HR609, S1, No.618 Squadron Narromine (Australia), June 1945. Medium Sea Grey overall with Dark Green camouflage on upper surfaces; Dull Red codes, Night serials. Dull Blue/white roundels on fuselage sides and above wings. Aircraft crashed at its base on 12th June 1945

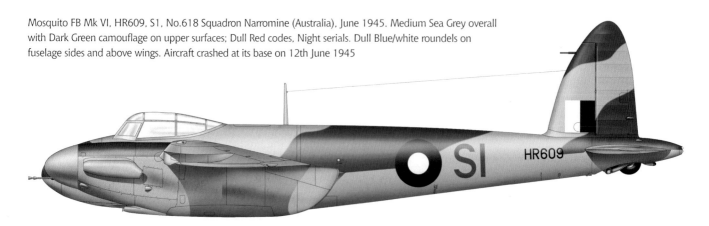

was always forward). The codes were applied in the usual size, format and location and these machines received an alpha-numeric code (e,g, C1, E1, S1) that was applied in Dull Red of approximately 24in high characters (this was always well aft of the roundel). The reason for this style of identification of the FB Mk VIs used by the squadron remains a mystery.

Post-War

The immediate post-war era saw the slackening of the wartime regulations as far as squadron markings were concerned, and a revision to the schemes applied to many types; initially though the overall schemes remained unchanged with a few revisions.

NF Mk XIX, MM669/G, YD•K, No 255 Squadron, Gianaclis (Italy), 1946. Medium Sea Grey/Dark Green finish with red codes and Night serial; Blue/White/Red upper wing roundel

This post-war machine has adopted the Type C roundel on the upper wings in place of the Type B, whilst the style of the squadron codes is more spaced out than was usually the case

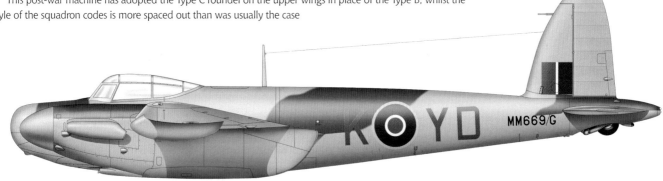

NF Mk 36, RL195, PS•A, No.264 Squadron, 1945. Medium Sea Grey overall with Dark Green on upper surfaces; Dull Red codes. Night serials (repeated below wings). Blue/Red roundels above wings; unit crest on fin

By this stage the application of squadron badges was becoming commonplace with the RAF, although in this instance the badge is quite small. Although no roundels have been applied under the wings by this stage, the serial number has been repeated in 30in high black characters, applied under each wing, read from the trailing edge on the starboard side and from the leading edge under the port; space was always made for the drop tank, so there is a gap between the alpha and numeric elements

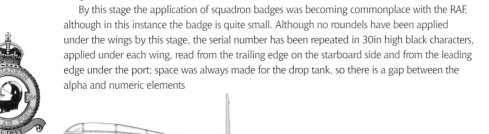

Mosquito FB Mk VI, PZ169, OM•R, No.107 Squadron, Gütersloh (Germany), 1947. Medium Sea Grey/Dark Green finish; yellow codes outlined in black. Yellow/Blue/White/Red roundels (same as on fuselage) above the wings

Whilst this BAFO machine has retained the wartime camouflage it has adopted the Type C roundel above the wings in place of the older Type B. The yellow codes are highly visible (probably black-edged to make them more so) and the squadron badge has been applied large on either side of the vertical fin

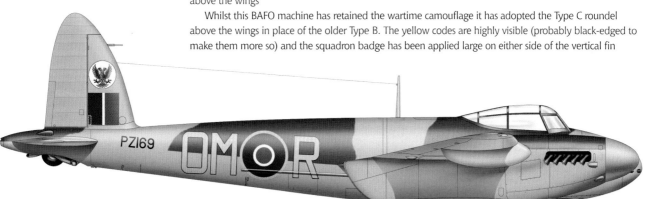

Mosquito FB Mk VI, TA471, YH•H, No.21 Squadron, Gütersloh (Germany), 1947. Medium Sea Grey overall with Dark Green camouflage on upper surfaces; yellow codes outlined in black. Spinners are silver/black/yellow; nose is silver with a black band. Blue/White/Red roundels above wings

This BAFO machine is in the wartime scheme but the upper wing roundels are now the new Type D, whilst those on the fuselage remain the wartime Type C1. Codes are once again outlined in black and the squadron badge, albeit smaller, is once again on the vertical fin. The silver nose and spinner caps are all part of the precursor to the move to removal of all camouflage from fighters in the post-war era, as promulgated in an order circulated on the 16th April 1946

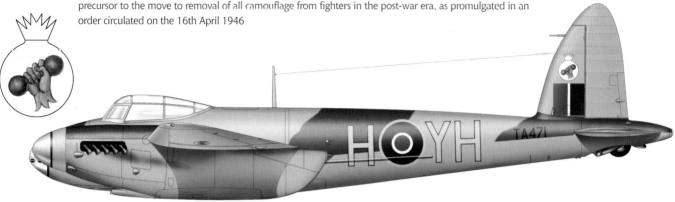

Mosquito NF Mk 36, RK985, TW•G, No.141 Squadron, Coltishall, 1949. Medium Sea Grey overall with Dark Green camouflage on upper surfaces; bright red codes. Night serial, night spinners with a white band; serial repeated below wings. Unit crest is carried on fin, over a black bar with white chevrons; roundels in bright colours on fuselage sides and above wings

The night-fighters remained in their wartime scheme, the only revisions here are the adoption of the new Type D roundels and fin flash in accordance with the 16th May 1947 instructions. Codes remained in red, although now this was a bright glossy version, not the wartime dull one. The application of the squadron badge on the vertical fin is pretty common, but No.141 has applied the pennants on either side of the badge, as this pre-war practice was reintroduced during 1948.

Mosquito NF Mk 36, LR148, No 85 Squadron, West Malling, 1951. Medium Sea Grey overall with Dark Green camouflage on upper surfaces; red/black checks around fuselage roundel. Blue spinners; roundels in bright colours on fuselage side and above wings. Serial in black, repeated below wings; unit markings in black/white on fin

An excellent example of the squadron colours being re-applied to the aircraft, as was the practice from 1948. In this instance the red/black squares are applied either side of the new Type D fuselage roundel and you will note they are parallel with the ground, not with that hypothetical line down the fuselage centre (the serial on the rear fuselage also follows the ground and the font/spacing is unusual). The serial number was now repeated under the wings in 30in high black characters, read from the leading edge under the port and from the trailing edge under the starboard; the gap between the alpha and numeric portions of the serial was to make space for a bomb carrier or drop tank

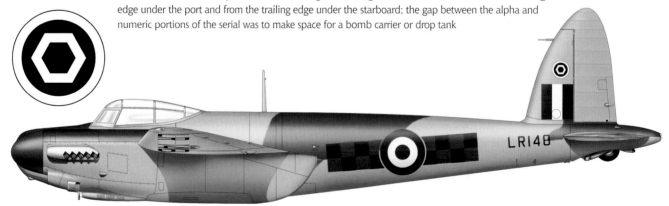

Mosquito NF Mk 36, RL239, No 199 Squadron, Hemswell, 1952. Medium Sea Grey with Night undersides; serials in white. National markings in bright colours in all positions; serial repeated below wings. Spinner is medium blue and white; squadron crest on fin

By the early 1950s the remaining night-fighter Mosquitos in use had adopted the grey/black 'bomber' scheme as seen here. The markings were still Type D but the serial was now applied in 24in white characters along the fuselage, split by the roundel at the alpha/numeric point. The codes were repeated in white under the wings, probably also in 24in characters, and this time there is no gap in them. The overall colours are toned down, with no fuselage bands etc., but the spinners repeat the white/blue/white/blue element of the squadron badge. This was the last scheme that an in-service fighter/night-fighter Mosquito would carry with the RAF

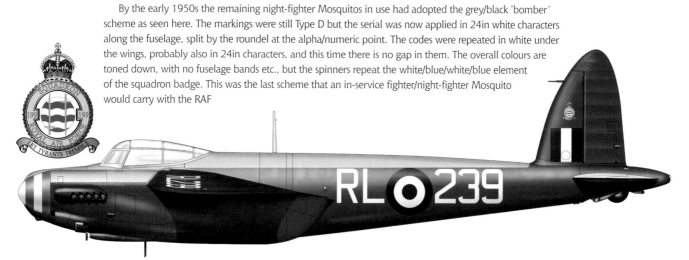

Mosquito FB Mk VI, PZ165, UP•E, No.4 Squadron, Celle, 1949. Dark Sea Grey upper surfaces and Night undersides; Red codes outlined in white. White serial; post-war roundels in bright colours on fuselage sides and above wings. Unit marking on fin within a white disc, outlined in black

This is not really a fighter scheme, what you have here is the bomber scheme that was adopted by many of the fighter-bombers that remained in service. The new scheme was introduced on the 15th May 1947 and although the new colours were initially matt, they were all soon replaced with a glossy version. The Type D roundel seen on the fuselage and also above the wings, came into use from the 16th May 1947, although for a while some aircraft used the wartime shades of Roundel Blue and red with white, whereas the Type D used Bright Red and Blue with white. Squadron codes were red, a common colour with the new scheme, and they were outlined in white for contrast. The serial number now also had to be in white and a 24in x 27in tail flash with equal portions of Bright Red, White and Bright Blue was applied to the vertical fin. At this stage underwing serial numbers had not been applied on this machine, but the new grey/black scheme was slow to be adopted in service, with most units not adopting it until well into 1948

Meteorological Flights (Met)

Very few images exist that are identified as Met machines, so it is difficult to be certain about the schemes applied to them. It is most likely that they retained their standard overall Medium Sea Grey scheme with Dark Green disruptive camouflage on the upper surfaces.

FB VI TA379 with the No.4 Squadron's sun and lightning crest on the vertical fin photographed during the immediate post-war months whilst the unit was in Germany
(©British Official)

Trainers

Mosquito T Mk III, HJ972, 'E', No.410 Squadron, Acklington, 1942. Finished in full day-fighter camouflage and markings: Ocean Grey/Dark Green/Medium Sea Grey with Sky spinners and rear fuselage band; Night serials. Yellow wing leading edges; Blue/Red roundels above wings

Most of the trainer versions used during WWII retained the then current fighter scheme. Here the Day Fighter Scheme is applied with the yellow wing leading edges and the Sky band around the rear fuselage but all other markings remain as per the fighter versions. The serial is centred on a line running forward from the tailplane centreline and yellow code letters and numbers were often used for trainer aircraft.

Mosquito T Mk III, VT620, FMO•C, No 204 Advanced Flying School, RAF Swinderby 1948. Trainer yellow overall with black serials and codes; serial repeated below wings. Roundels in bright colours above wings and on fuselage sides

By the post-war period some trainers reverted to the overall yellow (hi-vis) scheme, as seen here. These second line units adopted a three-character unit code, which was placed one side of the roundel, and the individual aircraft letter, which was placed the other. These were applied in big, 30in black characters and repeated under the wings in the usual manner. Roundels were Type D, as was the fin flash, but no roundels were applied under the wings.

Mosquito T Mk III, VA880/458.CW, No 762 Naval Air Squadron, Culdrose, October 1946. Yellow overall with black serials and codes; Blue/White/Red roundels in six positions

The FAA also operated the trainer variant and these carried two schemes, depicted here is the overall yellow scheme, which you can see is identical to VT620 depicted earlier with the addition of 'Royal Navy' above the serial number, the three-digit identification number aft of the fuselage roundel and the base codes above the fin flash. The serial number is not repeated under the wings

T Mk 3 RR308 of No.204 Advanced Flying School in the late 1940s-early '50s. This machine is in aluminium overall, with the fuselage and wing yellow bands instead of adopting an overall yellow scheme as we have shown for HJ972 operated by this unit. Note the dash added above the aircraft letter 'A' denoting it was the second aircraft to carry that identification letter in the squadron. This machine also apparently had a large 'F' on either side of the nose, no idea why, as 'A' would have seemed more appropriate?

Mosquito T Mk III, VT626/422/BY, operated by Airwork Fleet Requirements Unit (FRU), St. Davids. Aluminium overall with yellow band around rear fuselage; all lettering in black. Bright Blue/White/Red roundels in all positions

The simple aluminium scheme with the yellow bands around the wings and fuselage as used for all training aircraft in the post-war era. Roundels are now Type D, the serial is repeated in 30in black characters under the wings, but all the other markings remain much as they did with the overall yellow scheme. The lack of the 'Royal Navy' legend over the serial is unusual and you will find the three-digit squadron code can move about between the roundel and serial number, as is the case here, with it further aft than usual

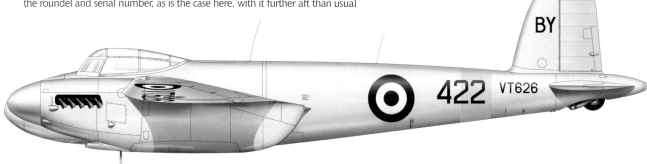

Fleet Air Arm

Navalised Mosquito FB Mk VI, LR359, the first twin-engined aircraft to land on an aircraft-carrier (HMS Indefatigable, 25 March 1944). Extra Dark Sea Grey/Dark Slate Grey upper surfaces with Yellow undersides; spinners and all lettering in black. Blue/White/Red roundels above and below wings

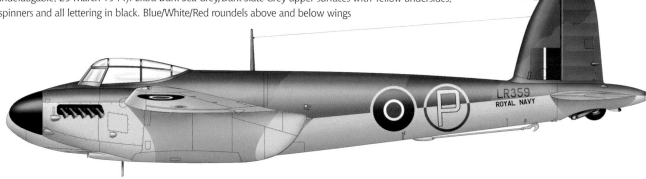

Mosquito FB Mk VI, TE711, FD•4L, No.811 Naval Air Squadron, Fleet Air Arm, 1946. Medium Sea Grey overall with Dark Green camouflage on upper surfaces; Blue codes ('FD' outlined in white) and spinners, the latter also having a white stripe. Night serial and Royal Navy legend; Blue/White/Red roundels above wings

The Fleet Air Arm operated the Mosquito FB Mk VI in its own right and these machines remained in the factory-applied scheme of grey/green overall with Type C1 roundel on the fuselage and a Type C above the wings. The codes here are applied in blue, with those that go over green given a thin white outline. The serial number is the usual size/location but above it was added the legend 'Royal Navy' in 4in characters

Mosquito TF/TR Mk 33, TW256, '593/LP', No.771 Naval Air Squadron, Lee-On-Solent, November 1948. Extra Dark Sea Grey/Dark Slate Grey/Sky finish with Night serials, codes and spinners; Blue/White/Red roundels above and below wings

When the TF/TR Mk 33 was adopted for service it initially had the Temperate Sea Scheme with a Type C1 fuselage roundel, Type C roundels above and below the wings and a Type C fin flash. The 'Royal Navy' legend was added above the serial in 6in characters and the two-alpha code for the unit operating the particular aircraft was applied in black 12in characters above the fin flash on either side of the vertical fin. Spinners usually remained black and the ASH radar pod could be unpainted, white or the camouflage colours

Mosquito TF/TR Mk 33, TW270/413/CW, No.790 Naval Air Squadron, Culdrose, 1948. Extra Dark Sea Grey/Sky finish with Night serials; white codes. Blue/White/Red roundels above and below wings

The other scheme carried by the TF/TR Mk 33 was the maritime strike scheme of Coastal Command, consisting of solid colours above and below. As you can see from this profile, the demarcation along the fuselage could be a little wavy, but that along the nose and tail followed that hypothetical line running along the fuselage centre. All roundels remained as the Temperate Sea Scheme, the serial and 'Royal Navy' were applied in a similar manner, although the former was often in 6in characters and a fin flash was applied. The dark nature of the grey meant that white was used to do the unit markings aft of the fuselage roundel and the base codes above the fin flash. In this instance the serial number is also repeated under each wing, inboard of the wing roundel (which is near the tip) and read from the trailing edge under the starboard and from the leading edge under the port; these were 30in high characters applied in black

TR Mk 33 TW248 probably with 790 NAS at Brawdy in the final TR Mk 33 scheme of aluminium overall, Type D roundels on the fuselage and above and below the wings. The codes are applied in 30in black characters under the wings, with the gap between the alpha-numeric elements to make space for a bomb rack or drop tank. Yellow bands are applied around the wing and rear fuselage, the former probably 18in and the latter 24in. No fin flash is carried, but the squadron code and base code, along with the serial number are applied on the fuselage and fin as per the camouflaged scheme

Mosquito TF/TR Mk 37 (Prototype), TW240 (converted from TR Mk 33). Extra Dark Sea Grey/Dark Slate Grey/Sky finish; Blue/White/Red roundels above and below wings. All lettering in Night

This prototype is in the Temperate Sea Scheme, as it was converted from a Mk 33, all markings remain as expected, the only thing to note is that period images prove the roundel under the starboard wing was partially painted over on its inboard region (roughly) and that the demarcation along the nose has a 'step' in it, where the access hatch is. We can only see this for sure on the starboard side, but doubt that it is on the port side (no hatch there)

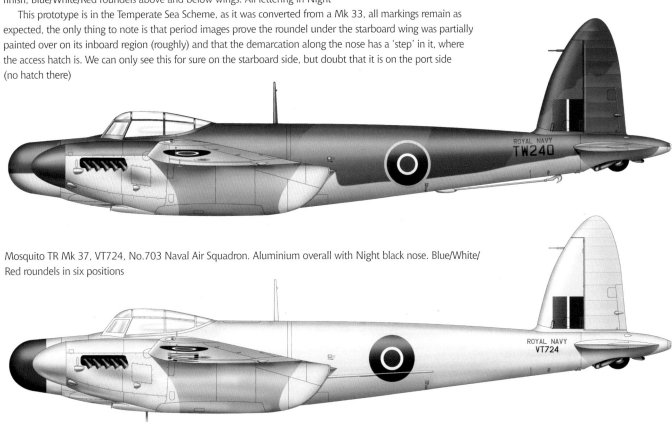

Mosquito TR Mk 37, VT724, No.703 Naval Air Squadron. Aluminium overall with Night black nose. Blue/White/ Red roundels in six positions

Foreign Production

Australia

The first Mosquito to arrive in Australia was NF Mk II DD664, which later became A52-1001. It arrived in its original Night Type S (Special Night) overall scheme, but had RAAF roundels on the fuselage and above and below the wings. A blue/white fin flash replaced the RAF one but the serial number remained in Dull Red.

The first Australian-produced FB Mk 40, A52-1 was finished with such haste, that it initially flew with an overall aluminium finish, except for the vertical fin and rudder, which were camouflaged in Foliage Green and Earth Brown. Roundels and fin flashes were as standard and the code was applied in black characters on each side of the rear fuselage, positioned mid-way between the roundel and the tail. This machine was later painted in a production scheme as stated below.

The next scheme to be applied to Mosquitos produced in Australia was Foliage Green and Earth Brown over Sky Blue. RAAF roundels were applied either side of the fuselage and above the wings. The camouflage pattern was identical to the RAF scheme, but you will see some with the demarcation high along the fuselage, with a steep sweep up from the wing to run it straight to the tailplane leading edge. A blue/white fin flash was

applied to the base of the fin in the RAF fashion and the serial number was applied in light grey in the same size/location as RAF machines.

In late 1944 the scheme for Australian-produced Mosquitos changed to Foliage Green overall with the national markings and serial number unchanged.

On the 24th March 1945 No.1 Squadron was the first to receive a Mosquito finished in aluminium overall. The official notification on the 5th March 1945 had stated that although all attack aircraft would be camouflaged Foliage Green, RAAF Mosquitos may be given "silver dope protective coating" and by the end of WWII all the RAAF Mosquitos (FB and PR variants), save for a few FB Mk 40s with OTUs, were in overall aluminium.

NF Mk II DD664 after its first flight in Australia
(©RAAF)

Mosquito FB Mk 40, A52-3, No.1 Air Performance Unit, RAAF, May 1944. Earth Brown and Foliage Green upper surfaces with Sky Blue undersides. Black spinners. Neutral Grey serials. National markings in six positions

The first FB Mk 40, A52-1, on an initial flight with only the tail painted in camouflage

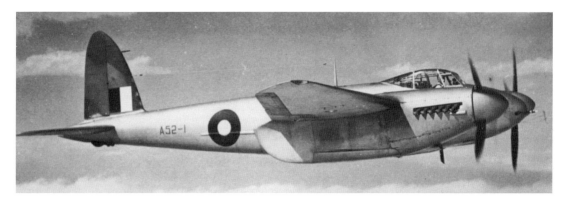

FB Mk 40 A52-1 after being repainted in in Foliage Green and Earth Brown over Sky Blue scheme, note the high fuselage demarcation line *(©BAE)*

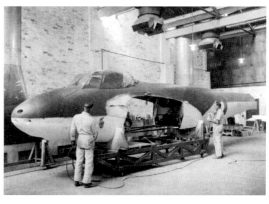

Sky Blue undersides being applied to FB Mk 40 A52-46 at Beale Piano Factory, Annandale, the factory having been requisitioned by D.H. Australia to make fuselages, tailplanes, flaps, wing leading edges and ailerons *(©Hawker-DH Austalia)*

New FB Mk 40s in the Flight Shed at Bankstown, two are in Foliage Green overall, while the remainder are Foliage Green and Earth Brown over Sky Blue

(©Hawker-DH Austalia)

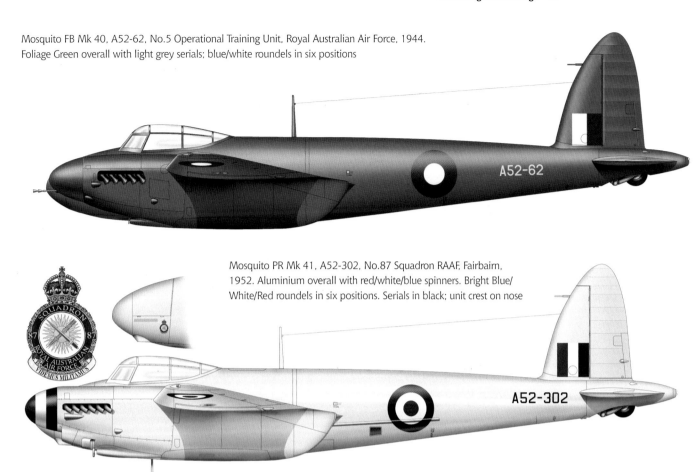

Mosquito FB Mk 40, A52-62, No.5 Operational Training Unit, Royal Australian Air Force, 1944. Foliage Green overall with light grey serials; blue/white roundels in six positions

Mosquito PR Mk 41, A52-302, No.87 Squadron RAAF, Fairbairn, 1952. Aluminium overall with red/white/blue spinners. Bright Blue/White/Red roundels in six positions. Serials in black; unit crest on nose

Canada

All Canadian-built Mosquitos were supplied in the standard RAF schemes that applied when they were built. The only exceptions you will find relate to the application of the yellow wing leading edges and 18in Sky band around the rear fuselage that was applied to fighters in the UK in 1944. As was often the case with the bomber variants built in Canada, the fighters also seem to often exhibit an odd demarcation on the engine cowls, whereby the upper line of the cowl is where the Dark Green ends, as is usual, but then the sides of the cowls down to their edge are a combination of Ocean Grey and Medium Sea Grey, often splitting the colours by the vertical panel line in the centre of this cowling and using the rear vertical panel line as the demarcation

FB VI A52-500 (ex-HR502) of No.1 Sqn RAAF in July 1945 seen in the overall aluminium scheme (©RAAF)

Mosquito T Mk 29, KA888, seen at the Downsview plant in 1944. Ocean Grey and Dark Green over Medium Sea Grey with Sky spinners and aft fuselage band. Yellow wing leading edges, yellow/blue/white/red fuselage roundel and blue/red roundel on upper wing. Note demarcation of colours on engine nacelle sides, this seems to be common practice on Canadian-built Mosquito fighters and bombers

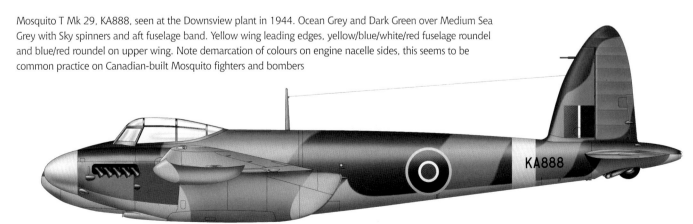

A little anomaly, this is FB Mk 26, KA133, with the Winter Experimental Establishment but still seen carrying the red nose markings from its previous operator, No.133 Squadron

(©Alberta Aviation Museum)

in that region. Many of the machines built in Canada received the Sky bands and yellow wing leading edges, but most were retained for service with the RCAF. Those that are seen in the UK are usually photographed on delivery and we therefore suspect, prior to allocation to a unit, they had the yellow and Sky markings removed.

Foreign Service

Belgium

The seven T Mk 3s used by the Belgian Air Force were in standard RAF trainer markings of aluminium overall with Trainer Yellow bands around the rear fuselage and wings. Belgian roundels were applied above and below the wings, and either side of the fuselage, with a fin flash of the same style. The markings comprised a serial number (MA-1 to 7) applied in small

black characters just ahead and slightly below the tailplane on either side of the rear fuselage. Squadron codes were allocated when with the Fighter Training School at Koksijde and these comprised 'B2' on one side of the fuselage roundel and an individual aircraft letter on the other. The markings were applied in black characters that were the same height as the diameter of the roundel. The single machine operated by No.10 Squadron, MA-7, was painted in the same manner, but carried that squadron's codes (ND) and the individual aircraft letter 'A' on the fuselage.

The three FB Mk VIs converted to TT Mk 6s (MC-1 to MC-3) were in the same overall aluminium scheme with the same style markings, but lacking any squadron codes.

The twenty-six NF Mk 30s were in the standard RAF night-fighter scheme of Medium Sea Grey overall with a disruptive camouflage pattern of Dark Green on the upper surfaces. The demarcation along the fuselage/nose was

Mosquito NF Mk 30, MB-24, ND•N, No.1 Wing, Royal Belgian Air Force, early 1950s. Medium Sea Grey overall with Dark Green camouflage on upper surfaces; white codes. Black serials, repeated below wings; black spinners anti-dazzle panel. Roundels in six positions, outlined in blue; 'N' repeated on nose below glazed radar housing

on a hypothetical line from the centreline of the trailing edge of the wing to the leading edge of the tailplanes and the upper panel in the radome was usually left unpainted on these machines. A black anti-dazzle panel was applied forward of the windscreen. Roundels were applied above and below the wings and on either side of the fuselage, they all look to be the same diameter (36in?) and were all usually thinly outlined in blue. A fin flash was applied in the usual manner and the serial number was applied in black characters ahead of the tailplane on either side of the rear fuselage and usually repeated under the wings (read from the trailing edge forward under the port and from the leading edge aft under the starboard). Squadron codes were applied in white characters that look to be approximately 24in high, and these were placed either side of the fuselage roundel in the usual manner, and sometimes the individual aircraft letter was repeated on the nose under the radome clear panel.

The NF Mk XVII and XIX used as Instructional Airframes at the Technical School at Tongere were in standard RAF camouflage, but we have failed to find any images that confirm if they retained RAF, or had been repainted with Belgian markings?

Czechoslovakia

The B-36s and LB-36s (FB Mk VI) used by the Ceskoslovenske Letectvo were finished in the standard RAF fighter scheme of Ocean Grey and Dark Green over Medium Sea Grey. Czech roundels with a white outline were applied above each wing and either side of the vertical fin, whilst those below the wing did not have the white outline. The RAF serial number was retained, still applied in 8in high black characters either side of the rear fuselage, forward of the tailplane. The squadron identification markings were applied in black-outlined white characters on either side of the fuselage, as there was no roundel in this location. The characters were large, probably 40in+, and the 1st Squadron of the 24th Bomber Regiment used 'IY-' followed by a number (e.g. '12'). This code was repeated under the wings, with the '-' element usually under the bomb/tank rack and the other bits either side of this. That did mean that the underwing

roundels were placed outboard of this code, putting them at about 4/5th span and the ones above the wings were placed in the same location, but lacked the squadron codes. Propeller spinners were dark red or black. The 2nd Squadron of the 24th Bomber Regiment used the codes 'JX', but all other markings remained the same as those of No.1 Squadron and this unit also had red spinners. The exception to the above was TE603, which was the personal aircraft of No.24 Bomber Regiment's commander and this was finished in aluminium overall with the codes 'KP-1' applied in black with a white outline on

Newly refurbished NF Mk 30 MB-17 at Fairey Aviation, Ringway in 1948 (©Westland)

either side of the rear fuselage. The RAF serial TE603 was applied in the same manner as the other machines, as were the roundels on the tail and above and below the wings. The machine had the spinners in aluminium.

Oddities include VR347, which was a No.2 Squadron machine, but was subordinate to the 25th Bomber Regiment and marked as JX-12. This machine was overall yellow, with the codes in black outlined in white, the serial number in black and the roundels applied in the usual manner (again with a white outline). This machine was damaged by protestors in Trecine in August 1948. A No.1 Squadron machine when subordinate to the No.25 Bomber Regiment was MM430, which carried the codes IY-7 and was finished in a dark grey overall (exact shade unknown). This had the codes applied in black with a white outline on either side of the fuselage and under the wings, plus the RAF serial in black on the aft fuselage and white-outlined roundels on the vertical fin and above and below the wings. The spinners were black.

Mosquito B-36, RF823, IY-5, 24th Bomber Regiment, Ceskoslovenske Letectvo. Ocean Grey/Dark Green/Medium Sea Grey finish with white codes, outlined in black; serials in black. National markings on fin and above wings outlined in white; black spinners

Mosquito FB Mk 26, FB•24, Chinese Nationalist Air Force, Hankow. Olive Green over Ocean Grey finish (see notes in accompanying text), with white codes; roundels on fuselage sides and above and below the wings; blue and white horizontal stripes on the rudder

China

This is a complex subject, as there is much conflicting information about the schemes and colours applied to these machines and it is made even worse by surviving photographs. The accepted story is that all of the FB Mk 26s and T Mk 27/29s bought from Canada for China were stripped of all their paint and markings, and repainted in a dark green (possibly olive green) over light grey scheme. However, there are images of airframes sealed and prepared for ship-

FB Mk 26 B-M016 of the Chinese Nationalist AF being ground handled

ment that are still in full RAF camouflage and markings, whilst there is a well-known shot of aircraft on the pan at Downsview, some of which are fully stripped of paint, others only partially? To muddy the waters even further, a recent decal sheet by Tiger Wings in China shows the aircraft to be in a mix of colours? The images of the airframes being re-assembled in Shangahi seem to show an overall aluminium scheme applied, whilst another shows an airframe that seems to have remnants of the camouflage on the engine nacelles, so what is the likely story?

I have to say that I feel that the large batch of airframes, sent over an extended period of time were sent in a mix of painted, partially painted and those repainted in aluminium. Once in China the airframes were reassembled and given a new paint scheme. Breaking this down further, you can see that the well-known shot of the airframe marked as 'FB1' seen in Canada was in an overall medium grey colour, with patches of dark green camouflage on the upper surfaces. This is therefore most likely a modification of the RAF

scheme, resulting in Ocean Grey overall with Dark Green camouflage, or local paint equivalents. These early machines also don't carry the Chinese roundels at this stage, instead they have the badge of No.1 Bombardment Group on each side of the fuselage comprising a Chinese character in a red disc. No roundels were carried on the wings, but the serial was applied under the wings in the same fashion as post-war RAF machines; FB1 and FB4 are thus far confirmed by period photographs in this scheme. The basic scheme was also applied to KA482 and KA892 when they were in China but by this stage they had the Chinese roundels applied (no tail stripes or codes, though – these machines had yellow spinners). The most common scheme, however, which Tiger Wings states applies to the FB Mk 26s and T Mk 27/29s was one of a light blue on the lower surfaces and an olive green on top. Tiger Wings states these are equivalent to RLM 76 underneath and RLM 80 on top. The use of RLM 80 on top can be explained as a rough equivalent to the olive green most accept was the upper surface colour; the use of a pale blue/grey underneath is not the accepted colour of light grey though, but it is still possible if you think about available colours and possible local mixing. The demarcation of the two colours in the latter scheme is straight and hard-edged, following the hypothetical line running through the centre of the wing and tailplane and projecting fore and aft. The demarcation of the engine nacelles is not the same as that seen on RAF and RCAF machines, in that it does not follow the upper panel line, instead if sweeps down from the wing leading edge to a line running through the centre of the exhaust stack opening in the cowl (there are some exceptions, so check reference photos). Roundels were applied above and below the wings, out towards the tips and on either side of the rear fuselage. The wing roundels are much smaller than those used on the fuselage and the fuselage one is well aft in comparison with RAF/RCAF practice. All of the machines received serial numbers in the 001 to 180 range with the type codes of 'FB' for the fighter-bombers and 'T' for the trainers being applied on the fuselage (e.g. T•19 or FB•40). The type also carried the serial on either side of the vertical fin, in the format of 'B-MO' [MO stands

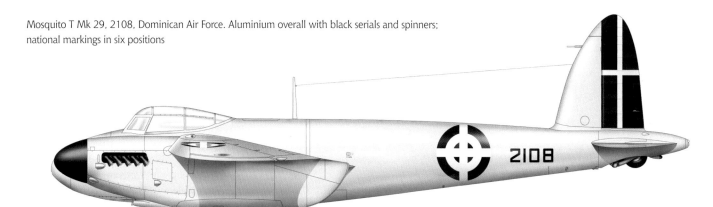

Mosquito T Mk 29, 2108, Dominican Air Force. Aluminium overall with black serials and spinners; national markings in six positions

for Mosquito] and then the full serial number, e.g 019; Tiger Wings disagrees with this, stating that the serial number was applied as 'B-' then an extended serial number (e.g. '0019'), but having seen close-up period images of the tail, the B-MOxxx format seems to correspond to what can be seen in these images. Exceptions to the rules on this include FB•73, which had a large '112' in white stencilled characters towards the top on each side of the vertical fin. The rudders of all Mosquitos seem to be universally painted in horizontal stripes of pale blue and white. A number of the FB Mk 26s adopted a different style of code when in squadron service, this being the last three of the serial number applied in white 45° stencil format characters aft of the fuselage roundel. Spinner colours could be blue, yellow, dark grey or aluminium (bare metal) depending on the unit they were used by at the time, and a squadron badge of a diving eagle dropping a bomb can be seen on the side of the nose on some machines of No.3 Squadron, No.1 Bombardment Group.

Dominican Republic

This nation purchased six FB Mk VIs and they were finished in aluminium overall, with black propellers and spinners. The Dominican roundel was applied either side of the fuselage and above the below the wings (these latter items being out towards the tips, probably at 4/5th span). The roundels were of small diameter, probably no more

than 24in. The national flag was applied either side of the vertical fin, at the mid-way point, with the rearmost edge on the hinge line A three-digit serial number was applied in small black characters either side of the rear fuselage, just forward of and below the tailplane. The serial numbers allocated were: 301 (ex-TE612), 302 (ex-T909), 303 (ex-TE822), 304 (ex-TE873), 305 (ex-RF939) and 306 (original serial number unknown).

Dominican FB Mk VI in the later style markings coded as '2102', this was previously '302' *(©D Hagedorn)*

The three ex-RCAF T Mk 29s (KA172, KA206 and KA423) obtained were in a similar overall aluminium scheme. They adopted a four-digit serial number in the 2100-range (2108 and 2109 are confirmed). The markings remained unchanged other than the roundels are bigger, the rudder is completely covered in the national flag and the new serial number is in a slightly larger size font.

Dominican FB Mk VI in original markings with the code '301' on the rear fuselage *(©D Hagedorn)*

FB Mk VI of the French AF RF876 in Indo-China, March 1947, with the 'Sharkmouth' motif on nose (©J-J. Petit)

France

The FB Mk VIs operated by the *Armée de l'Air* (French Army Air Force) were in the standard RAF scheme of overall Medium Sea Grey with a disruptive pattern of Dark Green on the upper surfaces. When GC 1/3 moved to Rabat and became GC 1/6 you will find some machines had the undersides (but not the wings) oversprayed in black, like the Mk II intruders used by the RAF; this was soft-edged and low on the fuselage sides, with sweeping lines up to the tailplane leading edge and wing trailing edge. The fuselage demarcation is as per RAF machines, but some French machines seem to have the very leading edge of the vertical fin sprayed in Dark Green with a soft edge (this may be shadow in period images, but we can't see how it would form in that area).

French roundels were applied either side of the rear fuselage and above the wings (none below) all thinly outlined in yellow. The squadron used a numeric identification system, so GC 2/6 had yellow characters outlined in black, whilst GC 1/3 (later becoming GC 1/6) had white characters outlined in black. This squadron number was applied aft of the fuselage roundel on both sides. A French fin flash was applied in the same manner as RAF machines and the RAF serial was retained on either side of the rear fuselage and also under the wings, again in the RAF style/location. GC 2/6 had the spinners with bands of blue (front), white and red (back), whilst GC 1/3 had red (front), white, red (back). The personal aircraft of the CO of GC 1/3, Capitaine Rupied carried the number '1' on the rear fuselage and on each side of the nose had the badges of SPA 69 and SPA 88 respectively.

The T Mk IIIs in French service were finished in Trainer Yellow overall, with the roundels and fin flash as per the FB Mk VI. The RAF serial number was applied to the rear fuselage and under each wing in the usual style/location. The spinners were usually also yellow.

The NF Mk 30s operated from Rabat were in standard RAF camouflage of Medium Sea Grey overall with disruptive Dark Green on the upper surfaces. The roundels and fin flash seem to all be as per the FB Mk VI and the RAF serial number was applied to the rear fuselage and under each wing in the usual style/location. The spinners were usually Medium Sea Grey.

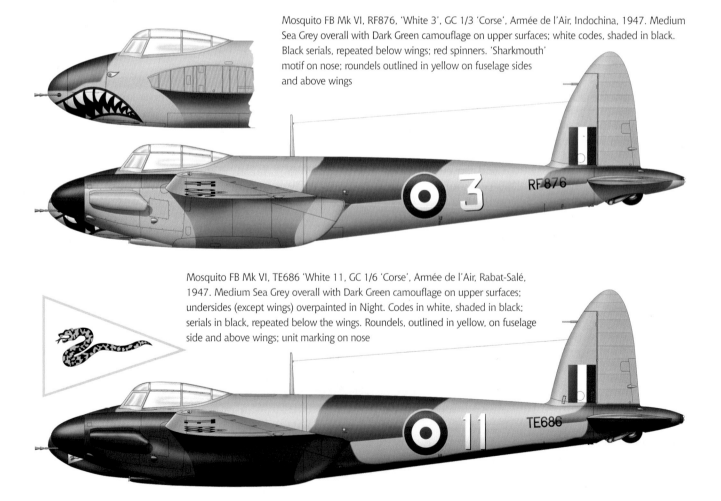

Mosquito FB Mk VI, RF876, 'White 3', GC 1/3 'Corse', Armée de l'Air, Indochina, 1947. Medium Sea Grey overall with Dark Green camouflage on upper surfaces; white codes, shaded in black. Black serials, repeated below wings; red spinners. 'Sharkmouth' motif on nose; roundels outlined in yellow on fuselage sides and above wings

Mosquito FB Mk VI, TE686 'White 11, GC 1/6 'Corse', Armée de l'Air, Rabat-Salé, 1947. Medium Sea Grey overall with Dark Green camouflage on upper surfaces; undersides (except wings) overpainted in Night. Codes in white, shaded in black; serials in black, repeated below the wings. Roundels, outlined in yellow, on fuselage side and above wings; unit marking on nose

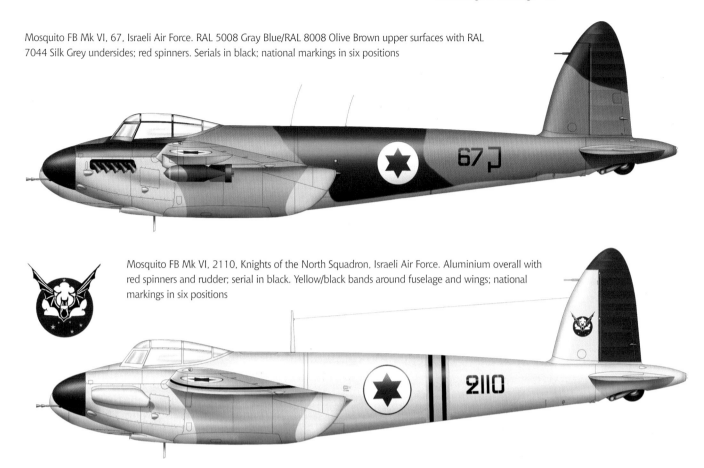

Mosquito FB Mk VI, 67, Israeli Air Force. RAL 5008 Gray Blue/RAL 8008 Olive Brown upper surfaces with RAL 7044 Silk Grey undersides; red spinners. Serials in black; national markings in six positions

Mosquito FB Mk VI, 2110, Knights of the North Squadron, Israeli Air Force. Aluminium overall with red spinners and rudder; serial in black. Yellow/black bands around fuselage and wings; national markings in six positions

Israel

The thirty-nine FB Mk 6s operated by the IAF were overall aluminium with the spinners and rudder in a dark red (No.109 Squadron) or black (No.110 Squadron). Roundels were applied either side of the rear fuselage and above and below the wings. The four-digit serial number was applied in a stylised form of stencil on the rear fuselage and initially this was followed by the prefix 'IAF'. After the incident with 2127 and 2129 in October 1951 however, this was removed and replaced with a Hebrew character instead. Some machines, 2146 being well-known, had the title 'IDFAF' aft of the serial on the port side and forward of it on the starboard side, plus the characters were big, filling nearly all the space between the roundel and the tailplane. When allocated to a unit (e,g, 109 and 110 Squadrons), their badge was usually applied on either side of the vertical fin, at the mid-point as well as often being painted on the access door on No.110 Squadron machines. You will also find stylised exhaust 'streaks' added as solid black areas projecting back from the exhausts on both sides of each engine nacelle. During Operation Kadesh, the FB Mk VIs received a new colour scheme to match the other front-line aircraft and this comprised Grey/Blue RAL 5008 and Olive Brown RAF 8008 upper surface camouflage over Silk Grey RAL 7044 undersides. The demarcation was low down the fuselage sides, soft-edged and wavy and although set half-way up on the nose and sweeping down behind the wing trailing edge, the demarcation did not sweep back up to the tailplane trailing edge, in-

stead it just projected to the tail cone, thus going under the tailplane. National markings remained the same, although most seem to have two- or three-digit identification numbers on the fuselage side and a different Hebrew symbol to that seen originally on the fighter-bombers. There are also examples at this time that remained their overall aluminium scheme, but just had the yellow and black bands around the mid-fuselage and wings that are associated with Operation Kadesh, so check your references.

The twenty NF Mk 30s (2141 to 2160) used by Israel were all painted black overall with the same style and location to the roundels

The two ex-Armée de l'Air T Mk 3s were

SNCAN staff pose with masks used to apply the David Shield to Mosquitos reconditioned by them at Chateaudun *(©SNCAN)*

FB Mk 6, S/No.2109 the starboard rear of the fuselage with the Hebrew K to denote Krav – fighter *(©IAF)*

FB Mk 6. S/No.2109 with the 'IAF' prefix applied up until 1951 *(©IAF)*

painted yellow overall with the same roundels as per the FB Mk VIs, red rudder and spinners and the same four-digit code on the rear fuselage, although as the role was different, the single Hebrew character after the serial was changed. The four FB Mk 6s (2161 to 2164) converted to dual-control probably remained in their fighter scheme, as we have been unable to unearth any photographs of them.

New Zealand

A number of T Mk IIs and T Mk 43s, along with FB Mk 40s were sold to New Zealand by Australia, however the bulk of the RZNAF's Mos-

quito force was made up of seventy-six ex-RAF FB Mk VIs, which were allocated serial numbers NZ2321 to NZ2396. Most, if not all, of these machines seem to be in aluminium overall. Roundels were applied either side of the fuselage and above and below the wings. When allocated to No.75 Squadron, codes of 'YC' were applied one side of the fuselage roundel, with an individual aircraft letter, on the other. A fin flash was applied to either side of the vertical fin in the RAF fashion and the serial number was also applied in the RAF manner either side of the rear fuselage, ahead of the tailplane. Spinners were black and usually glossy. Most of the RNZAF machines seem to have an anti-dazzle panel applied in black ahead of the windscreen, not all though, so check your references.

Exceptions we have found to these rules include NZ2325, which is seen with RAF Type C1 roundels applied to the fuselage and above and below the wings, with a Type C1 fin flash. The serial numbers are also applied under the wings in RAF style and as this machine is pictured with drop tanks installed, you can see how the tank creates a clear area in the code between 'NZ' and '2325' on each wing. This machine became YC•A with No.75 Squadron and by this stage it had roundels and fin flash as per all other machines, but for some reason retained the underwing serial numbers, even with rocket rails installed over them.

In July 1953 six RNZAF machines received civil registrations, these being ZK-BCT (ex-PZ413/NZ2381), BCU (ex-RF597/NZ2383), BCV (ex-PZ474/NZ2384), BCW (ex-PZ444/NZ2385), BCX (ex-RF849/NZ2386) and BCY (ex-PZ200/NZ23867). They were all acquired by Aircraft Supplies Ltd of Palmerston North and were painted aluminium overall with the civil registration applied in black characters on either side of the rear fuselage. The style of font used for this varies from aircraft to aircraft, so check photographs on the Internet to be sure.

An Israeli FB Mk VI from 110 Squadron forms a backdrop as Capt Hugo Marom (left) hands over to Capt Israel Kahav (right) on the 27th December 1953; note the unit badge on the crew door *(©IDF/IAF)*

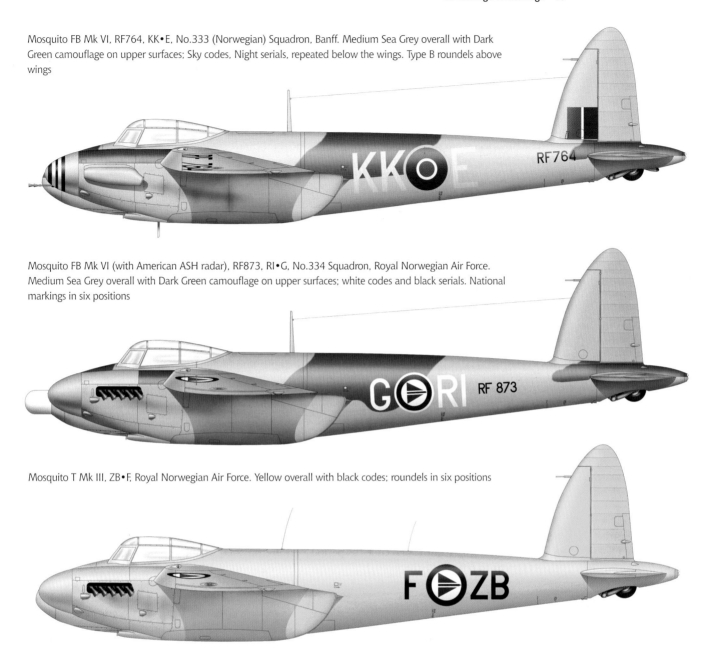

Mosquito FB Mk VI, RF764, KK•E, No.333 (Norwegian) Squadron, Banff. Medium Sea Grey overall with Dark Green camouflage on upper surfaces; Sky codes, Night serials, repeated below the wings. Type B roundels above wings

Mosquito FB Mk VI (with American ASH radar), RF873, RI•G, No.334 Squadron, Royal Norwegian Air Force. Medium Sea Grey overall with Dark Green camouflage on upper surfaces; white codes and black serials. National markings in six positions

Mosquito T Mk III, ZB•F, Royal Norwegian Air Force. Yellow overall with black codes; roundels in six positions

Norway

During WWII B Flight aircraft of No.333 (Norwegian) Squadron at RAF Leuchars were marked in standard RAF camouflage and carried the squadron codes KK applied in Sky. By this stage roundels were Type C1 on the fuselage and Type B on the wings, with a Type C1 fin flash on either side of the vertical fin. Once the aircraft were redesignated to No.334 Squadron in May 1945 the markings remained unchanged, even when the unit moved back to Norway two months later. Once under Luftforsvaret control in November 1945 the fuselage and wing roundels were over-painted with the Norwegian flag-style roundel and a much smaller diameter one was added under each wing, right out at the tip. The RAF serial number was, more often than not, applied under the wings in the usual manner, split by the drop tank between the second letter and first number. From August 1946 the RAF system of squadron codes was abandoned and a single-character

classification for the aircraft type was used (the Mosquito was 'F'), followed by a two-character identification codes for the specific aircraft (e.g. 'AD') and these were applied in the RAF style either side of the fuselage roundel. The RAF fin

An FB Mk VI possibly at Kjevik, which like many, has had the nose guns removed *(via Bjorn Olsen)*

flash was painted out and there seems to be a serial number or similar applied in small white characters on the tail, sometimes on the vertical fin, others have it on the rudder, but it is impossible from available images to determine what this is? The roundel under the wings was now applied in a larger diameter and was moved inboard, as no serial numbers seem to be applied, but the roundel is placed well forward, with the outer/front arc almost on the curve of the leading edge In January 1951 the squadron code system was reintroduced and ex-RAF units reverted to their original wartime code letters. No.334 Squadron however did not adopt 'KK' again, instead it used 'RI' the initial of its commanding office Major Reidar Isaken. The markings were applied in RAF-style, with RI to one side of the fuselage roundel and the individual aircraft letter on the other. All other markings remained as before, although the serial numbers looked to have been re-applied slightly further forward on the fuselage sides now, albeit still in 8in high black characters.

There are a number of profiles about that show an unidentified T Mk III marked as ZB•F, which is Trainer Yellow overall, with the national insignia either side of the fuselage and above and below the wings. The squadron codes, ZB, were applied in black one side of the fuselage roundel, with the individual aircraft letter the other. Although included here, we have found no period images to support this scheme and as it is listed by some as being operated by No.334 Squadron at Sola, when they did not use the type, nor the 'ZB' codes as far as we can tell, this scheme has to be considered an anomaly until such times as period images appear to prove its existence.

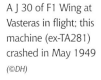

A crewman relaxes on the tail of 'Red O', just visible forward and below the new serial 30036 is the old RAF serial MM651 showing through the paint *(©Birger Lindberg)*

A J 30 of F1 Wing at Vasteras in flight; this machine (ex-TA281) crashed in May 1949 *(©DH)*

Sweden

The sixty surplus NF Mk XIXs supplied to the Flygvapnet (Swedish Air Force) were allocated serial numbers in the 30001 to 30060 range whilst in Flygvapnet service. The first two machines (30001 ex-TA286 and 30002 ex-TA275) were finished in aluminium overall, with the Swedish roundel either side of the fuselage (#30001 had these farther aft than usual) and above and below the wings; these latter markings were applied halfway between the carriers and the wing tips. The propellers and spinners were black and no other markings seem to have been applied (there may be a trace of the RAF serial on the rear fuselage, but photographs are not clear enough to know if these are showing through the paint or were actually applied onto the new aluminium). When taken on the strength of F1 at Hässlö they became 'Red A' (#30001) and 'Red B' (#30002), a small black '1' or '2' was applied aft of the fuselage roundel

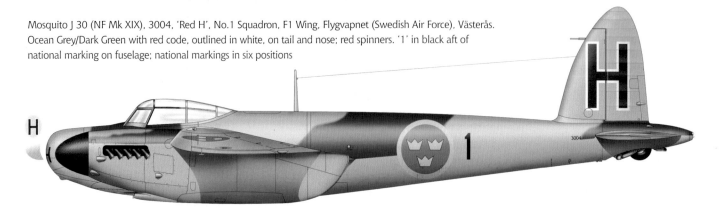

Mosquito J 30 (NF Mk XIX), 3004, 'Red H', No.1 Squadron, F1 Wing, Flygvapnet (Swedish Air Force), Västerås. Ocean Grey/Dark Green with red code, outlined in white, on tail and nose; red spinners. '1' in black aft of national marking on fuselage; national markings in six positions

and the 'A' and 'B' were applied in red with a white outline across the vertical fin and rudder. The spinners were now black tipped with red.

The remaining airframes were all supplied in standard RAF night-fighter camouflage of Medium Sea Grey overall with a disruptive pattern of Dark Green on the upper surfaces. The demarcation along the fuselage and nose was soft-edged and followed a line from the centreline of the tailplane, through the centre of the wing to the nose. It should be noted that some machines had the camouflage in this manner around the nose cone, whilst other machines had the tip painted in solid Medium Sea Grey, not following the lines of the nose cone cover and others had the entire nose cone cover in Medium Sea Grey, so check your references! Spinners were Medium Sea Grey, with black propeller blades. National markings were as per the first two machines, but period photos confirm that the RAF serial number can often be seen through the camouflage paint on the rear fuselage, while the new serial number in the 30001 to 30060 range was applied in black forward and just below it. When the type entered service with Nos.1, 2 & 3 Squadrons of F1 Wing each machine had a single alpha character to identify it and this was applied in a large format on the vertical fin and rudder, going across the hinge line. This character was applied in the squadron colour, so No.1 was initially white outlined in black, but later changed to red outlined in white, No.2 was blue outlined in white and No.3 was yellow outlined in white. Each squadron also had these colours applied to the spinners and the individual aircraft letter was usually repeated on the tip of the radome. Each squadron also designed its own squadron badge and these were usually applied to the crew access door on the starboard fuselage side.

Turkey

135 FB Mk VIs and ten T Mk IIIs were supplied to Turkey and all of the former were supplied in overall aluminium with the Turkish national insignia of a white-outlined red square on either side of the fuselage and above and below the wings. The RAF serial number

was retained and applied in small (probably 6in high) black characters on either side of the rear fuselage, just forward of the tailplane and centred on the centreline of the leading edge. The Turkish flag was applied either side of the vertical fin, half way up, with its rearmost edge on the hinge line. In Turkish service these machines adopted a two-digit identification number in black on the rear fuselage with this repeated in full (four-digit) much smaller sized characters on the nose, just below the machine-

The bat emblem of No.2 Squadron on the door of S/No.30053 'Blue O'
(©Björn Karlsson)

The emblem of No.1 Squadron on the door of S/No.30038 'Red A'
(©Harry Frohm)

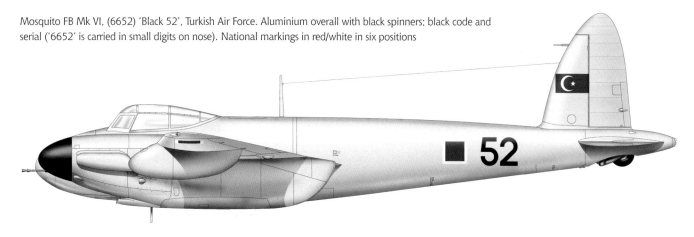

Mosquito FB Mk VI, (6652) 'Black 52', Turkish Air Force. Aluminium overall with black spinners; black code and serial ('6652' is carried in small digits on nose). National markings in red/white in six positions

T Mk III '542' was refurbished in January 1947 as a batch of ten for the Turkish Air Force and is seen here on a test flight from Hatfield *(©DH)*

gun access panel. The serial number system applied to all the FB Mk VIs was in the 6600 and 6700-series, e.g. '30' was 6730. This is confusing, though, as '52' is listed as 6652, whilst the already mentioned '30' was 6730? As yet we have not found any documents that cross-refer all the serial numbers allocated to the Turkish Air Force machines, so hopefully someone will have the necessary information (or access to such information) to compile one before too long and clear this whole thing up at last.

The T Mk IIIs were all finished in Trainer Yellow overall with national markings as per the FB Mk VIs. Production serial numbers 6601 to 6610 were allocated, but the aircraft were never marked with these, instead they received serial numbers 533 to 542, which were applied in the same style/location as those seen on the FB Mk VIs.

United States

NF Mk XXX, MN564/G of the 416th NFS was the first to arrive with unit on the 29th November 1944, which probably explains the '/G' prefix to the serial because it needed to be guarded at all times *(©Lippincott)*

The NF Mk XXXs operating in North Africa with the 416th NFS (Night Fighter Squadron) were in standard RAF night-fighter camouflage of overall Medium Sea Grey with Dark Green disruptive camouflage on the upper surfaces. The

RAF roundels were removed from the wings and fuselage and replaced with stars 'n' bars on either side of the fuselage and below the starboard and above the port wings. RAF fin flashes were overpainted, but the RAF serial number remained on the rear fuselage.

Yugoslavia

Seventy-six FB Mk VIs were allocated to the Yugoslavia Air Force under the Mutual Defence Air Programme in 1951. Surviving images of some of these machines en route seem to show a two-colour scheme, with solid Medium Sea Grey on top and a much darker shade underneath. The exact colour underneath is unknown, but was most likely Ocean Grey. The spinners are in this dark shade, whilst the blades are black. The demarcation along the fuselage is odd, in that it is obviously very soft, but on the nose it swoops up and cuts off just ahead of the windscreen, leaving the whole nose region in the lower colour, whilst the rear fuselage has a high demarcation that starts just above the wing trailing edge and then projects back to the tail cone (thus being slightly under the tailplane). Roundels are applied to either side of the fuselage and under the wings, these latter markings seem to be set halfway between the carriers and the tips and are not on the centreline (they are slightly forward of it and of 75cm diameter). Each aircraft was allocated a four-figure serial number in the 8000 range and this was applied either side of the vertical fin, half-way up, in black characters (these look to be 45° style, but not stencils, as no gaps can be seen). The last two of this serial was applied in white characters between the fuselage roundel and tail and these look to be approximately 12in tall and of a very 'boxy' style font. In service, the spinners also look to have been repainted in a lighter colour, so we presume this to relate to the operating unit's colours?

Later the remaining aircraft were apparently repainted using locally-produced paints, which resulted in a light grey on top and a bright blue underneath, and it has been said that the nearest matches to these two colours are Medium Grey FS26493 and Brilliant Medium Blue FS25466.

The three T Mk IIIs operated by the JRV were aluminium overall with the Trainer Yellow bands

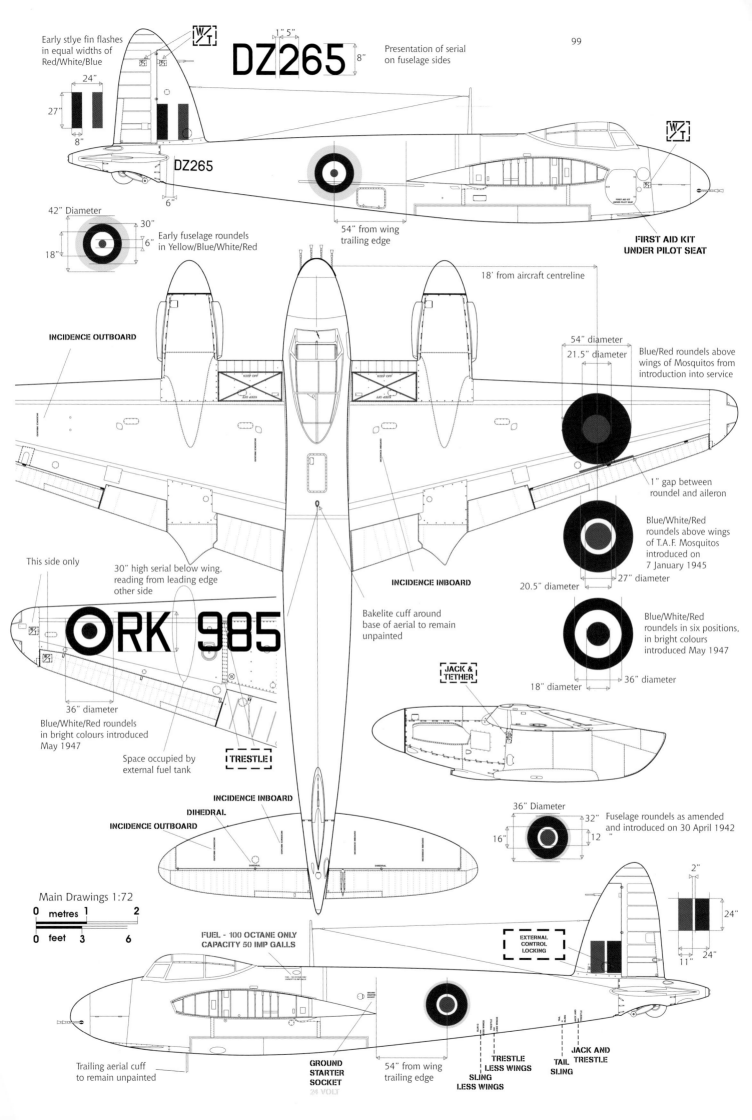

Early stlye fin flashes in equal widths of Red/White/Blue

24"
27"
8"

W/T

1" 5"
DZ265
8"

Presentation of serial on fuselage sides

DZ265

6"

42" Diameter
30"
6"
18"

Early fuselage roundels in Yellow/Blue/White/Red

W/T

FIRST AID KIT UNDER PILOT SEAT

54" from wing trailing edge

INCIDENCE OUTBOARD

18' from aircraft centreline

KEEP OFF
AID HERE

KEEP OFF
AID HERE

54" diameter
21.5" diameter

Blue/Red roundels above wings of Mosquitos from introduction into service

1" gap between roundel and aileron

Blue/White/Red roundels above wings of T.A.F. Mosquitos introduced on 7 January 1945

20.5" diameter
27" diameter

INCIDENCE INBOARD

Bakelite cuff around base of aerial to remain unpainted

Blue/White/Red roundels in six positions, in bright colours introduced May 1947

18" diameter
36" diameter

This side only

30" high serial below wing. reading from leading edge other side

ORK 985

36" diameter

Blue/White/Red roundels in bright colours introduced May 1947

Space occupied by external fuel tank

TRESTLE

JACK & TETHER

36" Diameter
32"
16"
12"

Fuselage roundels as amended and introduced on 30 April 1942

INCIDENCE INBOARD
DIHEDRAL
INCIDENCE OUTBOARD

DIHEDRAL

DIHEDRAL

Main Drawings 1:72

0   metres   1   2
0   feet   3   6

FUEL - 100 OCTANE ONLY
CAPACITY 50 IMP GALLS

EXTERNAL CONTROL LOCKING

2"
24"
11"
24"

Trailing aerial cuff to remain unpainted

GROUND STARTER SOCKET
24 VOLT

54" from wing trailing edge

TRESTLE
LESS WINGS

SLING
LESS WINGS

JACK AND TAIL SLING

JACK AND TRESTLE

Mosquito NF Mk 38, S/No.8020, 'White 20', Yugoslav Air Force, 1953. Night overall with white codes and serials; roundels on fuselage sides and below wings only. '20' repeated on nose in white

Mosquito FB Mk VI converted to dual-control, S/No.8169, 'Black 69', Yugoslav Air Force, Zadar, 1955. Aluminium overall with yellow bands around rear fuselage and wings; serials and codes in black. Roundels on fuselage sides and below wings only

around the wings and rear fuselage you will see on RAF machines. There were no roundels on top of the wings, just the RAF ones showing through the fresh paint, but there were 75cm diameter ones under each wing, placed well out towards the tip, just inboard of the panel line for the wing tip. Roundels were applied either side of the rear fuselage, halfway between the wing trailing edge and the fuselage band and the last two of the serial number (8101, 8102 or 8103) was applied in black stencil-style characters aft of the fuselage band; these look to be quite large characters, possibly 12in high. The serial was applied in full, in black (8in?) characters either side of the vertical fin, at the mid-point and the Yugoslavian flag was applied across the rudder, also at the mid-point. The three FB Mk VIs (8168, 8169 & unknown) converted to dual controls adopted the same scheme as applied to the T Mk IIIs.

The sixty NF Mk 38s operated by Yugoslavia were in standard RAF night-fighter colours of Medium Sea Grey overall with a disruptive pattern of Dark Green on the upper surfaces. The fuselage demarcation was soft-edged and high, running from the centreline of the wing trailing and tailplane leading edges. Roundels were applied to each side of the fuselage and below the wings (we have found no upper wing roundels on any of the photos we have seen). The fuselage ones look to be the same size as RAF examples, whilst those under the wing were smaller and located out towards the tip with the front arc just under the leading edge of the wing. No serial numbers are applied under the wing, but the

serial number in the 8001 to 8060 range was applied in black characters towards the top of the vertical fin. The last two of this serial were then repeated in white (12in) characters on either side of the rear fuselage 2/3rd of the way between the roundel and the tailplane. The only other marking was the Yugoslavia flag applied on either side of the rudder at the halfway point and covering the entire area from trailing edge to hinge line. Note that one machine, 8020 was finished in an overall black scheme, with all the markings as per the other machines, except the black serial number on the top of the fin was applied in white and it carried '20' in white on the tip of the radome and either side of the rear fuselage.

References
We would also recommend the following titles for those wishing to read more on this complex subject:

- British Aviation Colours of World War Two: The Official Camouflage, Colours and Markings of RAF Aircraft 1939-1945, RAF Museum Series Vol.3 (Arms & Armour Press 1976 ISBN: 0-85368-271-2
- Bombing Colours: British Bombers, Their Markings and Operations 1937-1973 by Michael J.F. Bowyer (Patrick Stephens Ltd 1973 SBN: 0-85059-128-7)

Chapter 5: Mosquito Kits

The Mosquito has been a popular subject with kit manufacturers over the years, with the fighter and fighter-based variants getting the biggest share of the coverage. We thought we would have a look through the kits that we could find of the type and give you our assessment of them.

Please note that we have only included those kits that have been released since I first covered the type back in 1998, assessments of all the older ones will be available as a downloadable PDF file from our website (www.valiant-wings.co.uk) once this title is on sale.

1/72nd Scale

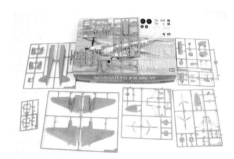

Hasegawa CP18

Hasegawa

Various

This Japanese company produced the fighter version of the Mosquito initially as the FB Mk VI (#CP18) in 1999, but since then has reissued it in a number of different guises and packaging, as well as revising it to offer some other variants as follows:
• NF Mk II 'Night Fighter' #00050 (2000)
• FB Mk VI 'Coastal Command' #00098 (2000)
• FB Mk VI 'SEAC' #00159 (2001)
• FB Mk VI 'RAAF' #00656 (2003)
• FB Mk VI '418 Sqn #00750 (2005)
• Mosquito 'Passenger Transport' #00268 (2001)
• Spitfire Mk VII & Mosquito FB Mk VI

Hasegawa 00050

Hasegawa 00739

'Operation Overlord' #02096 (2014)
• NF Mk XIII 'Night Fighter' #02198 (2016)
• FB Mk XVIII 'Anti-ship Attacker' #02024 (2013)

All share common basic tooling, so we will deal with the basic FB Mk VI version with notes relating to any changes made in specific issues or revisions for other version.

The components are moulded in Hasegawa's usual medium grey-coloured plastic and all feature engraved panel lines and access panels and raised details such as the reinforcing strip on the aft fuselage. The fuselage was split mid-way along the cockpit, to allow the

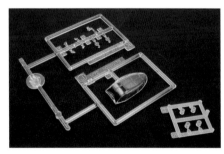

Hasegawa 1/72nd FB Mk VI_clear parts

Hasegawa 00159

Hasegawa 00750

bomber versions to be made and to mainly hide the resulting joint under the wing root radiators. Overall length and profile are spot on, the only area that could be a little skinny is around the ventral cannon bay region, but we are talking less than 1mm, so nothing to concern yourself with. The reinforcing strip is there on the starboard fuselage side (although when making the early W40-series machines offered in the NF Mk II kit, you may want to remove this, as some sources claim these machines did not have it) and the one around the fuselage is also depicted as raised detail. The cockpit interior is basic with floor, pilot's seat, bulkhead and instrument panel, rudder pedals, gunsight (in clear plastic), control column, navigator's seat and the rear stepped shelf with boxes to represent the radios. A decal is supplied for the instrument panel, but there is no sidewall detail at all and things like the rudder pedals are blocks mounted on the floor, whilst the pilot's seat lacks any real detail and the same applies to the radio equipment. Overall you get the very basics, but there is a lot of scope to improve things. The bomb bay roof is there, with moulded detail for the fuel tanks and is identical to the bomber versions.

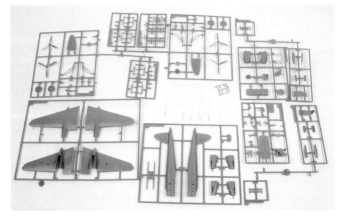

Hasegawa 1/72nd FB Mk VI

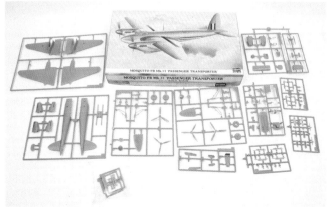

Hasegawa 00268 Transport

The fabric effect on the rudder is very nice and the pitot on the top of the vertical fin is a separate part. The tailplanes are correct in span and profile, the elevators are moulded in situ and all the panel lines match plans. The rivet detail on the elevators is nice and the trim tab linkage is the correct size and location and correctly positioned above the starboard and below the port. The tailwheel is moulded as one piece, but correctly depicts the twin-contact tyre and only really lacks depth due to being moulded as one (the side arms look 'flat'). Up front the nose cap is separate, with the machine gun barrels as separate parts that stick through from inside. The A.I. 'bow and arrow' antennae are also included on the sprues, as these were used with the NF Mk II kit. The ventral cannon ports are a separate part and include very impressively moulded barrels that are nicely inset into the ports and thus look very realistic. With the FB Mk XVIII you get two new resin inserts for the underside and a brass barrel for the 57mm Molins cannon. As Libor points out in his build elsewhere, though, the resin parts can be prone to shrinkage, making their fitment vague at best. Missing details include the downward ident lights underneath and you will need to rescribe the circular panel under the nose, as the sprue attachment is right in the middle of it. The camera port and cover under the rear fuselage from the bomber versions remains, so that has to be filled and the tail light is moulded grey plastic, so could be removed and replaced with one made from clear. The canopy is a single clear component and matches plans for overall shape and size. The clear sprue also includes the tip lights, downward identification lights and the gunsight.

Hasegawa 02096

The wing span and chord are perfect and all the panels lines and raised detail match scale plans, the only things missing are the bulges for the fuel pumps under the wings at mid-span, up against the fuselage. The hinge points for the control surfaces are nicely done and thus not over-accentuated, and the landing lights are supplied as clear parts (which you will need to back with chrome self-adhesive foil as Libor did in his builds). Upper surface detail also matches scale plans and the wing tip lights are supplied as separate clear parts, which are fine for those variants with twin tip lights, but for those that only had the front one installed, you will need to sand smooth and paint over the rear ones. The only real omission from the upper wing surface is the rear spar cap, although some may say in this scale it would best be depicted with engraved lines, Hasegawa have just omitted it, so you will either need to scribe them on, or as Libor did, created raised versions with layers of Mr Surfacer. The engine

Hasegawa 02024

nacelles are good in size and shape and the kit has the rear portion with the wheel wells in it moulded with the lower wing halves, so only the front section is separate (the upper cowl is moulded with the upper wing halves). All panel lines and rivets are correct and the fire extinguisher panel is engraved, which is fine in this scale, as its slight inset nature would not be discernible. The ice guards are supplied as separate parts, but they are designed with pegs that locate into holes ahead of the carburettor intake, when they were mounted on the lip of the intake. Both shrouded and exposed five-stack exhausts are included, the small bulge ahead of the lower edge visible in the latter arrangement, but covered by the former, are on the cowls and are covered by the shrouded exhausts, which is a nice touch. The propellers are of the correct diameter and both narrow and 'paddle' blades are included on the sprues. The spinners are moulded with separate back plates and have the correct diameter and profile. The undercarriage legs are moulded with the retraction arms and although the legs depict the rubber-in-compression units, they lack the prominent wire guards and the mudguards don't have the holes in the support brackets. The undercarriage doors are nicely moulded with the distinct curve to them and the oval raised cover in the middle, but the locating tabs are bulky, so many will remove them as Libor did in his builds. The wheels are very nice, with one half having a separate hub so that both five-spoke and plain units can be depicted. The tyres are the most common block pattern tread, although the circumferential joint will damage them. Most of the kits include the 3in RPs, even if not used, and these depict the 25lb SAP head, which makes a nice change. Each is moulded with the rail, whilst the tails are separate and all are commendably thin. The sprues do not contain drop tanks nor wing racks or bombs, however with releases such as the 'IDF' version, a new sprue was added for the wing racks and the bombs came from the bomb bay items that were included but not used in all the fighter variants, as they originate from the bomber version. The Mk XII night-fighter kit (#02198) had 50 Imp. Gal. drop tanks included, but these were resin parts and this kit also had the new radome supplied as a resin part as well, with

Hasegawa 02198

the gun camera on the starboard side also in resin. Hasegawa even include the altimeter 'T' antenna, should that variant require it under the wings, and with the night-fighter version you get the sloped antenna above the starboard wing at mid span and the dipoles above and below the tip; these latter items are single units that have to go through holes you drill through the wings.

The decal options for those kits we had to hand are as follows:

- **FB Mk VI (#CP18)**: NS850, TH•M, 'Black Rufe', No.418 Squadron, flown by Sqn Ldr R.A. Kipp, June 1944 and HX918 an unmarked machine of an unknown unit. Dragon-USA did a special version of this kit with markings for NT115, TH•J of No.418 Squadron added
- **NF Mk II 'Night Fighter' (#00050)**: W4082, RS•W, No.157 Squadron, RAF Castle Camps, late 1942 and DD739, RX•X, No.456 Squadron, September 1942. *The second option many claim would not have the reinforcing strip on the fuselage starboard side, although we can find no period images to confirm the W40-series did not have this fitted*
- **FB Mk VI 'SEAC' (#00159)**: RF784, UX•N, No.82 Squadron, Kumbhirgram, India and RF711, 'A', No.82 Squadron
- **FB Mk VI 'IDF' (#00739)**: 2015 and 2109 of No.109 'Valley' Squadron, 1953 and 2135 and 2121 of No.119 'Knights of the North' Squadron, 1953-5.
- **FB Mk VI '418 Sqn (#00750)**: HR241, TH•M, No.418 Squadron, November 1944 and PZ165, No.4 Squadron, 1949. The later option is in the post-war grey/black scheme with Type D roundels and white underwing codes
- **Mosquito 'Passenger Transport' (#00268)**: G-AGGD and G-AGGF operated by the BOAC from Leuchars
- **Spitfire Mk VII & Mosquito FB Mk VI 'Operation Overlord' (#02096)**: HR118, 'W', No.235 Squadron, June 1944 and MM403, B•V, No.464 Squadron, July 1944
- **NF Mk XIII 'Night Fighter' (#02198)**: HK382, RO•T, No.29 Squadron, January 1945 and HK429, RA•N, No.410 Squadron, February 1945
- **FB Mk XVIII 'Anti-ship Attacker' (#02024)**: NT225, 'O', No.248 Squadron, June 1944 and PZ468, QM•D, No.254

Squadron, April 1945. The decal sheet also includes serial numbers NT224 and HR138 plus red code letters 'D', 'Y' and 'E', but no indication of the schemes these apply to on the instructions.

In all cases the decal sheet also includes a full set of airframe stencils and a decal for the instrument panel. The decals are typical of Hasegawa, so well printed with good colour and limited carrier film, but this film can be a little on the thick side.

Verdict

A good kit, only let down by the lack of detail in the cockpit and the simplification of other aspects. The quality of the parts cannot be faulted and Hasegawa have done an excellent job with regard to the overall shape and dimensions, but with the Tamiya kit out there, this one has been considered as being in second place.

Tamiya

FB Mk VI/NF Mk II (#60747)

Produced by Tamiya in 2000 this is the most recent of any of the fighter Mosquitos in the scale. All the parts are moulded in their standard dark grey-coloured plastic with engraved panel lines etc. and as required raised detail for those elements that require it.

The fuselage is split in the middle of the cockpit, as Hasegawa did, and overall length and shape is excellent. The reinforcing strips along the starboard fuselage side and around the fuselage are both raised and all other panel lines match scale plans. The fuselage does include the ventral camera port under the rear fuselage as a clear part, although some options won't require it because it is most associated with the bomber version (the fuselage parts are common for both bomber and fighter, hence the inclusion). Cockpit detail is very nice, as you get an instrument panel with raised detail over which a decal can go and either the fighter-bomber vertical panel or the A.I. radar unit depending on which version you build. The gunsight is moulded in clear plastic and the rudder pedals are moulded with the front bulkhead, so they have nice deep relief. A fighter stick-style control column is included and the floor has the canvas boot at its base and the kneeling pad by the radar equipment The stepped nature of the rear bulkheads is correctly depicted and you get nicely a detailed 1154 and 1155 radio transmitter/receiver. The pilot's seat has separate armrests and decals for the seat belts, and the latter are also included for the navigator's seat, which is moulded to the step in the bulkheads. Interior detail on the sidewalls is excellent, with the electrical distribution panel, trailing aerial, throttle box, trim control and radio selector all moulded in situ. About all you can add is wiring and maybe a few smaller items such as cockpit lights etc., but the bulk of it is already there. The canopy is moulded in two parts, as you have the option of the bulged side panel on the starboard side. Thankfully the fit of the parts is so good that assembly should be without problem. The clear sprue also contains the gunsight, landing lights, tip lights and that camera port under the rear fuselage. The rear stepped region of the cockpit sits over a spar box unit to ease

wing attachment, but there is no detail within the bays below, so no cannon nor fuel tanks etc., the latter being something that Hasegawa did include in their kit. The nose cap is a separate item with the machine-guns correctly depicted below its centreline, and the instructions tell you to drill out the camera gun port because it's just moulded as a raised item on the part. The ventral cannon panel is also separate, with nice deep detail of the barrels within. The tailplanes are of the correct span and although the trailing edge and tip profile looks a bit too pointed, it is so marginal as not to be worth adjusting. All engraved detail matches plans, the trim tab linkage is the correct size and location and the riveting on the elevators is nicely done. The rudder features subtle fabric effect and the vertical fin has the pitot as a separate part. The tailwheel is split down the middle, to allow the twin-contact tyre to be depicted and it is well moulded with good relief to the detail.

The wings are of the correct span and chord, but Tamiya elected to chop the tips off and offer these separately, so they could do single and twin tip light arrangements (the fighter-bomber kits only include the single light arrangement, the twin is offered in the bomber kit). All the holes for the RPs, bombs

Tamiya 60747

and tanks are flashed over, so be aware of the notices on the instructions about when/if these need to be opened up. Most of the panel lines on the lower wing halves match scale plans, with a few additions, and the landing lights are separate clear parts. The lower halves of the radiator units are also moulded separately, so the matrices inside can be depicted, which is very nice touch. The upper wing halves also have panel lines and other details that match plans, but like Hasegawa, the rear spar cap is not depicted, either as engraved lines or raised detail, so you will need to add this if you wish. The undercarriage units are probably the most complete of any Mosquito kit, having the rubber-in-compression oleo legs complete with wire guards and retraction arms, plus the oil tanks mounted at the top in the wheel well and separate mudguards (lacking holes in the support bracket). The wheels have block-pattern tread and the hubs on one side are separate so that five-spoke or plain hubs can be depicted. The undercarriage doors are the correct size and shape, with interior detail even included, and they mount on lugs that project out from the sides of the wheel wells, thus more accurately depicting the hinges of the real thing. The

kit comes with 3in RPs fitted with 25lb SAP heads and these are nicely moulded to their rails with the tail fins separate. Also included are very nice bomb racks with 500lb bombs fitted with short tails, which is correct for the Mosquito. The nacelles are moulded as two halves, front to back and the detail matches scale plans, both shrouded and five-stack exhausts are included and the fire extinguisher panel is actually moulded in relief, just like the real thing. Propellers supplied are both narrow and 'paddle' blade types, but sand off the yellow tip markings from them before use, as there was no raised line at this point on the real thing! The spinners have separate backplates and are the correct diameter and profile. The last details include the A.I. 'bow and arrow' antenna on the nose and the two dipoles above and below the wing tips. These latter items are straight rods that have to be installed through holes drilled in the wing and the kit does not include the swept-back antenna on the upper surface of the starboard wing, so you will need to add this if making an NF Mk II.

The kit comes with these decal options:
• FB Mk VI, MM417, EG•T, No.487 Squadron
• FB Mk VI, RS625, NE•D, No.143 Squadron, Banff Strike Wing
• NF Mk II, W4087, RS•B, No.157 Squadron

Note that some sources state that W4087 does not have the reinforcing strip along the starboard side of the rear fuselage. The decals include airframe stencils, seat belts and an overlay for the instrument panel. They are well printed, with good colour and registration and although the carrier film is clear and limited, it is thick, but that is often the case with Japanese kits.

Verdict

It will probably come as no surprise to know that this is the choice for the fighter-bomber and night-fighter Mosquito in this scale. The level of detail coupled with the finesse of moulding and thus ease of assembly, make it the only choice for modellers working in this scale and I doubt it will be surpassed for many years to come.

Tamiya

NF Mk XIII/XVII (#60765)

This kit was based on the FB Mk VI and was released by Tamiya in 2001.

As the main kit is identical to the FB Mk VI accessed earlier, we will just look at

Tamiya 60765

the differences here. The bulk of the parts remain unchanged, all you do get is a new sprue containing new front fuselage halves that depict the Bullnose universal radome, the A.I. indicator, revised radio equipment and Gee unit for inside the cockpit plus some other cockpit parts that are actually the same as on the little sprue in the FB Mk VI kit, but are unique to a fighter, so have to be on this one too as the fighter-bombers sprue is not in this one. The only other revisions are the use of the dipoles above and below the wing tips and lack of things like the RPs under the wings, the rest remains unchanged. Tamiya do have you chop off the scoop under the tail, aft of the tailwheel but there is no Monica bulge to go here, although they are not always fitted.

The kit offers the following decal options:
• NF Mk XIII, DZ659 of the Fighter Interception Unit. Whilst the overall scheme is correct, this machine was later converted to an NF Mk XVII (ZQ•H) and period images show that the demarcation around the nose was low down, soft-edged and the upper radome region and oval access panel in the underside seem to be in different shades of grey to the Medium Sea Grey of the overall scheme
• NF Mk XVII, HK500, RA•I of No.410 Squadron.

The decal sheet is well printed with good colour and registration and it comes with all the markings plus a full set of stencils, seat belts and the overlay for the instrument panel.

Verdict

As with the FB Mk VI/NF Mk II kit, this is the choice for the later single-stage night-fighters, as it is so well detailed and produced that it is a joy to build. One can only hope Tamiya one day start making the two-stage variants.

1/48th Scale

Airfix

Mosquito NF Mk 30

This kit (#07111) was a revision of the FB Mk VI and was first released in 2003, when it was also issued as a 'Gift Set' (#97111) with paint, glue etc.

This kit combined the FB Mk VI with two new sprues, so all the comments on the FB Mk VI (see download version) also apply here. The new sprues are, oddly, moulded in a much lighter shade of grey than the remaining older parts, plus they offer engraved details, thus making them at odds with the fuselage etc. used from the older kit parts. The engraving itself is rather vague and 'soft' and the spar boxes on the wings this time are depicted as engraved lines for the front spar, whilst totally ignoring the rear spar, all of which is not very good. The new parts include the upper wing halves (remember the lower halves are from the old kit so still feature the raised front and rear box spars!), new two-stage engine nacelles, separate wing tips with the twin lights that will require cutting off the main wings to install, 50 Imp. Gal. drop tanks, the Bullnose radome and plain or slotted exhaust shrouds. The radome comes with the camera gun on the starboard side, plus the bulge in

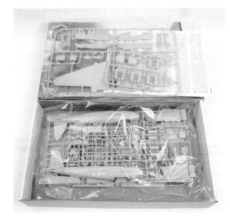

Airfix 07111

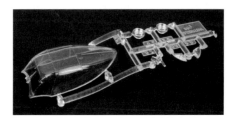

the access plate underneath, but sadly with the latter, because the radome is split vertically, there is a seam running right through the bulge that will make it hard to retain once you do any sanding.

The kit came with three decal options:
• **NT362**, HB•S, No.239 Sqn, 100 Group, RAF West Raynham, 1945. This machine is Dark Green and Medium Sea Grey over Night and being a 100 Group machine, it most likely had Monica tail-warning radar under the tail, which is not depicted in the kit.
• MM765 of the 416th Night Fighter Squadron, USAF 8th AF, Paris, 1944. This machine is Medium Sea Grey overall with Dark Green disruptive camouflage on the upper surfaces and red spinners.
• MB11, KT•D, 10th Squadron, 1st Wing, Belgian Air Force, Beauvechain, Belgium, 1952. This machine is also in Medium Sea Grey with Dark Green disruptive camouflage.

Verdict

To date this is still the only way to make a two-stage Merlin powered late-series night-fighter, without using resin conversions. The basis of the kit is now 35+ years old and the odd combination of new and old parts with raised or engraved detail makes this an oddball right from the start. You can probably cross-kit the new engine parts into the Tamiya kit, but there are better resin engines out there already, so there seems little point. Overall it is a sound kit, easy to build and reasonably priced even today, but it is just not really up to scratch as far as detail and quality is concerned for today's modeller, most likely.

Tamiya

FB Mk VI/NF Mk II (#61062)

This all-new tooling was released in 1998 and remains in the Tamiya catalogue to this day. It was also reissued in 2009 with their 10hp Tilly truck as a limited edition (#89786) and

as a special edition by the French importers T2M with French and Belgian markings in 2000 (#61062F).

The initial kit (#61062) comes in a medium grey-coloured plastic, whilst the special edition example (#89786) is moulded in black plastic, as it only depicts the NF Mk II. There are seven sprues of grey or black plastic, all featuring engraved panel lines etc., plus fixing as raised detail. The wings feature the front spar as a slightly raised area, whilst the rear spar is not shown at all; this is quite acceptable for both in this scale, and much more subtle than Airfix did with their kit. The elevators are metal skinned, whilst the rudder has a good fabric effect on it, but oddly Tamiya opted to not offer any of the control surfaces separate. The kit was designed to offer both fighter/fighter-bomber/night-fighter and bomber/PR versions, so the front end is separate, with a positive locating tab that is cleverly hidden within the wing root radiators. The breakdown of the kit also has to cope with a lot of variants, so the wing tips are separate, with both single and twin light options included (both with clear lens), five-spoke or plain wheel hubs, shrouded or

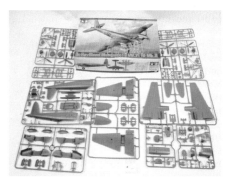

Tamiya 61062

exposed (five-stack) exhausts plus there are narrow and broad propellers. There are 500lb bombs and racks, plus 3in RPs that have the 25lb AP heads on them, which is a change from the usual 60lb HE versions. Overall detail in the kit is superb, with the machine-guns in the nose, so you can have the access cover removed, the racks and bombs in the bomb bay, with the fuel cells moulded in above them, the only thing you do not have is the forward bay with the cannon. Cockpit detail is very good, with moulded detail for all the instruments and separate 1154/1155 radio combination on the rear shelf. Tamiya

Tamiya 89786

opted to not mould the seat belts into each crew seat, instead they supply decals for these, which at least gives you the option of using aftermarket etched belts without the hassle of removing detail that is moulded in situ. The clear sprue contains a one-piece main canopy (with the frames that are only inside the glass depicted via decals, Tamiya being the first to do this), wing tip lenses, landing lights, gunsight and the glazed panel in the rear fuselage underside that only relates to the photo-reconnaissance versions and should be sanded smooth and painted over in this kit.

The two kits we have here offered the following decal options:

#61062
• FB Mk VI, MM417, EG•T, No.487 Squadron during the Amiens prison raid. This machine is Ocean Grey and Dark Green over Medium Sea Grey.
• FB Mk VI, RS625, NE•D of No.143 Squadron, Banff Strike Wing. This machine is listed as Dark Sea Grey over Sky, where it was more likely to be Extra Dark Sea Grey over Sky.
• NF Mk II, W4087, RS•B, No.157 Squadron, which is overall Night.

#89786
• NF Mk II, W4076, No.169 Squadron, 1944 in overall Night.
• NF Mk II, DD712, YP•R, No.239 Squadron, 1942, also in overall Night.
• F Mk II, DZ238, YP•H, No.23 Squadron, Malta, 1943. This machine is Ocean Grey and Dark Green over Night.

Verdict
Today, as it was back in 1998, this is THE choice for the NF Mk II and FB Mk VI in this scale. Sure, it can be improved and Tamiya have come a long way since then, so a Mosquito from them today would be different, but not a lot. It is therefore still the choice if you want to make either type in this scale, plus the best basis for any conversion of the fighter/fighter-bomber/night-fighter series.

Tamiya

NF Mk XIII/XVII (#61075)
Based on the FB Mk VI/NF Mk II kit, this one was released in 2000 and remains in the Tamiya catalogue to this day.

Inside the box you will find eight medium grey-coloured sprues, of which six are from the previous NF Mk II/FB Mk VI kit, which we have already covered. The two new sprues include revised a instrument panel and radar equipment, plus cockpit floor and bulkheads and the bomb/cannon bay doors, cannon port trough and a new Bullnose radome. All of these parts slot in to replace the existing ones and the radar detail is very good and nicely matches period photographs of this region in the Mk XIII or XVII. The only things to note are that DZ659 had the lower demarcation on the radome projecting forward around the access panel underneath, it was not a straight vertical demarcation of the nose cone as a whole, while both options are shown with a trailing aerial tube under the fuselage (#H3), when that should be a dipole on the centreline. The choice of HK415 for a late version of the Mk XIII may well be

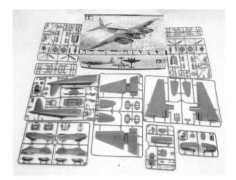

Tamiya 61075

contentious, as the change between the earlier thimble radome is claimed to have happened after HK499, but until we have seen a period image of HK415, we can't comment on the validity of this machine with a universal (Bullnose) radome?

The kit has the following two decal options:
• NF Mk XVII, DZ659, ZQ•H of the Fighter Interception Unit in Medium Sea Grey and Dark Green over Night.
• NF Mk XIII, HK415, KP•R, No.409 Squadron in Medium Sea Grey overall with Dark Green disruptive camouflage on the upper surfaces.

Verdict
As with the NF Mk II/FB Mk VI, this is THE choice for these versions in this scale. The level of detail combined with the ease with which this kit can be built makes them ideal for any skill level.

1/32nd Scale

Tamiya

FB Mk VI
There were rumours of this kit back in 2013, as representatives of Tamiya had been seen around the world measuring preserved examples, but the kit did not surface until 2015.

This is actually a very simple kit to assess, as it is very good. Dimensionally in this scale the FB Mk VI would have a 515.94mm (54ft 2in) span, would be 389.69mm (40ft 11in) long and have a height of 145.31mm (15ft 3in). It is difficult to measure the kit without having it built, but taking into account the various components all the dimensions are within 1-2mm, so that is well within acceptable levels for both shrinkage associated with injection moulding, the errors inherent in converting Imperial into Metric and my inadequacy in measuring! With the overall shapes and lengths all OK, the level of detail inside and out is superb, and it would seem in collecting data Tamiya has access to the example then being rebuilt to airworthiness in New Zealand. A couple of things therefore have to be understood, Tamiya correctly point out that some aspects of the restored aircraft differ from that of genuine wartime examples and, secondly, the restored one is a Canadian-built FB Mk 26, so it is not 100% representative of a British-built FB Mk VI and they have therefore probably made 'adjustments' in regard to certain details to try and correct this. The fact that this kit only offers single

wing tip lights and has only a 500lb bomb option under the wing, would indicate that it depicts the Series II machines, even the RAAF example is in the A52-500 to 537 range, so was a British-built FB Mk VI supplied to Australia to supplement their limited number of locally-built FB Mk 40s. Modifying back to Series I would not just be down to adding the second tip light and not putting a bomb under the wings, as the fairing around the carrier for the 250lb was different from that of the 500lb. You have both shrouded and exposed five-stack exhausts, along with narrow and 'paddle' blade propellers in the kit, although the wheel hubs only depict the later solid version, whilst most Series I machines usually had the older five-spoke hubs on the port side of each wheel. In the cockpit it is all good stuff, although some may argue that the RAAF option should have their AT5/AR8 installation, but I have not found confirmation if the British-supplied machines were fully kitted out with British radio equipment, or if these were only installed locally on arrival in Australia, so you choose? Detail overall though is excellent, some purists may say the Gee screen decal (#137) should just have the guide lines on it, as the 'zig-zag' would only be on the screen once it was actually working. The navigator's seat back armour plate is also something that did not remain the same

Tamiya 60326

shape throughout all variants and production, plus the layout of the switches etc. in this region is more akin to the FB Mk 26. Some of the detail moulded into the cockpit sidewalls is a little shallow, but again, this is only to be expected without making every part separate. The fuselage split at the front transit joint does hint that Tamiya may be considering a bomber version, along with a night-fighter in the near future. The rear fuselage region is good, the only thing to note is that the layout of lights, camera bays and/or access hatches on the underside of the Mosquito is a complex subject, not helped by the fact the manuals don't cover this region within the access and maintenance panels diagrams for most variants, so being pedantic about what light goes where, is pretty pointless. The tail region is good, with all detail accurate, although there are three round access panels on the tailplane underside (for the elevator hinges), when most diagrams in the manual of the

FB Mk VI show only two. The single tail light is moulded as a clear part, which is nice, but again some variants had a twin-light unit back here. The wings are also very good, you could get all picky and point out that the reinforcing plates inboard and outboard of the nacelle should have recessed screw-heads on all sides, so the raised 'rivets' on the front and back are not really accurate. On the upper surface the filler access panels are all slightly raised, when in fact engraved outlines would have been better as period images of the Mosquito under construction show these were flush with the upper skin surface. I also have to say at this point that I personally am not 100% convinced by the raised spar caps on the rear of the Mosquito wing, because again period images in detail of this region when the type was being built don't show a marked 'raised' area corresponding to this spar cap? The front one is there, but even that is only really visible as a very slight change in the contour of the upper skin, which a thicker layer of paint would suffice to represent, even in 1/32nd. I am sure the 'accuracy police' are probably up in arms at this point, and I admit it is my own view on the subject, but until I ever get the chance to get up on top of the wing of a Mossie and inspect it at close hand, my vote is for a less pronounced depiction of these two regions. The individual engines are extremely good but even with Tamiya's superb moulded detail you could probably spend months adding more and more detail to them. The big 'fault' with them those is that Tamiya obviously did not receive, or did not seek, copyright agreement to use the Rolls-Royce logo, so these are not cast into the rocker covers of each engine; never fear, BarracudaCast offer these as resin replacement parts (#BR32267). The cowlings (these were included in grey or clear plastic in the first European release of this kit) are very nice, with all the right lumps and bumps for the FB Mk VI. The lower cowls come in either standard of tropical versions, the latter with the longer carburettor intake and the lip projecting forward on which the ice guard is mounted. With full detail for the machine-gun (with gun camera), cannon and aft bomb bays you once again have everything in the box for a nice reproduction of these areas, but there is still scope to add even more detail should you desire. I really like the manner in which Tamiya offer the cannon/bomb bay doors in either closed, cannon bay only open or both bays open, as that should satisfy everyone. The only thing missing from the ventral doors is the cannon tool kit that sat in a pouch mounted on one side, but who is ever going to know that unless you are a real detail nut like me, and how would Tamiya have ever depicted it, so it is of no real concern. There are 50 gallon drop tanks included in the kit, the only issue here would be the RAAF option, as most, if not all, RAAF Mossies seem to have tanks with a prominent seam around the middle and the filler cap offset to port. I have no images of A52-518 to hand, so can't be 100% sure if it had these (locally-produced?) tanks fitted, but it does seem likely. Only 500lb bombs are included in the kit, as already stated, so it lacks 3in R.Ps, which we are sure will be added in a future release of the FB Mk VI in anti-shipping strike form,

and you also don't have 100 or 200 Imp. Gal. drop tanks either, but again hopefully these will be added in future incarnations and revisions of this kit.

In the box you get the following decal options:
• LR303, SM•A, NO.305 (Polish) Squadron
• HX922, EG•F, No.487 Squadron during Operation Jericho
• A52-518, NA•Y, No.1 Squadron, RAAF.

The decals are well printed with good colour and registration and you get a comprehensive set of stencils as well, not just for the airframe, but for the ordnance etc. Tamiya decals can be a little thick, but they always perform well, so they should not cause any problems for the majority of modellers.

The kit includes a booklet with a short history in Japanese, some nice drawings showing the major changes in the airframe and a series of colour photographs of the airworthy example in the USA. The kit is obviously heavily based on this example, which is a superb restoration, but as Tamiya point out, "some colours and details may differ from wartime aircraft", so check your references (I for one am not convinced by the numerous 'yellow dots' for armour plate markings in the cockpit region).

Verdict

This is a very comprehensive kit indeed and I think I can safely say that I doubt this kit will be surpassed for a considerable time, if ever. The UK RRP at the time of writing had risen to £199.99, so this is a very expensive kit, however the 'worth' of any product is purely personal, so I won't pass any comment about its potential value because that is something each modeller must decide for themselves. Certainly even for a quick builder, this would be a month or two's work, while anyone taking their time and really going to town with detail, could take as much as a year to complete it. It is THE choice for the fighter-bomber in this scale, forget converting the old Revell bomber, and it is of the highest quality so that anyone can build it, and I do mean anyone.

1/24th Scale

Airfix

NF Mk II/FB Mk VI

This kit was first announced in 2008 as #A20002, but it was actually released in 2009 as #A25001, the increase of fives series being as a result of the increase in price (which was first mentioned back in 2008 as being "around £80", but on release was £129.99.). This kit was reissued with revised decal options and only as an FB Mk VI (#A25001A) in late 2015, now costing £169.99.

The kit is massive, with the FB Mk VI scaling out at 687.92mm span, 519.58mm length and 193.75mm high in this scale. As with the Tamiya kit, this one is packed with details, so I won't go through them stage-by-stage, or we could be here all day, instead I will approach it overall, as I just did with the Tamiya example. I will also concentrate on the current release (#A25001A) and only point out any differences that exist between it and the original release (#A25001). Span is a tad over, but only by 2mm, so nothing

drastic, while the length works within the same sort of deficiency, so it would seem that is all down to the shrinkage rates. Comparison with the Tamiya kit is inevitable, so you can say this larger scale kit is not as complex/comprehensive as the smaller one, but it does still have a full interior, full machine-gun, cannon and bomb bays, plus both engines, so all it lacks is the sheer number of parts. The cockpit interior is pretty good, but no seat belts of any kind either in decal or etched (Tamiya have these as etched parts) are included, so you have to buy these elsewhere as their omission is very obvious in this scale. The back armour for the navigator does not have the upper extension seen on the Tamiya kit, which is right for some options, and it lacks the control levers on the port edge, which again is correct for some configurations (confusing, isn't it?). The multi-part rudder pedals are nice, while the use of clear plastic for the instrument dial 'glass' makes sense, especially with the inclusion of decals for each individual dial in the most recent release. I have to say that adding these decals on TOP of the clear parts, as shown in the painting and decalling guide at the very end of the instructions, seems a bit counterproductive to me? In the original release, Airfix did include different instrument panels for the NF Mk II and FB Mk VI versions, but these are ignored in the most recent incarnation even though the parts are all still on the sprues (yes, you can make an NF Mk II from the A25001A if you can source decals elsewhere). There is next to no detail moulded inside each cockpit half, which would be fine, but none of it is included separately either, plus there are very prominent ejector pin marks to deal with. What are included for the sidewalls are the main items such as the compass, throttle box and electrical distribution panel, along with all their associated wiring or linkage rods. Omissions in the fuselage include the very obvious lack of the access panel for the ground power socket on the port fuselage side, just aft of the wing trailing edge, which Airfix only depict as a decal that is not really on in this big scale, and a complete lack of the downward identification lamps under the rear fuselage; the instructions clearly show them on each decal option diagram, but there are not even engraved circles moulded into the actual kit parts that you could paint . The formation light at the very back of the fuselage, in the tail cone, is a separate clear part and if you look on the sprues you will find there is both the single- and twin-light unit, although only the latter is used/mentioned in #A25001A.

Airfix opted to go with a 'real' approach to creating the wings, as the lower half is moulded as one piece, with the interior of the rear bomb bay moulded into it (in reality, the wing was one-piece and the bomb bay region was built in situ once the wing and fuselage were mated). The inboard radiators have moulded detail that is OK, but with no etched parts in the kit, it lacks the finesse of this region seen in the Tamiya example. The wing tips are separate and although only the single light units are used here, the sprues still contain the twin-light tips needed for the NF Mk II etc. Obviously later versions were in mind when the kit was tooled because the outline for the landing light in the starboard wing can be seen inside the wing itself and the lens and interior parts are on the sprues, although ignored in the instructions. All control surfaces are separate but I have to say I personally think the raised rivet detail is overdone even in this large scale, so sand it all down a bit. The underside of the tailplanes have a single access panel for the hinge, which is correct if you look under the tail of the example on display in Australia, but the manual for the FB Mk VI shows two such panels under each tailplane? The fairing and linkage arm for each trim tab on the elevators is completely lacking, being almost flat as moulded. The rudder has nicely restrained fabric effect and the access panels etc., all of which match the manual diagrams and the example at Salisbury Hall. Once both nacelles are ready they can be joined to the wings and here they trap the flaps in place. These are separate assemblies, but because they are moulded with a flat connecting bar, they can't be positioned; the Tamiya approach here is thus infinitely better.

Each engine is included and is very nicely done, Airfix even did the 'Rolls-Royce' logos on the rocker covers. Of course there is huge potential to add more detail to the engine and engine bay regions, as the scale allows this, but from the box both areas are very well done. The main undercarriage (and tailwheel) use rubber tyres, but this is no problem as a number of aftermarket resin ones are out there to replace them if you don't like them. The main undercarriage units include the oil tank on the top, complete with pipework and drain cock (and stencil) and it all fits to the bulkhead that goes into the nacelle half and then the engine goes on in front. Details in the nacelle seems a little generic, as it's just regular boxed ribs, but that may be right, as I have not had my head in a Mossie wheel well for many a year! The undercarriage doors are the correct shape, but lack any real interior detail at all, which is not on in this scale (Tamiya have exterior and interior halves as separate parts), but they do have separate hinges. The cannon and bomb bay doors can be posed open and each has separate hinges and hydraulic rams, but the ejector chutes are moulded into the inside of the door, which makes them a little thick. The actual engine nacelles are spoilt in my eye by the over-scale fasteners all over them; yes, the type does have them, but in this scale they would be nowhere near that thick and prominent. The fire extinguisher panel (actually an 'Inconel heat resisting insert') on the side of the nacelle is shown via an engraved line and raised rivets, all of which are just wrong for depicting this region because the panel is, as stated, an 'insert' and is thus lower than the surrounding panel; cut it out and back the panel from the inside with plasticard for a more accurate look. Talking of the interior of the engines cowls, guess what, yes, no interior details at all! Finally I am not convinced by the size, location and number of intake and outlet scoops on the engine access panels, plus the jacking point access panel just below the leading edge of the wing is shown as a raised panel, but it was flush with the surrounding skin and is better thus depicted as an engraved outline.

The ventral gun/bomb bays have more detail than the Tamiya example with the bomb carrier frames and racks themselves being a lot better, while oddly the lack of etched metal means the bombs don't have the arming propellers separate but I actually think the moulded parts are more like the real thing. The ammo feeds for the 20mm cannon are lovely and are complete with actual shells moulded in feed tracks, plus each cannon barrel has the tip separate, so they could be moulded hollowed out. The rear bay can have the overload fuel tank added, or you can go with the standard tanks and two 500lb bombs with their associated racks. The nose armament contains all the guns, ammunition boxes and feeds and you get the G.45 gun camera but oddly (like Tamiya) the ammo chutes here don't seem to be moulded with any bullets inside them. You get the option of 500lb bombs and racks, 3in R.P.s with 25lb SAP heads or 50 Imp. Gal. drop tanks. As with the Tamiya kit, in the

Airfix A25001

original release the RAAF option should have tanks with the filler offset to port on top and a pronounced raised seam around them, none of which the kit parts depict. The rockets and rails are separate parts, but you will need to add the 'pig tails' in this scale. You get both 'saxophone' and five-stack exhausts, with all the latter pipes moulded separately and the former having the outlets separate so they can be hollow; the first two options use the exposed stacks, with only the post-war FB Mk VI using the 'saxophone' ones under shrouds (in the original release the first three options used the separate stacks, whilst the fourth option had the shrouded ones).

Final details include the propellers, which come with either narrow or 'paddle' blades. Each blade is separate to the hub, but what is really odd is that Airfix have you build and add the propeller boss early on in construction, once the engines were added to the nacelles. As a result the front plate in the nacelle is there, but there is no backplate to the actual spinner (this is inside the circumference of the spinner), which would make keeping them on rather difficult and may explain why that aspect of assembly is completely omitted in the instructions; stage 219 fits the blades, the next 15 stages deal with the interior, then the image returns to adding the wire guards to the undercarriage and low and behold, the spinners are on! Those 15 stages just mentioned include adding the 1154/1155 radio combination and these are nice mouldings

with a decal for the scale on the receiver; my comment about the radio fit in RAAF examples made in the Tamiya kit could well apply here also if you have the original kit with the option for A52-518 in it. The gunsight looks to depict the Mk IIIN and it has dimmer switch but lacks the hood over the clear lens that was associated with daylight operations. The choice of gunsight is odd, as most period images show the FB Mk VI with the Barr & Stroud GM2, which is the round one with the setting rings around the body and well-known in things like the Hurricane and Spitfire? The crew access door is separate and you get an access ladder, while the interior framework of the canopy is a single piece (which looks a bit heavy in comparison with Tamiya's treatment of this same area) and it has a separate signal pistol to lock into the socket, but there is no IFF unit, nor DF loop, so check your references because not all variants had them. The very last items to add are the canopy itself with the starboard side panel separate so Airfix can also depict the flat or bulged version, the windscreen wiper (yes, it is a separate part) and the aerial mast. The original release also had the A.I. 'bow and arrow' antenna in the nose, the swept-back dipoles on the starboard wing and the straight dipoles above and below each wing tip; although these are ignored in the latest release the parts are still on the sprues.

The original release (#A25001) offered the following decal options:
- FB Mk VI, HX922, EG•F, No.487 Squadron, 2nd TAF, RAF Hunsdon during Operation Jericho on the 18th February 1944
- FB Mk VI, HR405, NE•A, No.143 Squadron, Banff Strike Wing, Coastal Command, 1945
- FB Mk VI, A52-518, NA•Y, 'Bondi Blonde', No.1 Squadron, RAAF, Kingaroy QLD, Morotai and Labuan, 1945
- NF Mk II, W4087, RS•B, No.157 Squadron, RAF Castle Camps, December 1941

The revised reissue (#A25001A) offers the following decal options:
- FB Mk VI, RS823, VV-A flown by Fg Off W. Moffatt DFC and Flt Lt C. Hardy, No.235 Squadron, Banff Strike Wing, 4th May 1945
- FB Mk VI, RF838, EO•A, No.404 Squadron, Banff, April-May 1945
- FB Mk VI, RS679, No.4 Squadron, RAF Celle, Germany, September 1949.

Verdict
Huummm, an odd one to call, because its greatest strength is that it is a 1/24th scale Mosquito in mainstream injected plastic, and rumours/hopes of this have existed for decades. The kit overall is good and can form the basis of an impressive model, all I would say is that in many areas it is let down by the lack of, or poor depiction of, detail. This is certainly caused by the resources to spend on tooling and research, which were obviously restricted at times and this results in a kit that has to 'make do' with the depiction of some details, and omit others altogether (e.g. no seat belts in a kit this scale, shame on you Airfix). Regardless of my comments though, if you only ever make one 1/24th aircraft kit, make it this one, I don't think you will be disappointed.

Chapter 6: **Building a Selection**

All photos
© the authors 2017

Having looked at what kits are and have been available of the fighter Mosquitos in all scales, we thought it would be a good idea to build those that we felt were representative of all the manufacturers in 1/72nd, 1/48th and 1/32nd.

Hasegawa 1/72nd
FB Mk XVIII

by Libor Jekl

This kit is another variation of the Hasegawa tooling, it appeared fairly recently and uses the majority of components from previous releases. Anyway, the 'limited kit' label means there is something special about it and indeed the parts specific to the Mk XVIII, such as the bottom nose decking with cannon fairing, weapon bay doors, drop tanks and the nose tip are cast in grey-coloured resin, while the Molins 6-pdr (57mm) gun barrel is provided as a beautiful brass-turned item. Except for a set of fishtail exhaust stacks there are no changes to the sprue layout in comparison with the NF Mk II or FB Mk VI kits, which is expected because the Mk XVIII airframes were based on the latter version. The kit includes the complete

armament sprues with rocket projectiles and bombs, which is odd as the Mk XVIII could not carry them, but they will be a welcome addition in the spares box. In total four decal options are provided although only two are fully depicted in the instructions; these are NT225 'O' of No.248 Squadron, June 1944 and PZ468 QM•D operated in April 1945 by No.254 Squadron. Both options were camouflaged in the standard scheme of overall Medium Sea Grey with a Dark Green disruptive pattern on the upper surfaces. However, markings of the latter plane may seem a little suspicious as the 'Tse-Tse' serving with No.254 Squadron should have the squadron codes in black instead of red as supplied, and the roundel on the upper wing was changed to Type C in January 1945, so I doubt if the machine still had the Type B applied in April 1945 as depicted in the instructions. It is also probable that the spinners were Sky rather than Medium Sea Grey. There are also separate fuselage code letters 'Y' and 'E' provided along with the serial numbers, although no further information is provided. My references however state the serial number NT224 was 'E1' and not 'E', while the HR138 serial I could not even locate amongst the seventeen Mk XVIII airframes (the 'Y' being not mentioned in

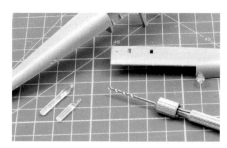

The missing lamps under the rear fuselage were reproduced with lengths of clear sprue glued into drilled holes

The rather basic cockpit interior was livened up with some elements from the Eduard Zoom fret for the Tamiya FB Mk VI kit

The etched detail from the Eduard set installed into the two nose halves

Here you can see the completed cockpit elements, as well as the 'dust catcher' built into the rear fuselage

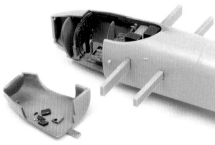

You can close up the rear fuselage halves with one nose half, then attach the other

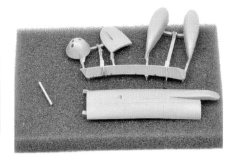

The resin and brass additional parts look gorgeous, I say 'look'!

there either), so I'm not sure what Hasegawa's intentions were with this part of the decal sheet.

At first I dealt with the missing signal lamps in the rear fuselage underside, which I drilled out and glazed with a piece of stretched clear sprue. Due to the lack of detail in the cockpit I used parts from the Zoom set by Eduard (#SS137) designed for Tamiya's FB Mk VI kit, but the main items such as the instrument panel, seat belts and control boxes are suitable for the Hasegawa kit as well. A few other items such as the throttle control box and similar were scratchbuilt from scraps of plastic and copper wire while other tiny items were sourced from an old etched fret. These parts together with the floor, seats and control stick were primed, airbrushed Akan Aircraft Grey/Green acrylic and glued to the cockpit bulkhead and/or the respective nose halves. In the rear fuselage I also cemented my own attempt at a 'dust catcher', as dust particles are unavoidable during any

kit build and especially annoying on kits with a closed canopy. The catcher was assembled from a piece of fine sponge and Tamiya tape, which was glued to the sponge with the adhesive side up. My idea was that the sponge should absorb fine dust particles, while the remaining larger particles should get stuck on the adhesive portion of the tape and thus the amount of particles sticking to the inside of the canopy would be kept to a minimum. Then I glued the fuselage nose halves, having attached

The painted cockpit interior elements

The resin inserts don't even manage to fit where they touch

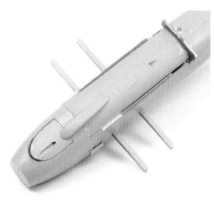

Lots of plasticard for the rear element and a load of cyanoacrylate for the front nose insert is the only way to deal with things

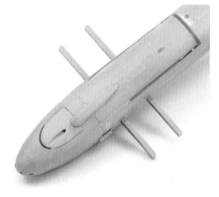

Much sanding later

Primer reveals just how much engraved detail has been lost

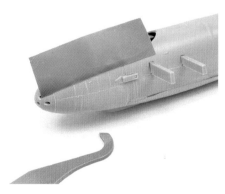

Out with the scribing tool and electrician's tape to rescribe all the panel lines

The big holes for mounting the ice guard on each nacelle are filled with sprue, as the guard should fit directly onto the front edge of the carburettor intakes themselves

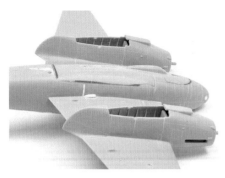

The missing fuel pump bulges are added to each side of the fuselage from profiled bits of resin, whilst the big tabs for the undercarriage doors are filled with plasticard because they just look so wrong on the completed model

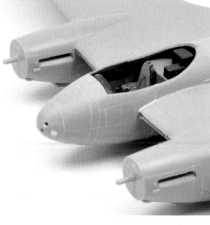

The outer two machine-gun ports in the nose need to be blanked off

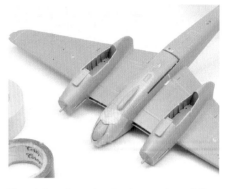

The reinforced panel under the nose is carefully masked with electrician's tape and standard masking tape, then layers of Mr Surfacer are applied to build up the area

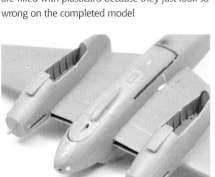

The completed raised area under the nose is subtle, but will show through the final paint

With the canopy on, masked and sprayed Interior Grey/Green, the model is primed with Mr Surfacer 1000 to highlight any problem areas

The black of the invasion stripes go on first then the demarcation is done for the white regions with fine masking tape, filled with wider versions

the starboard one first and once the fit of all parts looked good I closed up the fuselage. Now I turned my attention to the resin bits, which looked really nice, being cast without bubbles or other visible defects. Unfortunately, after sanding them off their casting blocks and trial assembly with the fuselage openings their glorious nature quickly faded. The fit was really awful with about 3mm gaps on the weapon bay decking, while the front gun cover was too small and could fall through the fuselage opening. The same was the case with the solid nose tip, which lacked about 1.5mm in diameter; obviously this was caused by excessive shrinkage of the resin material and hopefully this was just my bad luck having bought a defective example. Anyway, the situation still could be saved with a load of plastic strips and wedges that filled the gaps and plenty of cyanoacrylate. After a couple of sanding sessions the joints looked

acceptable, so I gave the affected areas a 'check' layer of Mr Surfacer 1000 and rescribed the panel lines. While having the scriber tool to hand I also added new panel lines on the sides of the cockpit and the nose, which should reproduce the armour and deflector panels added to the Mk XVIII airframe.

I continued with the wing and engine nacelles, which were assembled in the same fashion as on my previous Hasegawa kits. Underneath the wing I installed the missing fuel pump blisters and the weapon bay sides received new reinforcing strips cut from thin plastic sheet, as they had been damaged during the previous surgery with the bay doors. On the nose I bordered the oval-shaped deflector panel with thicker electrician's tape and sprayed inside several layers of Mr Surfacer 1000 to build up a subtly raised effect for this reinforcement feature. The construction was then easily finished without any surprises and

The white can now be applied, using the underlying black to create shadow-shading

The nose region is painted with Ocean Grey (in this case FS36118)

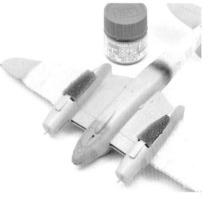

Medium Sea Grey is applied overall, post-shaded with a dark mix of the same

The Dark Green camouflage is applied freehand, with a soft demarcation

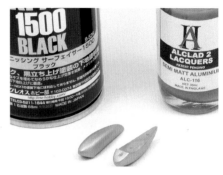

Mr Color Super Clear III is used to seal everything in prior to decaling

The decals behaved well on the whole, although those around the aileron mechanism bulges did get damaged whilst being positioned

The drop tanks were primed with black, then sprayed with semi-matt aluminium

once the canopy had been masked off, the kit received an overall layer of Mr Surfacer 1000 primer.

I selected NT225 for my build and this wore full invasion stripes, so these were masked off first and airbrushed on using H11 White and H12 Black. The black colour was applied first as this then allowed control over the shading and weathering effects of the white areas and some of the masking strips were intentionally cut unevenly, as can be seen in period photographs of NT225. The modified 'Tse-Tse' nose along with the cannon fairing was often oversprayed with a colour that looked a bit darker than the overall Medium Sea Grey, so I followed the instructions and went for Ocean Grey (H305). I continued with Medium Sea Grey (H306) and Dark Green (H72), which had been airbrushed freehand with softer transitions except on top of the nacelles where the dividing line followed the cowling panel line. A couple of thin layers of GX100 Super Clear III sealed the job and I could go ahead with decaling.

The kit's decals were of the usual Hasegawa standard, being a bit thick, but they responded well to the Gunze-Sangyo Mr Mark Setter and Softer and their final appearance was more than satisfying, even the tiny stencils. Only the wing roundel did not conform well over the aileron control mechanism blisters and I managed to damage it slightly, so some touch-up painting was needed to blend any damage in.

Next I dealt with the drop tanks, which were a regular instalment on the 'Tse-Tse' as the internal fuselage fuel tank volume was decreased due to the cannon mounting. The instructions suggested you paint them Medium Sea Grey, but they seem to be

a bit brighter on the period photos. I therefore went for semi-matte Aluminium from the Aclad II range airbrushed over Mr. Finishing Surfacer 1500 (Black) primer coat. I continued by scratchbuilding the wire guards along with other enhancements for the landing gear as described in the NF Mk II build that you can download off the Valiant Wings website and eventually installed each unit in the nacelles. The cannon barrel was primed with Mr Surfacer

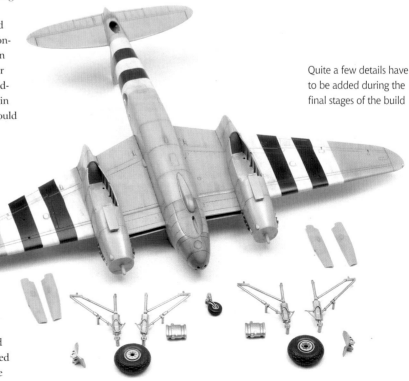

Quite a few details have to be added during the final stages of the build

units were snapped on via their poly caps and the remaining bits or tiny scratchbuilt items were added in line with my previous builds.

Verdict

Considering this is the only option for a 1/72nd scale 'Tse-Tse' Mosquito, leaving out the old Airfix kit, this isn't a bad choice, although a bit pricey. However, the resin parts seemed to be a real problem, although this could be just a problem of poor quality control in my example. While the Hasegawa Mosquito is still a pretty sound kit, it suffers from tricky fit of the individual sub-assemblies and lacks the detail in the most visible areas such as the cockpit and landing gear. Therefore I would recommend the kit to more skilled modellers, wanting to spend some extra time on this unique Mosquito version. Additionally, I would point out how this kit now shows its age; what was one of the class toppers almost 20 years ago, does not seem to be enough nowadays, plus the high prices of these kits move them into the collectors' market. More recent 1/72nd kits are miles ahead as far as the level of detail and construction features are concerned owing mainly to CAD/CAM technology, so let's hope a brand new tooling of this variant will arrive in near future - you listening, Airfix?

and painted in a light grey colour with a black muzzle, which was further polished with gunmetal pigment. It was then attached to a pre-drilled opening in the nose cover and its slightly sloped angle was approximately transferred from the scale drawing. The pair of nose machine guns was replaced with Quickboost resin items, the propeller

Tamiya 1/72nd

FB Mk VI converted to post-war Czechoslovakian B-36

by Libor Jekl

Similar to their B Mk IV/PR Mk IV kit that I built in the first volume of our coverage of the Mosquito, this kit covers more than one version. Therefore the kit includes the standard fighter-bomber variant with the option of building the anti-shipping attack variant armed with rocket projectiles, as well as the night-fighter NF Mk II. Compared to the B Mk IV/PR Mk IV there are two specific sprues (D and E) featuring the different parts, the former contains the separate fuselage front halves, nose tip with armament, gun covers, radar antennae plus other smaller parts, the second one provides the specific 'fighter' style canopy that is again moulded with a separate starboard side blister. Not surprisingly, all is moulded in Tamiya's usual excellent quality. You may consider replacing some

of the finest plastic parts such as the tiny radar antennae or adding the missing seat belts for etched, but I believe the majority of modellers will be happy with the kit as it is supplied in the box. In total, the kit provides three camouflage schemes: MM417, EG•T, of No.487 Squadron wearing the Day Fighter Scheme consisting of Dark Green, Ocean Grey and Medium Sea Grey; RS625, NE•D, from No.143 Squadron in the Special Coastal Duties scheme of Extra Dark Sea Grey and Sky; while W4087, RS•B is an all-black machine from No.157 Squadron.

One of the post-war operators of the Mosquito was by the re-established Czechoslovak Air Force, which received during 1946/47 a total of 24 FB Mk VIs supplied as settlement of the reciprocal military agreement signed between Great Britain and the exiled Czechoslovak government in 1940. Designated the B-36 in line with the then valid military coding system they served until 1953 until replacement with jet-propelled aircraft of Soviet origin took over.

I commenced work by filling the slot for the R.1155

The radio set used in these machines was of German origin, so one was scratchbuilt

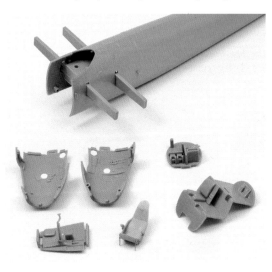

The cockpit as supplied is better detailed than the Hasegawa example, so little was added. The white discs are plasticard cut to fill the ejector pin marks

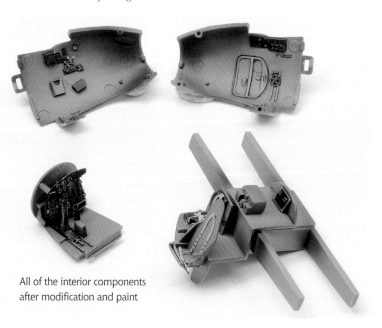

All of the interior components after modification and paint

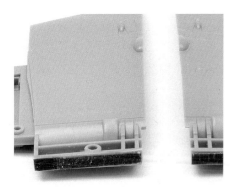

The radiator matrices as moulded are a little heavy, so they were replaced with etched versions

The clear landing lights are backed with chrome self-adhesive foil

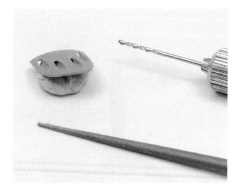

The cannon ports were drilled out, so that new barrels made from metal tubing could be added

The camera port and both inboard machine-gun ports in the nose were blanked off

moulded on the rear pilot's bulkhead with a piece of plastic strip, since the Czechoslovak machines received after major overhauls in 1949-50 LR 16ZY wireless sets of German (captured) origin. With the circles punched from thin plastic sheet I also addressed the ejector pin marks apparent on the cockpit sides and sprayed the interior with Aircraft Grey/Green from the Akan acrylics range (#72007). For the cockpit I used Eduard's Zoom set (#SS137), which also offered the seat belts that replaced the not very convincing decal items, the instrument panel and a couple of control boxes on the sidewalls. The new radio set was scratchbuilt from sheet plastic, painted dark grey and glued on the rear shelf. The front fuselage sides could then be glued together and mated with the rear fuselage that had been assembled earlier. The only area that needed some attention was the vertical joint line separating the front cockpit section, which was quickly filled with thin cyanoacrylate and sanded smooth. The signal lights engraved on the rear fuselage underside were drilled out, filled with pieces of clear stretched sprue and sanded flush with the surface before finally being polished.

The other prominent modification the Czechoslovak B-36 underwent during overhaul was the replacement of the armament with German examples due to lack of ammunition and spare parts for the British weapons. The four Hispano 20mm cannon were replaced with the MG151 of the same calibre and the quartet of Browning machine-guns in the nose was exchanged for two 13mm MG131s, while under the outer wing panels ETC 71A1 racks could be carried. The MG151 differed in comparison to the British gun in length and construction and this shifted the position of the spent ammunition chutes forward a bit. Due to a lack of detailed photographic material I based my work here on an armament scheme reprinted in the D.H. Mosquito monograph (No.7) issued by Jakab Publishing and the position of the individual chutes was appropriately estimated, while their configuration was taken from similar MG151 installations used on wartime German aircraft. The existing apertures on part D4 were therefore filled with piece of plastic and new ones cut using fine drill bits, scalpel blades and micro files. While working there I also improved the look of the protruding

The use of German 20mm cannon meant that the ejector ports were revised, so here the kit ones are filled with plastic off-cuts

The downward identification lamps along with the new access door on the centreline were all added

The larger ejector ports were added ahead of the now blanked-off original ones

The lower sections of the inboard radiator housings can be added once the wings are in place, thus ensuring they align properly

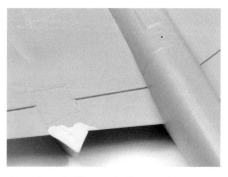

About the only filler required was on the upper rear element of each engine nacelle, just to level this area off

All the round lights were masked with tape punched to the correct size, the identification lamps having been first painted with the correct clear colour

The aft wing spar is missing in the kit, so this region is masked with electrician's tape (along with the region in front of the windscreen)

Mr Surfacer 1000 was used to fill the spar region, as it would result in a slightly raised area

The overall colour was RLM 02 lightened with white

barrels on the cannon decking, which incidentally did not correspond to the British weapon either. The barrels were removed with a scalpel, their openings deepened with a 1mm drill bit and new barrels were later cut from Albion Alloys brass tubing. The MG131s were mounted in the outer positions, so the inner apertures were filled along with the gun camera opening because this was not installed on these machines.

Now I paid attention to the wing, where I first sanded smooth the radiator raised faces and replaced them with finer etched items. The landing reflectors were backed with pieces of self-adhesive silver foil and the wing halves were then joined; the separately moulded radiator lower parts were added after the wing had been glued to the fuselage, so I could better control their fit. The only minor fit issue to worry about was the upper wing 'triangles' that

The canopy fit was so good, it could be secured with extra thin cement, with any gaps filled with Gator Glue

Post-shading was done with RLM 02 darkened slightly with matt black

Once glossed, the decals could be applied

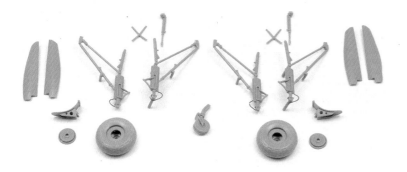

The undercarriage parts are quite comprehensive and accurate, all that needs to be added are the brake lines

matched the openings in the nacelles with some gaps and these were later filled with epoxy putty to avoid any future sink marks and then capped with a layer of Mr Surfacer 500. Joining the wing with the fuselage was easy thanks to the spars running through the fuselage, which ensured a strong joint and accurately set the position of the wing against the fuselage.

In the cockpit I installed the gunsight with its overly thick sight glass replaced with thin clear foil and then attached the canopy, which needs to be assembled out of two parts due to the separately moulded starboard blister. Thanks to its perfect fit I secured the canopy on the fuselage with a small amount of Mr Cement S and later filled the joint with Gator Grip white glue. This should prevent any fumes entering the cockpit area later during the spraying session, which may cause fogging of the clear part. The canopy was then masked off with the Eduard masks together with the fuselage identification lamps, which were previously brushed in corresponding transparent colours. The missing rear wing spar may be reproduced in the same way as the front one was moulded, which means slightly raised above the surface. The spar was defined with strips of electrical tape and oversprayed with several layers of Mr Surfacer 1000 and once the masks were removed, any sharp edges were removed with polishing clothes. In the

The completed undercarriage legs

same way I enhanced the front panel on the nose, which was partially sanded away when cleaning up the fuselage joint. The model was then primed with Mr Surfacer 1000 and I could go on with the painting.

The Czechoslovak Mosquitoes retained in service the original RAF camouflage, which was not retained after overhaul and they then received an overall light green-grey colour similar to RLM 02 (some sources state it could be light grey or light blue-grey). I used a mix of H70 RLM 02 toned with about 20% white H11 and the panel lines were then gently accentuated with post-shading using a darker mix of the base colour. The markings for the machine coded IY-7, serial number MM430 belonged in late 1949 to Air Regiment No.24 (at that time subordinate to Air Regiment No.25) based at Prague-Kbely were

The pale overall colour meant that MIG's Neutral Wash was the preferred choice for the panel lines

Scratches were applied with dark grey paint

The exposed five-stack exhausts came from Quickboost

MG131 barrels came from the Aires range

provided on the DK Decals sheet 'DH 98/B-36 Mosquito' (#72013). The decals worked fine, though a lot of patience was needed to assemble the fuselage code, as it consisted of two layers; the resulting white outline was rather thin so even the smallest upper decal displacement would mean the incorrect register of the code. At the end I gave some definition to the panel lines using an indistinctive wash that would match the light camouflage colour; eventually I used MIG Production's Neutral Wash. Any paint scratching and similar paint wear was applied using a fine brush and a dark grey mix of Vallejo acrylics.

Verdict

There is no reason to conclude otherwise than I did for the bomber variant of the Tamiya kit, this is again the best option in 1/72nd scale as far as the Mosquito fighter versions go. It beats its competitors due to the same attributes of excellent engineering, level of detail and ease of assembly. Despite its age (first released in 1999) this kit will remain a tough opponent for any potential new Mosquito kits, although I believe that a modern kit with a highly detailed interior including cockpit and weapon bay together with a cleverly designed canopy, a reasonable set of armament and well thought out assembly of this rather complex airframe would justify its place on the market. However, at the same time it is necessary to note that the Mosquito versions with the two-stage Merlin engines have still not been released, so let's hope the interest of any potential manufacturer of new Mosquito kits can be focused in that direction.

Airfix 1/48th

FB Mk VI converted to Chinese Nationalist FB Mk 26

by Steve A. Evans

The interior parts make a very neat looking cockpit. It's certainly a fine start if you want to do extra detailing yourself

There is no doubt that for such a famous aircraft, there is a severe lack of good kits of the Mosquito. It's a pity that Airfix seem to have ignored doing a new one as their old one is still amongst the best out there. The basics of this kit and half the contents of the box date back to 1980, which makes it about 37 years old! Shocking but true and even though it was updated in 2003 (I think) it's definitely showing its age. Luckily, when they decided to release this 'D-Day special', Airfix just jammed all of their

Yes, I know it's not a fighter on the lid but trust me, just about any version can be made from the contents of this box. Thank you Airfix

Mosquito sprues into the one box, making it very full indeed. Basically what this means is that you can do fighter, bomber and PR versions, either with single- or twin-stage Merlins, mixing and matching the bits to your heart's desire. This does leave you with some problems of course as the newer parts are of much better quality and do not necessarily fit the older parts too well. You have to understand also that due to the very nature of this chopped up kind of approach, you will need filler and probably plenty of it. Things like the fuselage centre joint are very nice but the wings and nacelles are far from it, with lots of gaps and mismatched bits to cope with.

Interior wise, it's a very pleasant surprise as it's actually got a lot of detail in there, most of it well moulded. It's a great place to start with your own detailing but careful painting is all you need for a pleasing result. You even get a couple of crew figures to put in there if you fancy but you will need some seat belts if you don't. One thing to mention is that the instructions that are in the box deal with the bomber and PR versions, so if you need the other fighter and night-fighter instructions then you can get copies from the Airfix website or from some of the online modelling forums.

So, what are the real problems with the kit? Firstly, re-

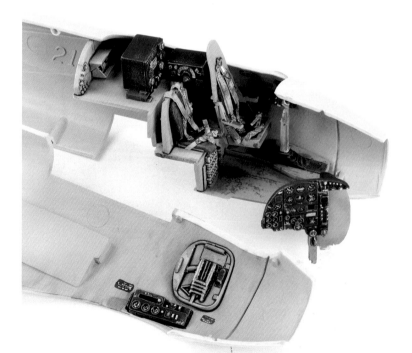

membering its age, it's surprisingly accurate, although the nose profile is a bit skinny from some angles. The worst bits are the clumsy raised panel lines and details, as well as the completely empty undercarriage bays. The latter are easy to deal with, as all you need to do is a little rescribing but adding detail to each bay is a bit more involved. To be honest, so little of this area will be seen on the finished kit that it seems a bit pointless to expend much energy and time on it. The only thing that really has to be done is the bulkhead at the rear of each nacelle, as that can be seen from directly ahead on the finished model. This is just a suitably shaped section of plasticard, with a single stiffener at the base, a curved piece at the top and two little spring assemblies between. The springs are the tensioners for the door retraction wires, which will also need to be added, of course.

The fit and finish of the main parts is OK, nothing special and yet nothing too troublesome either. You know just what you're getting when you buy this kit, so you have to expect to do a little more cosmetic work to the light blue plastic to get a good finish. There are some unsightly gaps around the nacelles and the wing-to-fuselage fit isn't the best, but show it some patience and tender loving care and you'll be fine.

The colour schemes in the box are both excellent, with one PRU Blue PR Mk XVI (which I modelled for you in Airframe and Miniature No.8) and one in silver dope. Doing the fighter version leaves you with the multitude of options that exist out there for it. For me I wanted something post-war and a little unusual, so Chinese Nationalist it was! I found some decals online in the right sizes and a

quick search found all the colour information and plenty of photographs to work from. Canada was the main supplier of Mosquitos to the Nationalist forces, most of which turned up in standard RAF style camouflage. These were quickly painted in their new scheme of Olive Drab over Neutral Grey. As always, the exact shade of these paints is difficult to pin down as there is no real consensus of opinion as to where the paint stocks came from. Suffice it to say that pretty much any dark olive green will do and pick any one of a dozen different neutral greys.

I opted for a darker version of the green, which seems to match the photographs and the standard USAAF Neutral Grey, both of which came from Gunze-Sangyo Mr Aqueous Hobby Color range, with H53 for the grey and H330 for the green. Suitably mucked up with varying shades of these two colours it looks scruffy enough, without looking completely worn out yet. The Mosquito did not have a happy life with the Nationalist Chinese, many

A serious weak point in the kit is the undercarriage bays. The oleos and tyres are very nice but the bay is completely devoid of any detail

Sorry about the rubbish picture but you really do have to make the rear bulkhead and the retention springs as they can be seen from some angles on the finished model

The canopy (one of three in the box), fits quite well but the nose is this kit's real downfall as it's too small and pinched looking

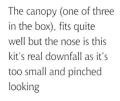

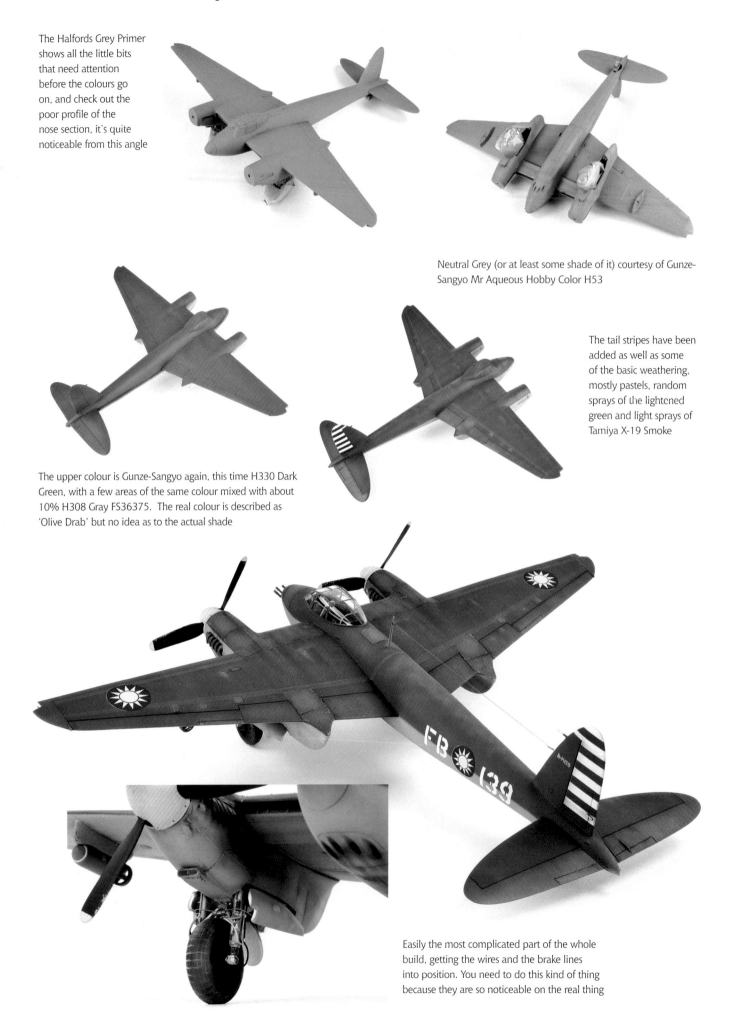

The Halfords Grey Primer shows all the little bits that need attention before the colours go on, and check out the poor profile of the nose section, it's quite noticeable from this angle

Neutral Grey (or at least some shade of it) courtesy of Gunze-Sangyo Mr Aqueous Hobby Color H53

The tail stripes have been added as well as some of the basic weathering, mostly pastels, random sprays of the lightened green and light sprays of Tamiya X-19 Smoke

The upper colour is Gunze-Sangyo again, this time H330 Dark Green, with a few areas of the same colour mixed with about 10% H308 Gray FS36375. The real colour is described as 'Olive Drab' but no idea as to the actual shade

Easily the most complicated part of the whole build, getting the wires and the brake lines into position. You need to do this kind of thing because they are so noticeable on the real thing

of the 150 or so in their inventory ended up crashed and on the scrap heap. When they were engaged properly they were some of the most effective ground-attack aircraft used in the fight against the Communist forces. Weathering was not too heavy, with the various shades of the main colours created with varying amounts of light grey added to the paint and plenty of pastel dust worked into the joints and the details. Sealed in under some Klear it was time for the decals.

I bought the decals from a company called Kora Models and they were rubbish! Sorry Kora, but I honestly could have printed better myself at home. The decals were thin to the point of transparency, were incredibly delicate and to make matter worse they were 'grabby'. This meant that they were really difficult to move around on the gloss surface, just inviting you to tear them. Thankfully the thinness made them easy to settle down over the few details they crossed, so silvering was non-existent, but this also made it all too easy for the underlying paint to show through and completely ruin the colour. If I had known in advance then I would have sprayed a light grey circle in place for each of the roundels. The decals even had a slight white 'haze' around the edge of each one, most of which I managed to remove but some remained stubbornly attached. The fuselage codes came from a sheet of 45° stencils by Carpena and the tail number was hand painted, along with the tail stripes of course. Once these were weathered with a touch of grey pastel dust, a thin coat of Klear was applied to seal it all in and the final touches could be added.

Finishing off any WWII aircraft is always tricky due to the amount of delicate bits to cope with. This one was no exception and the trickiest part of the whole kit was to come with getting the undercarriage doors and all the wires into place. The doors themselves are a little on the thick side but that's in keeping with the rest of the kit, but the retraction wires are some of the things that people seem to forget and yet they are so noticeable on the real aircraft. This one also got two brake lines for each main wheel, making the whole thing look quite busy indeed.

Other bits to go on are the wing tip lights, the spinners (Sky-coloured for this one) the exhausts and the armament, bombs and machine-guns. The 0.303in. nose guns are rather chunky so a replacement set would be wise if your pocket can stretch to it. With the aerial mast in place it was time for the final finish of Xtracolor XDFF matt varnish. Once dry the masking was peeled off the canopy, with a sigh of relief that it was still pretty clear, and the single aerial wire put into place to make this one finished.

Verdict

Old and tired it may be but you can still make a pretty good-looking Mosquito out of the jam-packed box. Just make sure you know what you're buying with this kit, as you will have your work cut out with the filler and sanding sticks. In all honesty, if you want the slim-line single-stage engines then the Tamiya kit is the preferred choice but if the bigger two-stage Merlins are what you're after then this kit gives you a multitude of great options for not a lot of cash. Remember that in this box are two sets of engines, two fuselages and three noses, so night-fighters, fighter-bombers, bombers and PR versions are all in there waiting for you to make the choice.

The fiddly bits at the end make it all come to life. Note the brake lines (two per wheel) and the wire for the door retraction mechanism

Tamiya 1/48th
FB Mk VI converted to BOAC configuration

by Steve A. Evans

This kit could be one of the most perfect marriages in the history of kit making. The iconic brand of Tamiya meets the truly classic form of the Mosquito, what's not to love? This kit has been around for some time with this particular box released in 1998. Considering that makes it 19 years old, it's not doing too badly. The box art is a little old fashioned looking but instantly recognisable as Tamiya from this time period. Also instantly recognisable is the presentation of parts and instructions in the box. The medium grey-coloured plastic comes in stapled plastic bags on eight sprues, a single sprue of very clear transparent

The box is a classic by now as just about everyone in the modelling world has held one of these in their hands. The Vingtor decals look good too

The modifications to the kit plastic for the BOAC version is pretty simple; the addition of the thermos of tea is an optional extra

The bomb bay has to be altered as well to make the cramped passenger compartment. The plywood cladding was painted white to give an illusion of a bit more space

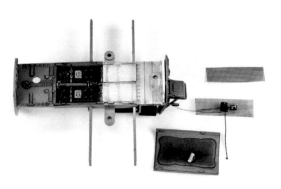

parts and a tiny bag with two poly caps. The instructions are beautifully drawn and are of the usual fold-out variety, with ten pages and 22 construction steps. The paint and marking guide is split into two sheets, one with all the decal placements and one showing the full camouflage pattern. The decal sheet is the usual kind of Tamiya thing from this period with matt carrier film and they are a little bit thick looking. They are nicely printed though, with very sharp detail, perfect register and good colours too. All three options in the box are absolute classics with a standard fighter-bomber, a Coastal Command type scheme and a night-fighter. All of which I completely ignored! I have a soft spot for the BOAC Mossies and their excellent markings, so when I was asked to make a Mosquito this was my first choice. In this case, the markings are supplied by Vingtor Decals, sheet #48-107. This decal sheet is researched by Nils Mathisrud and allows you to model most of the Mk VIs used by BOAC on their ball bearing and passenger runs to Sweden. These decals are sharply printed, with good colour and very little carrier film on the large lettering. More on these in a minute, of course.

To begin with, the BOAC Mosquitoes are a little

different from standard, with the guns removed and the forward section of the bomb bay converted into a tiny little passenger pod. This is where I started, by blanking off the gun ports and making the bits for the bomb bay. The bay was boarded up with plywood on the real thing and painted white to make it seem a little less cramped. The passenger had a mattress and padded bits to lie on, with an oxygen regulator and intercom unit to play with and he even had a flask of tea to warm him up. Not the most comfortable way to fly but certainly one of the fastest at the time.

The construction of the standard parts of the interior is, as usual with Tamiya, faultless. The detail is sharp and well moulded and everything fits together in exemplary fashion. To be honest, if it's not fitting properly, then you're not doing it right, because Tamiya moulds really are very precise, no wonder they were always more expensive than their rivals. The cockpit is made up of a separate nose section to allow for the variants and only twenty-seven parts to make all this detail. You get two crew figures as well and the main instrument panel and seat belts are supplied as decals on the main sheet. The cockpit attaches to the bomb bay section and to the main spar. This unit is neatly moulded too with very good fuel tank detail and of course, on the standard build, the breeches for the 20mm cannon. The fuselage halves close up around this and it may take a little wiggling and gentle persuasion to get it all to fit but when it does it 'clicks' into place with barely a joint line on show.

The wings, nacelles and undercarriage come first on the instruction sheet, oddly enough, but considering the modular nature of the build this isn't a problem. You do get a few options here, with the rockets or bombs under the wings and, even though they are not mentioned at all in the instructions, the slipper tanks as well. You also get the shrouded or unshrouded exhausts for the nacelles and the rather fiddly undercarriage units. The parts for the undercarriage are quite fine in places and although it all fits together well enough, because you are trying to get three or four bits to all line up at once, it does get a bit tricky. At least, once built, they can be put aside for later so they don't get in the way during spraying. A mention has to be made of the way in which the wings attach to the fuselage. Basically you slide the assembled wing onto the spar then push it up against the fuselage and locate

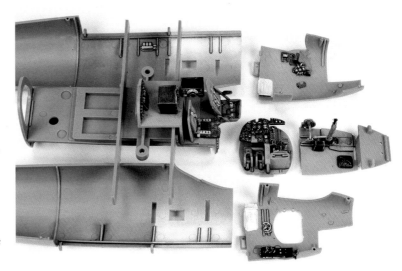

it securely in place with a small pin on the underside. If Tamiya's moulds were anything less than perfect, this would be a recipe for disaster, as it is, it's a glorious bit of plastic engineering that works beautifully.

The three options in the box are all very nice but as mentioned, will be completely ignored for this one. The

The Tamiya mouldings are superb, making up a pretty decent interior, and I even used the decal seat belts

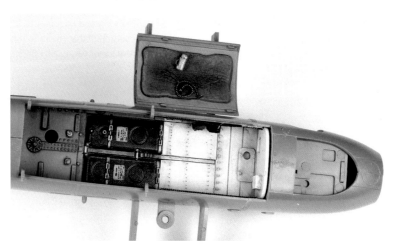

instructions for all three are perfectly adequate with nice drawings to follow on the separate sheets and luckily the Vingtor sheet is equally as good and it's even in full colour. The BOAC colour schemes went through a number of changes; starting as Dark Earth and Dark Green over Sky for the original aircraft but the next six FB Mk VIs got the Extra Dark Sea Grey/Dark Slate Grey over Sky version. This lasted for about 6 months before the underside was

The fuselage closes up perfectly around the plastic bits and you begin to get a sense of just how little space there was in the forward compartment for the passenger

The wings join the fuselage with a slightly complicated arrangement of spars and pins but due to Tamiya's excellent mouldings, it works perfectly

The wings are made up with the nacelles, all of which are neatly detailed and fit just about perfectly. The only filler on show is the little bit used to get rid of the joint line on the carburettor intake

The primer is used as fine filler for all the little blemishes, and then it's on with the real colours

Humbrol 123 Extra Dark Sea Grey to begin with and note the complete lack of any kind of shading at this point; it's all going to be done post-paint

The camouflage pattern is transposed from the Vingtor decal instructions because it's not the standard pattern at all, being the 'Civil Sea' pattern instead

Humbrol again, this time 31 Slate Grey, which gives a good contrast to the colours

Tamiya XF-21 Sky and I'd forgotten how 'rich' that particular version of that colour is. I should have gone for a shade or two paler, I think?

The Vingtor decals are good and bad. Good lettering and perfect printing are offset by their brittle nature

painted Night, more in keeping with the night time runs. This means that any of the markings on the Vingtor sheet can be done with either Sky or Night undersides, apart from G-AGGF, which never got the Night underside due

This is an instantly recognisable version of the famous Mosquito but you don't see it that often on the modelling tables

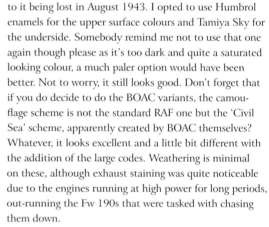

to it being lost in August 1943. I opted to use Humbrol enamels for the upper surface colours and Tamiya Sky for the underside. Somebody remind me not to use that one again though please as it's too dark and quite a saturated looking colour, a much paler option would have been better. Not to worry, it still looks good. Don't forget that if you do decide to do the BOAC variants, the camouflage scheme is not the standard RAF one but the 'Civil Sea' scheme, apparently created by BOAC themselves? Whatever, it looks excellent and a little bit different with the addition of the large codes. Weathering is minimal on these, although exhaust staining was quite noticeable due to the engines running at high power for long periods, out-running the Fw 190s that were tasked with chasing them down.

I used Johnson's Klear for the gloss surface and the decals were then applied, as per the Vingtor instructions. The decals look great but are a little brittle and the carrier film is noticeable on the fuselage codes. I would sug-

gest masking and painting the red, white and blue stripes and just using the codes. A little bit of grey pastel dust can be used to fade them all in a bit but not too much as you still want the markings to stand out, then it's on to the final assembly.

There is a lot to do at this point, starting with the undercarriage and doors. Basically the main units are very nice but there are a few prominent details still missing. In the nacelle, against the rear bulkhead, there are two spring units that are the closing mechanism for the doors. They attach to the interior of the nacelle and wires run from them up to the inside of the door. As the main unit retracts, these springs compress and pull the doors closed behind them, simple, lightweight and effective. The springs were made by winding some wire around a pin and then stretching them out a little, while the retraction wires are just slightly finer fuse wire. The front of each undercarriage unit also needs some wires, this time attached to the front of the door and wrapped around the oleos over small roller units. It also needs brake lines of course, one running down the back of each of the main stanchions and attached to the brake unit in the wheel. The bomb bay needs attention too, with the doors being cut open and the delicate actuator units attached. This allows a tiny view into the passenger compartment but you still can't see much in there.

The propeller units are next and you get two types of propeller in the kit, although all of the BOAC versions used the narrow blades. The spinners are Slate Grey and once again, minimal weathering is the order of the day. The poly caps in them will even allow the propellers to turn if you like that kind of thing.

The final tiny bits are added, like the pitot tube, aerial mast and carb intake screens, while the crew access door and ladder will be left off until after the final surface finish of Xtracolor XDFF Flat Varnish is applied. Once that's well and truly dried, the masks can be removed and the aerial wire added and it's looking done to me.

Quite a few bits to be sorted at the end. The bunch of wiry things on the right is the collection of spring units and retraction wires for the undercarriage doors

Verdict

The Tamiya kit of the Mosquito comes in a number of different boxes, any and all of which are just superb. The mouldings are clean, well thought out and precise, while the build process remains straightforward. This really is a kit for all levels of modelling as the new-borns will find it easy to build and delightfully

quick, while the old hands will love the engineering and the fact that there's so much you can do to the kit to make it shine.

The Vingtor decals make a wonderful machine (and model) into something just a little bit different. The instructions are comprehensive with some excellent information and they work perfectly well. If you fancy something a little off the beaten track I can heartily recommend them.

Tamiya 1/32nd
FB Mk VI

by Dani Zamarbide

For my personal taste, all aircraft powered by Merlin engines are beautiful and so the Mosquito, which uses two, is amongst my favourites. Tamiya's mew 1/32nd scale kit is certainly an engineering marvel, the quality of the parts is sublime and the moulding itself is so gorgeous that sometimes I feel a little sorry to have to start separating the pieces from the sprues! The instructions are clear and perfectly detailed but need to be studied closely because the amount of choice required for each step can lead you to make an error or omission of some small detail, such as opening holes or removing parts which do not correspond

to the model you wish to build. With this kit you can make two sub-variants and you have two colour options, an RAF example in the European theatre, or an Australian one in the Pacific.

The Australian option will be the choice of those of you not wanting to make yet another green/grey Mosquito, but I wanted an SEAC scheme in green and brown, with blue undersides and white stripes around the wings and rudder. This can luckily be obtained from the Xtradecal range, which are of excellent quality. Apart from the aftermarket decals, I only added a few more items: machine-guns, cannon and pitot from the Master range (whom I thank for kindly supplying them) and air intakes screen from the Brengun range of etched brass.

To build this model you do not need to follow the instructions in the order shown because each element can

The box spar unit makes for a sturdy model and you can see the levels of detail Tamiya have moulded into the central (fuel tanks) and outboard (wheel well) regions

The engines are little works of art in their own right

Assembly of the engines and nacelles is straight-forward if you take care to follow the instructions

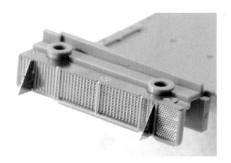

The photo-etched metal parts that create the radiators are very effective indeed

All the detail you see is from the kit parts, all that has been added is the cover, which was made from lead sheet

The wiring was all added to each sidewall, but the moulded level of detail is impressive nonetheless.

be constructed individually before finally adding all these sub-assembles to create the entire model. After studying the instructions I therefore decided to start with the engines and wings. The engines are wonderful with superior detail and as is often the case with kits from Tamiya, they are designed so that they can be exposed or covered thanks to the separate side cowlings that are held in pace with tiny magnets. I decided that for this build I would keep the engine cowls closed because the Mosquito has very elegant lines and at some point in the future I intend to buy another and build it with all the cowls off. You need to work methodically, to ensure that you know what parts are for the port or starboard engines, then when they are completed you will not have any unpleasant surprises when attaching them onto the wings. Once the engines are built, I moved on to the wings. The wing itself comes with a one-piece spar that gives rigidity to the model and is further reinforced by a series of screws so that the assembly is very quick and simple because all the pieces fit together perfectly. Among the many options in this kit, you have the capacity to have the flaps up or down and in my case I chose the latter. At each wing tip the formation lights are separate clear components, and the deep area for the undercarriage bay could be improved, but in my opinion, the level of detail Tamiya are offering will be enough for nearly all modellers. The final items to add to the wings, aside from the flying surfaces, are high-quality photo-etched grilles for the radiators in the wing root, which add greatly to the realism of this model. Once the engines were attached to the wings I closed up the various cowling panels and here Tamiya supplied the first examples sold in the UK with both grey-coloured and clear plastic side cowls, so that all the details of the engines can be seen without the need to remove the side panels. The

A lot of careful painting will pay dividends, as the moulded detail really pops out at you

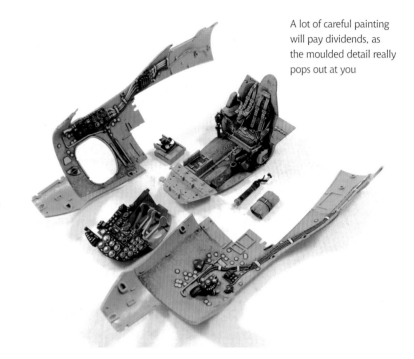

use of these clear panels is purely one of personal taste. The SEAC version chosen by me has the tropicalised air intakes fitted that are longer and wider than the European model. All that was now left was the hubs and propellers and again you must take note of the comments in the instructions, as Tamiya supply two types of propellers, the narrow and 'paddle' (wide) versions, the latter being the type I used on my model.

Now, I focused on the fuselage and started assembly of the cockpit interior, which shows detail of the highest quality. Everything you see in the cockpit interior is from

Tamiya have not cut corners here, the interior framework of the real thing is supplied in this kit, thus allowing you to paint it, as well as thus depicting those bars that are only inside the Perspex (and there are a couple on the Mosquito)

The brass gun barrels from Master are a real must for this kit, as they are exquisite

The 1154/1155 radio units are another region that will look a great deal better after painting

Careful painting and weathering of things like the wheels and bombs just add to the overall feel of quality you get from this kit

Just washes to enhance the moulded detail combined with mud and dirt splatter, give the undercarriage a well used look

Wear on the propellers and spinners take time, but are well worth it with a subject this big

kit parts, with the exception of some additional wiring, which was all added from scratch. I started with the seats and their harnesses, which are supplied as metal parts and to install them is not without some difficulty. I recommend that you flex the belts a bit, so they are not so rigid, as this will make them more fabric-like. Once again check the instructions because there are differences in the some of the flight instruments between the European and Australian variants. The option to add the armour plate behind the seat of the navigator is included in this kit, but I opted not to install it on my example. Additional references are a must when building any model, the bigger the scale and thus level of detail, the more so. The kit already includes a small booklet with a brief history of the type and a detailed series of walk-around photographs that come in handy, especially as it allows you to see the colours of certain details that instructions just cannot hope to impart. After installing all the components in the cockpit it was time to start thinking about painting. As

you know the Mosquito was built of about 80% wood and the floor of the cockpit is made with this material, and so the first thing I did was paint wood-effect in the region using a guide for the pattern of fibres in a wood plank. At this point, using the walk-around photographs and additional documentation, the rest of the cockpit interior and instruments were all carefully painted. Once complete this region forms a focal point on the model, because the large dome of the canopy allows you to see inside. I then pressed ahead with the installation of the guns, bomb bay and fuel tanks that are inserted into the fuselage and, like the engines, come with great detail so that you could leave the bomb doors open if you wanted. That said, the amount of detail would mean that it would take you four times longer due to all the careful painting required. The fuselage is split into two parts, the central (common) fuselage for all Mosquito variants and the forward fuselage, cockpit and machine-gun bay. This latter item is again very highly detailed, so you could leave it open,

With the model quickly assembled, the first paints to go on are the Interior Grey-Green over the cockpit and the white above each radiator

Next red is applied over the white, before the box and 'X are made up with lengths of micro tape

The first main colour applied is the lightest, therefore it is Azure Blue on the undersides

The demarcations along the wings, nacelles and fuselage are all defined with tape before the upper colours can be applied

The first upper camouflage colour is Dark Earth…

…followed by Dark Green, both applied freehand to give soft demarcation between the two

Weathering and fading of the upper colours is done with random applications of a sand colour

The white SEAC theatre bands are masked then sprayed around the wings and tail, the underlying dark colours help to ease shading effects

Paint chipping is done with aluminium (where applicable), various shades of grey and even a yellow for certain areas, such as the nose machine-gun access panels

Once the weathering is complete, the whole model is sealed with acrylic gloss varnish

Decals came from the Xtradecals sheet #32058

A dark brown panel wash was used on the upper surfaces, with a lighter shade for the undersides

but I closed it having only enhanced it with the brass gun barrels from Master in Poland.

With wings and fuselage joined you can attach the separate control surfaces, which will bring more realism to the model when completed. The need for putty on any of the joints was almost non-existent due to the accuracy of the fit of the parts, so I could quickly move on and start the painting stage.

Before beginning the painting stage you have to mask the canopy, wheel wells and the radiators. Thoughtfully Tamiya provide us with the masks for the canopy and once carefully cut out, they are a perfect fit. Painting started therefore with a layer of grey-green on the outside of the canopy, and then on the top of the wing above the radiators, first I applied white, then over the white I applied red to ensure the red was vibrant because red (and yellow) are notorious for being weak colours. Once dry I cut pieces of tape to create the typical 'X' markings carried in this region to denote it was a 'no step' zone. Once done, I could then start with the camouflage colours. The

paints I chose for this were from the AK-Interactive range and were Dark Green and Dark Earth on top and Azure Blue underneath. I always start with the lightest colour, so in this case it was the Azure Blue. Once that was dry the demarcations along the nose, wings and fuselage were all masked with tape, so I could start with the upper camouflage colours. First on was Dark Earth, followed by the Dark Green and each was applied freehand so that the edges between the two colours were soft. The potential to weather an SEAC subject was one of the reasons I chose it, so I applied a filter of sand over all the green and brown regions, whilst with the rivets and panel lines I applied a dark brown wash. AK-Interactive produce a range of washes that are often used by armour modellers to create such things as fluid loss or general dirt and dust. On the underside, especially in the region of the tail wheel, you get dirt and mud along with small splashes created by the moment of the aircraft whilst taxiing, so this type of wash is ideal. Finally with brown and black, both heavily diluted with about 96% thinners, I created exhaust stain-

Weathering comprised washes, filters and various products that replicate oil and grime, all of which were used to make a very 'messy' Mossie

Splatter of mud and grime across the front of the wing and tail bands is done using weathering products from the AK-Interactive range

There is not a great deal to add at the very end of the build, as seen here, about all that is not included is the single aerial lead from the mast to the vertical fin

ing from the engines and around the gun ports to give the model a more battered appearance.

Finishing the model, once I'd done the painting phase, consisted of attaching the wheels and undercarriage, along with the undercarriage doors and the crew access hatch. The bombs supplied in the kit are of high quality with the inclusion of a small propeller at the back in etched, although also included are drop tanks if you prefer. All I had to do now was remove the masks, attach the photo-etched ice guards that are missing from the kit, and thus

came from the Brengun range, attach the antenna cable (there is only a single lead on this SEAC machine), the windscreen wiper and the various lenses in the lamps to complete this build.

Verdict

One of the best models Tamiya have ever produced, certainly in the near future I will buy another one so that I can have all that wonderful detail in view, plus there are just so many potential schemes for the type both during WWII and by many nations in the immediate post-war era. The model is a delight to build and I recommend it most highly because you are really going to enjoy building this one, I know I did.

Chapter 7: Building a Collection

All artwork
©Wojciech Sankowski

With so many versions of the Mosquito as potential modelling subjects we thought it would be useful to show you the difference between all the variants based on the fighter airframe to assist you in making them.

Fighter & Night-Fighter

Note: This initial section is not in chronological order, as the prototype (W4052) was always considered a fighter, even though it was painted black and in its initial and revised forms had some or all of the dipoles associated with A.I. radar

F Mk II prototype (W4052) – Initial Form

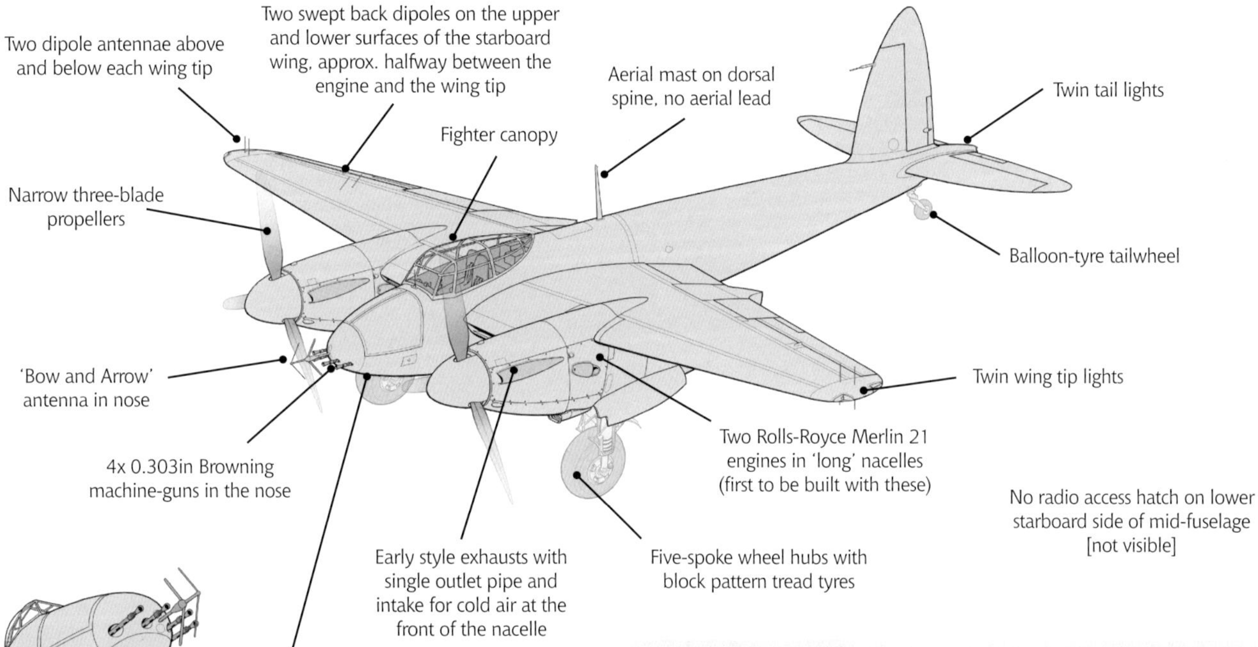
Two dipole antennae above and below each wing tip
Two swept back dipoles on the upper and lower surfaces of the starboard wing, approx. halfway between the engine and the wing tip
Aerial mast on dorsal spine, no aerial lead
Twin tail lights
Fighter canopy
Narrow three-blade propellers
Balloon-tyre tailwheel
'Bow and Arrow' antenna in nose
Twin wing tip lights
Two Rolls-Royce Merlin 21 engines in 'long' nacelles (first to be built with these)
4x 0.303in Browning machine-guns in the nose
No radio access hatch on lower starboard side of mid-fuselage [not visible]
Early style exhausts with single outlet pipe and intake for cold air at the front of the nacelle
Five-spoke wheel hubs with block pattern tread tyres

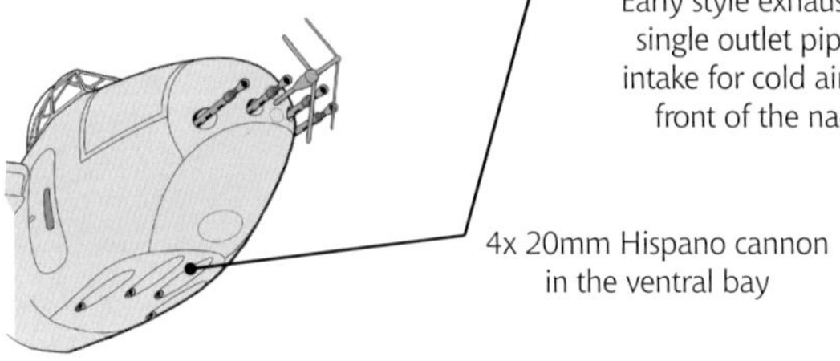
4x 20mm Hispano cannon in the ventral bay

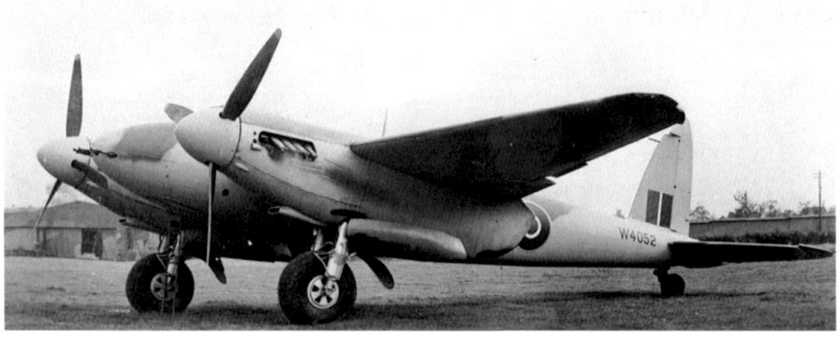
W4052

A nice shot of prototype W4052 in its final colour scheme *(©DH)*

F Mk II prototype (W4052) – Revised Form

Same as F Mk II prototype (W4052) – Initial Form except:

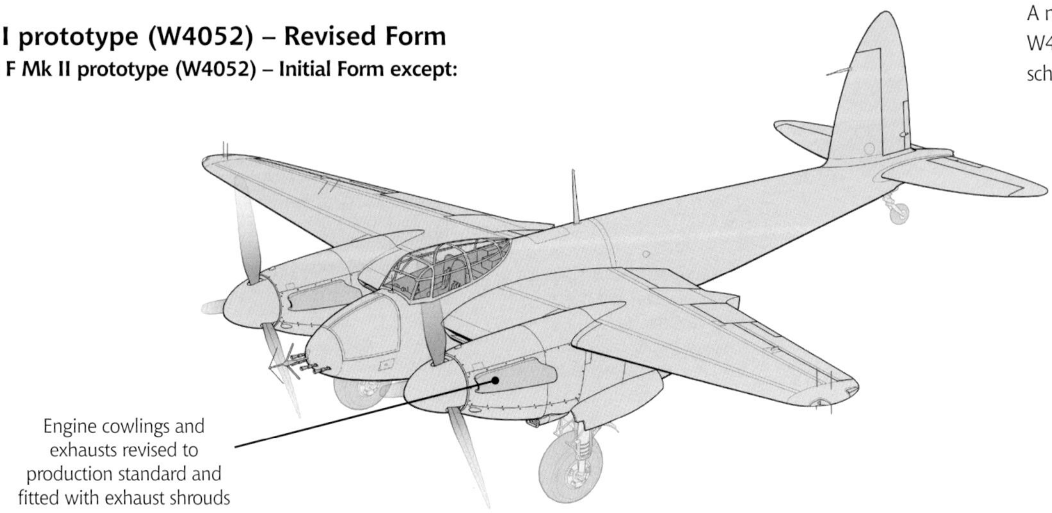
Engine cowlings and exhausts revised to production standard and fitted with exhaust shrouds

This view of the port side of W4052 with the Youngman 'frill' speed brake installed, shows the segmented nature of the unit, the rods that link to each petal and the fact that on this side, the frill is continual *(©DH)*

F Mk II with 'frill ' speed brake (W4052 – experimental)
Same as F Mk II prototype (W4052) – Revised Form except:

The frill was later modified by the removal of a section on the dorsal spine, to reduce buffeting of the vertical fin and rudder [not shown – see photo opposite]

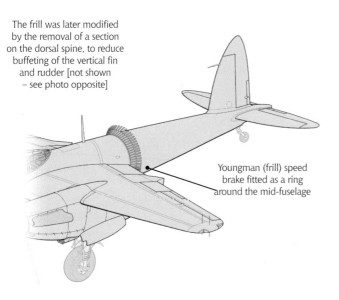

Youngman (frill) speed brake fitted as a ring around the mid-fuselage

In this shot of the starboard side of the Youngman speed brake, you can see that it is only partial, plus you can also see the radio hatch added directly behind it, but the lack of any strengthening strake. Note the unpainted panel at the base of the aerial mast and the cut-out at the top of the frill *(©DH)*

By this stage a radio access hatch had definitely been added on the starboard side of the mid-fuselage (no strengthening strake was fitted, though) [not shown]

F Mk II with bellows-style speed brake (W4052 – experimental)
Same as F Mk II prototype (W4052) – Revised Form except:

Bellows-style speed brake fitted in two sections above and one section below the mid-fuselage; lower set was approx. 180°, the upper two were 70°

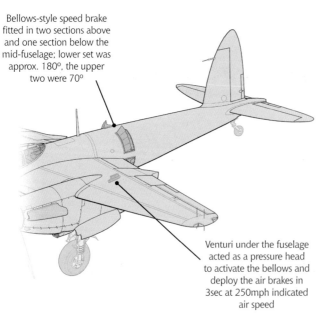

Venturi under the fuselage acted as a pressure head to activate the bellows and deploy the air brakes in 3sec at 250mph indicated air speed

Note: Found to cause severe buffeting and vibration, which some felt might lead to structural failure, so the air brake was never adopted

This is the port side of W4052 with the bellows-style speed brake in the stowed position; note that the lower arc would be closed by air pressure when the aircraft was in flight

(©DH Aircraft Museum Trust)

This shot shows the bellow speed brake in the fully open position. The venturi that acts to pressurise the system in flight can be seen under the fuselage directly in front of the lower segment of the speed brake *(©DH Aircraft Museum Trust)*

F Mk II with dorsal turret (W4053 – experimental)
Same as F Mk II prototype (W4052) – Revised Form except:

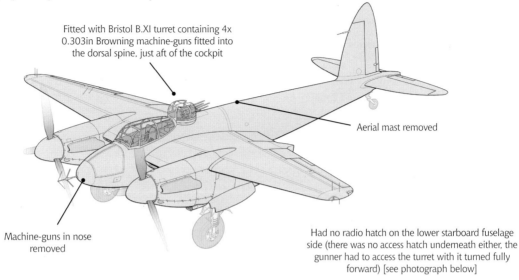

Fitted with Bristol B.XI turret containing 4x
0.303in Browning machine-guns fitted into
the dorsal spine, just aft of the cockpit

Aerial mast removed

Machine-guns in nose
removed

Had no radio hatch on the lower starboard fuselage
side (there was no access hatch underneath either, the
gunner had to access the turret with it turned fully
forward) [see photograph below]

As far as we are aware, this is the only image of the experimental turret installation in
W4053, it shows the turret and also the lack of radio hatch and reinforcing strake on this
side of the lower fuselage, the hatch area being patched and filled

This close-up of W4052 in its final form highlights the oval
Perspex observation panel added to the crew access door
(©D.H./BAe)

F Mk II prototype (W4052) – Final Form
Same as F Mk II prototype (W4052) – Revised Form except:

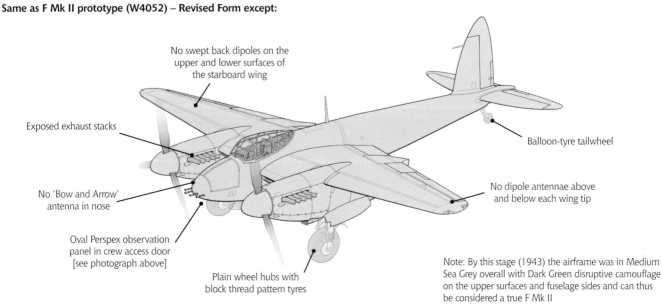

No swept back dipoles on the
upper and lower surfaces of
the starboard wing

Exposed exhaust stacks

Balloon-tyre tailwheel

No 'Bow and Arrow'
antenna in nose

No dipole antennae above
and below each wing tip

Oval Perspex observation
panel in crew access door
[see photograph above]

Plain wheel hubs with
block thread pattern tyres

Note: By this stage (1943) the airframe was in Medium
Sea Grey overall with Dark Green disruptive camouflage
on the upper surfaces and fuselage sides and can thus
be considered a true F Mk II

NF Mk II with A.I. Mk IV radar
Same as F Mk II prototype (W4052) – Revised Form except:

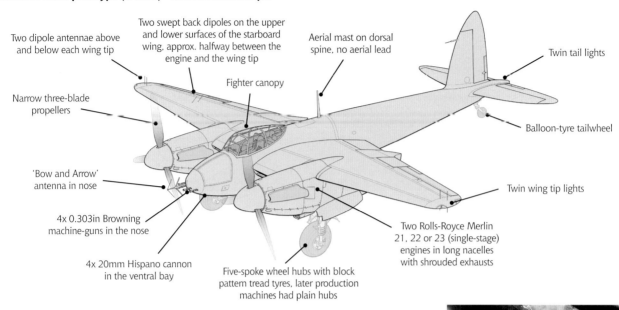

Two dipole antennae above and below each wing tip

Two swept back dipoles on the upper and lower surfaces of the starboard wing, approx. halfway between the engine and the wing tip

Aerial mast on dorsal spine, no aerial lead

Twin tail lights

Fighter canopy

Narrow three-blade propellers

Balloon-tyre tailwheel

'Bow and Arrow' antenna in nose

4x 0.303in Browning machine-guns in the nose

Twin wing tip lights

Two Rolls-Royce Merlin 21, 22 or 23 (single-stage) engines in long nacelles with shrouded exhausts

4x 20mm Hispano cannon in the ventral bay

Five-spoke wheel hubs with block pattern tread tyres, later production machines had plain hubs

NF Mk II with tropical filters (W4096 – prototype)
Same as NF Mk II with A.I. Mk IV radar except:

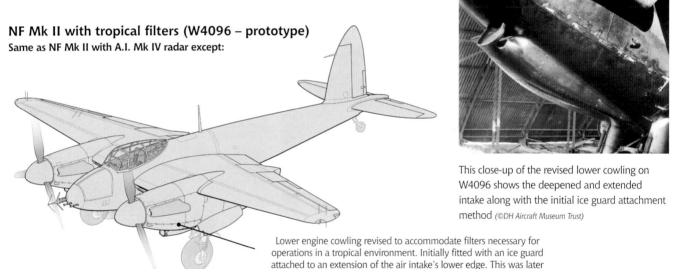

This close-up of the revised lower cowling on W4096 shows the deepened and extended intake along with the initial ice guard attachment method *(©DH Aircraft Museum Trust)*

Lower engine cowling revised to accommodate filters necessary for operations in a tropical environment. Initially fitted with an ice guard attached to an extension of the air intake's lower edge. This was later changed to the standard version mounted via four attachment lugs (two above and two below) on the intake lip

NF Mk II with Helmore/GEC Turbinlite
Same as F Mk II prototype (W4052) – Revised Form except:

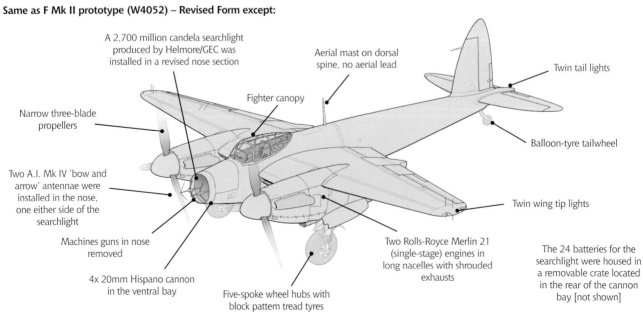

A 2,700 million candela searchlight produced by Helmore/GEC was installed in a revised nose section

Aerial mast on dorsal spine, no aerial lead

Twin tail lights

Fighter canopy

Narrow three-blade propellers

Balloon-tyre tailwheel

Two A.I. Mk IV 'bow and arrow' antennae were installed in the nose, one either side of the searchlight

Machines guns in nose removed

Twin wing tip lights

Two Rolls-Royce Merlin 21 (single-stage) engines in long nacelles with shrouded exhausts

4x 20mm Hispano cannon in the ventral bay

Five-spoke wheel hubs with block pattern tread tyres

The 24 batteries for the searchlight were housed in a removable crate located in the rear of the cannon bay [not shown]

F Mk II (Intruder)
Converted from NF Mk II for daytime use, all details as per the NF Mk II except:

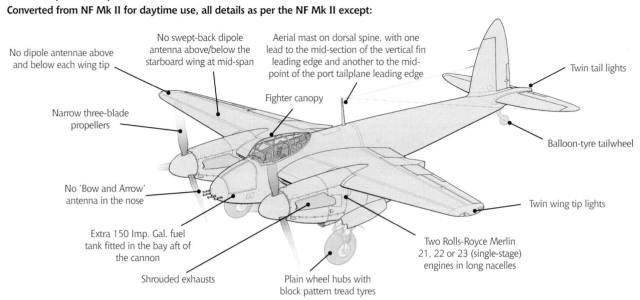

No dipole antennae above and below each wing tip

No swept-back dipole antenna above/below the starboard wing at mid-span

Aerial mast on dorsal spine, with one lead to the mid-section of the vertical fin leading edge and another to the mid-point of the port tailplane leading edge

Twin tail lights

Fighter canopy

Narrow three-blade propellers

Balloon-tyre tailwheel

No 'Bow and Arrow' antenna in the nose

Twin wing tip lights

Extra 150 Imp. Gal. fuel tank fitted in the bay aft of the cannon

Two Rolls-Royce Merlin 21, 22 or 23 (single-stage) engines in long nacelles

Shrouded exhausts

Plain wheel hubs with block pattern tread tyres

F Mk II (DD723) with Merlin XX engines

Same as F Mk II except:

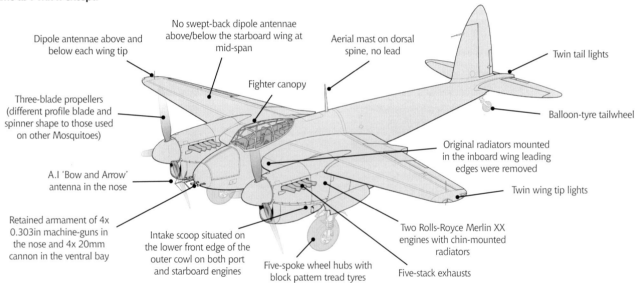

Dipole antennae above and below each wing tip

No swept-back dipole antennae above/below the starboard wing at mid-span

Aerial mast on dorsal spine, no lead

Twin tail lights

Fighter canopy

Three-blade propellers (different profile blade and spinner shape to those used on other Mosquitoes)

Balloon-tyre tailwheel

A.I 'Bow and Arrow' antenna in the nose

Original radiators mounted in the inboard wing leading edges were removed

Twin wing tip lights

Retained armament of 4x 0.303in machine-guns in the nose and 4x 20mm cannon in the ventral bay

Intake scoop situated on the lower front edge of the outer cowl on both port and starboard engines

Five-spoke wheel hubs with block pattern tread tyres

Two Rolls-Royce Merlin XX engines with chin-mounted radiators

Five-stack exhausts

F Mk II with SCR 720 radar (DZ659/G)
Same as F Mk II except:
(See photo next page)

Revised nose radome containing an American SCR 720 radar scanner plus associated equipment in the cockpit

Twin-contact, anti-shimmy tailwheel tyre

Small blister on centreline under new radome, probably to clear some form of projection below the scanner dish

Nose-mounted machine guns removed

Five-spoke wheel hubs with block pattern tread tyres

NF Mk XII
Developed from the NF Mk II

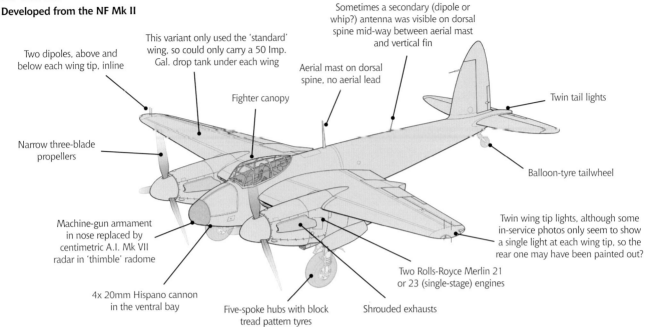

Two dipoles, above and below each wing tip, inline

This variant only used the 'standard' wing, so could only carry a 50 Imp. Gal. drop tank under each wing

Sometimes a secondary (dipole or whip?) antenna was visible on dorsal spine mid-way between aerial mast and vertical fin

Aerial mast on dorsal spine, no aerial lead

Fighter canopy

Twin tail lights

Narrow three-blade propellers

Machine-gun armament in nose replaced by centimetric A.I. Mk VII radar in 'thimble' radome

Balloon-tyre tailwheel

Twin wing tip lights, although some in-service photos only seem to show a single light at each wing tip, so the rear one may have been painted out?

4x 20mm Hispano cannon in the ventral bay

Five-spoke hubs with block tread pattern tyres

Shrouded exhausts

Two Rolls-Royce Merlin 21 or 23 (single-stage) engines

(See previous page) A front port side view of F Mk II DZ659/G fitted with A.I. Mk X (SCR 720) radar in nose taken in March 1943 *(©DH)*

This close-up under the nose of Mk XIII, HK382 (RO•T) of No.29 Squadron at Hunsdon, clearly shows the dipole antenna fitted on the centreline, aft of the cannon ports

(©British Official)

NF Mk XIII (Early)
Developed from the FB Mk VI

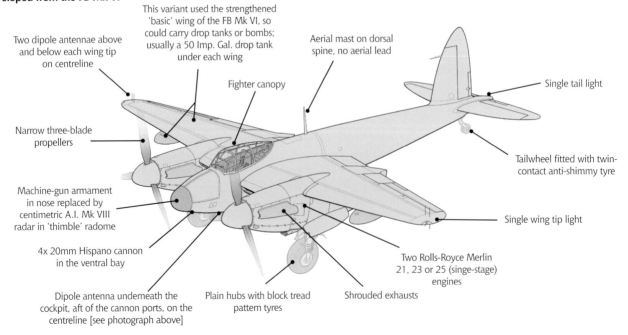

Two dipole antennae above and below each wing tip on centreline

This variant used the strengthened 'basic' wing of the FB Mk VI, so could carry drop tanks or bombs; usually a 50 Imp. Gal. drop tank under each wing

Aerial mast on dorsal spine, no aerial lead

Fighter canopy

Single tail light

Narrow three-blade propellers

Machine-gun armament in nose replaced by centimetric A.I. Mk VIII radar in 'thimble' radome

Tailwheel fitted with twin-contact anti-shimmy tyre

4x 20mm Hispano cannon in the ventral bay

Single wing tip light

Dipole antenna underneath the cockpit, aft of the cannon ports, on the centreline [see photograph above]

Plain hubs with block tread pattern tyres

Shrouded exhausts

Two Rolls-Royce Merlin 21, 23 or 25 (single-stage) engines

NF Mk XIII (Late)
Same as NF Mk XIII (Early) except:

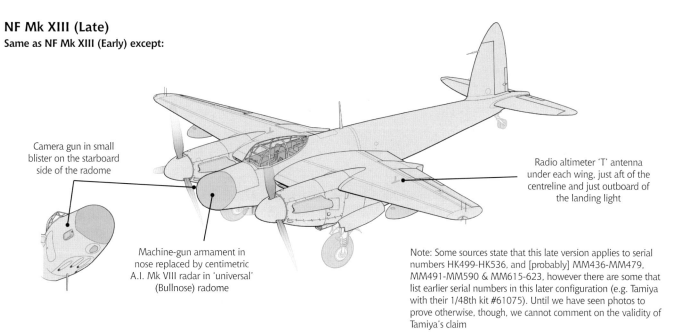

Camera gun in small blister on the starboard side of the radome

Machine-gun armament in nose replaced by centimetric A.I. Mk VIII radar in 'universal' (Bullnose) radome

Radio altimeter 'T' antenna under each wing, just aft of the centreline and just outboard of the landing light

Note: Some sources state that this late version applies to serial numbers HK499-HK536, and [probably] MM436-MM479, MM491-MM590 & MM615-623, however there are some that list earlier serial numbers in this later configuration (e.g. Tamiya with their 1/48th kit #61075). Until we have seen photos to prove otherwise, though, we cannot comment on the validity of Tamiya's claim

NF Mk XIV (Project only)
Proposed high-altitude development of the NF Mk XIII with Merlin 67 engines, never built

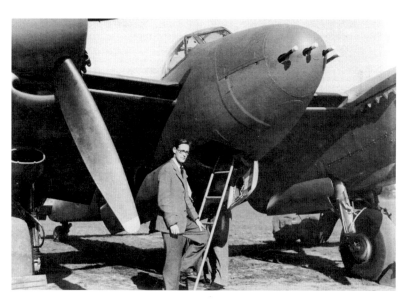

NF Mk XV MP469 in its initial form with J. P. Smith of the Mosquito Design Team by the ladder. You can see the grafted fighter nose from F Mk II DD715, along with the strengthening rib on this side of the lower nose and the bomber-style access hatch in the underside (©BAe)

NF Mk XV prototype (MP469) – Initial Form
High-altitude variant developed (in 7 days) from a PR Mk VIII

Raised strengthening rib can be seen on the starboard side of the lower nose, there may be another one on the port side, but no photo exists to show that region [see photograph above]

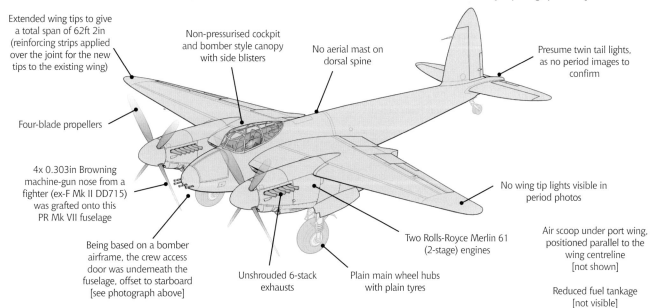

Extended wing tips to give a total span of 62ft 2in (reinforcing strips applied over the joint for the new tips to the existing wing)

Non-pressurised cockpit and bomber style canopy with side blisters

No aerial mast on dorsal spine

Presume twin tail lights, as no period images to confirm

Four-blade propellers

4x 0.303in Browning machine-gun nose from a fighter (ex-F Mk II DD715) was grafted onto this PR Mk VII fuselage

Being based on a bomber airframe, the crew access door was underneath the fuselage, offset to starboard [see photograph above]

Unshrouded 6-stack exhausts

Plain main wheel hubs with plain tyres

Two Rolls-Royce Merlin 61 (2-stage) engines

No wing tip lights visible in period photos

Air scoop under port wing, positioned parallel to the wing centreline [not shown]

Reduced fuel tankage [not visible]

NF Mk XV prototype (MP469) – Revised Form
Same as NF Mk XV prototype (MP469) – Initial Form except:

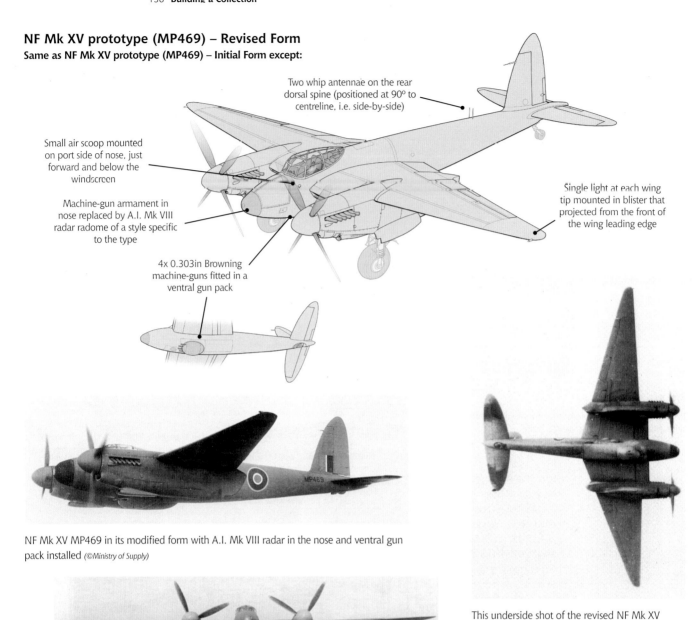

Two whip antennæ on the rear dorsal spine (positioned at 90º to centreline, i.e. side-by-side)

Small air scoop mounted on port side of nose, just forward and below the windscreen

Machine-gun armament in nose replaced by A.I. Mk VIII radar radome of a style specific to the type

Single light at each wing tip mounted in blister that projected from the front of the wing leading edge

4x 0.303in Browning machine-guns fitted in a ventral gun pack

NF Mk XV MP469 in its modified form with A.I. Mk VIII radar in the nose and ventral gun pack installed *(©Ministry of Supply)*

This underside shot of the revised NF Mk XV MP469 shows the ventral gun pack, as well as the intake situated on the starboard fuselage side at mid-chord *(©BAe)*

Front view of NF Mk XV MP469 in its initial form at Hatfield 16th September 1942, clearly showing the extended wing span and four-blade propellers first tested on W4050 and fitted to MP469 on the 13th September 1942 *(©DH/BAE)*

NF Mk XV (Production)
Four converted from B Mk IVs
Same as NF Mk XV prototype (MP469) – Revised Form except:

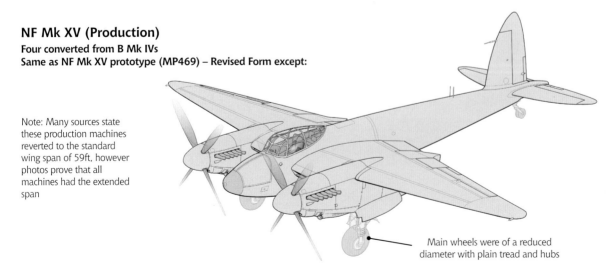

Note: Many sources state these production machines reverted to the standard wing span of 59ft, however photos prove that all machines had the extended span

Main wheels were of a reduced diameter with plain tread and hubs

NF Mk XVII
Similar to NF Mk XII

Two dipole antennae above and below each wing tip on centreline

Narrow three-blade propellers

Shrouded exhausts

Machine-gun armament in nose replaced by American A.I. Mk X (SCR.720) radar in 'universal' (Bullnose) radome

4x 20mm Hispano cannon in the ventral bay

Fighter canopy

Whip antenna for Gee fitted on dorsal spine, just aft of canopy (not always fitted)

Aerial mast on dorsal spine, no aerial lead

Plain main wheel hubs with block pattern tread tyres

Two Rolls-Royce Merlin 21 or 23 (single-stage) engines

Twin tail lights

Twin-contact, anti-shimmy, tailwheel tyre

Single wing tip lights

Small blister in oval access panel under radome

Dipole antenna on fuselage centreline directly aft of the cannon ports

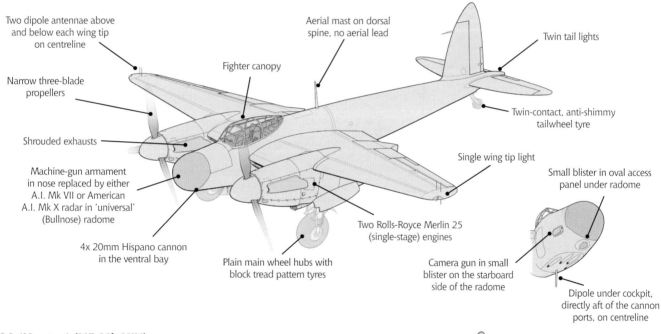

NF Mk XIX

Two dipole antennae above and below each wing tip on centreline

Narrow three-blade propellers

Shrouded exhausts

Machine-gun armament in nose replaced by either A.I. Mk VII or American A.I. Mk X radar in 'universal' (Bullnose) radome

4x 20mm Hispano cannon in the ventral bay

Fighter canopy

Aerial mast on dorsal spine, no aerial lead

Plain main wheel hubs with block tread pattern tyres

Two Rolls-Royce Merlin 25 (single-stage) engines

Twin tail lights

Twin-contact, anti-shimmy tailwheel tyre

Single wing tip light

Small blister in oval access panel under radome

Camera gun in small blister on the starboard side of the radome

Dipole under cockpit, directly aft of the cannon ports, on centreline

J 30 'Hunter' (NF Mk XIX)
Same as NF Mk XIX except:

Fighter canopy with bulged side panels

Whip antenna out of the back of the canopy

Four-blade propellers

First three machines had shrouded exhausts, the rest had exposed exhaust stacks

Radio altimeter 'T' antenna under each wing, just aft of the centreline

Landing light in leading edge of starboard wing

Universal shackles for bombs and drop tanks carried under each outer wing panel (rarely see anything attached to these)

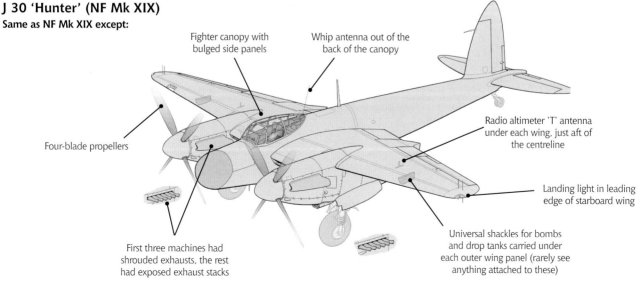

NF Mk XXX (Designated 'Mk 30' after 1948)

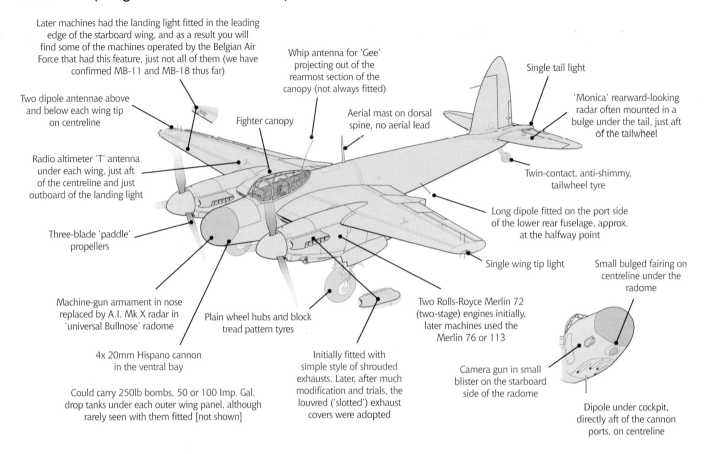

Later machines had the landing light fitted in the leading edge of the starboard wing, and as a result you will find some of the machines operated by the Belgian Air Force that had this feature, just not all of them (we have confirmed MB-11 and MB-18 thus far)

Two dipole antennae above and below each wing tip on centreline

Radio altimeter 'T' antenna under each wing, just aft of the centreline and just outboard of the landing light

Three-blade 'paddle' propellers

Machine-gun armament in nose replaced by A.I. Mk X radar in 'universal Bullnose' radome

4x 20mm Hispano cannon in the ventral bay

Could carry 250lb bombs, 50 or 100 Imp. Gal. drop tanks under each outer wing panel, although rarely seen with them fitted [not shown]

Fighter canopy

Whip antenna for 'Gee' projecting out of the rearmost section of the canopy (not always fitted)

Aerial mast on dorsal spine, no aerial lead

Plain wheel hubs and block tread pattern tyres

Initially fitted with simple style of shrouded exhausts. Later, after much modification and trials, the louvred ('slotted') exhaust covers were adopted

Single tail light

'Monica' rearward-looking radar often mounted in a bulge under the tail, just aft of the tailwheel

Twin-contact, anti-shimmy, tailwheel tyre

Long dipole fitted on the port side of the lower rear fuselage, approx. at the halfway point

Single wing tip light

Two Rolls-Royce Merlin 72 (two-stage) engines initially, later machines used the Merlin 76 or 113

Small bulged fairing on centreline under the radome

Camera gun in small blister on the starboard side of the radome

Dipole under cockpit, directly aft of the cannon ports, on centreline

NF Mk XXXI

Reserved for a Packard Merlin 69-powered night fighter, but never produced

NF Mk 36

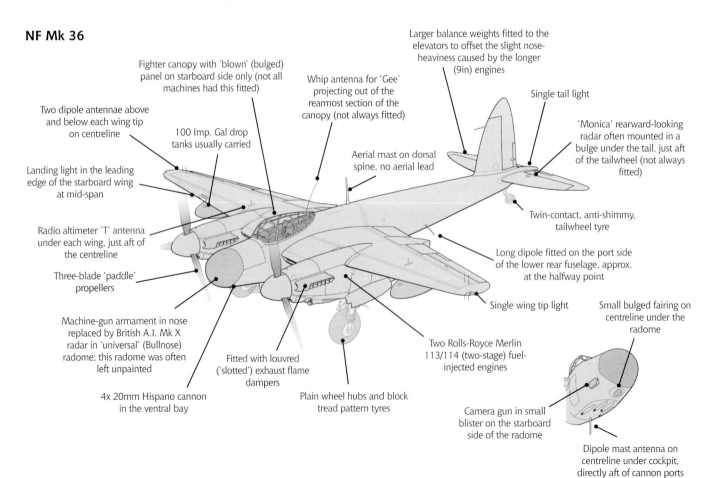

Fighter canopy with 'blown' (bulged) panel on starboard side only (not all machines had this fitted)

Two dipole antennae above and below each wing tip on centreline

100 Imp. Gal drop tanks usually carried

Landing light in the leading edge of the starboard wing at mid-span

Radio altimeter 'T' antenna under each wing, just aft of the centreline

Three-blade 'paddle' propellers

Machine-gun armament in nose replaced by British A.I. Mk X radar in 'universal' (Bullnose) radome; this radome was often left unpainted

4x 20mm Hispano cannon in the ventral bay

Whip antenna for 'Gee' projecting out of the rearmost section of the canopy (not always fitted)

Aerial mast on dorsal spine, no aerial lead

Fitted with louvred ('slotted') exhaust flame dampers

Plain wheel hubs and block tread pattern tyres

Larger balance weights fitted to the elevators to offset the slight nose-heaviness caused by the longer (9in) engines

Single tail light

'Monica' rearward-looking radar often mounted in a bulge under the tail, just aft of the tailwheel (not always fitted)

Twin-contact, anti-shimmy, tailwheel tyre

Long dipole fitted on the port side of the lower rear fuselage, approx. at the halfway point

Single wing tip light

Two Rolls-Royce Merlin 113/114 (two-stage) fuel-injected engines

Small bulged fairing on centreline under the radome

Camera gun in small blister on the starboard side of the radome

Dipole mast antenna on centreline under cockpit, directly aft of cannon ports

NF Mk 36 (Hookah)

Same as NF Mk 36 except:

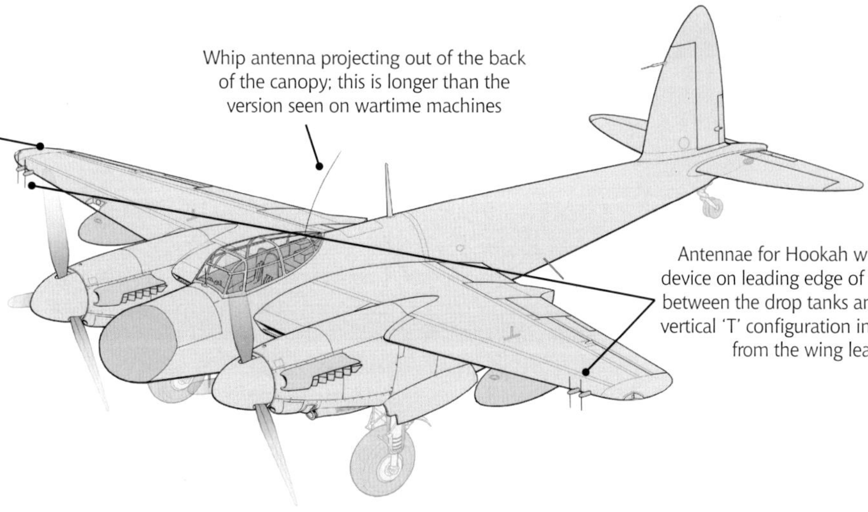
Whip antenna projecting out of the back of the canopy; this is longer than the version seen on wartime machines
No antennae above and below each wing tip, on centreline
Antennae for Hookah wide-band homing device on leading edge of each wing, halfway between the drop tanks and tips, mounted as vertical 'T' configuration in bulges that project from the wing leading edge

NF Mk 38

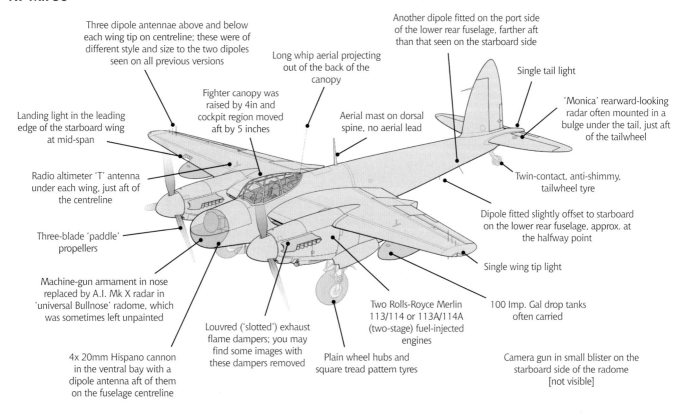

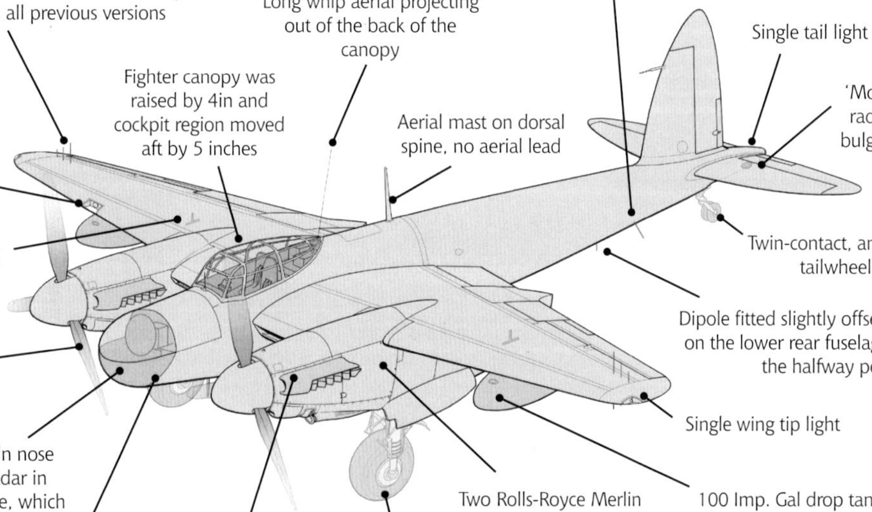
Three dipole antennae above and below each wing tip on centreline; these were of different style and size to the two dipoles seen on all previous versions
Another dipole fitted on the port side of the lower rear fuselage, farther aft than that seen on the starboard side
Long whip aerial projecting out of the back of the canopy
Single tail light
Fighter canopy was raised by 4in and cockpit region moved aft by 5 inches
'Monica' rearward-looking radar often mounted in a bulge under the tail, just aft of the tailwheel
Landing light in the leading edge of the starboard wing at mid-span
Aerial mast on dorsal spine, no aerial lead
Radio altimeter 'T' antenna under each wing, just aft of the centreline
Twin-contact, anti-shimmy, tailwheel tyre
Dipole fitted slightly offset to starboard on the lower rear fuselage, approx. at the halfway point
Three-blade 'paddle' propellers
Single wing tip light
Machine-gun armament in nose replaced by A.I. Mk X radar in 'universal Bullnose' radome, which was sometimes left unpainted
Two Rolls-Royce Merlin 113/114 or 113A/114A (two-stage) fuel-injected engines
100 Imp. Gal drop tanks often carried
Louvred ('slotted') exhaust flame dampers; you may find some images with these dampers removed
4x 20mm Hispano cannon in the ventral bay with a dipole antenna aft of them on the fuselage centreline
Plain wheel hubs and square tread pattern tyres
Camera gun in small blister on the starboard side of the radome [not visible]

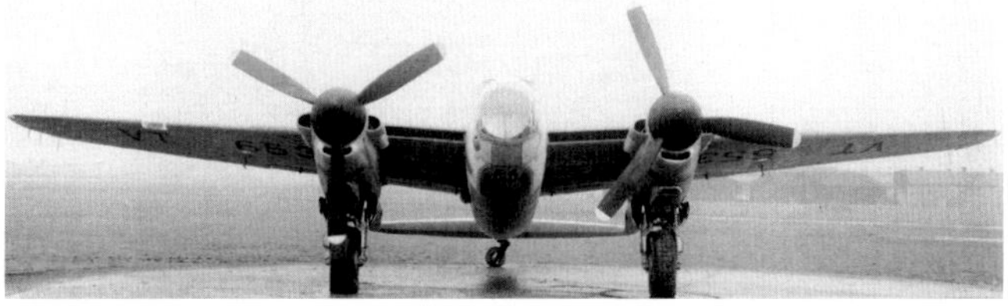

VT653 was the third production airframe and is seen here prior to collection from Hatfield in Jan 1948 *(©DH)*

NF (Met) Mk 38

Same as the NF Mk 38 except:

Note: Very few images of this version exist, so it is impossible to create anything more than a purely speculative isometric

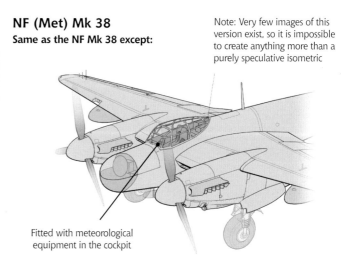

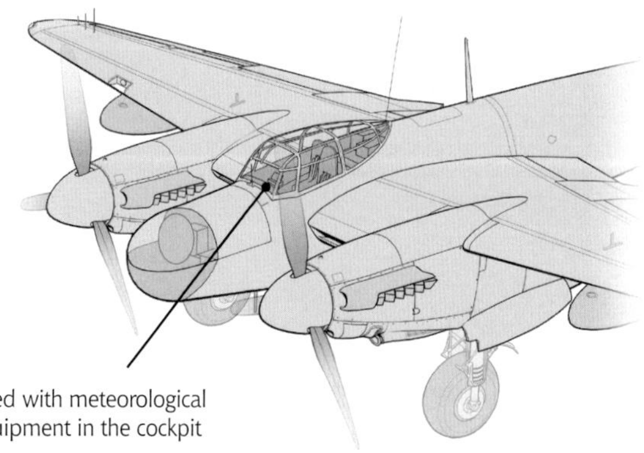
Fitted with meteorological equipment in the cockpit

Fighter-Bombers

FB Mk VI (Series I)

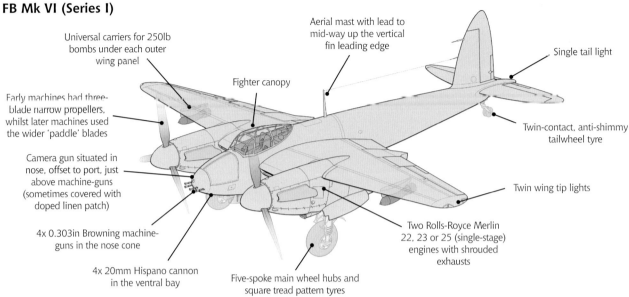

Universal carriers for 250lb bombs under each outer wing panel

Aerial mast with lead to mid-way up the vertical fin leading edge

Single tail light

Fighter canopy

Early machines had three-blade narrow propellers, whilst later machines used the wider 'paddle' blades

Twin-contact, anti-shimmy tailwheel tyre

Camera gun situated in nose, offset to port, just above machine-guns (sometimes covered with doped linen patch)

Twin wing tip lights

4x 0.303in Browning machine-guns in the nose cone

Two Rolls-Royce Merlin 22, 23 or 25 (single-stage) engines with shrouded exhausts

4x 20mm Hispano cannon in the ventral bay

Five-spoke main wheel hubs and square tread pattern tyres

FB Mk VI (Series II)
Same as FB Mk VI (Series I) except:

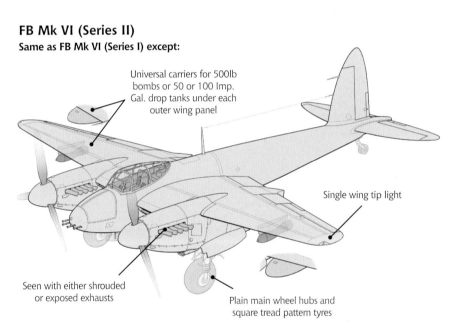

Universal carriers for 500lb bombs or 50 or 100 Imp. Gal. drop tanks under each outer wing panel

Single wing tip light

Seen with either shrouded or exposed exhausts

Plain main wheel hubs and square tread pattern tyres

FB Mk VI (RP)
Same as FB Mk VI (Series II) except:

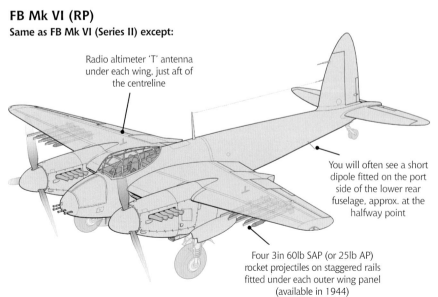

Radio altimeter 'T' antenna under each wing, just aft of the centreline

You will often see a short dipole fitted on the port side of the lower rear fuselage, approx. at the halfway point

Four 3in 60lb SAP (or 25lb AP) rocket projectiles on staggered rails fitted under each outer wing panel (available in 1944)

FB Mk VI, MM403, SB•V of No.464 Squadron at Hunsdon being loaded with 500lb MC bombs

(©Crown Copyright)

FB Mk VIs attack the Norwegian vessel Lysaker (under German control) in the little harbour of Tetgenaes at Stadlandet, Dalsfjord 23rd March 1945 *(©Air Ministry)*

FB Mk VI (Banff – Series I)
Same as FB Mk VI (Series I) except:

Whip antenna projecting out the rearmost section of the canopy

Aerial mast on dorsal spine, no lead

Whip antenna on dorsal spine, midway between the aerial mast and vertical fin

Aerial lead from high up on the leading edge of the vertical fin to a point 3/4rds the way back along the dorsal spine

Short dipole fitted on the port side of the lower rear fuselage, approx. at the halfway point

Seen with either shrouded or exposed exhausts

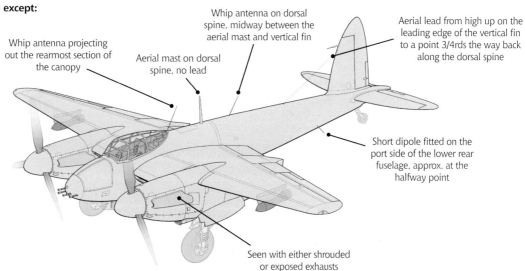

FB Mk VI (Nos.23, 141 & 515 Squadrons, 100 Group, early 1945)
Same as FB Mk VI (Banff – Series I) except:

Two dipoles mounted above and below the wing tips, on the centreline

'Monica' rearward-looking radar often mounted in a bulge under the tail, just aft of the tailwheel

Machine-gun armament in nose replaced with ASH radar pod

100 Imp. Gal. drop tank carried under each outer wing panel

Seen with either 5-spoke or plain wheel hubs

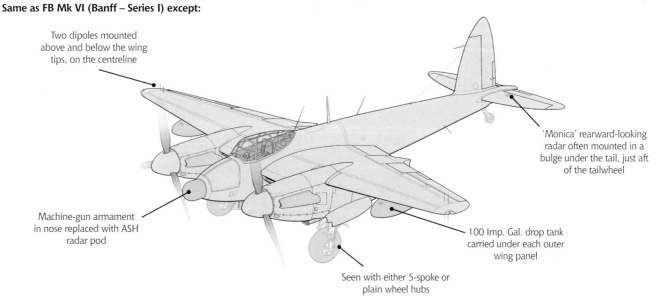

FB Mk VI (Banff – Series II) – Initial Form
Same as FB Mk VI (Banff – Series I) except:

(See photo next page)

Gun/rocket camera relocated to centre of nose cone with raised edge to top as lens cover projected out of the cone, not recessed back into it, as had previously been the case

Plain main wheel hubs with block tread pattern tyres

Strengthening underneath outer wing panels to accept rocket projectile Mk IIIA rails to carry either eight 25lb AP or 60lb HE 3in rockets

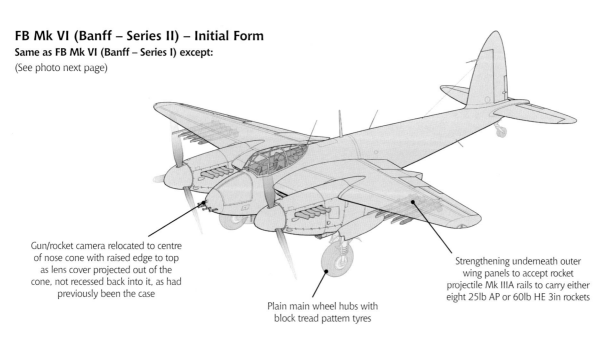

A close-up of the nose of this Banff Wing FB Mk VI clearly shows the pronounced ring around the camera gun in the top of the nose cone

FB Mk VI (Banff – Series II) – Final Form
Same as FB Mk VI (Banff – Series II) – Initial Form except:

To stop the drop tank hitting the RP rails on separation, there was a metal frame situated between the inner rails and the tank under each wing

FB Mk VI, PZ446 of No.143 Squadron being rearmed at Banff with 3in 60lb RPs; note that the entire background has been removed by the wartime censors *(©British Official)*

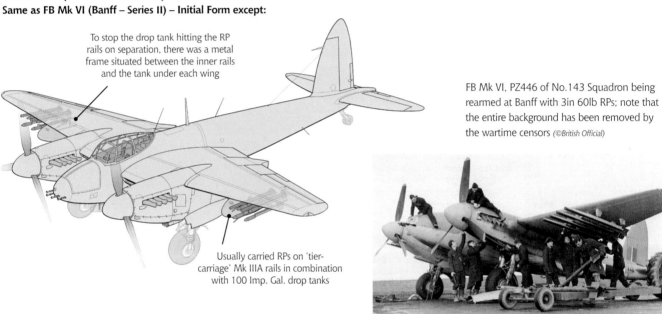

Usually carried RPs on 'tier-carriage' Mk IIIA rails in combination with 100 Imp. Gal. drop tanks

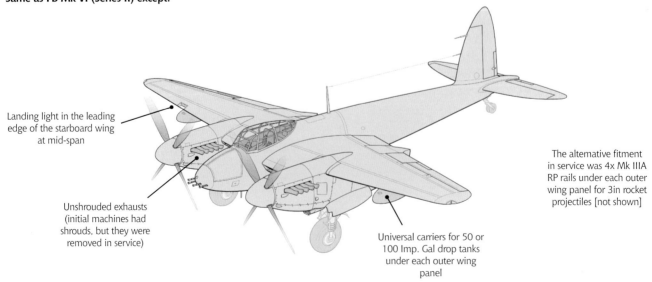

FB Mk VI (Turkish Air Force)
Same as FB Mk VI (Series II) except:

Landing light in the leading edge of the starboard wing at mid-span

Unshrouded exhausts (initial machines had shrouds, but they were removed in service)

Universal carriers for 50 or 100 Imp. Gal drop tanks under each outer wing panel

The alternative fitment in service was 4x Mk IIIA RP rails under each outer wing panel for 3in rocket projectiles [not shown]

FB Mk VI (Royal Norwegian Air Force)
Same as FB Mk VI (Series II) except:

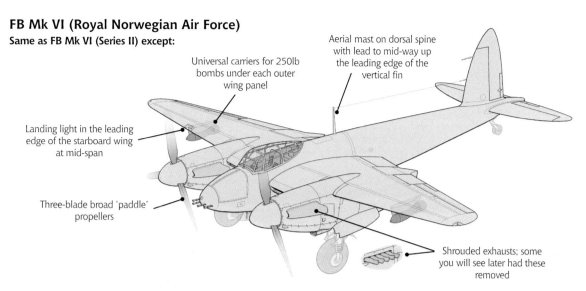

Universal carriers for 250lb bombs under each outer wing panel

Aerial mast on dorsal spine with lead to mid-way up the leading edge of the vertical fin

Landing light in the leading edge of the starboard wing at mid-span

Three-blade broad 'paddle' propellers

Shrouded exhausts; some you will see later had these removed

FB Mk VI (Dominican Air Force)
Same as FB Mk VI (Series II) except:

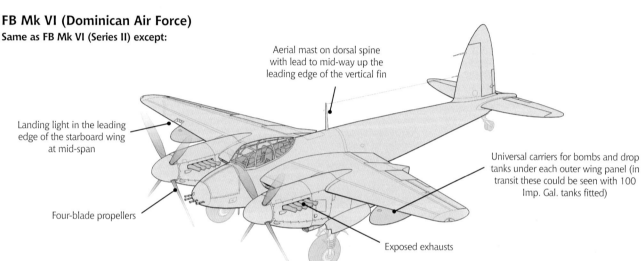

Aerial mast on dorsal spine with lead to mid-way up the leading edge of the vertical fin

Landing light in the leading edge of the starboard wing at mid-span

Universal carriers for bombs and drop tanks under each outer wing panel (in transit these could be seen with 100 Imp. Gal. tanks fitted)

Four-blade propellers

Exposed exhausts

FB Mk VI (RAAF)
Same as FB Mk VI (Series II) except:

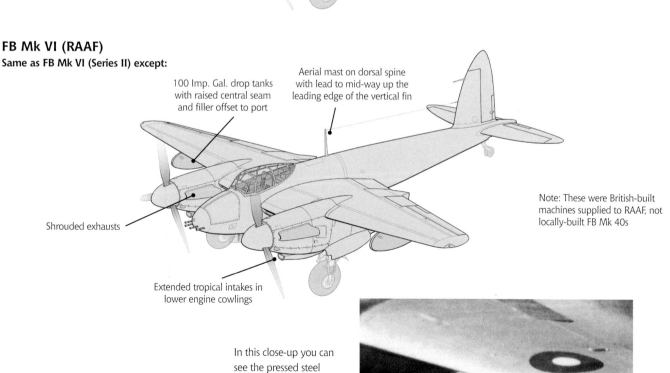

100 Imp. Gal. drop tanks with raised central seam and filler offset to port

Aerial mast on dorsal spine with lead to mid-way up the leading edge of the vertical fin

Shrouded exhausts

Note: These were British-built machines supplied to RAAF; not locally-built FB Mk 40s

Extended tropical intakes in lower engine cowlings

In this close-up you can see the pressed steel drop tanks with the pronounced seam down the middle, plus the filler cap offset to port
(©RAAF Official)

FB Mk X (Project Only)

This was to be a Packard Merlin 67 powered version of the FB Mk VI but it was never built

FB Mk XVIII (Early)

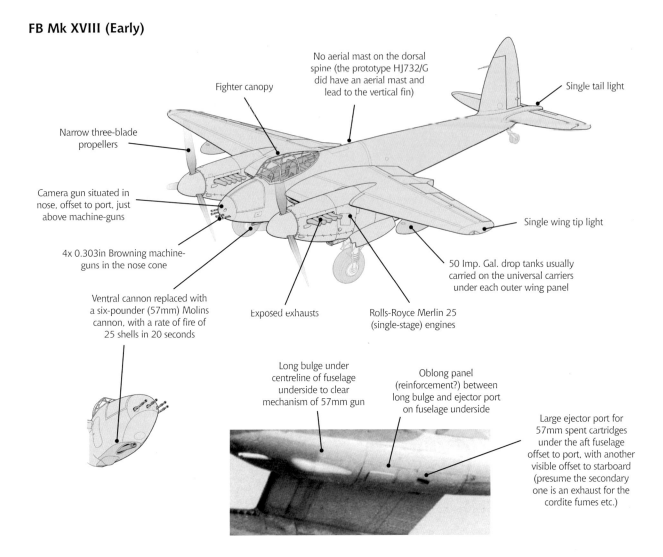

No aerial mast on the dorsal spine (the prototype HJ732/G did have an aerial mast and lead to the vertical fin)

Fighter canopy

Single tail light

Narrow three-blade propellers

Single wing tip light

Camera gun situated in nose, offset to port, just above machine-guns

50 Imp. Gal. drop tanks usually carried on the universal carriers under each outer wing panel

4x 0.303in Browning machine-guns in the nose cone

Ventral cannon replaced with a six-pounder (57mm) Molins cannon, with a rate of fire of 25 shells in 20 seconds

Exposed exhausts

Rolls-Royce Merlin 25 (single-stage) engines

Long bulge under centreline of fuselage underside to clear mechanism of 57mm gun

Oblong panel (reinforcement?) between long bulge and ejector port on fuselage underside

Large ejector port for 57mm spent cartridges under the aft fuselage offset to port, with another visible offset to starboard (presume the secondary one is an exhaust for the cordite fumes etc.)

FB Mk XVIII (Late)
Same as FB Mk XVIII (Early) except:

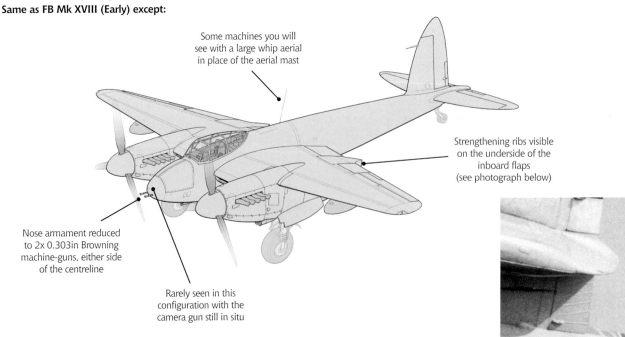

Some machines you will see with a large whip aerial in place of the aerial mast

Strengthening ribs visible on the underside of the inboard flaps (see photograph below)

Nose armament reduced to 2x 0.303in Browning machine-guns, either side of the centreline

Rarely seen in this configuration with the camera gun still in situ

FB Mk 21 (Canada)
Canadian-built FB Mk VI, only three built, same as FB Mk VI except:

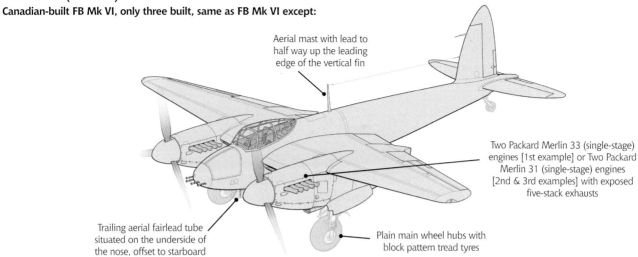

Aerial mast with lead to half way up the leading edge of the vertical fin

Two Packard Merlin 33 (single-stage) engines [1st example] or Two Packard Merlin 31 (single-stage) engines [2nd & 3rd examples] with exposed five-stack exhausts

Trailing aerial fairlead tube situated on the underside of the nose, offset to starboard

Plain main wheel hubs with block pattern tread tyres

FB Mk 24 (Canada)
Canadian-built high-altitude fighter-bomber developed from the FB Mk 21
Same as FB Mk 21 except:

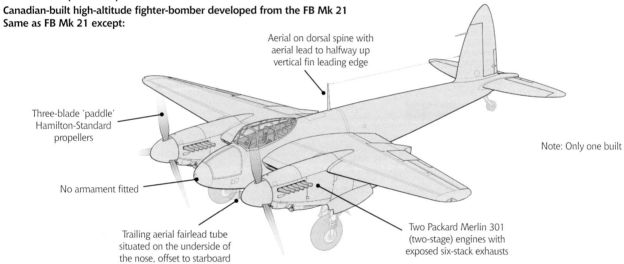

Aerial on dorsal spine with aerial lead to halfway up vertical fin leading edge

Three-blade 'paddle' Hamilton-Standard propellers

No armament fitted

Note: Only one built

Trailing aerial fairlead tube situated on the underside of the nose, offset to starboard

Two Packard Merlin 301 (two-stage) engines with exposed six-stack exhausts

FB Mk 26 (Canada including Chinese operated examples)

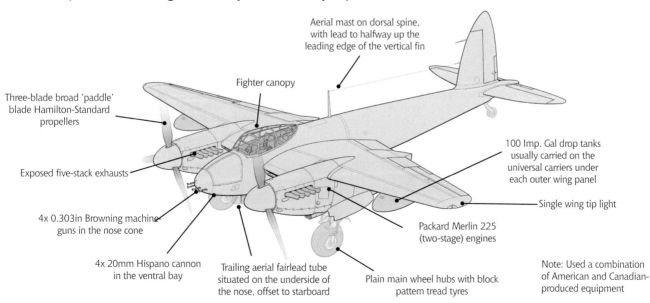

Aerial mast on dorsal spine, with lead to halfway up the leading edge of the vertical fin

Fighter canopy

Three-blade broad 'paddle' blade Hamilton-Standard propellers

Exposed five-stack exhausts

4x 0.303in Browning machine guns in the nose cone

4x 20mm Hispano cannon in the ventral bay

Trailing aerial fairlead tube situated on the underside of the nose, offset to starboard

Plain main wheel hubs with block pattern tread tyres

Packard Merlin 225 (two-stage) engines

100 Imp. Gal drop tanks usually carried on the universal carriers under each outer wing panel

Single wing tip light

Note: Used a combination of American and Canadian-produced equipment

FB Mk 28 (Canada)
Mark allocated to Canadian production but never taken up

FB Mk 40 (Australia)

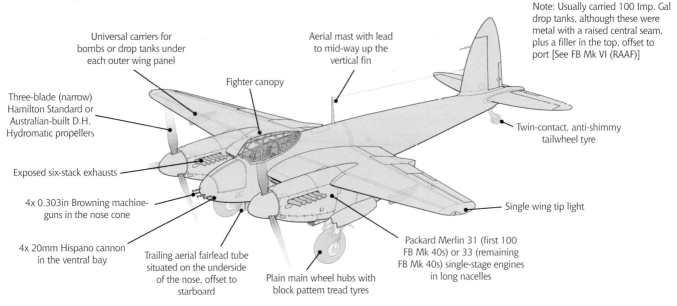

Universal carriers for bombs or drop tanks under each outer wing panel

Aerial mast with lead to mid-way up the vertical fin

Note: Usually carried 100 Imp. Gal drop tanks, although these were metal with a raised central seam, plus a filler in the top, offset to port [See FB Mk VI (RAAF)]

Fighter canopy

Three-blade (narrow) Hamilton Standard or Australian-built D.H. Hydromatic propellers

Twin-contact, anti-shimmy tailwheel tyre

Exposed six-stack exhausts

4x 0.303in Browning machine-guns in the nose cone

Single wing tip light

4x 20mm Hispano cannon in the ventral bay

Trailing aerial fairlead tube situated on the underside of the nose, offset to starboard

Plain main wheel hubs with block pattern tread tyres

Packard Merlin 31 (first 100 FB Mk 40s) or 33 (remaining FB Mk 40s) single-stage engines in long nacelles

FB Mk 42 (Australia)
Same as FB Mk 40 except:
• Two Packard Merlin 69 engines
After testing this variant was dropped and converted to become the PR Mk 41(see later in this section)

Photo-Reconnaissance

PR Mk 40 (Australia) A52-2 – converted from FB Mk 40
Same as FB Mk 40 except:

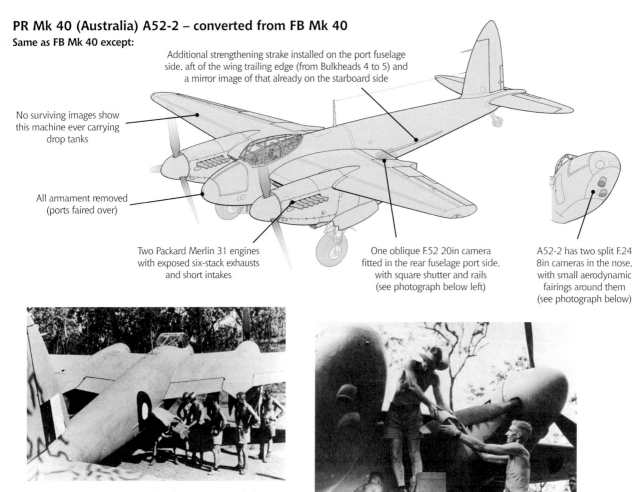

Additional strengthening strake installed on the port fuselage side, aft of the wing trailing edge (from Bulkheads 4 to 5) and a mirror image of that already on the starboard side

No surviving images show this machine ever carrying drop tanks

All armament removed (ports faired over)

Two Packard Merlin 31 engines with exposed six-stack exhausts and short intakes

One oblique F.52 20in camera fitted in the rear fuselage port side, with square shutter and rails (see photograph below left)

A52-2 has two split F.24 8in cameras in the nose, with small aerodynamic fairings around them (see photograph below)

PR Mk 40 A52-2 during one of its first missions, with the crew loading film cassettes for the F.24 camera in the rear fuselage *(©J. Love)*

PR Mk 40 A52-2 with crew loading film cassettes for the F.52 cameras in the nose *(©J Love)*

PR Mk 40 (Australia) remainder – converted from FB Mk 40
Same as FB Mk 40 except:

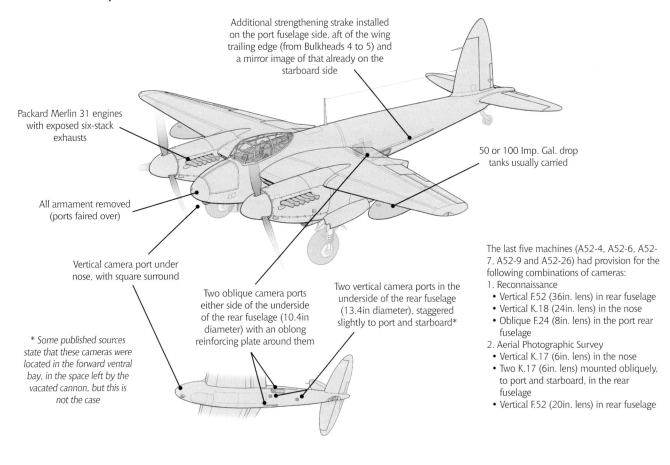

Additional strengthening strake installed on the port fuselage side, aft of the wing trailing edge (from Bulkheads 4 to 5) and a mirror image of that already on the starboard side

Packard Merlin 31 engines with exposed six-stack exhausts

50 or 100 Imp. Gal. drop tanks usually carried

All armament removed (ports faired over)

Vertical camera port under nose, with square surround

Two oblique camera ports either side of the underside of the rear fuselage (10.4in diameter) with an oblong reinforcing plate around them

Two vertical camera ports in the underside of the rear fuselage (13.4in diameter), staggered slightly to port and starboard*

Some published sources state that these cameras were located in the forward ventral bay, in the space left by the vacated cannon, but this is not the case

The last five machines (A52-4, A52-6, A52-7, A52-9 and A52-26) had provision for the following combinations of cameras:
1. Reconnaissance
   • Vertical F.52 (36in. lens) in rear fuselage
   • Vertical K.18 (24in. lens) in the nose
   • Oblique F.24 (8in. lens) in the port rear fuselage
2. Aerial Photographic Survey
   • Vertical K.17 (6in. lens) in the nose
   • Two K.17 (6in. lens) mounted obliquely, to port and starboard, in the rear fuselage
   • Vertical F.52 (20in. lens) in rear fuselage

PR Mk 41 (Australia)
Originally intended as the FB Mk 41, but project dropped and developed as this photo-reconnaissance version instead

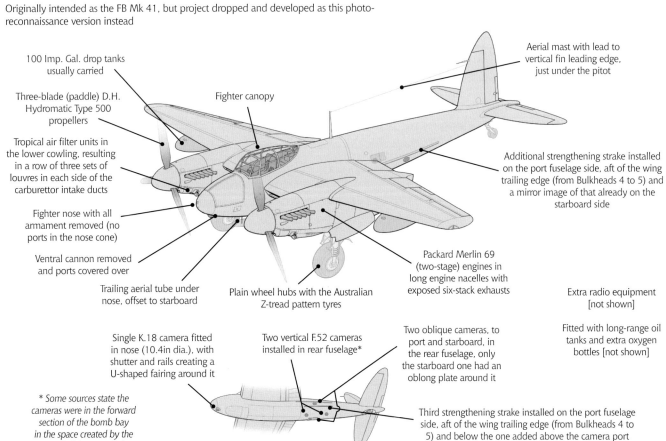

100 Imp. Gal. drop tanks usually carried

Three-blade (paddle) D.H. Hydromatic Type 500 propellers

Tropical air filter units in the lower cowling, resulting in a row of three sets of louvres in each side of the carburettor intake ducts

Fighter nose with all armament removed (no ports in the nose cone)

Ventral cannon removed and ports covered over

Trailing aerial tube under nose, offset to starboard

Fighter canopy

Aerial mast with lead to vertical fin leading edge, just under the pitot

Additional strengthening strake installed on the port fuselage side, aft of the wing trailing edge (from Bulkheads 4 to 5) and a mirror image of that already on the starboard side

Packard Merlin 69 (two-stage) engines in long engine nacelles with exposed six-stack exhausts

Plain wheel hubs with the Australian Z-tread pattern tyres

Extra radio equipment [not shown]

Fitted with long-range oil tanks and extra oxygen bottles [not shown]

Single K.18 camera fitted in nose (10.4in dia.), with shutter and rails creating a U-shaped fairing around it

Two vertical F.52 cameras installed in rear fuselage*

Two oblique cameras, to port and starboard, in the rear fuselage, only the starboard one had an oblong plate around it

Some sources state the cameras were in the forward section of the bomb bay in the space created by the removal of the cannon, but this is not the case

Third strengthening strake installed on the port fuselage side, aft of the wing trailing edge (from Bulkheads 4 to 5) and below the one added above the camera port

Trainer & Target-Tug

T Mk III (Early)

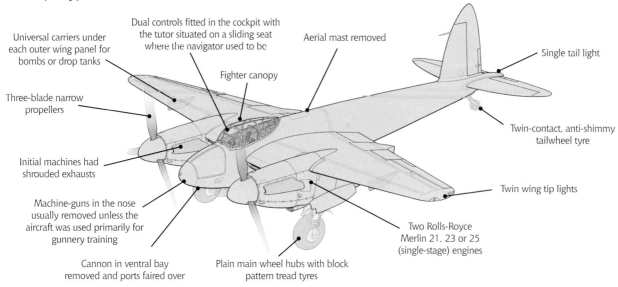

Universal carriers under each outer wing panel for bombs or drop tanks

Dual controls fitted in the cockpit with the tutor situated on a sliding seat where the navigator used to be

Aerial mast removed

Single tail light

Fighter canopy

Three-blade narrow propellers

Twin-contact, anti-shimmy tailwheel tyre

Initial machines had shrouded exhausts

Twin wing tip lights

Machine-guns in the nose usually removed unless the aircraft was used primarily for gunnery training

Two Rolls-Royce Merlin 21, 23 or 25 (single-stage) engines

Cannon in ventral bay removed and ports faired over

Plain main wheel hubs with block pattern tread tyres

T Mk III (Late)
Same as T Mk III (Early) except:

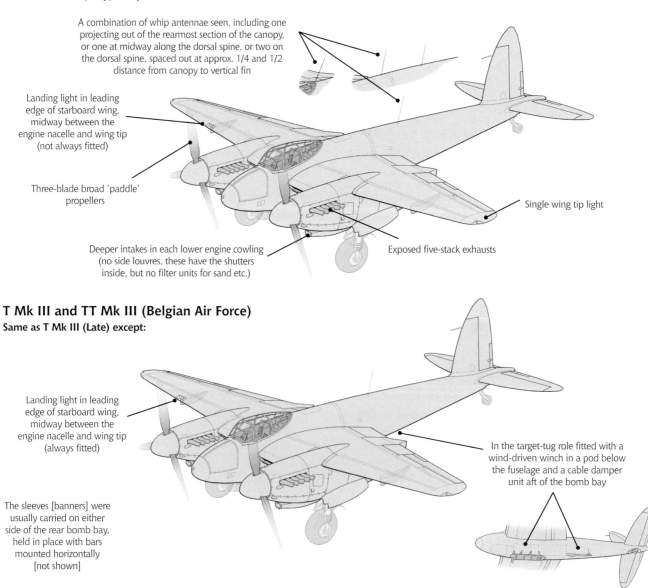

A combination of whip antennae seen, including one projecting out of the rearmost section of the canopy, or one at midway along the dorsal spine, or two on the dorsal spine, spaced out at approx. 1/4 and 1/2 distance from canopy to vertical fin

Landing light in leading edge of starboard wing, midway between the engine nacelle and wing tip (not always fitted)

Three-blade broad 'paddle' propellers

Single wing tip light

Deeper intakes in each lower engine cowling (no side louvres, these have the shutters inside, but no filter units for sand etc.)

Exposed five-stack exhausts

T Mk III and TT Mk III (Belgian Air Force)
Same as T Mk III (Late) except:

Landing light in leading edge of starboard wing, midway between the engine nacelle and wing tip (always fitted)

In the target-tug role fitted with a wind-driven winch in a pod below the fuselage and a cable damper unit aft of the bomb bay

The sleeves [banners] were usually carried on either side of the rear bomb bay, held in place with bars mounted horizontally [not shown]

TT Mk 6 (Belgian Air Force)
Same as FB Mk VI (Series II) except:

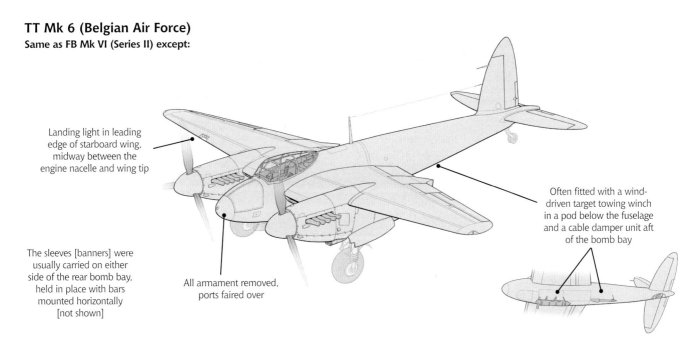

Landing light in leading edge of starboard wing, midway between the engine nacelle and wing tip

Often fitted with a wind-driven target towing winch in a pod below the fuselage and a cable damper unit aft of the bomb bay

The sleeves [banners] were usually carried on either side of the rear bomb bay, held in place with bars mounted horizontally [not shown]

All armament removed, ports faired over

T Mk 22 (Canada)
Dual-control trainer based on the FB Mk 21
Only six built

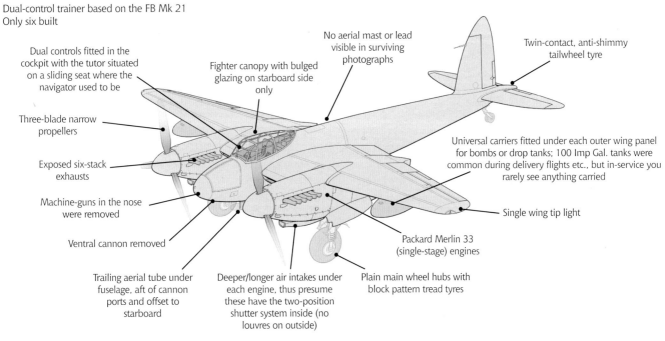

Dual controls fitted in the cockpit with the tutor situated on a sliding seat where the navigator used to be

Fighter canopy with bulged glazing on starboard side only

No aerial mast or lead visible in surviving photographs

Twin-contact, anti-shimmy tailwheel tyre

Three-blade narrow propellers

Exposed six-stack exhausts

Machine-guns in the nose were removed

Ventral cannon removed

Universal carriers fitted under each outer wing panel for bombs or drop tanks; 100 Imp Gal. tanks were common during delivery flights etc., but in-service you rarely see anything carried

Single wing tip light

Packard Merlin 33 (single-stage) engines

Trailing aerial tube under fuselage, aft of cannon ports and offset to starboard

Deeper/longer air intakes under each engine, thus presume these have the two-position shutter system inside (no louvres on outside)

Plain main wheel hubs with block pattern tread tyres

T Mk 27 (Canada)
Same as T Mk 22 (Canada) except:

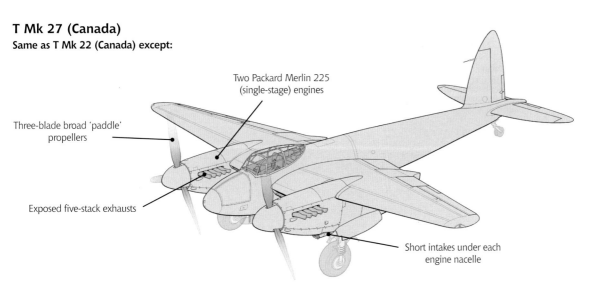

Two Packard Merlin 225 (single-stage) engines

Three-blade broad 'paddle' propellers

Exposed five-stack exhausts

Short intakes under each engine nacelle

T Mk 29 (Canada) – Early
Dual-control trainer developed from the FB Mk VI
(many were FB Mk 26s built without armament due to shortages of cannon)

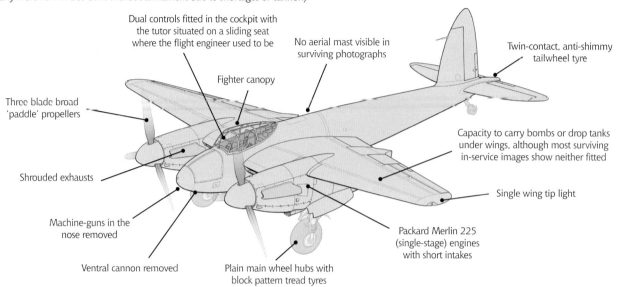

Dual controls fitted in the cockpit with the tutor situated on a sliding seat where the flight engineer used to be

No aerial mast visible in surviving photographs

Fighter canopy

Twin-contact, anti-shimmy tailwheel tyre

Three blade broad 'paddle' propellers

Capacity to carry bombs or drop tanks under wings, although most surviving in-service images show neither fitted

Shrouded exhausts

Single wing tip light

Machine-guns in the nose removed

Packard Merlin 225 (single-stage) engines with short intakes

Ventral cannon removed

Plain main wheel hubs with block pattern tread tyres

T Mk 29 (Canada) – Late
Same as T Mk 29 (Canada) – Early except:

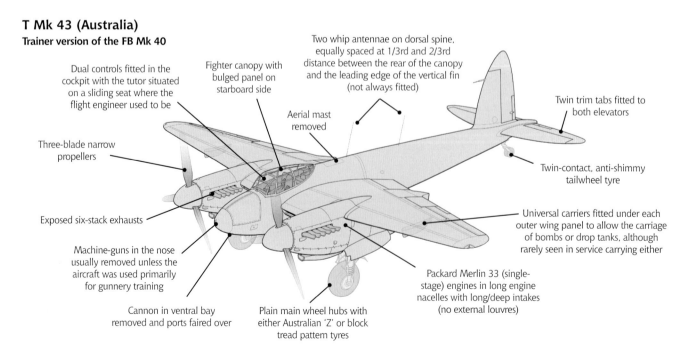

Aerial mast on dorsal spine with lead to halfway up the leading edge of the vertical fin

Exposed six-stack exhausts

100 Imp. Gal drop tanks usually carried on the universal carriers fitted under each outer wing panel

T Mk 43 (Australia)
Trainer version of the FB Mk 40

Dual controls fitted in the cockpit with the tutor situated on a sliding seat where the flight engineer used to be

Fighter canopy with bulged panel on starboard side

Two whip antennae on dorsal spine, equally spaced at 1/3rd and 2/3rd distance between the rear of the canopy and the leading edge of the vertical fin (not always fitted)

Twin trim tabs fitted to both elevators

Three-blade narrow propellers

Aerial mast removed

Twin-contact, anti-shimmy tailwheel tyre

Exposed six-stack exhausts

Universal carriers fitted under each outer wing panel to allow the carriage of bombs or drop tanks, although rarely seen in service carrying either

Machine-guns in the nose usually removed unless the aircraft was used primarily for gunnery training

Packard Merlin 33 (single-stage) engines in long engine nacelles with long/deep intakes (no external louvres)

Cannon in ventral bay removed and ports faired over

Plain main wheel hubs with either Australian 'Z' or block tread pattern tyres

Sea Mosquito

Navalised FB Mk VI (LR359) – TR Mk 33 prototype

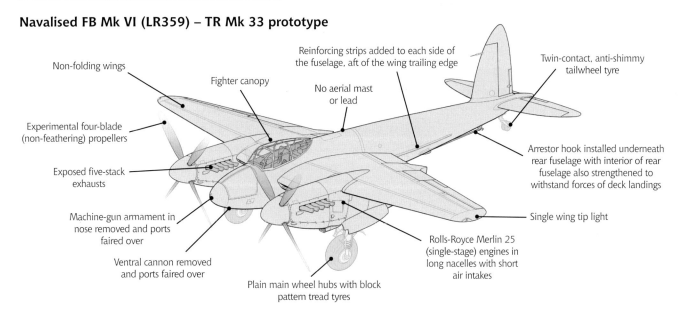

Non-folding wings

Fighter canopy

Reinforcing strips added to each side of the fuselage, aft of the wing trailing edge

Twin-contact, anti-shimmy tailwheel tyre

No aerial mast or lead

Experimental four-blade (non-feathering) propellers

Exposed five-stack exhausts

Arrestor hook installed underneath rear fuselage with interior of rear fuselage also strengthened to withstand forces of deck landings

Machine-gun armament in nose removed and ports faired over

Single wing tip light

Ventral cannon removed and ports faired over

Rolls-Royce Merlin 25 (single-stage) engines in long nacelles with short air intakes

Plain main wheel hubs with block pattern tread tyres

Navalised FB Mk VI (LR387) – TR Mk 33 second prototype
Same as Navalised FB Mk VI (LR359) TR Mk 33 prototype except:

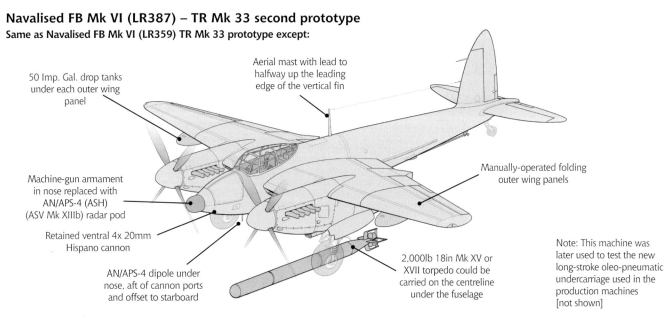

50 Imp. Gal. drop tanks under each outer wing panel

Aerial mast with lead to halfway up the leading edge of the vertical fin

Machine-gun armament in nose replaced with AN/APS-4 (ASH) (ASV Mk XIIIb) radar pod

Manually-operated folding outer wing panels

Retained ventral 4x 20mm Hispano cannon

AN/APS-4 dipole under nose, aft of cannon ports and offset to starboard

2,000lb 18in Mk XV or XVII torpedo could be carried on the centreline under the fuselage

Note: This machine was later used to test the new long-stroke oleo-pneumatic undercarriage used in the production machines [not shown]

TF/TR Mk 33 (inc. pre-production TS444 & TS449)
Same as Navalised FB Mk VI (LR387) TR Mk 33 2nd prototype except:

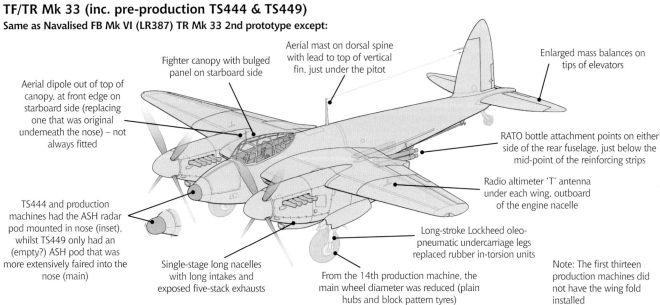

Fighter canopy with bulged panel on starboard side

Aerial mast on dorsal spine with lead to top of vertical fin, just under the pitot

Enlarged mass balances on tips of elevators

Aerial dipole out of top of canopy, at front edge on starboard side (replacing one that was original underneath the nose) – not always fitted

RATO bottle attachment points on either side of the rear fuselage, just below the mid-point of the reinforcing strips

Radio altimeter 'T' antenna under each wing, outboard of the engine nacelle

TS444 and production machines had the ASH radar pod mounted in nose (inset), whilst TS449 only had an (empty?) ASH pod that was more extensively faired into the nose (main)

Single-stage long nacelles with long intakes and exposed five-stack exhausts

Long-stroke Lockheed oleo-pneumatic undercarriage legs replaced rubber in-torsion units

From the 14th production machine, the main wheel diameter was reduced (plain hubs and block pattern tyres)

Note: The first thirteen production machines did not have the wing fold installed

TF/TR Mk 33 – Late
Same as TF/TR Mk 33 (inc. pre-production TS444 & TS449) except:

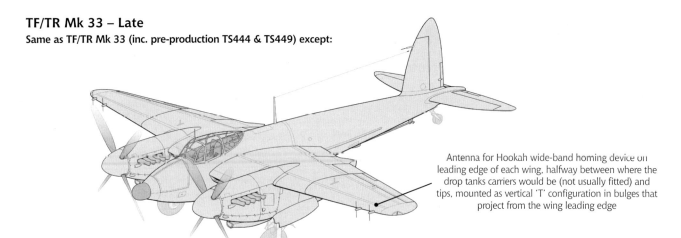

Antenna for Hookah wide-band homing device on leading edge of each wing, halfway between where the drop tanks carriers would be (not usually fitted) and tips, mounted as vertical 'T' configuration in bulges that project from the wing leading edge

TR Mk 33 TW250 with No.751 NAS at Watton as the Radio Warfare Unit, the RN element of the Central Signals Establishment (©FAA/FAAM)

TF/TR Mk 37 (inc. prototype TW240)

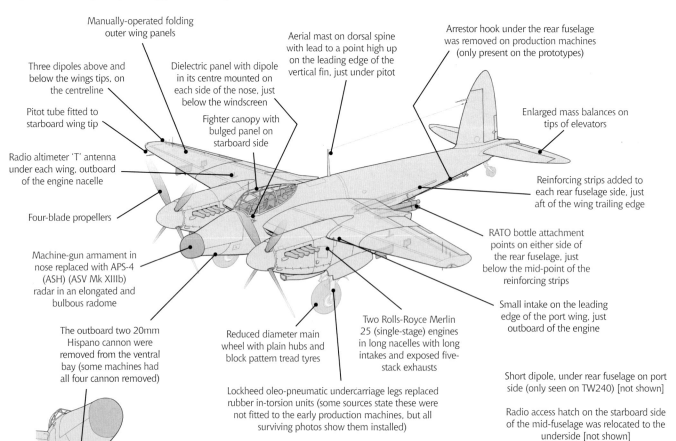

Manually-operated folding outer wing panels

Three dipoles above and below the wings tips, on the centreline

Pitot tube fitted to starboard wing tip

Radio altimeter 'T' antenna under each wing, outboard of the engine nacelle

Four-blade propellers

Machine-gun armament in nose replaced with APS-4 (ASH) (ASV Mk XIIIb) radar in an elongated and bulbous radome

The outboard two 20mm Hispano cannon were removed from the ventral bay (some machines had all four cannon removed)

Dielectric panel with dipole in its centre mounted on each side of the nose, just below the windscreen

Fighter canopy with bulged panel on starboard side

Aerial mast on dorsal spine with lead to a point high up on the leading edge of the vertical fin, just under pitot

Arrestor hook under the rear fuselage was removed on production machines (only present on the prototypes)

Enlarged mass balances on tips of elevators

Reinforcing strips added to each rear fuselage side, just aft of the wing trailing edge

RATO bottle attachment points on either side of the rear fuselage, just below the mid-point of the reinforcing strips

Small intake on the leading edge of the port wing, just outboard of the engine

Reduced diameter main wheel with plain hubs and block pattern tread tyres

Two Rolls-Royce Merlin 25 (single-stage) engines in long nacelles with long intakes and exposed five-stack exhausts

Lockheed oleo-pneumatic undercarriage legs replaced rubber in-torsion units (some sources state these were not fitted to the early production machines, but all surviving photos show them installed)

Short dipole, under rear fuselage on port side (only seen on TW240) [not shown]

Radio access hatch on the starboard side of the mid-fuselage was relocated to the underside [not shown]

Bulge situated under the starboard fuselage side, parallel to the wing centreline (not an intake, as it has no opening in the front) [not shown]

Note: Designed to carry a 1,000lb 'Uncle Tom' rocket projectile on a special rack under each outer wing panel. Only TW240 is photographed with either racks or rockets installed, though; Uncle Tom was the British designation for the American Tiny Tim rocket and was probably never adopted for use due to the damage the big rocket motor's exhaust blast was found to cause to the launch aircraft

Chapter 8: # In Detail

What follows is an extensive selection of images and diagrams that will help you understand the physical nature of the fighter variants, as well as all other versions based upon it.

Cockpit & Canopy

An overall shot of the instrument panel of an FB Mk VI taken by D.H. on the 7th July 1943 *(©DH)*

This diagram from the Pilot's Notes shows the instrument panel and is applicable to the FB Mk VI, XVIII, 24 and 26 *(©Crown Copyright)*

1. Coolant temperature gauges.
2. Compass.
3. Oil temperature gauges.
4. Oil pressure gauges.
5. Fuel pressure warning lights.
6. Boost pressure gauges.
7. Floodlights.
8. R.P.M. indicators.
9. Floodlight rheostats.
10. Stowage for R.I. compass repeater.
11. Exciter button for U.V. lighting.
12. Boost control cut-out.
13. Instrument flying panel.
14. Gun sight bracket.
15. Radiator flap switches.
16. Air intake filter switch.
17. Ultra-violet lamp.
18. Magneto switches.
19. Rudder trimming tab and indicator.
20. Electrical services switch.
21. Immersed pump warning light.
22. Engine starter switches.
23. Booster-coil switches.
24. Ventilators.
25. Feathering buttons.
26. Bomb doors warning light.
27. Bomb containers jettison button.
28. Bombs or tanks/camera change-over switch.
29. Flaps selector.
30. Bomb selector switches.
31. Bomb fusing switches.
32. Undercarriage selector.
33. Gun master switch.
34. Bomb doors selector.
35. Oxygen regulator.
36. Triple pressure gauge.
37. Flaps position indicator.
38. Undercarriage position indicator.
39. Landing lamp switches.

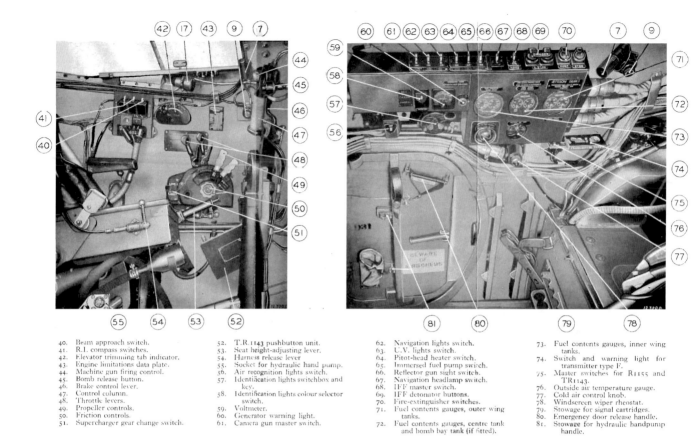

40. Beam approach switch.	52. T.R.1143 pushbutton unit.
41. R.I. compass switches.	53. Seat height-adjusting lever.
42. Elevator trimming tab indicator.	54. Harness release lever.
43. Engine limitations data plate.	55. Socket for hydraulic hand pump.
44. Machine gun firing control.	56. Air recognition lights switch.
45. Bomb release button.	57. Identification lights switchbox and
46. Brake control lever.	key.
47. Control column.	58. Identification lights colour selector
48. Throttle levers.	switch.
49. Propeller controls.	59. Voltmeter.
50. Friction controls.	60. Generator warning light.
51. Supercharger gear change switch.	61. Camera gun master switch.

62. Navigation lights switch.	73. Fuel contents gauges, inner wing
63. U.V. lights switch.	tanks.
64. Pitot-head heater switch.	74. Switch and warning light for
65. Immersed fuel pump switch.	transmitter type F.
66. Reflector gun sight switch.	75. Master switches for R1155 and
67. Navigation headlamp switch.	TR1143.
68. IFF master switch.	76. Outside air temperature gauge.
69. IFF detonator buttons.	77. Cold air control knob.
70. Fire-extinguisher switches.	78. Windscreen wiper rheostat.
71. Fuel contents gauges, outer wing	79. Stowage for signal cartridges.
tanks.	80. Emergency door release handle.
72. Fuel contents gauges, centre tank	81. Stowage for hydraulic handpump
and bomb bay tank (if fitted).	handle.

The port and starboard sidewalls, once again applicable to the FB Mk VI, XVIII and 26 *(©Crown Copyright)*

1. Beam approach visual indicator
2. Blind flying instrument panel
3. Rudder trim control
4. Switches for radiator flaps and tropical air intake (if fitted)
5. Gun reflector sight
6. Boost cut-out handle
7. Instrument board lamp and dimmer
8. Compass floodlamp and dimmer
9. Gunsight spare lamp holder
10. U/c and engine data plates
11. Ultra-violet lamps
12. Tail trim indicator
13. Accessories panel
14. Engine control box
15. Card holders
16. Compass
17. Landing lamp control switches
18. Radio controller. T.R.1133 or T.R.1143
19. Time of flight clock holder
20. Pilot's cold air punkah louvre
21. Undercarriage and flap indicators
22. Pilot's oxygen regulator and pipe
23. Fireman's axe
24. Pressure venting cock
25. Oxygen high pressure valve
26. Fuel drop tanks pressurising cock
27. Cabin heater control
28. Oil dilution switches
28A. Junction box "B" lamp and dimmer
28B. Blind flying panel lamp and dimmer
29. Fuel cocks
30. Observer's oxygen regulator
31. Sanitary tank and funnel
32. Torch
33. Hydraulic handpump
34. First-aid equipment
35. Hydraulic selector unit
36. Gun "fire" and "safe" switch
37. Engine slow running cut-outs
38. Incendiary bomb stowage
39. Aileron trim control
40. Windscreen de-icer
41. Footage indicator
42. Bomb switch panel
43. Bomb container jettison switch
44. "Bomb doors open" warning light
45. Observer's parachute stowage
46. Chart board and map stowage
47. Drift recorder
48. Drift recorder door
49. Lamp extension lead stowage
50. U/c emergency selector valve
51. Entrance ladder
52. Door stay
53. Fire extinguisher
54. Signal cartridge stowage
54A. Fuzes, type "F" transmitter
55. Lamp and lead stowage
56. Hydraulic handpump lever
57. Trailing aerial lead in
58. Trailing aerial winch
59. Gun heater control
60. Gun heater duct
61. Observer's oxygen pipe
62. Observer's armour
63. Observer's intercommunication panel
64. Radio and intercommunication switches
65. Cold air control
66. Door jettison handle
67. Chart board lamp and dimmer
68. Junction box "B"
69. Windscreen wiper control
70. Downward ident. lamp switches
71. Generator warning lamp
72. Downward ident. lamp colour control
73. Resin lamp switch
74. Long range fuel tank warning lamp
75. Observer's cold air punkah louvre
76. Propeller feathering press switches
77. Starter and booster coil press switches
78. Ignition and master switches
79. Beam approach indicator lamp dimmer
80. Beam approach indicator floodlamp
81. Brake pressure gauge
82. Fuel drop tank jettison switch
83. Switch and warning lamp, type "F" transmitter
84. R.P. salvo switch
85. R.P. firing switch
86. R.P. master switch

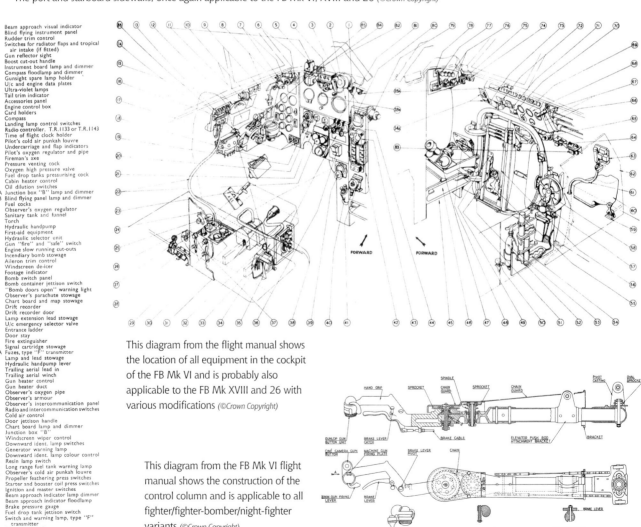

This diagram from the flight manual shows the location of all equipment in the cockpit of the FB Mk VI and is probably also applicable to the FB Mk XVIII and 26 with various modifications *(©Crown Copyright)*

This diagram from the FB Mk VI flight manual shows the construction of the control column and is applicable to all fighter/fighter-bomber/night-fighter variants *(©Crown Copyright)*

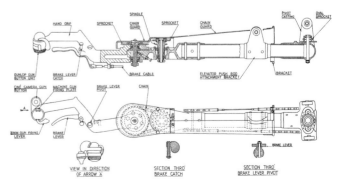

A wartime image of the port sidewall of an FB VI viewed from low-level through the access hatch
(©DH/BAE)

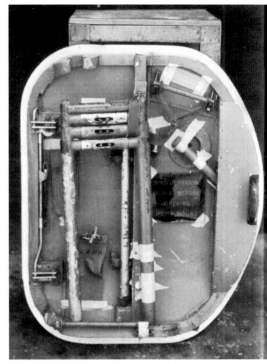

This is the inside of the crew access hatch as seen on all variants based on the fighter airframe. The access ladder, held under the floor with the bomber versions, has to be within the door on the fighters; all parts are tacked in place with tape when this photo was taken back in the early 1970s
(©Stuart Howe†)

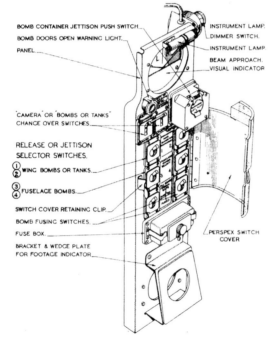

BOMB CONTAINER JETTISON PUSH SWITCH
BOMB DOORS OPEN WARNING LIGHT.
PANEL.
INSTRUMENT LAMP.
DIMMER SWITCH.
INSTRUMENT LAMP.
BEAM APPROACH.
VISUAL INDICATOR
'CAMERA' OR 'BOMBS' OR 'TANKS' CHANGE OVER SWITCHES.
RELEASE OR JETTISON SELECTOR SWITCHES.
①② WING BOMBS OR TANKS.
③④ FUSELAGE BOMBS.
SWITCH COVER RETAINING CLIP.
BOMB FUSING SWITCHES.
FUSE BOX.
BRACKET & WEDGE PLATE FOR FOOTAGE INDICATOR.
PERSPEX SWITCH COVER

In the FB Mk VI, on the right of the main instrument panel, is this bomb switch panel
(©Crown Copyright)

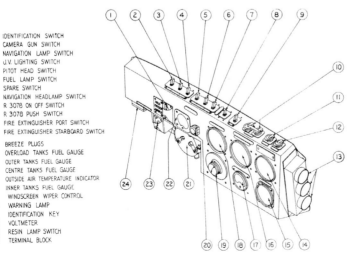

1   IDENTIFICATION SWITCH
2   CAMERA GUN SWITCH
3   NAVIGATION LAMP SWITCH
4   U.V. LIGHTING SWITCH
5   PITOT HEAD SWITCH
6   FUEL LAMP SWITCH
7   SPARE SWITCH
8   NAVIGATION HEADLAMP SWITCH
9   R 3078 ON OFF SWITCH
10 R 3078 PUSH SWITCH
11 FIRE EXTINGUISHER PORT SWITCH
12 FIRE EXTINGUISHER STARBOARD SWITCH
13 BREEZE PLUGS
14 OVERLOAD TANKS FUEL GAUGE
15 OUTER TANKS FUEL GAUGE
16 CENTRE TANKS FUEL GAUGE
17 OUTSIDE AIR TEMPERATURE INDICATOR
18 INNER TANKS FUEL GAUGE
19 WINDSCREEN WIPER CONTROL
20 WARNING LAMP
21 IDENTIFICATION KEY
22 VOLTMETER
23 RESIN LAMP SWITCH
24 TERMINAL BLOCK

The electrical distribution panel, known as 'Box B' is situated on the starboard sidewall of all variants *(©Crown Copyright)*

Crew access on all versions based on the fighter airframe, except the NF Mk XV, was via the hatch on the starboard side, using the ladder as seen here

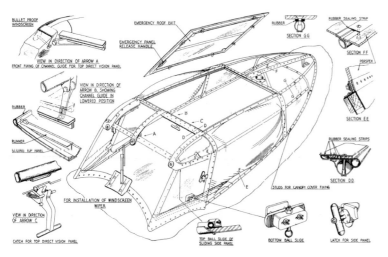

This period image shows the earlier FB Mk VI canopy with the flat side panels; you can also see how the 'clear vision' panel slides back

From the FB Mk VI flight manual comes this diagram of the canopy. This depicts the later version with the bulged side panels *(©Crown Copyright)*

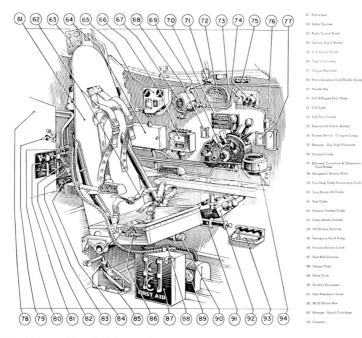

This is the port sidewall of the FB Mk 26 *(©Crown Copyright)*

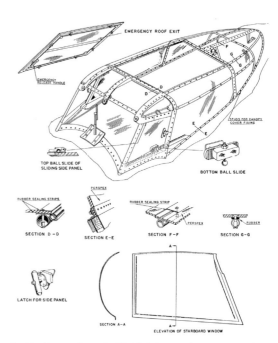

In this diagram from the FB Mk 26 manual you can see the canopy with only the starboard side panel bulged; this was probably the most common configuration *(©Crown Copyright)*

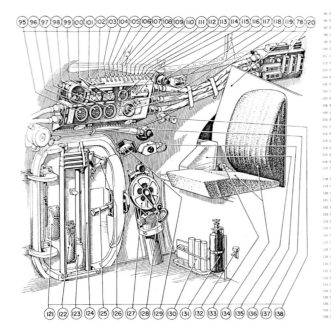

Here is the starboard sidewall of the FB Mk 26 *(©Crown Copyright)*

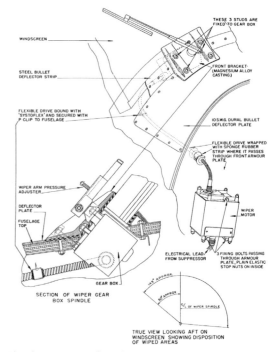

This diagram comes from the FB Mk 26 manual and shows the windscreen wiper unit that is applicable to all variants with the flat-armoured windscreen *(©Crown Copyright)*

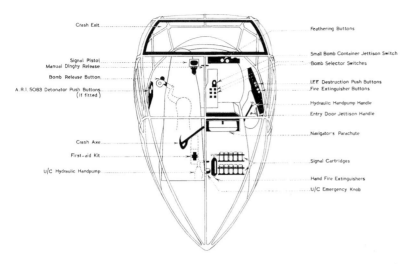

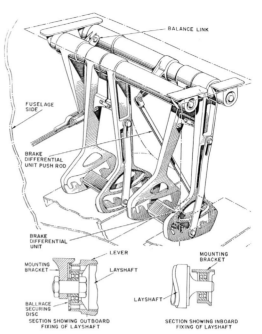

This emergency equipment diagrams comes from the FB Mk 26 manual, but is applicable to most fighter/fighter-bomber variants *(©Crown Copyright)*

The design of the rudder pedals remained unchanged throughout Mosquito production, here you have them illustrated in the FB Mk 26 flight manual *(©Crown Copyright)*

The instrument panel in the F/NF Mk II

(©Crown Copyright)

21. Radiator temperature gauges
22. Oil temperature gauges
23. Oil pressure gauges
24. Boost pressure gauges
25. Fuel pressure warning lights
26. Engine r.p.m. indicator
27. Ventilator
28. Port instrument panel light
29. Boost control cut-out
30. Instrument flying panel
31. Centre instrument panel light
32. Rudder trimming tab control and indicator
33. Main services switch
34. Magneto switches
35. Engine starter switches
36. Booster coil switches
37. Propeller feathering switches
38. Undercarriage position indicator
39. Undercarriage selector lever
40. Flap selector lever
41. Flap position indicator
42. Gun master switch
43. Aileron trimming tab control and indicator
44. Triple pressure gauges
45. Oxygen regulator
46. Remote contact switch
47. Machine-gun firing control

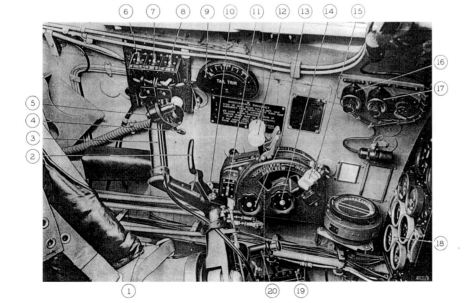

Port sidewall of the F/NF Mk II *(©Crown Copyright)*

1. Elevator trimming tab control
2. Brake control lever
3. Control column
4. Cannon trigger
5. Camera gun button
6. Radio normal/speech switch
7. Intercommunication switch
8. Beam approach switch
9. Elevator trim indicator
10. Mixture control lever
11. Supercharger gear change switch
12. Throttle levers
13. Mixture control friction adjuster
14. Throttle control friction adjuster
15. Propeller speed control levers
16. Compass light switch
17. Port instrument panel light switch
18. Engine instrument panel
19. Radio control box
20. Sea adjusting lever

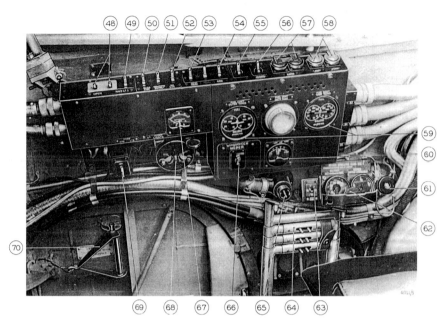

Starboard sidewall of the F/NF Mk II *(©Crown Copyright)*

48. Radiator shutter switches
49. Navigation lamps switch
50. Camera gun switch
51. Contactor supply switch
52. Ultra-violet light switch
53. Pressure head heater switch
54. Generator switch
55. Navigation headlamp switch
56. R.3078 switch
57. R.3078 destruction switches
58. Fire extinguishers switches
59. Fuel contents gauges
60. Air temperature gauge
61. High pressure oxygen control valve
62. Oxygen regulator
63. Observer's inter-communication switch
64. Collapsible ladder
65. Cold air ventilating control
66. Windscreen wiper switch (replaced by rheostat on later aircraft)
67. Voltmeter
68. Identification switchbox
69. Formation lights switch
70. Emergency door release handle

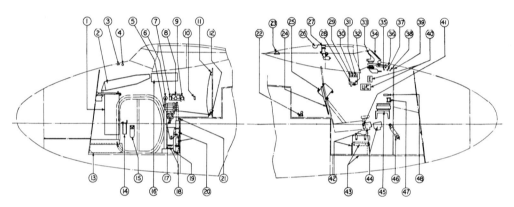

This diagram shows the placement of all the equipment in the cockpit of the NF Mk XII, XIII and XIX and probably also relates to the Mk XVII, although the flight manual does not say so, it does with just about every other item after the various amendments have been included

(©Crown Copyright)

① SPECIAL EQUIPMENT	⑬ OBSERVER'S PARACHUTE	㉕ MAP CASE	㊲ L.H. FLOOD LAMP DIMMER SWITCH
② SPECIAL EQUIPMENT	⑭ INSPECTION LAMP	㉖ COCKPIT ROOF LAMP	㊳ REFLECTOR SIGHT PLUG
③ DIMMER SWITCH FOR R.H. FLOOD LAMP	⑮ EXTENSION LEAD	㉗ SIGNAL PISTOL	㊴ INSTRUMENT PANEL SEE SECT. I
④ R.H. FLOOD LAMP	⑯ ELECTRICAL BOX 'B' SEE FIG.2	㉘ PILOT'S INTERCOMMUNICATION JACK	㊵ ENGINE AND U/C DATA PLATES
⑤ TELESCOPIC STEPS	⑰ FILM FOOTAGE INDICATOR	㉙ T.R. 1133 RADIO SWITCH	㊶ PILOT'S HARNESS RELEASE CATCH
⑥ COLD AIR VENTILATION CONTROL	⑱ POCKET FOR NAVIGATIONAL INSTRUMENTS	㉚ INTERCOMMUNICATION SWITCH	㊷ SANITARY TANK AND FUNNEL
⑦ INTERCOMMUNICATION SWITCH	⑲ FIRE EXTINGUISHER	㉛ BLIND APPROACH SWITCH	㊸ FIRST AID BOX AND ELECTRIC TORCH
⑧ OBSERVER'S OXYGEN REGULATOR	⑳ SIGNAL CARTRIDGES	㉜ PILOT'S OXYGEN CLIP	㊹ T.R. 1133 RADIO CONTROLLERS
⑨ OBSERVER'S OXYGEN CONTROL	㉑ HYDRAULIC HAND PUMP HANDLE	㉝ REFLECTOR SIGHT	㊺ COMPASS
⑩ OBSERVER'S INTER-COM. JACK	㉒ COCKPIT HEATING CONTROL	㉞ WINDSCREEN WIPER	㊻ DE – ICING PUMP
⑪ OBSERVER'S OXYGEN CLIP	㉓ UPWARD IDENTIFICATION LAMP	㉟ COMPASS LAMP DIMMER SWITCH	㊼ COMPASS DEVIATION CARD
⑫ GUN HEATER CONTROL	㉔ FIREMAN'S HATCHET	㊱ L.H. FLOOD LAMP	㊽ COMPASS FLOOD LAMP

Here is all the operational equipment in the cockpit of the NF Mk XII and XIX and although not stated, we suspect this is also similar to that in the NF Mk XIII and XVII

(©Crown Copyright)

1. NAVIGATION LAMP SWITCH.
2. RESIN LAMP SWITCH.
3. IDENTIFICATION LAMP SWITCH.
4. GENERATOR WARNING LAMP.
5. IDENTIFICATION KEY.
6. WINDSCREEN WIPER ON-OFF SWITCH.

BEAM APPROACH SWITCH.
COMPASS SWITCH.
NEGATIVE SWITCH.
R.3121. DISTRESS SWITCH.

MK. XIII
MK. XIX

PILOT'S INTERCOMMUNICATION SOCKET.

SWITCHES :
A CAMERA GUN.
B PITOT HEAD.
C REFLECTOR SIGHT.
D R.3121.MASTER.

TYPE "F" RECEIVER
GUN 'FIRE'& 'SAFE' UNIT.

REFLECTOR GUNSIGHT.
CAMERA PUSH SWITCH.
GUN FIRING PUSH.
SWITCH.
LANDING LIGHT.
SWITCHES.

R.3121.SWITCHES.
AUTOMATIC.
MANUAL.

T.R.1430.CONTROLLERS.
T.R.1430.MIXING SWITCH.

MK XIII
MK XIX } CLOCK.

A.R.I.5093. OR
S.C.R.720. { RECEIVER UNIT.
INDICATOR UNIT.
SCANNER CONTROL LEVER
[A.R.I. 5093. ONLY.]
FLASHER UNIT.

CAMERA FOOTAGE INDICATOR.
TYPE "F" TRANSMITTER SWITCH & WARNING LAMP.
OBSERVER'S INTERCOMMUNICATION SOCKET.

An interesting shot of what is almost certainly the prototype (W4052) complete with the initial style canopy with flat side panels on both sides, but in this instance, also fitted with a pole antenna in the rear/middle, with what looks like a transmitter/receiver dipole mounted on it? No idea what it was for, probably early A.I. trials, but it's an interesting addition to the airframe's life. Note all radar equipment has been covered with a canvas sheet, which is why you can't see it through the Perspex *(©DH)*

For years these photos have been identified as various fighter or bomber variants, but the fact that this cockpit shot clearly shows the installation of a fighter control column, radar equipment on the right of the instrument panel and yet has a bomber-style access door in the cockpit floor means this can only be the interior of the NF Mk XV *(©DH/BAE)*

This accompanying image, shows the port side of the cockpit in the NF Mk XV during conversion, the racks to the right are for the radar equipment and the instrument panel lacks the blind flying element *(©DH/BAE)*

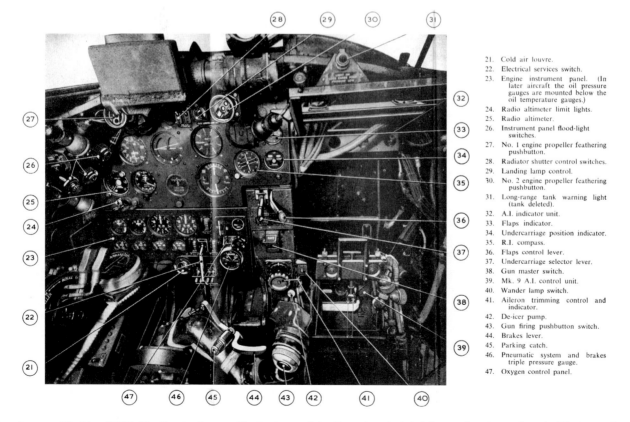

21. Cold air louvre.
22. Electrical services switch.
23. Engine instrument panel. (In later aircraft the oil pressure gauges are mounted below the oil temperature gauges.)
24. Radio altimeter limit lights.
25. Radio altimeter.
26. Instrument panel flood-light switches.
27. No. 1 engine propeller feathering pushbutton.
28. Radiator shutter control switches.
29. Landing lamp control.
30. No. 2 engine propeller feathering pushbutton.
31. Long-range tank warning light (tank deleted).
32. A.I. indicator unit.
33. Flaps indicator.
34. Undercarriage position indicator.
35. R.I. compass.
36. Flaps control lever.
37. Undercarriage selector lever.
38. Gun master switch.
39. Mk. 9 A.I. control unit.
40. Wander lamp switch.
41. Aileron trimming control and indicator.
42. De-icer pump.
43. Gun firing pushbutton switch.
44. Brakes lever.
45. Parking catch.
46. Pneumatic system and brakes triple pressure gauge.
47. Oxygen control panel.

Although you can't build an NF Mk 38 without serious modification to an existing kit, we have included the next three images from the Pilot's Notes because they are similar to the NF Mk 36; this is the instrument panel *(©Crown Copyright)*

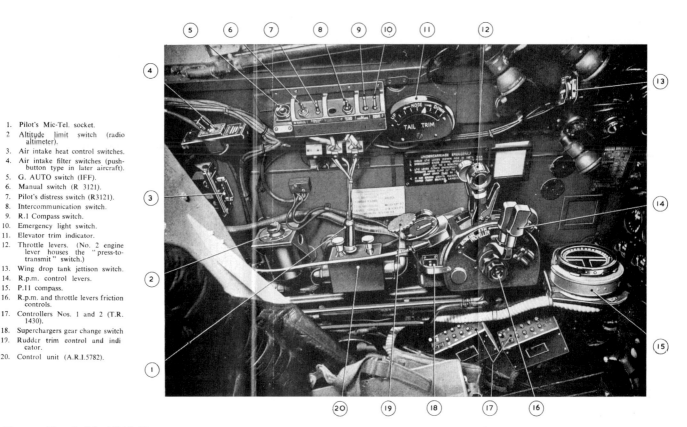

1. Pilot's Mic-Tel. socket.
2. Altitude limit switch (radio altimeter).
3. Air intake heat control switches.
4. Air intake filter switches (push-button type in later aircraft).
5. G. AUTO switch (IFF).
6. Manual switch (R 3121).
7. Pilot's distress switch (R3121).
8. Intercommunication switch.
9. R.1 Compass switch.
10. Emergency light switch.
11. Elevator trim indicator.
12. Throttle levers. (No. 2 engine lever houses the "press-to-transmit" switch.)
13. Wing drop tank jettison switch.
14. R.p.m. control levers.
15. P.11 compass.
16. R.p.m. and throttle levers friction controls.
17. Controllers Nos. 1 and 2 (T.R. 1430).
18. Superchargers gear change switch
19. Rudder trim control and indi cator.
20. Control unit (A.R.I.5782).

The port sidewall of the NF Mk 38 *(©Crown Copyright)*

48. Cold air louvre.
49. Generator warning lights.
50. Pressure head heater switch.
51. Reflector sight switch.
52. Cine-camera master switch.
53. Booster pump switch—port.
54. Booster pump switch—starboard.
55. Long-range tank fuel pump switch (tank deleted).
56. Windscreen wiper switch.
57. R3121 switch.
58. Fire - extinguisher pushbutton switches for port, centre and starboard tank bays.
59. Fire - extinguisher pushbutton switches for Nos. 1 and 2 engines.
60. Electrical panel lighting rheo-stat.
61. Fuel contents gauges.
62. Transmitter, type "F."
63. No. 2 engine starter and booster coil switches.
64. No. 1 engine starter and booster coil switches.
65. Cockpit cold air control.
66. Control tuning unit (A.R.I. 5782).
67. Windscreen wiper rheostat.
68. Identification lights switch box (morse signalling).
69. Identification lights switch.
70. Resin lights switch.
71. Navigation lights switch.

The starboard sidewall of the NF Mk 38 *(©Crown Copyright)*

11. Oil pressure gauges.
12. Boost pressure gauges.
13. Fuel pressure warning lights.
14. R.p.m. indicators.
15. Ventilators.
16. Boost control cut-out.
17. Instrument flying panel.
18. Generator warning light.
19. Rudder trimming tab control.
20. Fuel pump ON-OFF switch.
21. Air temperature gauge.
22. Voltmeter (if fitted).
23. Radiator shutter switches.
24. Identification lights switch box (morse).
25. Propeller feathering pushbuttons.
26. Engine starter pushbuttons.
27. Booster coil pushbuttons.
28. Electrical services switch.
29. Ignition switches.
30. Navigation lights and windscreen wiper switches.
31. Resin lights switch.
32. Cine-camera master switch.
33. I.F.F. master switch.
34. Identification lights selector switch.
35. I.F.F. destruction pushbuttons (not in circuit).
36. Fire-extinguisher pushbuttons.
37. Pressure-head heater.
38. Navigation head-lamp switch.
39. Windscreen wiper rheostat.
40. Fuel contents gauges.
41. Dual throttle levers.
42. Windscreen de-icer pump.
43. Aileron trimming tab control and indicator.
44. Flap selector lever.
45. Undercarriage selector lever.
46. Triple pressure gauge.
47. Flaps position indicator.
48. Undercarriage position indicator.
49. Landing lamp switches.
50. Coolant temperature gauges.
51. Oil temperature gauges.

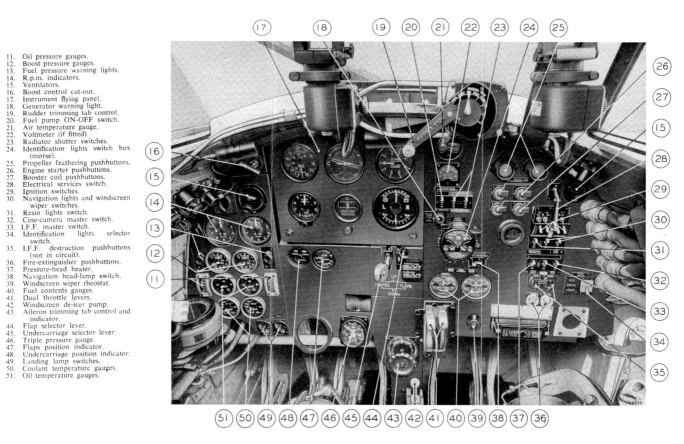

The instrument panel of the T Mk III from the Pilot's Notes *(©Crown Copyright)*

A nice wartime overall shot of the instrument panel etc. in a T Mk III *(©DH/BAE)*

1. Pilot's seat raising lever.
2. V.H.F. controller.
3. Supercharger gear change switch.
4. Mixture control lever (see para. 22).
5. Beam approach switch.
6. Elevator trimming tab indicator.
7. Throttle levers.
8. R.p.m. control levers.
9. Control column.
10. Compass.
11. Oil pressure gauges.
12. Boost pressure gauges.
13. Fuel pressure warning lights.
14. R.p.m. indicators.
50. Coolant temperature gauges.
51. Oil temperature gauges.

The port sidewall of the T Mk III from the Pilot's Notes *(©Crown Copyright)*

32.	Rudder trim tab control and indicator
33.	Starboard switch panel
36.	Dual throttle levers
42.	Propeller feathering controls
43.	Engine starter switches
44.	Booster coil switches
45.	Ventilator
46.	Main services switch
47.	Magneto switches
48.	Navigation lights switch
49.	Formation lights switch
50.	Camera gun switch
51.	R.3078 switch
52.	Pressure head heater switch
53.	R.3078 destruction switches
54.	Fire extinguisher switches
55.	Navigation headlamp switch
56.	Windscreen wiper switch (rheostat on later aircraft)
57.	Fuel contents gauges
58.	Identification switchbox
59.	Radio normal/special switch
60.	Radiator shutter switches
61.	Generator switch
62.	Voltmeter
63.	Contactor supply switch
64.	Air temperature gauge

The switch panel on the starboard side of the T Mk III from the Pilot's Notes; there are no illustrations of the starboard sidewall as a whole for the T Mk III in either the Pilot's Notes nor the Flight Manual *(©Crown Copyright)*

Although not the clearest image, this is the only one we have found that shows the sliding/folding second seat used in the T Mk III and all foreign-produced two-seat trainer variants

(©DH/BAE)

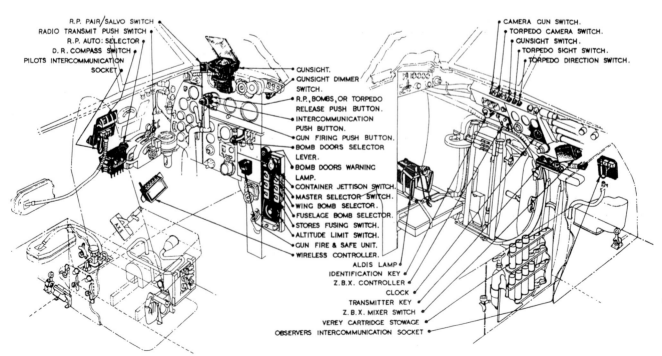

This diagram shows the placement of the operational controls in the cockpit of the Sea Mosquito TR Mk 33 *(©Crown Copyright)*

Although of poor quality, this image of the port sidewall of FB Mk 40 A52-3 does show the limited number of changes in the equipment of this Australian version *(©RAAF)*

This is the starboard sidewall of FB Mk 40 A52-3, again with few changes from the British versions *(©RAAF)*

The instrument panel of A52-3, the only changes seem to concern the items to the right of the instrument panel *(©RAAF)*

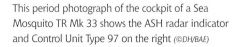

This period photograph of the cockpit of a Sea Mosquito TR Mk 33 shows the ASH radar indicator and Control Unit Type 97 on the right *(©DH/BAE)*

This shot inside the Sea Mosquito TR Mk 37 prototype TW240 shows the ASV Mk XIII radar indicator in the stowed position on the right *(©DH/BAE)*

While this shot shows the ASV Mk XIII radar deployed and with the rubber hood attached to the scope *(©DH/BAE)*

Radio & Radar

The nose of an early production NF Mk II photographed in early 1942 with the A.I. Mk IV Type 19 'bow and arrow' antenna in the nose; this machine is in the Special Night finish, so is one of the first production batch in the W40xx-range *(©DH/BAE)*

This is the indicator unit for the A.I. Mk IV inside the cockpit of the NF Mk II *(©Crown Copyright)*

When the Mosquito intruders adopted Serrate II, these black boxes were installed in the nose in place of the machine-guns, although the Type 19 'bow and arrow' transmission aerial for the A.I. IV remained *(©Crown Copyright)*

As well as the 'bow and arrow' antenna, there were the azimuth and elevation dipoles mounted on the wings, as seen here on DD758 at Hatfield in the summer of 1942 *(©DH/BAE)*

F Mk II DZ659 was used for SCR 720 radar installation trials, with the initial bulged radome specific to this prototype seen here *(©DH/BAE)*

Later, when the Mosquito adopted the Gee system, this was installed behind the pilot's seat to be operated by the navigator, with the associated RF Unit above it on the spar shelf; this is an early installation, hence the grey fronts to each unit, in service the whole unit was black and the routes of the power lines differed slightly from those seen here *(©Crown Copyright)*

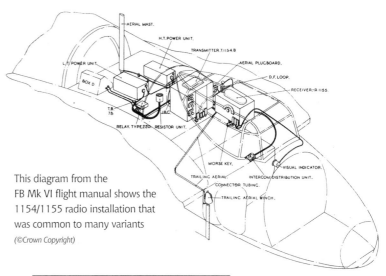

This diagram from the FB Mk VI flight manual shows the 1154/1155 radio installation that was common to many variants *(©Crown Copyright)*

A close-up, taken on the 31st March 1943, of the SCR720 installation in the nose of F Mk II DZ659, the large round drum is the frequency unit *(©DH/BAE)*

This is the Type 315 dipole associated with the Boozer III warning system that identified the aircraft was being 'painted' by Wurburg or FuG 202-212 transmissions; it is situated on the port side of the front/rear fuselage *(©Crown Copyright)*

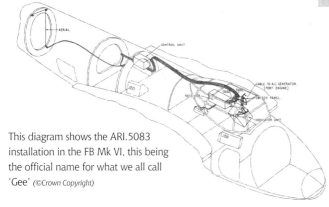

This diagram shows the ARI.5083 installation in the FB Mk VI, this being the official name for what we all call 'Gee' *(©Crown Copyright)*

A close-up of the fitment of A.I. Mk XV ASH in the nose of an FB Mk VI from No.515 Squadron, operating as part of 100 Group

This is the dipole associated with Carpet and is seen under the starboard rear fuselage of LR302; this system was aimed at countering enemy GCI (ground-control interception) radar *(©Crown Copyright)*

An unusual image, this seems to show the test fitment of ASV radar into the nose of a fighter variant that may be an FB Mk VI or a Sea Mosquito TR Mk 33? *(©R.C. Sturtivant)*

The Type 73 indicator unit (without its prominent rubber hood) and receiver unit for the A.I. Mk VIIIB in the cockpit of an NF Mk XII taken at Hullavington *(©Crown Copyright)*

The A.I. Mk VIIIB power unit, modulator and voltage control regulator on the spar shelf in the rear of the cockpit of an NF Mk XIII *(©Crown Copyright)*

The A.I. Mk VIIIB signal processor and receiving units in the rear fuselage, they were put there to keep the balance, and because there was no room in the cockpit, and to stop interference with the processor units *(©Crown Copyright)*

A small but nice image into the starboard side of the radome of an NF Mk XIII, showing the A.I. Mk VIIIB

The indicator unit of the A.I. Mk X with a Monica VIII CRT mounted below it in the cockpit of an NF Mk XXX *(©Crown Copyright)*

Here you can see the 'thimble' radome used initially on the NF Mk XII, seen here on HK117 *(©DH/BAE)*

Not the best quality image, but this shows the 'universal' radome on the NF Mk XXX, with its plastic upper section, the round item is the high frequency unit for the A.I. Mk X *(©Crown Copyright)*

The antenna RC-94D of the SCR 720 (A.I. X) radar system

The Monica bulge under the tail of NF Mk XXX MM474/G with No.406 Squadron in late 1944 *(©G. Cruickshank via S. Howe†)*

In the post-war era the upper plastic section of the radome was often left unpainted, as seen here on an NF Mk 36

The unpainted section of the radome for the A.I. Mk IXb in the NF Mk 38 (seen here on VX196 as it reaches the end of the production line in late 1950) was slightly different in comparison with that of the NF Mk 36 *(©DH)*

The Hookah broadband system was tested on the Mosquito from November 1944 and continued in the post-war period. Here you can see one style of antenna on the starboard wing *(©Crown Copyright)*

In this close-up of NF Mk 36 (RL201, YP•C) of No.23 Squadron you can see a different style of Hookah radar antenna on the leading edges of each wing *(via Internet)*

No.23 Squadron also did tests with this style of Hookah radar antenna installation, seen here on NF Mk 36, RK998, YP•A; this is the style of antenna later adopted by the FAA for the TR Mk 33 *(via Internet)*

Although of poor quality, this wartime image does show the AT5 transmitter (L) and AR8 receiver (R) plus the aerial coupling unit in the middle fitted to FB Mk 40 A52-3; this radio installation is unique to RAAF Mosquitos and was not exported to other nations *(©RAAF)*

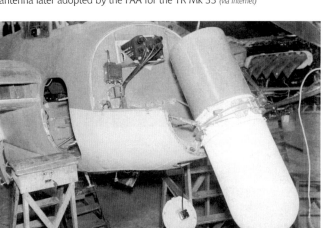

The AN/APS-2 radar known in the UK as ASH (Air-Surface-Home), pod seen here in the nose of a Sea Mosquito TR Mk 33, probably TS449, hinged down in the servicing position *(©DH/BAE)*

The 'Hookah' antenna on the wing of Sea Mosquito TR Mk 33 TW241 of No.703 NAS *(via Internet)*

The view through the open access hatch of a Sea Mosquito TR Mk 33; use in conjunction with early images of the radar installation to work out the layout of this region
(©DH/BAE)

The ASV Mk XIII radar in the nose of the TR Mk 37 prototype *(©DH/BAE)*

The elongated nose of the Sea Mosquito TR Mk 37 prototype TW240; note the relocated radio hatch in the underside of the fuselage in the open position *(©DH/BAE)*

Cameras

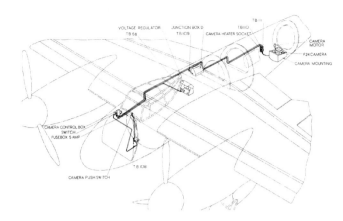

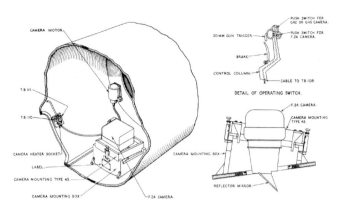

The F.24 with a reflector mirror was installed in the rear fuselage of the FB Mk VI (©Crown Copyright)

This is a close-up of the F.24 in the rear fuselage of the FB Mk VI, along with the trigger on the control column (©Crown Copyright)

This photographs shows (left to right) Reg Duncan, Phil Spielvogel and Neil Ray of No.87 (PR) Squadron, RAAF with the various American and British camera used by their aircraft; these comprise (left to right, top to bottom: K17 with 6in lens (PR Mk 40 and 41), K17 with 12 inch lens (PR Mk 40 & 41), F.24 with 8 inch lens (not used in the Mosquito), K18 with 24in lens (PR Mk 40), F.24 with 5 inch lens (PR Mk XVI), F.52 with 36in lens (PR Mk 40 & 41), F.24 with 14 inch lens (PR Mk XVI) and F.52 with 20 inch lens (PR Mk 40 and 41) (©RAAF)

The PR Mk 41 had an F.52 camera mounted vertically in the nose (©P. Skulski)

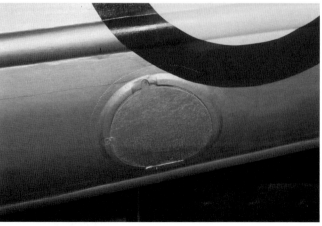

The PR Mk 41 also had two cameras mounted in the rear fuselage, this is the one on the port side, the one on the starboard is in the radio access hatch, and there was provision to carry more underneath the rear fuselage (©P. Skulski)

Miscellaneous

The Swedish Air Force tested the use of infra-red binoculars in their J 30s, and here you can see the PS20/A indicator in the top left of the instrument panel *(via The Military Archives)*

This is the IR binocular placed through the windscreen, and viewed from the front *(via The Military Archives)*

The IR binocular through the windscreen, seen from the side *(via The Military Archives)*

The Swiss Mamba SM-1 turbojet being tested under FB Mk VI (ex-NS993) in Switzerland *(via Stuart Howe†)*

FB Mk VI, NS993 landed in Switzerland, where it was interned and later used by the Swiss Air Force (as '20-10'). It is seen here with the aerodynamic test shape prior to Swiss Mamba SM-1 turbojet tests *(via Stuart Howe†)*

A close-up of the Swiss Mamba SM-1 turbojet underneath the FB Mk VI with the front cowls removed *(via Stuart Howe†)*

In Belgium target towing was undertaken by the FB Mk 6 and TT Mk 3, this is a close-up of the port side of the winch under a TT Mk 3 of the Belgian Air Force (*©Rudy Binnemans*)

The cable buffer aft of the bomb bay underneath a Belgian Air Force FB Mk VI (*©Rudy Binnemans*)

The target-towing sleeve under the belly of an FB Mk VI of the Belgian Air Force – the installation is similar to that used on the TT Mk 35 by the RAF

(*©Rudy Binnemans*)

Access Panels

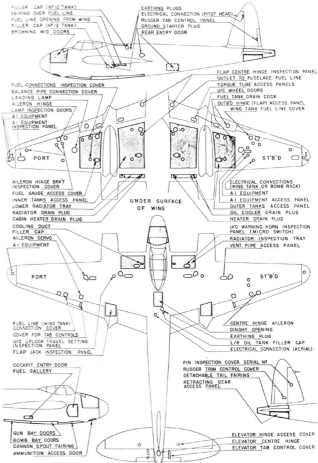

Here are the inspection and access panels for the FB Mk 26 (*©Crown Copyright*)

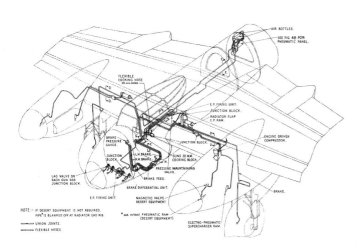

This diagram shows the pneumatic system of the FB Mk VI, but is applicable to all fighter-based variants (*©Crown Copyright*)

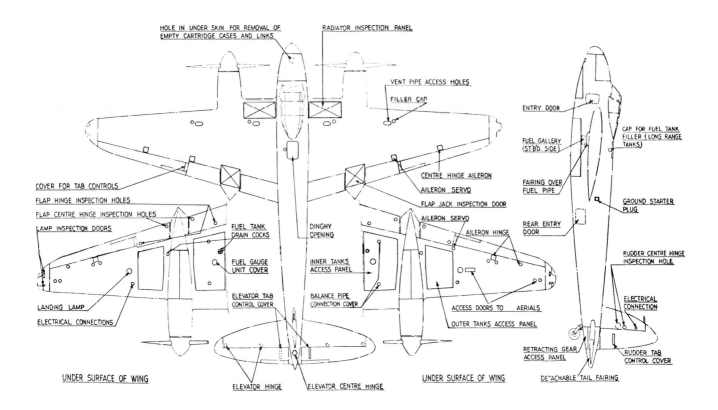

This diagram shows the various inspection and access panels for the FB Mk VI – this diagram you will also find in the NF Mk XII, XIII, XVII and XIX manual, even though all the details around the nose area are not applicable to the night-fighters? *(©Crown Copyright)*

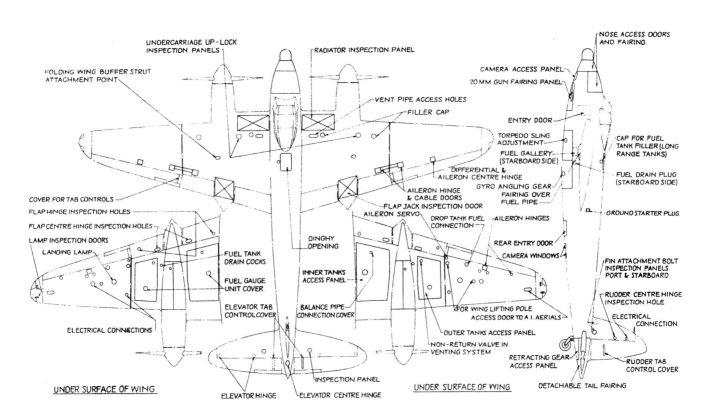

These are the inspection covers and access panels on the Sea Mosquito TR Mk 33 *(©Crown Copyright)*

Wings

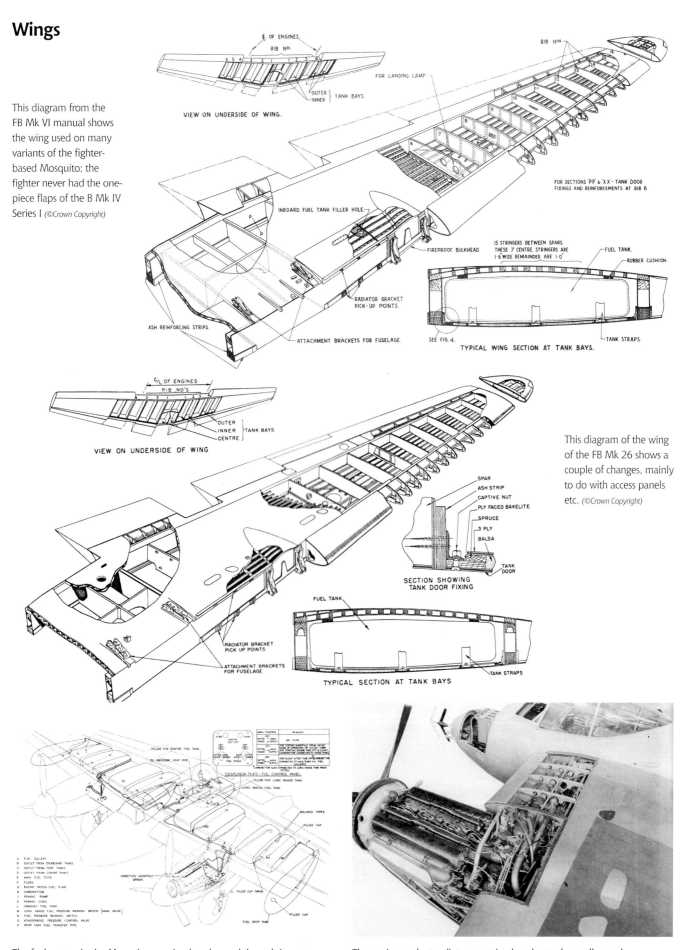

This diagram from the FB Mk VI manual shows the wing used on many variants of the fighter-based Mosquito; the fighter never had the one-piece flaps of the B Mk IV Series I (©Crown Copyright)

This diagram of the wing of the FB Mk 26 shows a couple of changes, mainly to do with access panels etc. (©Crown Copyright)

The fuel system in the Mosquito remained unchanged through its career, although the wing fold of the Sea Mosquito necessitated a change around the fold point – this diagram is from the FB Mk VI manual (©Crown Copyright)

The engine coolant radiators remained unchanged as well, seen here on NF Mk II, DD612 with the covers off; only the test-fitting of the Merlin 23 in DD723 saw a change here, as the XX-series engines had a Marston radiator slung underneath (©DH/BAE)

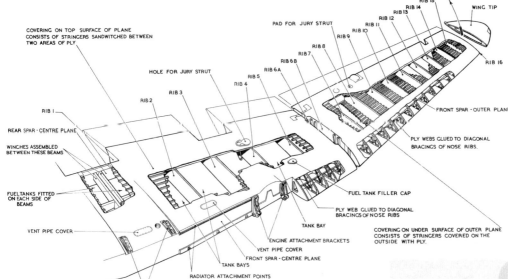

COVERING ON TOP SURFACE OF PLANE CONSISTS OF STRINGERS SANDWITCHED BETWEEN TWO AREAS OF PLY

HOLE FOR JURY STRUT

PAD FOR JURY STRUT

RIB 15
RIB 14
RIB 13
RIB 12
RIB 11
RIB 10
RIB 9
RIB 8
RIB 7
RIB 6B
RIB 6A
RIB 5
RIB 4
RIB 3
RIB 2
RIB 1

WING TIP

FRONT SPAR - OUTER PLANE

RIB 16

PLY WEBS GLUED TO DIAGONAL BRACINGS OF NOSE RIBS.

REAR SPAR - CENTRE PLANE

WINCHES ASSEMBLED BETWEEN THESE BEAMS

FUELTANKS FITTED ON EACH SIDE OF BEAMS

VENT PIPE COVER

FUEL TANK FILLER CAP

PLY WEB GLUED TO DIAGONAL BRACINGS OF NOSE RIBS

TANK BAY

ENGINE ATTACHMENT BRACKETS

VENT PIPE COVER

FRONT SPAR - CENTRE PLANE

TANK BAYS

RADIATOR ATTACHMENT POINTS

FUSELAGE ATTACHMENT BRACKETS

COVERING ON UNDER SURFACE OF OUTER PLANE CONSISTS OF STRINGERS COVERED ON THE OUTSIDE WITH PLY.

Here is the wing of the Sea Mosquito TR Mk 33, showing the modifications made to accommodate the wing-fold *(©Crown Copyright)*

Manual fold of the TR Mk 33 required seven men, as insufficient hydraulic power for powered wing fold was available because fitted it would have been expensive and require a major modification to the existing hydraulic system *(©DH/BAE)*

Prototype (Naval) FB Mk VI LR387 with its wings in the fully folded position *(©DH/BAE)*

Here is a close-up of the fold hinge area on the Sea Mosquito *(©DH/BAE)*

This shot of the first FB VI (HJ662/G) on jacks with the rear of the nacelle off exposes the aileron control linkage and differential control *(©DH/BAE)*

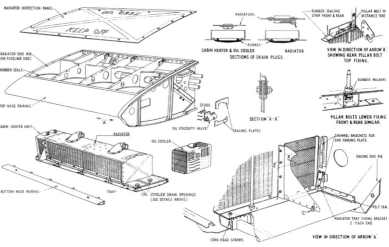

This is the radiator set-up and it applies to all variants with just a few minor modifications to fixtures in some of the post-war machines *(©Crown Copyright)*

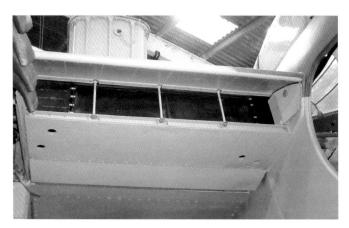

A nice view into the starboard radiator of the FB Mk VI at Salisbury Hall, where you can see the split nature of the radiator matrices inside (the cabin heater unit it on the left) and their associated screens *(©Nigel Perry)*

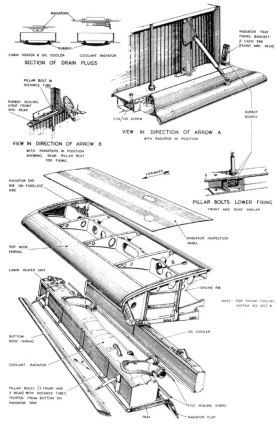

This is how the radiators were dismantled and assembled, which gives you an idea of what was behind them in the wing *(©Crown Copyright)*

The same region in the PR Mk 41 in Australia, seems to show that there were some differences in the foreign-built machines *(©P. Skulski)*

Here you can see the flap region on the wing trailing edge without the flaps themselves installed, here on the FB Mk VI at Salisbury Hall *(©Nigel Perry)*

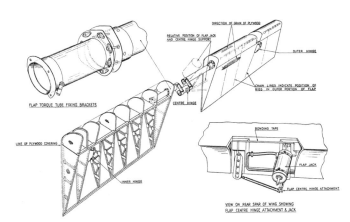

This diagram shows the construction of the two-part flaps and it applies to all versions *(©Crown Copyright)*

Here you can actually see how the flaps are built, as these are constructed at Salisbury Hall for their FB Mk VI *(©Nigel Perry)*

Both inboard and outboard flap elements have prominent hinge lines, which you can see here on the underside of the outboard port flap on the PR Mk 41 in Canberra *(©P. Skulski)*

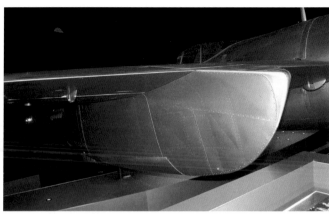

The rear of the nacelle region did not change once the two-part flaps were adopted with the B Mk IV Series II and thus apply to all fighter-based variants, seen here on the PR Mk 41 at Canberra *(©P. Skulski)*

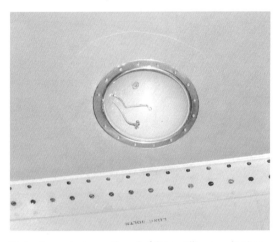

Under the port wing, outboard of the nacelle, was a landing light, that hinged flush with the wing surface when not in use and seen here on the PR Mk 41 at Canberra, which has a different style one to that used in British-built machines *(©P. kulski)*

Here is a close-up of the landing light in a British-built machine, this being the FB Mk VI at Salisbury Hall

(©Nigel Perry)

In the latter stages of WWII and into the post-war era, the landing light on many late production machines, as well as many machines refurbished and sold abroad, had the landing light removed from under the port wing and this two-lamp unit built into the leading edge of the starboard outer wing panel

This diagram shows the Type L landing lamp (sometimes called a 'Grime's' lamp) and is applicable to all British-built variants *(©Crown Copyright)*

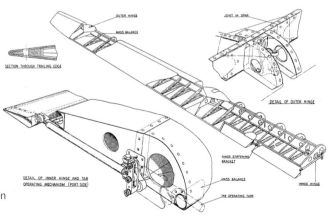

The aileron remained unchanged throughout the Mosquito production and this diagram shows how it was constructed *(©Crown Copyright)*

Mid & Aft Fuselage

W4052 in flight from A&AEE in late 1941, note the lack of the strengthening strake above the radio hatch aft of the wing trailing edge, this was added to all machines from December 1942 to strengthen the area and stop water ingression into the fuselage, the strake working as a gutter to direct water fore and aft (©British Official)

An overall shot of the starboard fuselage side on the FB Mk VI being restored at Salisbury Hall (©Nigel Perry)

This is the starboard side of the PR Mk 41 (A52-319) on display in Canberra, where you can see the camera port built into the radio hatch on this side (©P. Skulski)

Another shot of PR Mk 41 A52-319 in Australia, this time showing the port side above the wing trailing edge with the ground starter cover on the right and the transit joint covered in the middle (©P. Skulski)

A close-up of the radio hatch area on the FB Mk VI at Salisbury Hall, the hatch itself has not been fitted yet as the hinges are curved and mount inside the top edge of the opening (©Nigel Perry)

If you look forward along the fuselage of PR Mk 41 A52-319, you can see the dinghy pack stowage in the upper decking, just aft of the canopy *(©P. Skulski)*

If you go underneath the wing, you will find this bulge over the fuel transfer pump on either side, just forward of the flap hinge line; this is PR Mk 41, A52-319 *(©P. Skulski)*

Most photos will show the gun and bomb bay regions with the tanks installed, the NF Mk 30 in Belgium however has these removed, so you can see the raised bay in the rear region for the standard tanks; you are looking forward

(©George Papadimitriou)

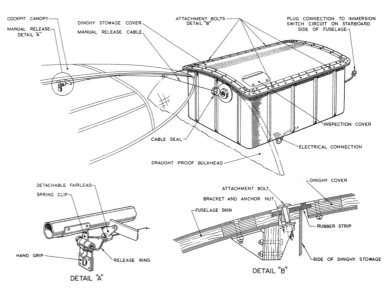

This diagram shows the the dinghy pack installation, and is applicable to all versions
(©Crown Copyright)

The gun bay and bomb doors are similar on all versions of the fighter-based variants; this shows the diagram for these from the FB Mk VI flight manual *(©Crown Copyright)*

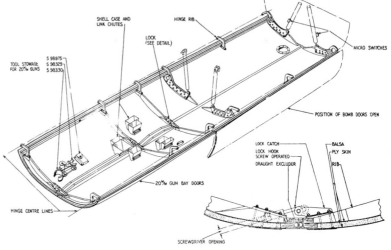

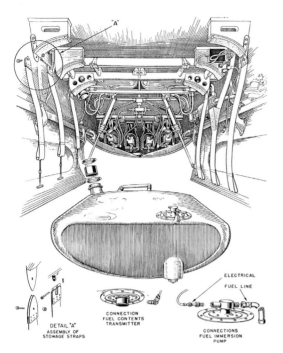

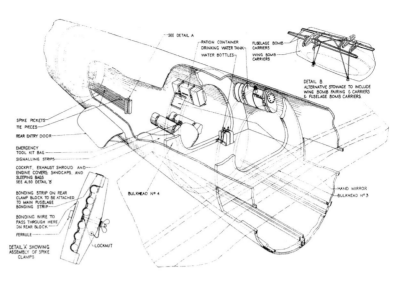

When used in a tropical or desert environment, auxiliary equipment could be stowed in the rear fuselage, as seen here in a diagram from the FB Mk VI manual *(©Crown Copyright)*

In place of bombs in the rear bay, many versions of the Mosquito could carry a long-range fuel tank instead. This diagram comes from the FB Mk 26 manual, but applies to numerous other versions as well *(©Crown Copyright)*

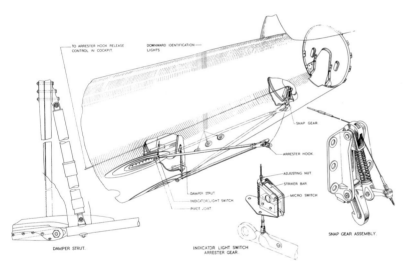

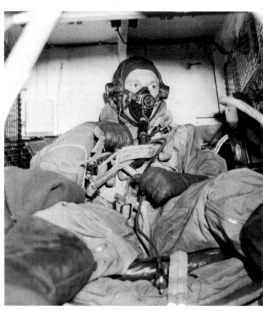

The Sea Mosquito was fitted with an arrestor hook under the rear fuselage, this diagram of it comes from the TR Mk 33 manual *(©Crown Copyright)*

As recounted in Steve's build of a BOAC FB Mk VI, these carried a poor passenger in the bomb bay, as seen in this period image *(©British Official)*

This photo of the first FB Mk VI converted for carrier operations, LR359, clearly shows the arrestor hook and its attachments under the rear fuselage *(©DH/BAE)*

In service, the Sea Mosquito TR Mk 33 also had RATO bottles on either side of the fuselage, as seen here on the 2nd pre-production machine TS449 *(©DH/BAE)*

Tail

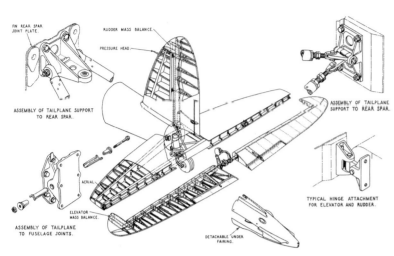

This diagram from the FB Mk VI flight manual shows the tail unit and it applies to most variants of the Mosquito (©Crown Copyright)

This shot shows the vertical fin and rudder of FB Mk VI TA122 at Salisbury Hall, you can also see the tailplane without the elevators fitted (©Nigel Perry)

This shot of the tail on PR Mk 41 A52-319 at Canberra shows little difference from the British-built example, save for how the fabric covering is applied and how the ribs are dealt with on the rudder, all of which may be due to modern methods of restoration and preservation (©P. Skulski)

The only difference on the other side of the vertical fin is the lack of the various access panels seen on the starboard side, and the fitment on the fairing around the trim tab linkage (©P. Skulski)

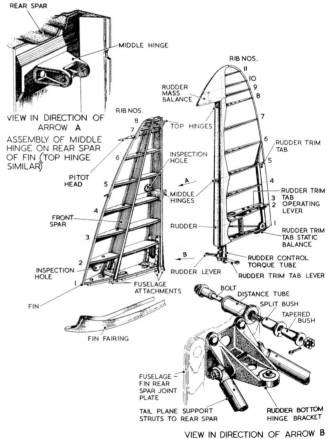

This diagram shows the construction of the fin and rudder unit, and comes from the NF Mk 38 manual, but applies to all Mosquito variants (©Crown Copyright)

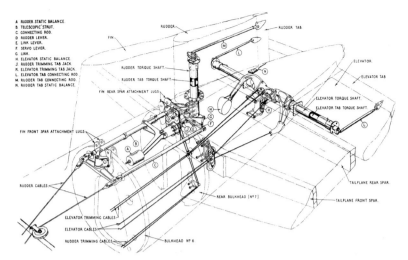

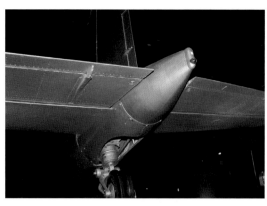

In this shot under the tail of PR Mk 41 A52-319, you can see the trim tab actuator on this side (it is above on the starboard side) as well as the single formation light on the tail cone of this machine *(©P. Skulski)*

Here are all the control linkages within the tail region, which applies to all variants *(©Crown Copyright)*

This is the pitot head installation diagram and it applies to all versions *(©Crown Copyright)*

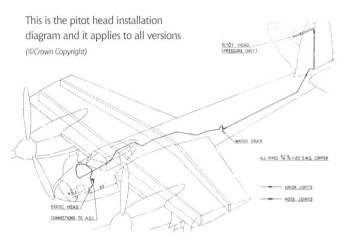

This view under the starboard tailplane and elevator on the PR Mk 41 (A52-319) at Canberra shows the metal skinning of both elements, plus the lack of any trim tab actuator fairing on this side *(©P. Skulski)*

Much is written about the elevator mass balance weights on different versions, here you can see the standard units on this shot from behind W4052 ar A&AEE in 1941 – note the profile of the tip leading edge *(©Crown Copyright)*

The NF Mk 38 had enlarged elevator mass balance weights to deal with the changed CofG, this shot under 8030 with the 103rd Recon Regiment as it comes in to land clearly shows the 'kink' in the leading edge profile of each elevator tip *(©M. Micevski via Stuart Howe†)*

The Sea Mosquito TR Mk 33 had an enlarged elevator mass balance, but the prototype (LR387) certainly did not, as this shot proves – same profile to the tip leading edge *(©DH/BAE)*

Engines, Propellers & Cowlings

The Merlin 21 in the starboard nacelle of a T Mk III, probably HJ886 after roll-out at Leavesden in 1942 *(©Crown Copyright)*

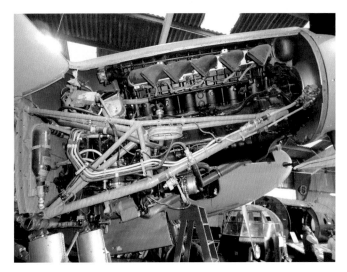

Outer view of the starboard engine in the FB Mk VI being restored at Salisbury Hall, this has the five-stack ejector exhaust system fitted *(©Nigel Perry)*

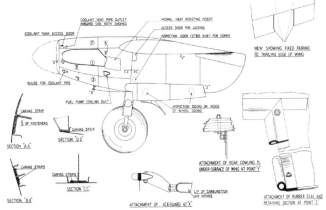

Here you have the cowls associated wth the shrouded exhaust system, seen here in the FB Mk VI manual *(©Crown Copyright)*

When the five-stack exhaust system was used, these were the cowls fitted *(©Crown Copyright)*

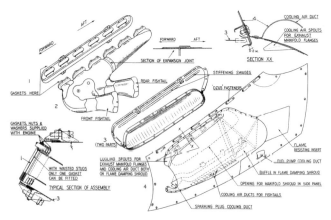

This is the initial style of exhaust, associated with the shrouded exhausts and called 'saxophone' due to the shape of the collector pipes inside the shroud *(©Crown Copyright)*

This is the inner view of the starboard engine of the FB Mk VI at Salisbury Hall, and you can more clearly see how the last two exhaust outlets share a common exhaust stack *(©Nigel Perry)*

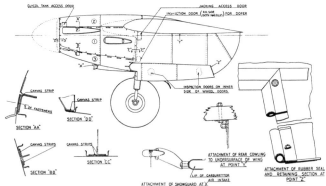

A useful diagram as it shows the engine panels and exhaust set-up for the prototypes, and early W40-series Mk IIs *(©Crown Copyright)*

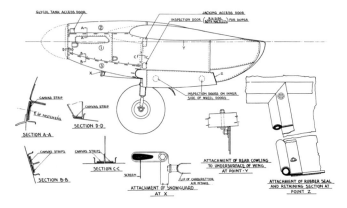

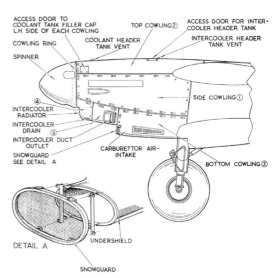

When the Merlin 72 was adopted, being a two-stage engine, these are the cowlings used, seen here with the louvres in the lower intake associated with tropical operations; these are the early cowls with the fuel pump cooling duct *(©Crown Copyright)*

These are the later two-stage cowls, used on the Merlin 113/114 powered machines, without the fuel pump cooling duct; neither versions have the inset fire extinguisher panels seen on the single-stage cowls *(©Crown Copyright)*

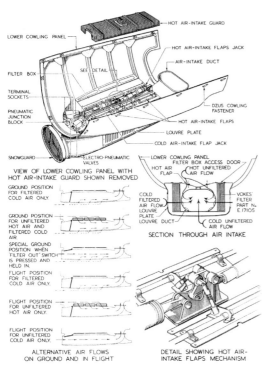

This is the lower cowling incorporating the air intake and filter unit used in the later two-stage Merlin variants *(©Crown Copyright)*

Here is a close-up of the intake and intercooler duct outlets on the PR Mk 41 A52-319 at Canberra; note the inner sections of the latter are aluminium castings held within the aluminium aerodynamic outer skin of the scoop *(©P. Skulski)*

The first trials of a tropical air intake on a two-speed, single-stage supercharged Merlin Mosquito took place with NF Mk II W4096 in 1943; note how the ice guard is mounted as a separate part, later it would be affixed to the lip of the intake itself *(©DH Aircraft Museum Trust)*

B Mk IV Series II DK290/G was the first to test six individual fish tail exhausts at A&AEE in 1943 *(©Crown Copyright)*

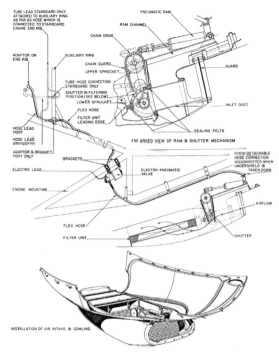

Here is the production tropical air intake, seen here in the FB Mk 26 manual, but applicable to various variants

(©Crown Copyright)

The adoption of the six-stack exhaust system became common in the latter stages of WWII and in the post-war era, this diagram shows how the individual stacks fitted *(©Crown Copyright)*

Here is a side view of the armour plates added to the engine of the FB Mk XVIII *(©DH/BAE)*

Due to its low-level role, the FB Mk XVIII had extra armour plate fitted, this shot shows the plates fitted to the engine, viewed from the front *(©DH/BAE)*

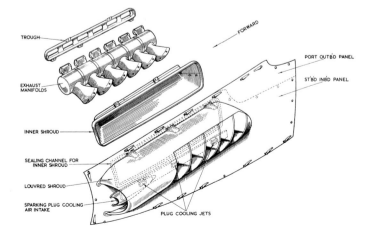

The final exhaust system used on the Mosquito was the 'slotted' flame damper, seen here in the NF Mk 38 manual, but also applicable to the late-production NF Mk 30 and all NF Mk 36s

(©Crown Copyright)

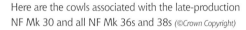

ACCESS DOOR TO
COOLANT TANK FILLER CAP
L.H. SIDE OF BOTH COWLINGS

TOP COWLING②

ACCESS DOOR FOR INTER-
COOLER HEADER TANK

COWLING RING

COOLANT HEADER
TANK VENT

INTERCOOLER HEADER
TANK VENT

SPINNER

B   B

④

B

INTERCOOLER
RADIATOR

A

SIDE COWLING①

INTERCOOLER
DRAIN

A

⑤

A

INTERCOOLER DUCT
OUTLET

SNOW GUARD
SEE DETAIL C

CARBURETTOR AIR
INTAKE

BOTTOM COWLING

COWLING RING

SECTION A–A

CANVAS STRIP

DETAIL C

UNDERSHIELD

SNOWGUARD

SECTION B–B

CANVAS STRIP

Here are the cowls associated with the late-production
NF Mk 30 and all NF Mk 36s and 38s *(©Crown Copyright)*

The only other engine tested in a Mosquito fighter was the Merlin 23 with its underslung
Marston radiator fitted to F Mk II DD723 for tests by Rolls-Royce at Hucknall *(©DH/BAE)*

Early machines used the narrow blade propellers seen at
the beginning of this section on the T Mk III prototype,
later machines all went over to the broad 'paddle' blade of
the Type 500, seen here as P. W. Stanfield, foreman of the
Mosquito running sheds at Hatfield, adjusts the backplate of
a new FB Mk VI in March 1945 *(©DH/BAE)*

The other blade type was the
Hamilton-Standard paddle
propeller, used on all the
Canadian and Australian-
built machines and seen here
on FB Mk 26, KA133, with
the Winter Experimental
Establishment

(Alberta Aviation Museum)

Here you can see the blade root cut-outs for the broad blades
on the FB Mk VI at Salisbury Hall *(©Nigel Perry)*

Undercarriage

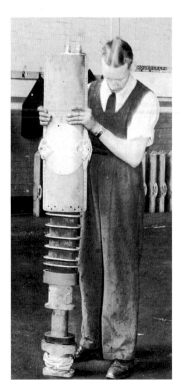

From very early on oleo-pneumatic dampers for the main undercarriage were dispensed with and these rubber blocks in compression were used instead *(©DH/BAE)*

These are the shock absorber blocks in the oleo leg, which remained for all versions of the *Mosquito*, except some Sea Mosquito variants *(©Crown Copyright)*

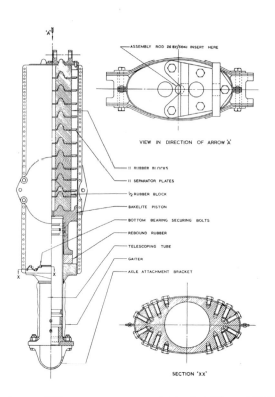

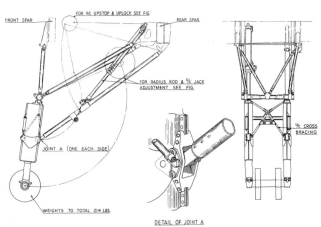

This diagram shows the overall assembly and operation and applies to all variants bar the Sea Mosquito *(©Crown Copyright)*

Overall view of the rear linkage on a Mosquito being restored at Salisbury Hall; this is the starboard leg, looking inboard *(©Nigel Perry)*

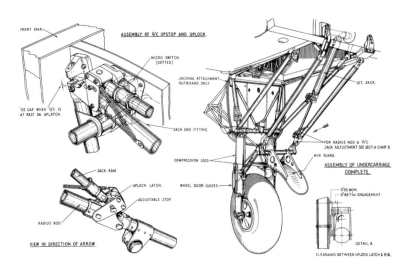

This diagram of the undercarriage system comes from the FB Mk VI manual, but applies to nearly all Mosquito variants *(©Crown Copyright)*

This is another shot of the undercarriage rear linkage of the FB Mk VI at Salisbury Hall, this time the port leg, looking inboard *(©Nigel Perry)*

A nice shot of the main legs of the FB Mk VI at Salisbury Hall, showing the wire guards that are retained on all variants but often missing from kits of the type *(©Nigel Perry)*

This is the top of the main legs on the NF Mk 30 in Belgium, which lacks the wires that close the doors, but this means you can see the buffer blocks and pulleys associated with it

(©George Papadimitriou)

In this view of the side of the main leg on the Belgian NF Mk 30 you can see that the gauge of the pipe used for the wire guard is greater at the bottom and for the front regions, than it is for the back/upper parts *(©George Papadimitriou)*

Going up above the main struts, again in the Belgian NF Mk 30, you can see the linkage at the top of the legs and the oil tank in this region *(©George Papadimitriou)*

If you turn around in the bay this is the rear area, with the different lengths to the rear struts caused by the angle the rear spar travels through the area *(©David Willis)*

These are the Lockheed oleo-pneumatic legs used on the Sea Mosquito TR Mk 33 and 37, seen here on TW249; note the lack of any mudguard on this particular machine, which was not usual

The early machines used a 'balloon' tyre on the tailwheel, but to reduce shimmy a twin-contact tyre was soon adopted and is seen here on the PR Mk 41 at Canberra *(©P. Skulski)*

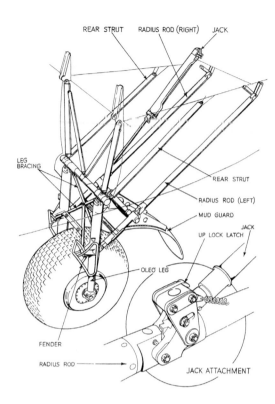

From this angle, you can see the twin-contact points of the tailwheel tyre, as well as the mudguard built up inside the tail region *(©P. Skulski)*

This diagram from the Sea Mosquito TR Mk 33 manual shows the oleo-pneumatic undercarriage used by it and the TR Mk 37 *(©Crown Copyright)*

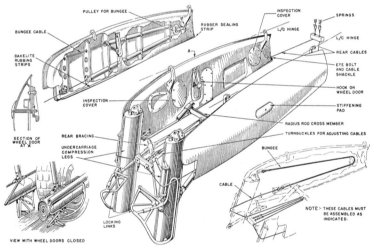

This diagram shows the undercarriage doors used on all Mosquito variants, with the bungee chords built inside the doors to operate the wires that pulled the doors closed on retraction *(©Crown Copyright)*

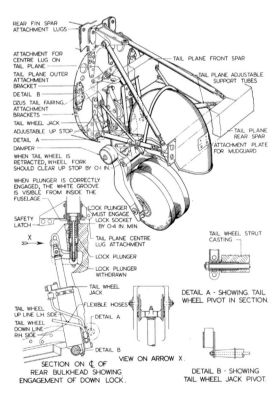

This shows how the tailwheel attaches to the rear of the fuselage and except for the TC tyre (where some early machines had a standard tyre without the ridges), this installation is applicable to all variants *(©Crown Copyright)*

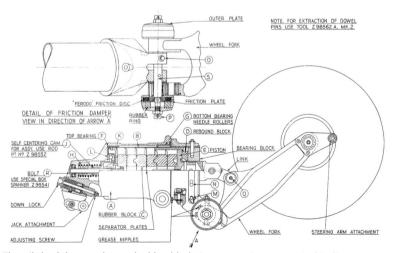

The tailwheel damper also used rubber blocks in compression, as seen in this diagram *(©Crown Copyright)*

Armament, Ordnance & Drop Tanks

NF Mk II W4052 in final assembly at Salisbury Hall on the 25th April 1941, this close-up of the nose armament shows the one-part upper access doors originally intended for the type; these were quickly replaced with the two-part doors hinged on the centreline that all production machines had (©DH)

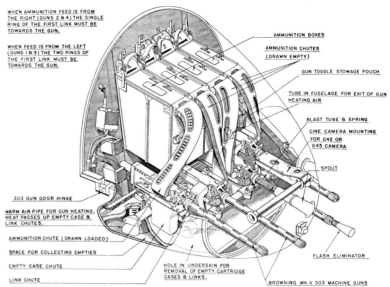

This diagram shows the installation of the Browning 0.303in machine-guns in the nose from the FB Mk 26 manual, but applicable to all variants (©Crown Copyright)

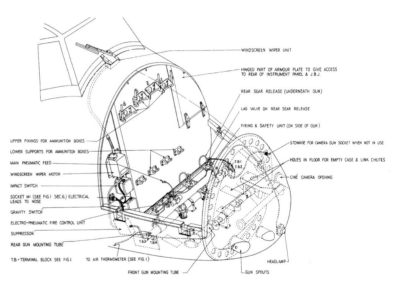

This diagram shows the various wiring relating to the machine-guns in the nose (©Crown Copyright)

Lovely period close-up under the nose of an FB Mk VI, the round panel under the nose allows access to spent 0.303in rounds and links (retained to stop slipstream damage to the cannon ports): W-T means Wired Throughout and DTD is the paint standard (©DH/BAE)

Here you can see the machine-guns without their ammo boxes in an NF Mk II, complete with A.I. Mk IV antenna in the nose (©DH/BAE)

Close-up of the muzzle flash eliminators on the guns in the nose of the FB Mk VI at Salisbury Hall *(©Nigel Perry)*

An armourer loads 0.303in rounds into the ammo bins in the nose of a Mosquito *(©British Official)*

Period photo of the 20mm cannon ports in the underside of an NF Mk XII, note the dipole in the centre of the panel behind them *(©British Official)*

When used in the PR role by the RAAF, the machine-gun ports were plated over, as was the camera gun port above and to the port side; this is the PR Mk 41 A52-319 at Canberra *(©P. Skulski)*

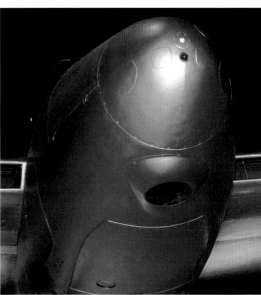

The 20mm cannon installation photographed in an NF Mk II in February 1942 *(©DH/BAE)*

This diagram shows the 20mm cannon installation that applies to all fighter-based variants *(©Crown Copyright)*

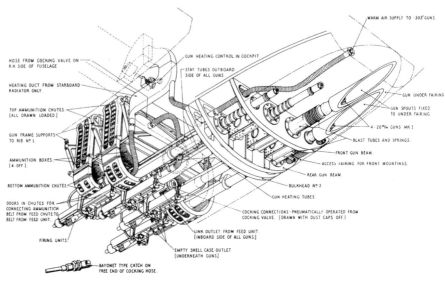

This is the forward bulkhead under the nose, looking forward, and you can see the tunnels for the Hispano cannon barrels plus the various hydraulic and pneumatic pipework; the black oblongs on either side of the roof are oxygen economisers *(©DH/BAE)*

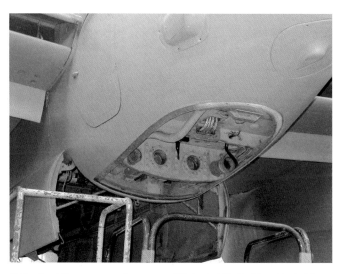

At the front if you remove the cannon, this is what the bulkhead looks like; this is the NF Mk 30 in Belgium *(©George Papadimitriou)*

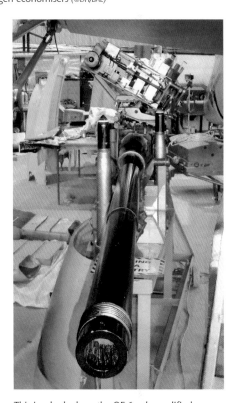

This is a look along the QF 6-pdr modified by Molins for installation in the FB Mk XVIII *(©Nigel Perry)*

This is the QF 6-pdr (57mm) anti-tank gun alongside an FB Mk XVIII of No.248 Squadron at Portreath on the 5th August 1944 *(©Air Ministry)*

An FB Mk XVII with an armourer holding a 57mm shell *(©Air Ministry)*

Photos relating to the installation of the 57mm cannon in the FB Mk XVIII are rare, this shows the inside of the gun bay looking forward; note the modification made to the starboard doors, the bulge at the front and the ejector scoop at the rear *(©DH/BAE)*

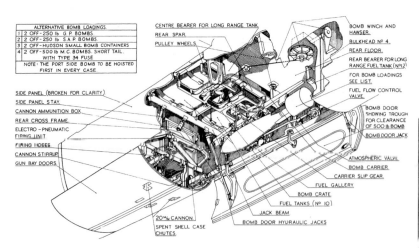

This diagram from the FB Mk VI manual shows the installation of bombs in the aft ventral bay *(©Crown Copyright)*

Armourers H. 'Smithy' Smith and Col Davies guiding a 500lb bomb as it is winched into the bomb bay of a No.464 Squadron FB Mk VI *(©British Official)*

Bombs on their carrier prior to loading into FB Mk VI SM•Q (either NS999 or LE262) of No.29 Squadron at Lasham *(©Polish Institute and Sikorski Museum)*

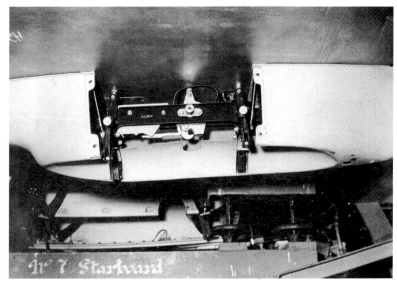

Close-up of the bomb carrier within the bomb rack fairing under the wing of FB Mk VI prototype HJ662/G; the starboard side (mid) cover has been removed *(©DH/BAE)*

This is the 250lb fairing, seen in the FB Mk 26 manual *(©Crown Copyright)*

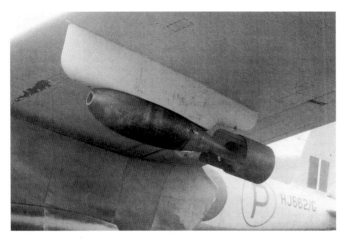

A 250lb bomb under the wing of FB Mk VI prototype HJ662/G at A&AEE during handling and diving trials in June-July 1942; note the shape of the fairing at the rear, which denotes the type suitable for the 200lb bomb – odd light colours are caused by use of orthochromatic film *(©Crown Copyright)*

A 500lb bomb is winched up under a No.140 Wing FB Mk VI – both bomb sizes used the Mk III universal carrier, but required different style outer fairings *(©British Official)*

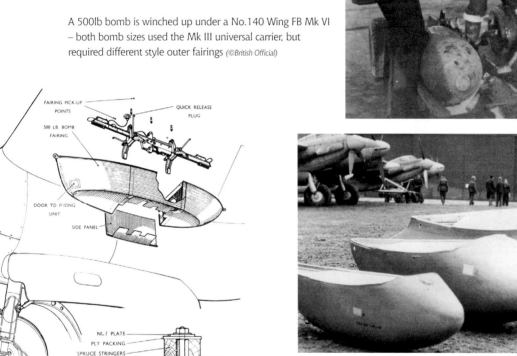

This is the 500lb fairing *(©Crown Copyright)*

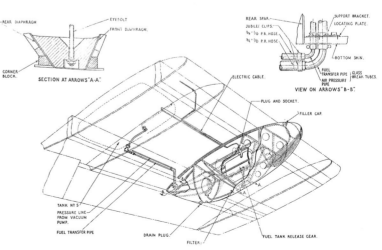

The Mosquito could carry the 50, 100 and 200 Imp. Gall. drop tanks, although the early machines could only use the first two *(©British Official)*

Australian-built machines seemed to use a locally manufactured tank that had a prominent raised seam around the middle, plus the filler cap was off-set to port as a result

This diagram shows the installation of the drop tank under the wing *(©Crown Copyright)*

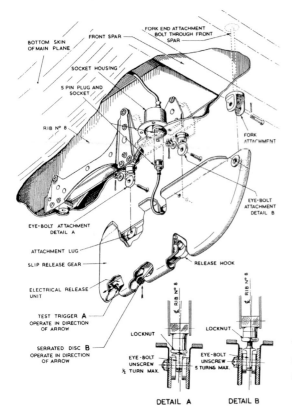

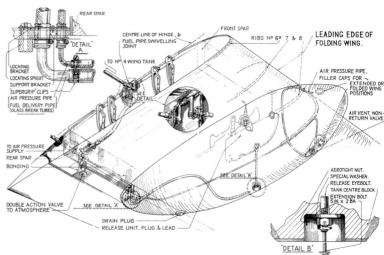

The Sea Mosquito, with its wing fold, had to have a slightly revised system for the installation of wing tanks *(©Crown Copyright)*

The tank was held in place with this drop tank release mechanism and it is applicable to all variants capable of carrying such tanks *(©Crown Copyright)*

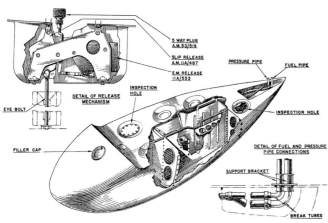

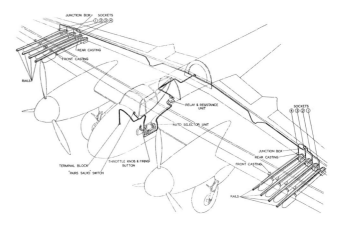

This diagram shows the RP installation in the FB Mk VI *(©Crown Copyright)*

This diagram shows the construction of the drop tank and is applicable to all but the Australian-produced ones *(©Crown Copyright)*

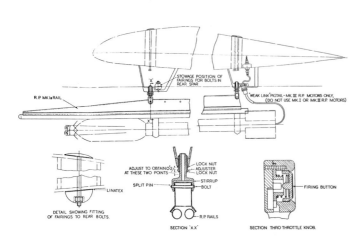

This diagram shows RP installation details for the FB Mk VI using Mk IA rails *(©Crown Copyright)*

Here RPs are being loaded onto Mk IIIA rails *(©British Official)*

A rear view of RPs with 25lb SAP heads, under the wing of a No.143 Squadron FB Mk VI at Banff *(©C.E. Brown)*

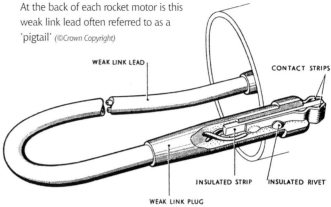

At the back of each rocket motor is this weak link lead often referred to as a 'pigtail' *(©Crown Copyright)*

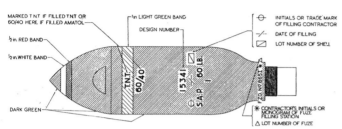

These are the identification markings on a 60lb HE/SAP No 1 Mk 1 head; the 25lb is similar *(©Crown Copyright)*

The two-tier Mk IIIa RP installation without the rockets fitted; note the blast/separation guard between the rails and the drop tank *(©British Official)*

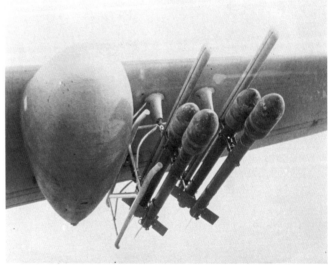

The two-tier Mk IIIa RP installation with the rockets fitted *(©British Official)*

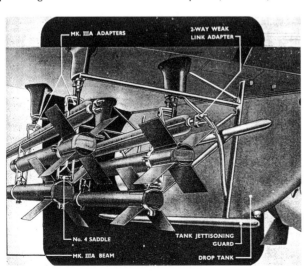

Here is the rear of the Mk IIIa two-tier RP installation *(©Crown Copyright)*

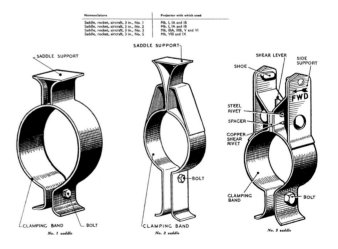

Each rail required a different style of saddle, this diagram shows the No.1, 2 and 3 versions as used in WWII, along with details of the rails to which they were applicable *(©Crown Copyright)*

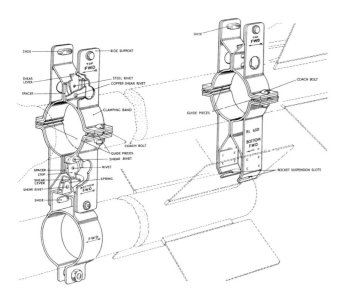

This is the No.4 Mk 2 saddle, which was used with the two-tier Mk IIIa installation *(©Crown Copyright)*

FB Mk 6 '2109' of the IDF was experimentally fitted with 5in rockets for tests on the 31st August 1951 *(©IDF/IAF)*

In Yugoslavia various types of torpedo were tested under the FB Mk VI, the TR-45/A version is seen here installed in October 1953

(©M. Micevski via Stuart Howe†)

FB Mk VI NT220 at Farnborough with 'Tiny Tim' missiles underneath, ML901 also tested these between May 18th and June 22nd 1945 *(©RAE/Crown Copyright)*

Although not the best quality image, this does show the 'Triplex' (three 3in RP tubes) projectiles under the wing of Sea Mosquito TR Mk 33 TS444 at A&AEE in July 1946 *(©Crown Copyright)*

The 11in 'Uncle Tom' rocket was tested under the Mosquito at A&AEE Boscombe Down, although the type was never adopted for service use

(©Crown Copyright)

The only British variant designed to carry a torpedo was the Sea Mosquito, an 18in example is seen here under the FB Mk VI (Naval) prototype LR387 *(©DH/BAE)*

Appendix: I **Kit List**

Below is a list of all static scale construction kits produced to date of the D.H. Mosquito (fighter, fighter-bomber, night-fighter and Sea Mosquito variants). This list is as comprehensive as possible, but if there are amendments or additions, please contact the author via the Valiant Wings Publishing address shown at the front of this title.

Note: All kits are injection moulded plastic unless stated otherwise

1/72nd

- D.H. Mosquito FB.VI #Patt. No.281 (1957) – Reissued in 1977 as #02001-9, new box in 1981 as # 9 02001, reissued in 1983 (same number) reverted to box art seen in 1977, as #902001 in 1985 and as #02001 in 1986 {released late 1987}
- Airfix D.H. Mosquito VI #1-49 (1964) – *American market version of Patt No.281*
- Airfix D.H. De Havilland Mosquito #Patt. No.399 (1972) Made the NF Mk II/FB Mk VI & XVIII – Renumbered #03019-3 in 1973, #03019 in 1983, reissued in early 1990 as #03019, new box art in 1994 (#03019), issued in the 'All in One' series in 1995 and as #93019 in 1998 (#03019), issued with the RAF Refuelling set, paints & glue in 2002 as #93302, issued as part of the 'VE-Day Anniversary Set' as #10301 in 2005 and with revised box art as #03019, renumbered in 2008 as #A03019
- Airfix D.H. Mosquito & Me 262 'Dogfight Double' #Patt No.D362F (1967) – Renumbered #03142-2 in 1973, issued as a 'Starter Set' in 2001 as #93019 and issued as the new-style Gift Set in 2009 as #A50068
- Airfix D.H. Mosquito NF Mk XIX/J.30 #03062 (1995) – Renumbered in 2008 as #A03062
- AMT (ex-Frog) D.H. Mosquito IV/VI #A-631 (1967-1970s)
- Frog D.H. Mosquito Mk IV/VI #F187 (1968-1977)
- Frog 'Penguin' 1/72nd D.H.98 Mosquito FB Mk VI #117P (1946-1949) – *The first 'plastic' Mosquito kit*
- Hasegawa (ex-Frog) D.H. Mosquito Mk IV/VI #JS-045 (1967-1973/4)
- Hasegawa D.H. FB Mk VI #CP18 (1999)
- Hasegawa D.H. NF Mk II 'Night Fighter' #00050 (2000) – *Limited edition*
- Hasegawa D.H. FB Mk VI 'Coastal Command' #00098 (2000) – *Limited edition*

- Hasegawa D.H. FB Mk VI 'Asia Theater' #00159 (2001) – *Limited edition*
- Hasegawa D.H. FB Mk VI 'RAAF' #00656 (2003) – *Limited edition*
- Hasegawa D.H. FB Mk VI 'IDF' #00739 (2004) – *Limited edition*
- Hasegawa D.H. FB Mk VI '418 Sqn #00750 (2005) – *Limited edition*
- Hasegawa D.H. Mosquito 'Passenger Transport' #00268 (2001) – *Limited edition*
- Hasegawa Spitfire Mk VII & Mosquito FB Mk VI 'Operation Overlord' #02096 (2014) – *Limited edition*
- Hasegawa D.H. Mosquito NF Mk XIII 'Night Fighter' #02198 (2016) – *Limited edition*
- Hasegawa D.H. Mosquito FB Mk XVIII 'Anti-ship Attacker' #02024 (2013) – *Limited edition*
- Hi-Tech (updated ex-Airfix) [inj/res/mtl/pe/vac] D.H. Mosquito FB Mk VI #018 (1993) – *This kit has resin and photo-etched detail and conversion parts (two-stage engine nacelles & canopies) to update the base Airfix kit, which was also included*
- Igrushka (ex-Frog) D.H. Mosquito #N/K (1980s)
- InTech (ex-Frog) D.H. Mosquito #T22 (1992->)
- Kikoler/Kiko (ex-Airfix) D.H. Mosquito #3019 (early 80s)
- Lodela (ex-Airfix) D.H. Mosquito Mk II #RH-3019
- Maestro Models J30 Mosquito #72-001 (1990s) – *This was the Airfix FB Mk VI kit with resin, metal, photo-etched and vacformed parts to convert to the NF Mk XXX/J 30*

Airfix Pat No 281 (1963)

Airfix Patt No D362F

Airfix 03062 (1995)

Airfix 03062

Airfix USA 1-49

Airfix A50068

Hasegawa CP18

Hasegawa CP18 (SE)

Frog F187 (1968)

Hasegawa 00050

Hasegawa 00098 (2005)

Hasegawa 00159

Hasegawa 00268

Hasegawa 00739

Hasegawa 00750

Hasegawa 02024

Airfix 02001 (1977)

Airfix 02001 (1983)

Airfix 03019 (1975)

Airfix 03019 (1990)

Airfix 03019 (1994)

Airfix 03019 (1998)

Airfix 03019 (2005)

Airfix A03019 (2013)

Hasegawa 02096

Hasegawa 02198

Hasegawa JS-045

Matchbox 40116 (1992)

Matchbox PK-116 (1976)

MPC 2-0211 (1976)

MPC Profile series

Tamiya 60747

Tamiya 60765

Tamiya 89786

Airfix 07100

Airfix 07111

Airfix 07111 (2003)

Tamiya 61062

Tamiya 61075

Tamiya 60326

Airfix A25001

Airfix A25001A

- Matchbox D.H. Mosquito #PK-116 (1976) – *This made the B Mk IX or NF Mk 30* – Reissued, same kit number new box art in 1982, reissued as 'de Havilland Mosquito Mk IX/NF.30' under Revell's control in 1989 as #40116 and reissued again with the same kit number but revised boxart in 1992
- Mavi (Model Aviation) [vac] D.H. Mosquito NF.II/FB.VI #7016 (1993->)
- MPC (ex-Airfix) D.H. Mosquito #7017 (1965-1985) Also #2-0211 (with 6 ground-crew figures from the RAF Personnel set) in 1976 & 2-7017 – *This is a reboxing of the #Patt. No.399*
- MPC (ex-Airfix) D.H. Mosquito 'Profile Series' #2-1516 (1965-1985) – *This is a reboxing of the #Patt. No.399, but the kit offers a USAAF example that is a PR version and should thus be two-stage engines, which are not in the kit, also shown with a fighter (solid) nose, should be glazed (bomber) one, again not in the kit*
- Novo (ex-Frog) D.H. Mosquito IV/VI #78082 (1979-1980)
- Obit (ex-Frog) D.H. Mosquito IV/VI #N/K (1993)
- Tamiya D.H. Mosquito FB Mk VI/NF Mk II #60747 (2000)
- Tamiya/TMA D.H. Mosquito FB Mk VI/NF Mk II #60747F (2001) – *Limited edition with T2M in France with French markings*
- Tamiya D.H. Mosquito NF Mk XIII/XVII #60765 (2001)
- Tashigrushka (ex-Frog) D.H. Mosquito IV/VI #N/K – *The release of this kit by this firm is possible but unconfirmed*
- USAirfix (ex-Airfix) D.H. Mosquito II/VI/XVIII #30040 (1980-1981)

1/48th
- Airfix D.H. Mosquito Mk VI #06100-7 (1977) – *Not released as this number, eventually released in 1980 as #07107-7* – Renumbered as #07100 in 1983, reissued in 1988 as #07100 (£6.95), reissued again (same number) in 1990

- Airfix D.H. Mosquito NF Mk 30 #07111 (2003) – Also issued as a 'Gift Set' as #97111
- Hasegawa (ex-Monogram) Mosquito FB Mk VI #HM9 (1980s)
- Hasegawa (ex-Monogram) Mosquito FB Mk VI Part 2 #HM83 (1990s) – *With AeroMaster decals*
- Hi-Tech (ex-Airfix) D.H. Mosquito FB Mk VI #N/K – *Planned but never released*
- Tamiya D.H. Mosquito FB Mk VI/NF Mk II #61062 (1998)
- Tamiya D.H. Mosquito NF Mk II & 10hp Tilly #89786 (2009) – *Limited edition*
- Tamiya/T2M D.H. Mosquito FB Mk VI/NF Mk II 'France/Belgium' #61062F (2000) – *Limited edition in France*
- Tamiya D.H. Mosquito NF Mk XIII/XVII #61075 (2000)

1/32nd
- Tamiya D.H. Mosquito FB Mk VI #60326

1/24th
- Airfix D.H. Mosquito NF.II/FB.VI/NF.30 #A20002 – *Announced as this kit number in 2008 (£79.99), but in 2009 this was changed to just the NF.II/FB.VI as #A25001 (£129.99) see separate listing below*
- Airfix D.H. Mosquito NF.II/FB.VI #A25001 (2009)
- Airfix D.H. Mosquito FB Mk VI #A25001A (2015) – *Just the FB Mk VI parts out of #A25001 plus new decals*
- Heritage Aviation [vac] D.H. Mosquito #24001 (2007) – *Announced for 2006 as a resin kit and although 'masters' of the kit were displayed it was released in 2007 as a vac-formed kit with resin and metal parts*

Colour shot of F Mk II, DZ231, YP•R of No.23 Squadron over Malta 27th June 1943

Appendix: II **Accessory List**

Below is a list of all accessories for static scale construction kits produced to date for the D.H. Mosquito fighter and fighter-based variants. We have refrained this time from including those items that are out of production as we write, however these will be available as a free download from our website (www.valiant-wings.co.uk) once this title is produced. This list is as comprehensive as possible, but if there are amendments or additions, please contact the author via the Valiant Wings Publishing address shown at the front of this title.

Notes

br	–	Brass
dec	–	Decal
flm	–	Acetate Film
Inj	–	Injection-moulded Plastic (limited-run)
ma	–	Self-adhesive Tape Paint Masks
mtl	–	White-metal (including Pewter)
pa	–	Paper (or Fabric)
pe	–	Photo-etched Brass
rb	–	Rubber
res	–	Resin
vac	–	Vacuum-formed Plastic
vma	–	Vinyl Self-adhesive Paint Masks
{Academy} –		Denotes the kit for which the set is intended

Aires 7067

1/72nd

- Aires [res/pe] Mosquito Mk II/VI Cockpit Set #7067 {Tamiya}
- Aires [res/pe] Mosquito FB Mk VI Gun Bay #7091 {Tamiya}
- Aires [res/pe] Mosquito FB Mk VI Bomb Bay #7099 {Tamiya}
- Airwaves [pe] Mosquito Mk II/VI/XVIII Detail Set #AC72166 {Airfix}
- Armory [res] Mosquito Weighted Wheels #AW72406
- Attack Squadron [res] TR.1143 Radio Set for Spitfire, Mosquito, P-51D & P-47D #72076
- Attack Squadron [res] Two-stage Merlin Nacelle Set #72104 {Tamiya}
- Attack Squadron [res] Mosquito Wheels – 5-spoke Hub, Block Tread Pattern #72105
- Attack Squadron [res] Mosquito Wheels – 5-spoke Hub, Radial Tread Pattern #72106
- Aviaeology [pe] Mosquito 3-tier R.P rig for Coastal Strike FB Mk VIs #AES72001
- Aviaeology [res] ARI 5083 Gee Mk II for Mosquito, Beaufighter etc. #AES72002
- CMK [res] Mosquito FB Mk VI Engine #7036 {Hasegawa}
- CMK [res] Mosquito Control Surfaces #7038 {Hasegawa}
- CMK [res] Mosquito B Mk IV/FB Mk VI Detail Set #7047 {Hasegawa}
- CMK [res] Mosquito FB Mk VI Bomb Bay #7227 {Tamiya}
- CMK [res] Mosquito Exterior Set #7228 {Tamiya}
- CMK [res] Mosquito Control Surfaces #7229 {Tamiya}
- CMK/Quick & Easy [res] Mosquito B Mk IV/FB Mk VI Oil Coolers #Q72024 {Hasegawa}
- Eduard [ma] Mosquito FB Mk VI Canopy & Wheel Masks #CX119 {Tamiya}
- Eduard [pe] Mosquito FB Mk VI Detail Set 'Zoom' #SS137 {Tamiya}
- Eduard [pe] Mosquito FB Mk VI Detail Set #72-072 {Airfix}
- Eduard [pe] Mosquito FB Mk VI/NF Mk II Detail Set #72-323 {Tamiya}
- Eduard [pe] Mosquito NF Mk II Detail Set #72-389 {Hasegawa}
- Equipage [res/rb] Mosquito Wheel Set #72084

Aires 7091

- Falcon [vac] RAF Fighters WWII; inc. Fighter canopy #Set No.2 {Airfix}
- LF Models [vma] Mosquito FB Mk VI Camouflage Masks – Ocean Grey/Dark Green Scheme #M7217 {Airfix or Tamiya}
- LF Models [vma] Mosquito FB Mk VI Camouflage Masks – Ocean Grey/Dark Green/Medium Sea Grey Scheme #M7218{Airfix or Tamiya}
- LF Models [vma] Mosquito FB Mk VI Camouflage Masks – Ocean Grey/Dark Green/Night Scheme #M7219 {Airfix or Tamiya}
- Maestro Models [res] Mosquito 4-blade Propellers #K7278
- Master [br] Mosquito NF Mk II/FB Mk VI Pitot Tube & Armament Set #AM-72-091
- Montex [vma] Mosquito FB Mk VI Exterior Canopy Masks #SM72068 {Hasegawa}
- Montex [vma] Mosquito FB Mk VI Exterior Canopy Masks #SM72079 {Tamiya}
- PART [pe] Mosquito FB Mk VI/NF Mk II Detail Set #S72-139 {Tamiya}
- PART [pe] Mosquito FB Mk VI Detail Set #S72-132 {Hasegawa}
- Pavla Models [res] Mosquito T Mk III Cockpit Set #C72038 {Tamiya}
- Pavla Models [res] Mosquito Merlin 73/72 Engine Cowlings x2 #U72-62 {Tamiya}
- Pavla Models [vac] Mosquito Fighter Canopy #V72-09 {Airfix}
- Pmask [vma] Mosquito National Insignia Masks #Po72004
- Quickboost [res] Mosquito Undercarriage Doors #QB72121 {Tamiya}
- Quickboost [res] Mosquito FB Mk VI Nose – 2-gun #QB72204 {Tamiya}

Eduard SS137

Master AM-72-091

CMK 7047

CMK 7227

CMK 7228

CMK 7229

CMK Q72024

Eduard 72-323

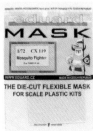

Eduard CX119

Pavla Models C72038

Quickboost QB72121

Quickboost QB72204

Quickboost QB72425

Squadron 9156

Aires 4086

Rob Taurus 48068

- Quickboost [res] Mosquito Exhausts #QB72301 {Tamiya}
- Quickboost [res] Mosquito Oil Radiators #QB72425 {Tamiya}
- Quickboost [res] Mosquito Seats with Safety Belts #QB72550 {Tamiya}
- Rob Taurus [vac] Mosquito NF Mk II/FB Mk VI Canopy #72071 {Tamiya}
- Red Roo Models [res] Mosquito 100 Gallon Drop Tanks – RAAF #RRR72118 {Airfix or Tamiya}
- Rob Taurus [vac] NF Mk II/FB Mk VI Canopy #72071 {Tamiya}
- Squadron [vac] Mosquito FB Mk VI Canopy #9156 {Airfix}
- True Details [res] Mosquito Wheels, Spoked Hubs, Block Tread Pattern #72033
- Warhawk Productions [vac] Mosquito FB Canopy #V72012 {Airfix}
- Warhawk Productions [vac] Mosquito FB (Late) Canopy #V72013 {Airfix}
- Yahu Models [pe] Mosquito FB Mk VI/NF Mk II Instrument Panel #7260 {Hasegawa or Tamiya}

1/48th

- Aires [res] Mosquito FB Mk VI/NF Mk II Cockpit Set #4086 {Tamiya}
- Aires [res] Mosquito FB Mk VI Bomb Bay #4152 {Tamiya}
- Aires [res] Mosquito FB Mk VI Gun Bay #4177 {Tamiya}
- Aires [res] Mosquito NF Mk II/FB Mk VI Engine Set #4200 {Tamiya}
- Aires [res] Mosquito Wheel Bays #4208 {Tamiya}
- Armory [res] Mosquito Wheels – Checkerboard Tyre Pattern, Weighted #48402
- Aviaeology [pe] Mosquito 3-tier R.P. rig for Coastal Strike FB Mk VIs #AES18001
- Aviaeology [res] ARI 5083 Gee Mk II for Mosquito, Beaufighter etc. #AES48002
- CMK [res/pe] Mosquito FB Mk VI* Interior #4036 {Tamiya} *States 'Mk IV' on box top, but this is for the fighter version
- CMK [res/pe] Mosquito Merlin Engine Set #4038
- CMK [res] Mosquito B Mk IV/FB Mk VI Exterior Set #4106 {Tamiya}
- CMK [res/pe] Mosquito Wing Mounted Coolers #4241 {Tamiya}
- CMK [res/pe] Mosquito Control Surfaces #4260 {Tamiya}
- CMK/Quick & Easy [res] Mosquito Tailwheel Strut and Wheel #Q48114 {Tamiya}
- Eduard [vma] Mosquito FB Mk VI/NF Mk II Canopy & Wheel Masks #XF010 {Tamiya}
- Eduard [ma] Mosquito FB Mk VI/NF Mk II Canopy & Wheel Masks #EX029 {Tamiya}
- Eduard [pe] Mosquito FB Mk VI/NF Mk II 'Zoom' Detail Set #FE239 {Tamiya}
- Eduard [pe] Mosquito FB Mk VI Detail Set #48-157 {Airfix}
- Eduard [pe] Mosquito FB Mk VI/NF Mk II Detail Set #48-271 {Tamiya}
- Eduard [pe] Mosquito FB Mk VI/NF Mk II Detail Set #49-239 {Tamiya}
- E-Z Masks [vma] Mosquito Fighter Canopy Masks x2 #102 {Tamiya}

- Freightdog Models [res] Mosquito NF Mk XII Conversion #FDR48M02 {Tamiya}
- Freightdog Models [res] Mosquito FB Mk VI No.100 Group Conversion #FDR48M03 {Tamiya}
- Falcon [vac] RAF Fighters WWII; contains FB Mk VI (Late) Canopy #Set No.31 {Airfix}
- Falcon [vac] RAF Part 2; contains FB Mk VI (Bulged) Canopy #Set No.40 {Tamiya}
- HGW [pe/pa] Mosquito Seat Belts #148543
- LF Models [vma] Mosquito FB Mk VI Camouflage Masks – Ocean Grey/Dark Green Scheme #M4815 {Airfix or Tamiya}
- LF Models [vma] Mosquito FB Mk VI Camouflage Masks – Ocean Grey/Dark Green/Medium Sea Grey Scheme #M4816 {Airfix or Tamiya}
- LF Models [vma] Mosquito FB Mk VI Camouflage Masks – Ocean Grey/Dark Green/Night Scheme #M4817 {Airfix or Tamiya}
- Maestro Models [res] Mosquito 4-Blade Propellers x2 #K4880 {Tamiya}
- Master [br] Mosquito NF Mk II/FB Mk VI Pitot Tube & Armament Set #AM-48-111 {Tamiya}
- Montex [vma] Mosquito FB Mk VI/NF Mk II Canopy & Insignia Masks #MM48004 {Tamiya}
- Montex [vma] Mosquito FB Mk VI/NF Mk II Canopy Masks #SM48004 {Tamiya}
- Montex [vma] Mosquito FB Mk VI/NF Mk II Canopy Masks #SM48228 {Airfix}
- PART [pe] Mosquito FB Mk VI/NF Mk II Detail Set #S48-052 {Tamiya}
- Pmask [vma] Mosquito FB Mk VI/NF Mk II National Insignia Masks #Po48004
- Quickboost [res] Sea Mosquito Stabilisers #QB48030 {Tamiya}
- Quickboost [res] Mosquito Undercarriage Doors #QB48140 {Tamiya}
- Quickboost [res] Mosquito FB Mk VI Nose, 2-Gun Version #QB48252 {Tamiya}
- Quickboost [res] Mosquito Exhausts #QB48306 {Tamiya}
- Quickboost [res] Mosquito Fenders #QB48325 {Tamiya}
- Quickboost [res] Mosquito Seats with Safety Belts #QB48593 {Tamiya}
- Resin 2 Detail [res] Mosquito 5-stack Exhausts #AC48045 [Tamiya]
- Res-IM [vma] Mosquito FB Mk VI Marking Masks #G4810 {Tamiya}
- REXx [mtl] Mosquito FB Mk VI Exhausts #48015 {Tamiya}
- Rob Taurus [vac] Mosquito NF Mk II/FB Mk VI Canopy #48068 {Tamiya}
- Scale Aircraft Conversions [mtl] Mosquito Landing Gear #48038 {Tamiya}
- Squadron [vac] Mosquito FB Mk VI Canopy x2 #9532 {Airfix}
- Squadron [vac] Mosquito FB Mk VI Standard & Bulged Canopies #9600 {Tamiya}
- True Details [res] Mosquito Wheels, Plain Hubs, Block Tread Pattern #48017
- True Details [res] Mosquito Wheels, Spoked Hubs, Block Tread Pattern #48093

Aires 4152

Aires 4200

Eduard 49-239

CMK 4036

Freightdog FDR48M02

Verlinden 1474

Eduard 48-157

Quickboost QB48252

Freightdog FDR48M03

Maestro Models K4880

PART S48-052

Quickboost QB48030

BarracudaCast
BR32265

Brassin 632 065

Brassin 632 066

Brassin 632 077

Eduard 32-849

Eduard 32-379

Eduard JX184

Master AM-32-083

SAC 32099

Cammett Camb24007

- True Details [res] Mosquito FB Mk VI/NF Mk II Cockpit Set (ex-KMC) #48489 {Tamiya}
- True Details [res] Mosquito FB Mk VI Cockpit Set #48532 {Airfix}
- Ultracast [res] Mosquito Seats, Late Pattern Harness #48033
- Ultracast [res] Mosquito Control Surfaces #48034 {Tamiya}
- Ultracast [res] Mosquito Detailed Crew Access Door #48035 {Tamiya}
- Ultracast [res] Mosquito Tailwheel Assembly #48045 {Tamiya}
- Ultracast [res] Mosquito Mudguards #48046 {Tamiya}
- Ultracast [res] Mosquito Flame Damper Exhaust Shrouds #48047 {Tamiya}
- Ultracast [res] Mosquito 5-Stack Exhausts #48104 {Tamiya}
- Ultracast [res] Mosquito 100 Gallon Tanks #48118 {Tamiya}
- Ultracast [res] Mosquito Wheels, Spoked Hubs and Block Tread #48246
- Ultracast [res] Mosquito Wheels, Plain Hubs and Block Tread #48247
- Ultracast [res] Mosquito Wheels, Spoked Hubs and Diamond Tread Pattern #48248
- Ultracast [res] Mosquito Wheels, Plain Hubs and Diamond Tread Pattern #48249
- Ultracast [res] Mosquito Wheels, Spoked Hubs and Australian 'Z' Block Tread Pattern #48250
- Verlinden [res/pe] Mosquito Cockpit Detail Set #1460 {Tamiya}
- Verlinden [res/pe] Mosquito Gun Bay & Control Surfaces #1474 {Tamiya}
- Xtraparts [res] Mosquito Universal Radome #XP4843 {Airfix} *Same as Paragon Designs set*
- Yahu Models [pe] Mosquito NF Mk II/FB Mk VI Instrument Panel #YMA4830 {Tamiya}

1/32nd

- Aviaeology [pe] Mosquito 3-tier R.P. rig for Coastal Strike FB Mk VIs #AES32001
- Aviaeology [res] ARI 5083 Gee Mk II for Mosquito, Beaufighter etc. #AES32002
- BarracudaCast [res] Mosquito FB Mk VI Ammo Feed Chutes #BCR32265 {Tamiya}
- BarracudaCast [res] Mosquito FB Mk VI R-R Merlin Rocker Covers #BCR32267 {Tamiya}
- Brassin [res] Mosquito FB Mk VI Wheels #632 065 {Tamiya}
- Brassin [res] Mosquito FB Mk VI Exhaust Stacks #632 066 {Tamiya}
- Brassin [res/pe] Mosquito FB Mk VI Nose Gun Bay #632 077 {Tamiya}
- Brassin [res/pe] Mosquito FB Mk VI Gun Bay #632 078 {Tamiya}
- Brassin [res/pe] Mosquito FB Mk VI Engines #632 091 {Tamiya}
- Brassin [res/pe] Mosquito FB Mk VI Starboard Engine #632 092 {Tamiya}
- Brassin [res/pe] Mosquito FB Mk VI Port Engine #632 093 {Tamiya}
- Eduard [pe/ma] Mosquito FB Mk VI 'Big ED' Detail & Mask Set #BIG3359 {Tamiya} – Inc. 32-379, 32-845, 32-849 & JX184
- Eduard [pe] Mosquito FB Mk VI Seat Belts #32-845 {Tamiya}
- Eduard [pa] Mosquito FB Mk VI Seat Belts – Fabric #32-846 {Tamiya}
- Eduard [pe] Mosquito FB Mk VI Interior Detail Set #32-849 {Tamiya}
- Eduard [pe] Mosquito FB Mk VI Interior 'Zoom' Detail Set #33148 {Tamiya}
- Eduard [pe] Mosquito FB Mk VI Exterior Detail Set #32-845 {Tamiya}
- Eduard [ma] Mosquito FB Mk VI Canopy & Wheel Masks #JX1845 {Tamiya}
- Grey Matter Figures (ex-Paragon) [res] FB Mk VI Conversion #GMAE3201 {Revell}

- Heritage Aviation [res] Mosquito Singe-stage Merlin Nacelles #N/K {Revell}
- Heritage Aviation [vac] Mosquito FB Mk VI Canopy #N/K {Revell}
- HGW [pe/pa] Mosquito FB Mk VI Seat Belts #132568 {Tamiya}
- HGW [pe/pa/ma] Mosquito FB Mk VI Seat Belts & Decal Option Masks #132809 {Tamiya}
- Master [br] Mosquito NF Mk II/FB Mk VI Pitot Tube & Armament Set #AM-32-083 {Tamiya}
- MasterCasters [pe] Mosquito Grilles and Fasteners #MST32021 {HK Model or Revell}
- Montex [vma] Mosquito FB Mk VI Canopy & Markings Masks #MM32163 {Tamiya}
- Montex [vma] Mosquito FB Mk VI Canopy Masks #SM32163 {Tamiya}
- Pmask [vma] Mosquito Insignia Masks #Po32004 {Tamiya}
- Profimodeller [br] Mosquito Pitot Tube #32241
- Quickboost [res] Mosquito Exhausts #QB32066 {Revell}
- RB Productions [pe] Mosquito Radiators #RB-P32040
- Scale Aircraft Conversions [mtl] Mosquito Landing Gear #32099 {Tamiya}
- Warbird Productions [vac] Mosquito Bomber Canopy Set #None {Revell}
- Yahu Models [pe] Mosquito NF Mk II/FB Mk VI Instrument Panel #YMA3210

1/24th

- Aviaeology [pe] Mosquito 3-tier R.P. rig for Coastal Strike FB Mk VI #AES24001
- Aviaeology [res] ARI 5083 Gee Mk II for Mosquito, Beaufighter etc. #AES24002
- Airscale [pe] Mosquito FB Mk VI/NF Mk II Instrument Panel #24MOSA {Airfix}
- BarracudaCast [res] Mosquito Late Wheels, Plain Hub, Square Tread Pattern #BC24281 {Airfix}
- Cammett [pe] Mosquito Intake Grilles & Cowling Fasteners #BC24281 {Airfix}
- Eduard [pe] RAF WWII Seat Belts – Early Version #23005
- Eduard [pe] RAF WWII Seat Belts – Late Version #23006
- HGW [pe/pa] Sutton QK Harness (Early) #124505
- HGW [pe/pa] Mosquito NF Mk II/FB Mk VI Seat Belts #124509 {Airfix}
- Maestro Models [res] Mosquito NF Mk XIX/J 30 Radar Nose #K2401 {Airfix}
- Master [br] British M2 Browning 0.303 Calibre Machine-gun Barrels x4 #AM-24-001 {Airfix}
- Master [br] British Hispano Mk II 20mm Cannon Barrels x4 #AM-24-002 {Airfix}
- Master [br/pe] British 3in Rocket Projectiles with 60lb SAP Heads x8 for early Mk I rails #AM-24-011 {Airfix}
- Master [br/pe] British 3in Rocket Projectiles with 60lb SAP Heads x8 for late Mk III rails #AM-24-012 {Airfix}
- MasterCasters [res] Mosquito Weighted Wheels, Square Tread Pattern #MST24001 {Airfix}
- MasterCasters [res] Mosquito Weighted Wheels, Covered Hubs #MST24002 {Airfix}
- MasterCasters [res] Mosquito Weighted Wheels, Diamond Tread Pattern #MST24003 {Airfix}
- Montex [vma] Mosquito FB Mk VI/NF Mk II Canopy & Markings Masks #MM24015 {Airfix}
- Montex [vma] Mosquito FB Mk VI/NF Mk II Canopy Masks #SM24015 {Airfix}
- Top Notch [vma] Mosquito FB Mk VI/NF Mk II Camouflage Pattern Masks #24-M030 {Airfix}
- RB Productions [pe] Radiator Detail Set #RB-P24003 {Airfix}
- Scale Aircraft Conversions [mtl] Landing Gear #24002 {Airfix}

Appendix III: **Decal & Mask List**

DK Decals 72013

Thunderbird 72-004

Xtradecal X72232

DK Decals 48005

DK Decals 48007

Below is a list of all the decal sheets and marking paint masks (those purely for masking canopies and/or wheels are in the Accessories appendix) produced to date for the D.H. Mosquito fighter and fighter-based variants that we could find. This list only covers those sheets that remain in production at the point of writing; all out-of-production sheets will be available (in the same style) as a free download from our website (www.valiant-wings. co.uk) once this title is available. If there are any amendments or additions, please contact the author via the Valiant Wings Publishing address shown at the front of this title.

1/72nd

Aviaeology

#AOD72005M RCAF Mosquitoes – Canadians in Fighter Command #1
- FB Mk VI (Series I), HJ719, TH•U, No.418 Squadron, early-mid 1944
- FB Mk VI, HR147, TH•Z, No.418 Squadron, late 1944
- FB Mk VI, NS850, TH•M, No.418 Squadron, mid-1944
- FB Mk VI, SZ976m TH•V, No.418 Squadron, spring 1945

#AOD720023 Banff Strike Wing Mosquitoes
Due 2017

#AOD72033 The Coastal Strike Wings – The Outriders: 333 (RNoAF) Squadron 1943-45
- F Mk II, DZ700, •H, summer 1943
- F Mk II, DZ744, 3•G, spring 1944
- FB Mk VI, HR904, 3•E, autumn 1944
- FB Mk VI, HR864, 3•H, summer 1944
- FB Mk VI, HR116, 3•F, late 1944
- FB Mk VI, HR596, KK•F, November 1944 – January 1945
- FB Mk VI, HR129, KK•Q, spring 1945
- FB Mk VI, RF769, KK•P, November 1944 – January 1945

#AOD72S05 Mosquito Airframe Stencils/Data Markings

BarracudaCals

#BC72165 Mosquito Airframe Stencils

Berna Decals

#BD 72-99 De Havilland Mosquito FB Mk VI in French & Foreign Service
- RS534, '1', GC I/6 'Corse', Tan Son Nhut, Indochina, 1947
- RF836, '6', GC I/6 'Corse', Rabat, Morocco, 1947-48
- TE794, '33', GC 2/6 'Normandie-Niemen', Rabat, Morocco, 1947-48
- PZ381, '5', GC 2/6 'Normandie-Niemen', Rabat, Morocco, 1947-48
- '301', Dominican Air Force, 1949
- '30' & '55', Turkish Air Force, 1949

Carpena Decals
#72.30 de Havilland Mosquito Part 1 – Inc:
- W4082, RS•W, No.157 Squadron
- NF 30, NB11, KT•O, No.11 Squadron, Belgian Air Force
- FB Mk VI, RF838 IY-12, No.311 Sqn, Czechoslovakian AF
- FB Mk VI '2110', Israeli Air Force

#72.31 de Havilland Mosquito Part 2 – Inc:
- FB Mk VI, TE605, '31', Groupe de Chasse 2/6, 6 Escadre de Chasse, Rabat, Morocco, 1947-9
- FB Mk VI, A52-526, NA•E, No.1 Squadron, RAAF, July 1945
- FB Mk VI, HP910, KK•L, No 333 (RNoAF) Sqn, Jan 1945
- FB Mk VI, TE711, FD•4L, No.811 Squadron, FAA, 1946

DK Decals
#72013 Mosquitos used by Czechoslovak Airmen – Inc:
- NF Mk II, flown by Flt Lt Karel Kuttelwascher, DFC & bar, No.23 Squadron, , July 1942
- NF Mk XVII, flown by F/O Miroslav Štandera & W/O Karel Bednařik, No.68 Squadron, autumn 1944
- NF Mk XIX, flown by Sqn Ldr Miloslav Mansfeld, DFC & Flt Lt Slavomil Janáček, DFM, No.68 Squadron, autumn 1944
- NF Mk XXX, flown by Flt Lt Josef Vopálecký & F/O Rudolf Husár, No.68 Squadron, March 1945
- FB Mk VI, flown by Sqn Ldr Josef Stránský DFC & F/O František Bouda, No.21 Squadron, June 1944
- NF Mk XII, flown by W/O Vladimír Kepák, No.307 Squadron, October 1944

- NF Mk XXX, flown by F/O Pavel Kudláč, No.125 Squadron, March 1945
- B-36 (FB Mk VI), TE603, flown by pplk. Vlastimil Veselý, Air Regiment No.24, Ruzyně Air Show, 7th September 1947
- B-36 (FB Mk VI), PZ247, flown by npor. Alois Štanc, 2nd Squadron, Air Regiment No.24, 1947
- B-36 (FB Mk VI), MM430, Air Regiment No.25, 1950
- CB-36 (T Mk III), VR347, flown by ppor. Krucký & rt. Štýdler, Air Regiment No.25, November 1949
- B-36 (FB Mk VI), RF823, 1st Squadron, Air Regiment No.24, 1947
- B-36 (FB Mk VI), RF838, Air Regiment No.25, 1948
- FB Mk VI, RF838, No.404 Squadron (Banff Strike Wing), April 1945

#72016 No.100 Group RAF – Inc:
- FB Mk VI, PZ459, 3P•D, No.515 Squadron, 1945

EagleCals

EC#168 Mosquito FB Mk VI
- MM417, EG•T, 487 Squadron, February 1944
- NT137, 'Lady Luck', TH•H, No.418 Squadron, October 1944
- HR352, SB•S, No.464 Squadron, March 1945
- NS838, 'Wag's "War-Wagon"', UP•J, No.605 Sqn, March 1944

EC#169 Mosquito FB Mk VI
- HR551, UX•P, No.82 Squadron, summer 1945
- HP913, SM•W, No.305 Squadron, November 1944
- NS927, SM•C, No.305 Squadron, autumn 1944
- MM403, SB•V, No.464 Squadron, September 1944

Freightdog Models

#FSD72003S Weekend Warriors – RAuxAF 1948-1953 – Inc:
- T Mk 3, VT588, RAO-L, No.608 Squadron, RAF Manston

#FSD72004S Brits Abroad Pt.II – RAF Post-war Conflicts – Inc:
- FB Mk 6, RS679, AU•P, No.4 Squadron, RAF Celle, West Germany, 1949

IsraDecal

#IAF-73 Israeli Air Force Mosquito & T-6 Texan/Harvard
Markings for numerous T Mk 3, FB Mk 6, NF Mk 30 and Sea Mosquito TR Mk 33 options

LF Models

#C7281 Mosquito over Switzerland Part 1
- FB Mk 6, (ex-NS993), B-5, Kriegtechnische Abteilung, Eidgenössiches Flugzeugwerke, Emmen, 1949

#C7293 Mosquito over Dominican Rep.
- FB Mk 6, '2102', Esquadron de Caza Bombarderom 1948-1954

Model Alliance

#MA-72204 2nd Tactical Air Force 1944-45 – Inc:
- NF Mk XXX, MM788, RA•Q, No.410 Squadron based at Amiens/Glisy

Moose Republic Decals

#72012 NF Mk XXX/J 30 Mosquito
Options for eleven J 30s in Swedish Air Force service

Print Scale

#72-159 de Havilland Mosquito
- FB Mk VI, NS838, UP•J, No.605 Squadron, March 1944
- FB Mk VI, HJ808, UP•O, No.605 Squadron, November 1943
- NF Mk XXX, NT325, HU•N, No.406 Sqn, November 1944
- NF Mk II, DZ230, YP•A, No.23 Squadron, December 1942
- FB Mk VI, NT115, TH•J, No.416 Squadron, October 1944
- NF Mk XXX, NT242, RS•F, No.157 Squadron, January 1945
- NF Mk XII, HK425, KP•R, No.409 Squadron, October 1944
- NF Mk XVII, HK286, RX•A, No.456 Squadron, March 1944
- FB Mk VI, RS575, 3P•V, No.515 Sqn, February-April 1945
- NF Mk XIII, MM465, NG•X, No.604 Squadron, July 1944
- FB Mk VI, HJ914, SB•O, NO.464 Squadron, December 1943

Thunderbird Models

#72-003 Mosquito Racer
- FB Mk VI, CF-FZG of World Wide Airways

#72-004 Mosquito Racer
• FB Mk VI, CF-GKL of Kenting Aviation Ltd

Xtradecals

#72093 No.617 (Dambusters) Squadron 1943-2000 – Inc:
• FB Mk VI, NT202, AJ•N, used by the squadron in the pathfinder role

#72148 The History of No.4 Squadron – Inc:
• FB Mk 6, TA540, UP•G, RAF Wahn, 1948

#X72195 D-Day 70th Anniv. June 1944-2014 Part 2 – Inc:
• FB Mk VI, MM403, SB•V, No.464 Squadron, RAF Gravesend

#X72232 Mosquito FB Mk VI/B.IV/B.XX/T.III – Inc:
• T Mk 3, VT588, RAO-L, No.608 Sqn, RAF Manston 1948
• FB Mk VI, RF838, EO•A, No.404 Squadron, RAF Banff, 1945
• FB Mk VI, RS623, VV•A, No.235 Squadron, RAF Banff, 1945
• FB Mk VI, HR399, OB•R, No.45 Squadron, India, 1945
• FB Mk VI, RF751, •B, No.211 Squadron, India, 1945
• FB Mk VI, NT233, SM•X, No.138 Wing, flown by Gp Capt Bower & Flt Lt Cairns, No.305 Sqn, RAF Hartford Bridge, 1944
• FB Mk VI, HR623, •CI, No.618 Squadron, RAAF, Narromine, NSW, 1945

1/48th

Airframe Decals

#AF-72199 Coastal Command WWII – Part 2 – Inc:
• FB Mk VI, RS623, VV-A, No.235 Squadron, RAF Banff, 1945

Aviaeology

#AOD48005M RCAF Mosquitoes – Canadians in Fighter Command #1
Same options as #AOD72005M

#AOD48023 Banff Strike Wing Mosquitoes
Due 2017

#AOD48033 The Coastal Strike Wings – The Outriders: 333 (RNoAF) Squadron 1943-45
Same options as #AOD72033

#AOD48S05 Mosquito Airframe Stencils/Data Markings

BarracudaCals

#BC48166 Mosquito Airframe Stencils

Berna Decals

#BD 48-121 De Havilland Mosquito FB Mk VI in French & Foreign Service
Same options as #BD 72-99

Carpena Decals

#48.22 de Havilland Mosquito Part 1 – Inc:
• W4082, RS•W, No.157 Squadron
• FB Mk VI, TE605, '31', Groupe de Chasse 2/6, 6 Escadre de Chasse, Rabat, Morocco, 1947-9

#48.96 de Havilland Mosquito Part 2
• FB Mk VI, A52-526, NA•E, No.1 Squadron, RAAF, July 1945
• FB Mk VI, RF838 IY-12, No.311 Sqn, Czechoslovakian AF
• FB Mk VI '2110', Israeli Air Force

#48.97 de Havilland Mosquito Part 3
• NF.30, NB11, KT•O, 11 Escadrille de Chasse de Nuit, 1R Wing de Chasse, Beauvechain, 1947-53
• FB Mk VI, HP910, KK•L, No 333 (RNoAF) Squadron, January 1945
• FB Mk VI, TE711, FD•4L, No.811 Squadron, FAA, 1946

DK Decals

#48005 Mosquito used by Australian pilots in the RAAF and RAF – Inc:
• FB Mk VI, A52-533, No.1 Squadron, RAAF, Borneo, 1945
• FB Mk VI, A52-513, No.1 Squadron, RAAF, Borneo, 1945
• FB Mk VI, A52-531, No.1 Squadron, RAAF, Borneo, 1945
• PR Mk 40, A52-6, No.87 Sqn, RAAF, Coomalee Creek, 1944
• FB Mk VI, HX914, No.464 Squadron, December 1943
• FB Mk VI, HR352, No.464 Squadron, March 1945
• NF Mk XVII HK290/G, No.456 Squadron, Ford, 1944

#48007 Mosquito used by Czechoslovak airmen – Inc:
• NF Mk II, flown by Flt Lt Karel Kuttelwascher, DFC & bar, No.23 Squadron, July 1942
• NF Mk XVII, flown by F/O Miroslav Štandera & W/O Karel Bednařík, No.68 Squadron, autumn 1944
• NF Mk XIX, flown by Sqn Ldr Miloslav Mansfeld, DFC & Flt Lt Slavomil Janáček, DFM, No.68 Squadron, autumn 1944
• NF Mk XXX, flown by Flt Lt Josef Vopálecký & F/O Rudolf Husár, No.68 Squadron, March 1945

• B-36 (FB Mk VI), TE603, flown by pplk. Vlastimil Veselý, Air Regiment No.24, Ruzyně Air Show, 7th September 1947
• B-36 (FB Mk VI), PZ247, flown by npor. Alois Štanc, 2nd Squadron, Air Regiment No.24, 1947
• B-36 (FB Mk VI), MM430, Air Regiment No.25, 1950
• CB-36 (T Mk III), VR347, flown by ppor. Krucký & rt. Štýdler, Air Regiment No.25, November 1949
• B-36 (FB Mk VI), RF823, 1st Sqn, Air Regiment No.24, 1947

#48009 No.100 Group RAF
Same options as #72016

EagleCals

EC#168 Mosquito FB Mk VI
Same options as 1/72nd version

EC#169 Mosquito FB Mk VI
Same options as 1/72nd version

LF Models

#C4838 Mosquito over Switzerland Part 1
Same option as #C7281

#C4840 Mosquito over Dominican Rep.
Same option as #C7293

Model Alliance

#MA-48198 Coastal Command WWII Part I – Inc:
• FB Mk VI, RF838, EO•A, No.404 Squadron, RAF Banff, 1945

#MA-48204 2nd Tactical Air Force 1944-45
Same option as #MA-72204

Montex

#K48173 Mosquito NF Mk II/FB Mk VI
• NF Mk II, EW•R, No.307 Squadron, December 1942
• FB Mk VI, OM•Q, No.107 Sqn, Cambrai-Epinoy, Oct 1944
Note: This is a set of vinyl self-adhesive masks

#K48174 Mosquito FB Mk VI
• FB Mk VI, OB•C, No.45 Squadron, Kumbhirgram, India, January 1945
• FB Mk VI, HR558, UX•X, No.82 Squadron, Kumbhirgram, India, early 1945
Note: This is a set of vinyl self-adhesive masks

#K48322 Mosquito FB Mk VI
• FB Mk VI, NT198, SM•U, No.305 Squadron, September 1944
• FB Mk VI, NS837 TH•E, No.418 Squadron, October 1944
Note: This set of vinyl self-adhesive masks includes all the national markings and codes, with serial number and artwork etc. supplied as decals

Owl Decals

#48014 Nightfighter Experts – Inc:
• FB Mk VI, HR417, TH•Z, flown by Sqn Ldr Russell Bannock, No.418 Squadron

Print Scale

#48-085 de Havilland Mosquito Part 1
• FB Mk VI, NS838, UP•J, No.605 Squadron, March 1944
• FB Mk VI, HJ808, UP•O, No.605 Squadron, November 1943
• NF Mk XXX, NT325, HU•N, No.406 Sqn, November 1944
• NF Mk II, DZ230, YP•A, No.23 Squadron, December 1942
• FB Mk VI, NT115, TH•J, No.416 Squadron, October 1944
• NF Mk XXX, NT242, RS•F, No.157 Squadron, January 1945

#48-086 de Havilland Mosquito Part 2
• NF Mk XII, HK425, KP•R, No.409 Squadron, October 1944
• NF Mk XVII, HK286/G, RX•A, No.456 Sqn, March 1944
• FB Mk VI, RS575, 3P•V, No.515 Sqn, February-April 1945
• NF Mk XIII, MM465, NG•X, No.604 Squadron, July 1944
• FB Mk VI, HJ914, SB•O, NO.464 Squadron, December 1943

Moose Republic Decals

#48008 NF Mk XXX/J 30 Mosquito
Same options as #72012

Thunderbird Models

#72-003 Mosquito Racer
• FB Mk VI, CF-FZG of World Wide Airways

Xtradecals

#X48071 No.23 Squadron 1943-1990 – Inc:
• NF Mk II, DZ230, YP•A, RAF Luqa, Malta, 1943
• FB Mk VI, HJ675, YP•V, Italy, 1943

#X48075 No.617 (Dambusters) Squadron 1943-2000
Same option as #X72093

Moose Republic 48008

Print-Scale 48-085

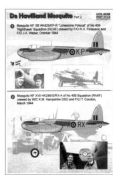

Print-Scale 48-086

Xtradecal X48156

Aviaeology AOD32005

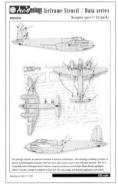

Aviaeology AOD32S05

EagleCal 32#169

#48148 100 Years of No.4 Squadron Part 1 – Inc:
• FB Mk 6, TA540, UP•G, RAF Wahn, 1948

#X48156 de Havilland Mosquito FB Mk VI/B Mk IV/T Mk III – Inc:
• T Mk III, TV970, FK-V, No.20 Squadron, RAF Wittering, 1946
• T Mk 3, VT588, RAO-L, No.608 Sqn, RAF Manston 1948
• FB Mk VI, RF838, EO•A, No.404 Squadron, RAF Banff, 1945
• FB Mk VI, RS623, VV•A, No.235 Squadron, RAF Banff, 1945
• FB Mk VI, HR399, OB•R, No.45 Squadron, India, 1945

1/32nd
Aviaeology

#AOD32005M RCAF Mosquitoes – Canadians in Fighter Command #1
Same options as #AOD72005M

#AOD32011 RCAF Coastal Strike Mosquitoes
• FB Mk VI, RF838, RF851, RF856 & RF882

#AOD32231 Banff Strike Wing Mosquitoes – Nos.143, 235 & 248 Squadrons Part 1
Due release in 2017

#AOD32232 Banff Strike Wing Mosquitoes – Nos.143, 235 & 248 Squadrons Part 2
Due release in 2017

#AOD32033 The Coastal Strike Wings – The Outriders: 333 (RNoAF) Squadron 1943-45
Same options as #AOD72033

#AOD32S05 Mosquito Airframe Stencils/Data Markings

Berna Decals

#BD 32-39 De Havilland Mosquito FB Mk VI in French & Foreign Service
Same options as #BD 72-99

EagleCals

EC#168 Mosquito FB Mk VI
Same options as 1/72nd version

EC#169 Mosquito FB Mk VI
Same options as 1/72nd version

HGW

#232011 Mosquito FB Mk VI Airframe Stencils

Montex

#K32322 Mosquito NF Mk II/FB Mk VI
Same options as #K48173

#K32329 Mosquito FB Mk VI
Same options as #K48322

Ventura Decals

#V3265 Israeli Mosquitos – Inc:
• FB Mk VIs '2109' and '2114'

Xtradecals

#X32058 de Havilland Mosquito FB Mk VI
• FB Mk VI, RF838, EO•A, No.404 Squadron, RAF Banff, 1945
• FB Mk VI, RS623, VV•A, No.235 Squadron, RAF Banff, 1945
• FB Mk VI, HR399, OB•R, No.45 Squadron, India, 1945
• FB Mk VI, RF751, •B, No.211 Squadron, India, 1945

#X32059 de Havilland Mosquito B Mk IV/B.XX/T.III – Inc:
• T Mk 3, TV970, FK•V, No.219 Sqn, RAF Wittering, 1946

1/24th
Aviaeology

#AOD24005M RCAF Mosquitoes – Canadians in Fighter Command #1
Same options as #AOD72005M

#AOD24023 Banff Strike Wing Mosquitoes – Nos.143, 235 & 248 Squadrons Part 1
Due release in 2017

#AOD24033 The Coastal Strike Wings – The Outriders: 333 (RNoAF) Squadron 1943-45
Same options as #AOD72033

#AOD24S05 Mosquito Airframe Stencils/Data Markings

BarracudaCals

#BC24167 Mosquito Airframe Stencils

Berna Decals

#BD 24-02 De Havilland Mosquito FB Mk VI in French & Foreign Service
• RF836, '6', GC I/6 'Corse', Rabat, Morocco, 1947-48
• TE794, '33', GC 2/6 'Normandie-Niemen', Rabat, Morocco, 1947-48

Montex

#K24051 Mosquito NF Mk II/FB Mk VI
Same options as #K48173

#K24079 Mosquito FB Mk VI
Same options as #K48322

Xtradecals

#24-001 De Havilland Mosquito FB Mk VI
• NS850, TH•M, No.418 Squadron, circa 1944-45
• MM403, SB•V, No.464 Squadron, RAF Thorney Island, autumn 1944
• HR462, OB•J, No.45 Squadron, India, March 1945
• 3-W, No.235 Squadron, RAF Portreath, June 1944

A well-known shot of FB Mk VI PZ438 of No.143 Sqn, Banff Strike Wing being rearmed, this machine is fitted with the later Mk III rails

(©C.E. Brown)

Appendix IV: **Bibliography**

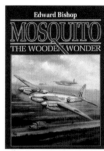

The below list of Mosquito related material is as comprehensive as possible, but there are bound to be omissions so if there are amendments or additions, please contact the author via the Valiant Wings Publishing address shown at the front of this title.

Official Publications

De Havilland Mosquito F Mk II – Air Publication 2019B
De Havilland Mosquito T Mk III – Air Publication 2019C
De Havilland Mosquito FB Mk VI – Air Publication 2019E
De Havilland Mosquito N.F. Mk XII – Air Publication 2019G
De Havilland Mosquito NF Mk XIII – Air Publication 2019H
De Havilland Mosquito N.F. Mk XVII – Air Publication 2019K
De Havilland Mosquito NF Mk XIX – Air Publication 2019R
De Havilland Mosquito FB Mk 26 – Air Publication 2019T
De Havilland Mosquito NF Mk 36 – Air Publication 2653P
De Havilland Mosquito TT Mk 37 – Air Publication 2653R
De Havilland Sea Mosquito T.R.33 – Air Publication 4088A
De Havilland Sea Mosquito T.F.37 – Air Publication 4088B

Publications

- Achtung! Moskito! by M.W. Bowman (Schiffer Publishing 2010 ISBN: 978-0-7643-3347-7)
- Aircraft Archive – Fighters of World War Two Volume 1 (Argus Books 1988 ISBN:0-85242-948-7)
- De Havilland Mosquito, Famous Aircraft of the World No.40 (Bunrin-do)
- De Havilland Mosquito: Polscy piloci na Mosquito cz.1 by R. Gretzyngier & L. Musialkowski, Monografie Lotnicze 101 (AJ-Press 2006 ISBN: 83-7237-178-4)
- De Havilland Mosquito: An Illustrated History by Stuart Howe (Aston Publishing Ltd 1992 ISBN: 0-946627-63-0)
- De Havilland Mosquito: An Illustrated History by Stuart Howe (Crécy Publishing Ltd 1999 ISBN: 0-947554-76-9) – Revised reprint of Aston Publishing (1992) title
- De Havilland Mosquito: An Illustrated History Vol 1 by Stuart Howe (Crécy Publishing Ltd 2007 ISBN: 0-947554-76-9)
- De Havilland Mosquito: An Illustrated History Vol 2 by Stuart Howe & Ian Thirsk (Crécy Publishing Ltd 2007 ISBN: 0-85979-115-7)
- De Havilland Mosquito, Aero Detail No.23 (Dia Nippon Kaiga Co., Ltd 1999 ISBN: 4-499-22695-3)
- De Havilland Mosquito by Mister Kit & J.P. De Cock, Special La Derniere Guerre (Editions Atlas 1979)
- De Havilland Mosquito by Martin W.Bowman (Crowood Press 1997, ISBN 1 86126 075 X)
- De Havilland Mosquito by R. Jackson, Combat Legend (Airlife Publishing Ltd 2003)
- De Havilland Mosquito in RAF, FAA, RAAF, SAAF, RNZAF, RCAF, USAF, French & Foreign Service. Aircam No.28 by Francis Mason, R.Ward & M.Roffe (Osprey Publications Ltd. 1972 SBN: 85045-043-8)
- Israeli Air Force de Havilland Mosquito The 'Wooden Wonder' in Heyl; Ha'Avir Service Part 1 – 1948 to 1953 by S. Aloni (AirDOC 2006 ISBN: 3-935687-61-3)
- l'Aviation Militaire Française en Indochine 1946-1954 Tome 1 by J-C Soumille (Association Airdoc 1994)
- Les Avions Britanniques aux Couleurs Françaises by J-J Petit (Avia Editions 2003 ISBN: 2-915030-04-9)
- Modelling the De Havilland Mosquito by R. Sutherland, Osprey Modelling No.7 (Osprey Publishing 2005)
- Mosquito by B.Sweetman & R.Watanabe (Janes Publishing Co. Ltd. 1981)
- Mosquito by C. Martin Sharp & Michael J.F. Bowyer (Faber & Faber Ltd. 1967 & 1971, ISBN: 0-571-04750-5 & 0-571-09531-3 and Crécy Publishing Ltd 1995 & 1997 ISBN: 0-947554-41-6)
- Mosquito Aces of World War 2 by A. Thomas, Aircraft of the Aces series No.69 (Osprey Publishing 2005 ISBN: 1-84176-878-2)
- Mosquito – A Pictorial History of the D.H.98 by Philip Birtles (Janes Publishing Company Ltd. 1980, ISBN: 0-7106-0065-8)
- Mosquito at War by Chaz Bowyer (Ian Allen Publishing 1973, The Promotional Reprint Co. Ltd. 1995, ISBN: 1-85648-227-8)
- Mosquito Bomber/Fighter-Bomber Units 1942-45 by M. Bowman, Combat Aircraft No.4 (Osprey 1998)
- Mosquito Fighter Squadrons In Focus by P. Birtles (Red Kite Books 2005 ISBN: 0-9546201-3-5)
- Mosquito Racer by D. McVicar (Airlife Publishing 1985 ISBN: 0-906393-58-2)
- Mosquito – The Illustrated History by P.J. Birtles (Sutton Publishing 1998 ISBN: 0-7509-1495-5)
- Mosquito; Their history and how to model them by Michael J.F.Bowyer and Bryan Philpott, Classic Aircraft No.7 (Patrick Stephens Ltd. 1980 ISBN-0-85059-432-4)
- Mosquito Monograph: A History of Mosquitoes in Australia and RAF Operations by D. Vincent (D. Vincent 1982 ISBN: 0-9596052-1-5)
- Mosquito Part 1, In Action No.127 by J. Scutts (Squadron/ Signal Publications Ltd 1992 ISBN: 0-89747-285-3)
- Mosquito Part 2, In Action No.139 by J. Scutts (Squadron/ Signal Publications Ltd 1993 ISBN: 0-89747-303-5)
- Mosquito Photo-Reconnaissance Units of World War 2 by M. Bowman, Osprey Combat Aircraft No.13 (Osprey Publishing 1999 ISBN: 1-85532-891-7)
- Mosquito Portfolio by Stuart Howe (Ian Allen Ltd 1984 ISBN: 0-7110-1406-X)
- De Havilland Mosquito Portfolio, A Brookland Aircraft Portfolio (Brookland Books/Business Press International Ltd 1986 ISBN: 0-948-207-914)
- Mosquito Squadrons of the Royal Air Force by C.Bowyer (Ian Allen Publishing 1984 ISBN: 0-7110-1425-6)

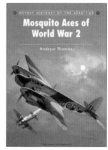

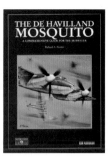

- Mosquito Survivors by Stuart Howe (Aston Publishing 1986 ISBN: 0-946627-11-8 – Marked as -04-5 on cover?)
- Mosquito – The Original Multi-role Aircraft by G.M. Simons (Arms & Armour Press 1991 ISBN: 0-85368-995-4)
- Mosquito – The Wooden Wonder by Edward Bishop (Max Parrish & Co. Ltd 1959, Pan/Ballantine 1971, Airlife Publishing Ltd 1980 & 1995 ISBN: 1-85310-708-5)
- Mosquito Thunder – No.105 Sqn RAF at War 1942-45 by S.R. Scott (Sutton Publishing Ltd 1999 ISBN: 0-7509-1800-4)
- Mosquito Victory by J.Currie (Goodall Press 1983)
- Mosquito, Walk Around No.15 by R. MacKay (Squadron/Signal Publications 1999 ISBN: 0-89747-396-5)
- One Man's "Mossie" – 'The Spirit of Val' by N. Spence in collaboration with T. Agar (Yorskhire Air Museum 1996 ISBN: 0-9512379-50)
- Polish Air Force 1939-1945 by Dr J. Koniarek (Squadron/Signal Publications 1994 ISBN: 0-89747-324-8)
- Racing Planes and Air Races A Complete History by R. Kinert Vol IV 1946-1967 (Aero Publishers Inc. 1968)
- RAF & RCAF Aircraft Nose Art in World War II by C. Simonsen (Hikoki Publications 2001 ISBN: 1-902109-20-1)
- Soumrak Králu Vzduchu – Ceskoslovenské vojenské letectvo 1945-1950 by J. Fidler & J. Rajlich (Ares/Deus 2000 ISBN: 80-86158-24-1)
- Soviet Air Power in World War 2 by Y. Gordon (Midland Publishing 2008, ISBN: 978-1-85780-304-4)
- The De Havilland Mosquito by M.J. Hardy (David & Charles Ltd 1977 ISBN: 0-7153-7367-6)
- The De Havilland Mosquito – An Illustrated History by Stuart Howe (Aston Publications Ltd 1992 ISBN: 0-946627-63-0)
- The De Havilland Mosquito, Modellers' Datafile No.1 by R.A. Franks (©1999) – Reprinted in 2013 as Modellers' Datafile No.20
- The Belgium Air Force by J. Pacco (JP Publications 1986, 87, 89, 90 & 96 ISBN: 90-801136-2-X)
- The Cold War Years: Flight Testing at Boscombe Down 1945-1975 by T. Mason (Hikoki Publications 2001 ISBN: 1-902109-11-2)
- The Mosquito Log by A. McKee (Souvenir Press 1988 ISBN: 0-285-62838-0)
- The Mosquito Manual (Arms & Armour Press 1977, Aston Publications Ltd. 1988 ISBN: 0-946627-32-0)
- The Mosquito 50 Years On: A report on the 50th Anniversary Symposium held at British Aerospace Hatfield on the 24th September 1990 (GMS Enterprises/Hatfield RAeS 1991 ISBN: 1-870384-11-3)
- The Secret Years: Flight Testing at Boscombe Down 1939-1945 by T. Mason (Hikoki Publications 1998 ISBN: 1-951899-9-5)
- Wings of Fame Volume 18 (Aerospace Publishing Ltd 2000 ISBN: 1-86184-046-2/1-86184-061-6)

Periodicals
- Airfix Magazine, Vol.8 No.10 June 1967
- Replic No.88 (December 1998)
- Scale Aircraft Modelling, Vol.8 No.6 March 1986, Vol.17 No.5 July 1995, Vol 18 No.10 July, No.11 August, No.12 September 1996, Vol.19 No.1 October 1996, Vol.20 No.10 December 1998, Vol.25 No.2 April 2003 & Vol.27 No.8 October 2005
- Scale Aviation Modeller Vol.2 Iss.7 July 1996, Vol.2 Iss.8 August 1996 & Vol.2 Iss.9 September 1996
- Scale Aviation Modeller International Vol.13 Iss.11 November 2007
- Scale Models, Vol.1 No.4 January 1970, Vol.12 No.144 September 1981, Vol.13 No.157 November 1982, Vol.13 No.158 December 1982 & Vol 20 Issue 6, June 1989
- Scale Models International, Vol.24 No.281 March 1993
- Zlinek (11/1992)
- 21st Profile Vol.1 No.2 (21st Profile Ltd)

NF Mk 38 VX196 was the last Mosquito built and is seen here as it reaches the end of the production line at Chester in late 1950 (©DH)